AF395820

THE KILLING FIELDS OF
PROVENCE

THE KILLING FIELDS OF
PROVENCE

OCCUPATION, RESISTANCE AND LIBERATION IN THE SOUTH OF FRANCE

JAMES BOURHILL

Pen & Sword

MILITARY

AN IMPRINT OF PEN & SWORD BOOKS LTD.
YORKSHIRE - PHILADELPHIA

First published in Great Britain in 2019 by
PEN AND SWORD MILITARY
An imprint of
Pen & Sword Books Ltd
Yorkshire – Philadelphia

Copyright © James Bourhill, 2019

ISBN 978 1 52676 132 3

Typeset in Times New Roman 11.5/14 by
Aura Technology and Software Services, India
Printed and bound in the UK by TJ International Ltd.

Pen & Sword Books Limited incorporates the imprints of Atlas, Archaeology,
Aviation, Discovery, Family History, Fiction, History, Maritime, Military, Military
Classics, Politics, Select, Transport, True Crime, Air World, Frontline Publishing,
Leo Cooper, Remember When, Seaforth Publishing, The Praetorian Press,
Wharncliffe Local History, Wharncliffe Transport, Wharncliffe True Crime and
White Owl.

For a complete list of Pen & Sword titles please contact
PEN & SWORD BOOKS LIMITED
47 Church Street, Barnsley, South Yorkshire, S70 2AS, England
E-mail: enquiries@pen-and-sword.co.uk
Website: www.pen-and-sword.co.uk

Or
PEN AND SWORD BOOKS
1950 Lawrence Rd, Havertown, PA 19083, USA
E-mail: Uspen-and-sword@casematepublishers.com
Website: www.penandswordbooks.com

Contents

List of Illustrations

1. One of the ninety or so French ships scuttled in the Toulon harbour on 27 November 1942, to prevent them from falling into German hands. (Dale Rooks / US Coast Guard)
2. Nancy Wake (married name Fiocca) started off in the Marseille underground and became a fully fledged SOE agent.
3. Eleven young resistants executed at Saint-Julien-du-Verdon on 11 June 1944.
4. Krystyna Skarbek, aka Christine Granville, described by one of her SOE assessors as 'a very smart-looking girl, simply dressed and aristocratic'. A fellow agent once said that she looked like 'an athletic art student'.
5. American B-17s drop weapons and supplies to the Maquis of the Vercors on Bastille Day, 14 July 1944. (USAF)
6. Victims of the massacres which took place on the Vercors Plateau being reinterred at what is now the National Nécropole near Vassieux-en-Vercors.
7. OSS Major Peter Ortiz, wearing a USMC uniform, inspecting members of the Resistance on 7 August 1944, at Col de la Forclaz, north of Les Saisies, during Mission UNION II. The second man on his right is Capitaine Jean Bulle. (Raymond Bertrand)
8. American B-24 Liberators directly over Saint-Jean-Cap-Ferrat with Nice to the back and Villefranche-sur-Mer on the right. (USAF)
9. Bombing mission over Fréjus Plage on Dragoon D-Day. Saint-Raphaël is on the right and the Base *aéronautique navale* runway is the diagonal strip on the left. (USAF)
10. Paratroopers of the 1st Airborne Task Force jump from C-47 'Dakota' aircraft near Le Muy during Operation Rugby, 15 August 1944.
11. Paratroopers walk through the vineyards to their assembly point. (US Signals Corps)

12. A paratrooper at the intersection of the Draguignan road and the RN 7. The villages of La Motte and Le Muy were at the epicentre of the drop zones. (US Signals Corps)
13. Infantrymen move inland from the beachhead through a pine forest. (US Signals Corps)
14. Glider pilots injured during the airborne operation receive medical attention at Le Mitan, a farm near the village of La Motte.
15. Corporal Burl J. Knapp of the 509th Parachute Infantry Batallion pictured with Nicole Célébonovitch, a resistant from Saint-Tropez, soon after the liberation. Burl Knapp was killed in action less than a week later. (US Signals Corps)
16. German prisoners, mostly *Osttruppen*, hot and thirsty under the August sun, but relieved that for them, the war is over. (Dale Rooks / US Coast Guard)
17. German PoWs being processed in Saint-Tropez. (US Signals Corps)
18. Wounded being evacuated by landing craft in the calm waters of the Gulf of Saint-Tropez. (Dale Rooks / US Coast Guard)
19. Support vehicles and supplies come ashore at Saint-Tropez. By the end of Dragoon, more than 130,000 men, 18,000 vehicles and 7,000 tons of supplies were landed. (Dale Rooks / US Coast Guard)
20. Audie Murphy, the most highly decorated American soldier in history, was awarded the Distinguished Service Cross (DSC) for his actions at Pampelonne Beach on 15 August 1944.
21. Relieved to be safely ashore, NCOs drive along the coastal road in their Jeep. (Dale Rooks / US Coast Guard)
22. American GMC 6x6 trucks move inland from the beachhead through wine country. (Dale Rooks / US Coast Guard)
23. An M7 (Priest) self-propelled gun passing through Brignoles, 20 August 1944. (US Signals Corps)
24. Vehicles of the US 3rd Infantry Division enter Aix-en-Provence on 21 August 1944. (US Signals Corps)
25. Shutters, lined with fabric for the blackout, are flung open as American troops pass along the street below. This image was snapped by South African photographer Constance Stuart as she looked up from a truck. (Constance Stuart / American University Museum)
26. As the Allies raced through the rustic beauty of the countryside, waving people appeared as a kaleidoscopic blur. (Dale Rooks / US Coast Guard)

List of Maps

The Provence-Alpes-Côte d'Azur (PACA) Region.

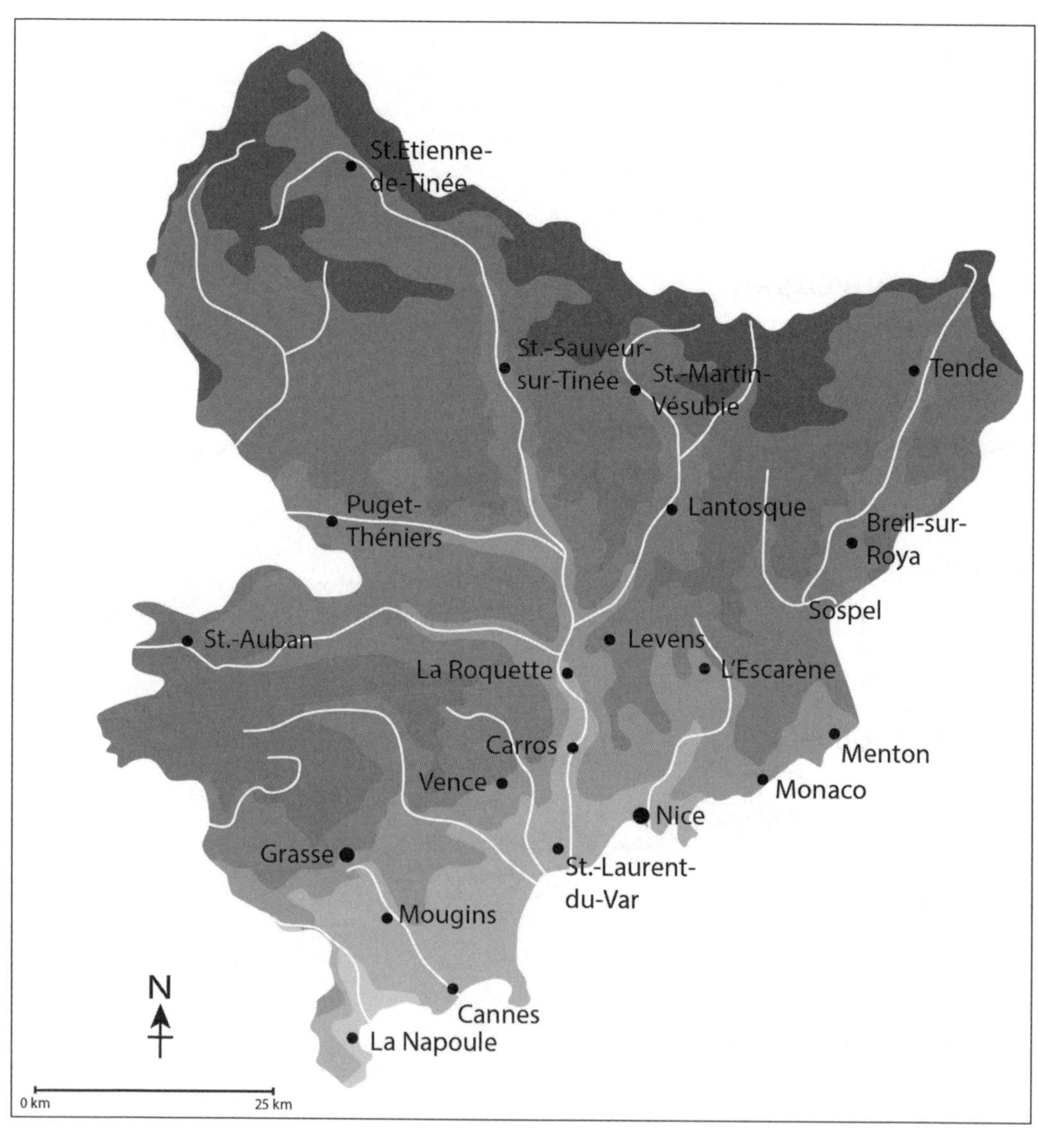

Department of the Alpes-Maritimes.

MAPS

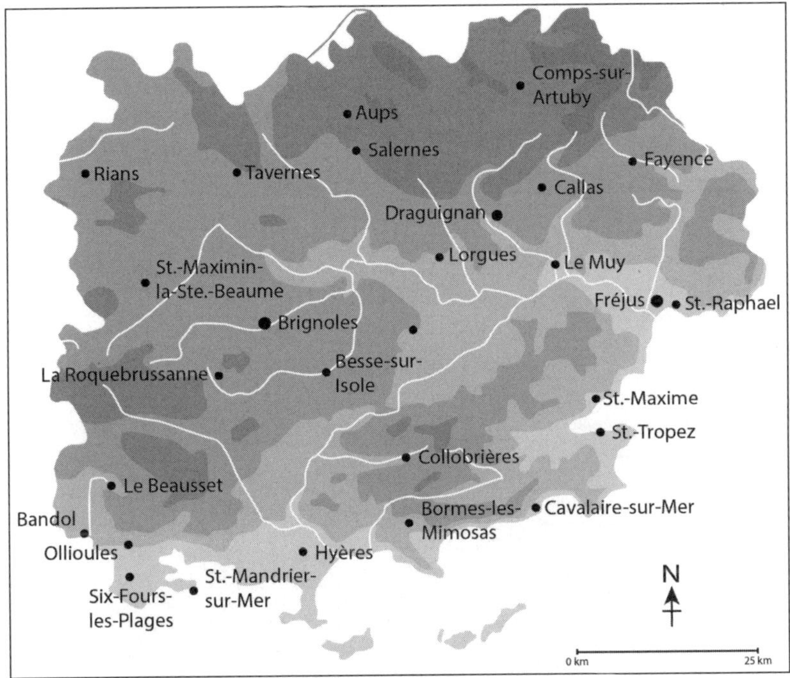

Department of the Var.

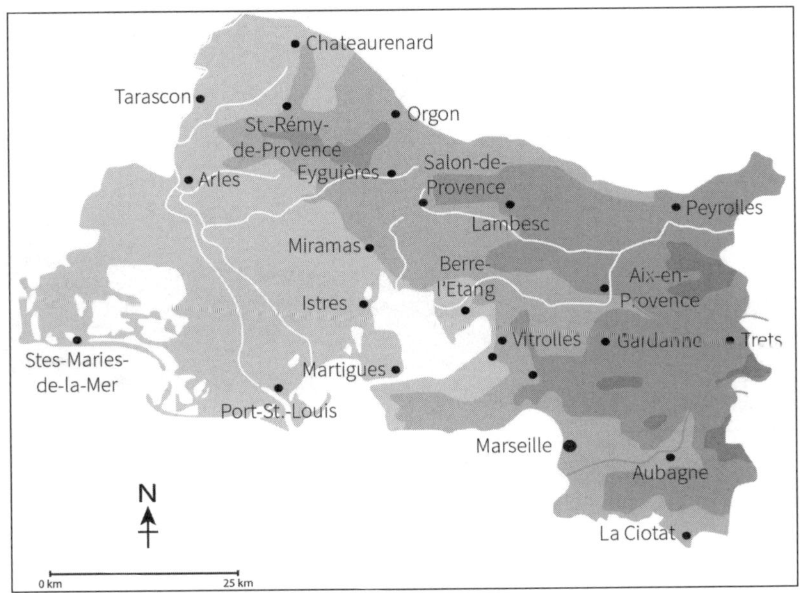

Department of the Bouches-du-Rhône.

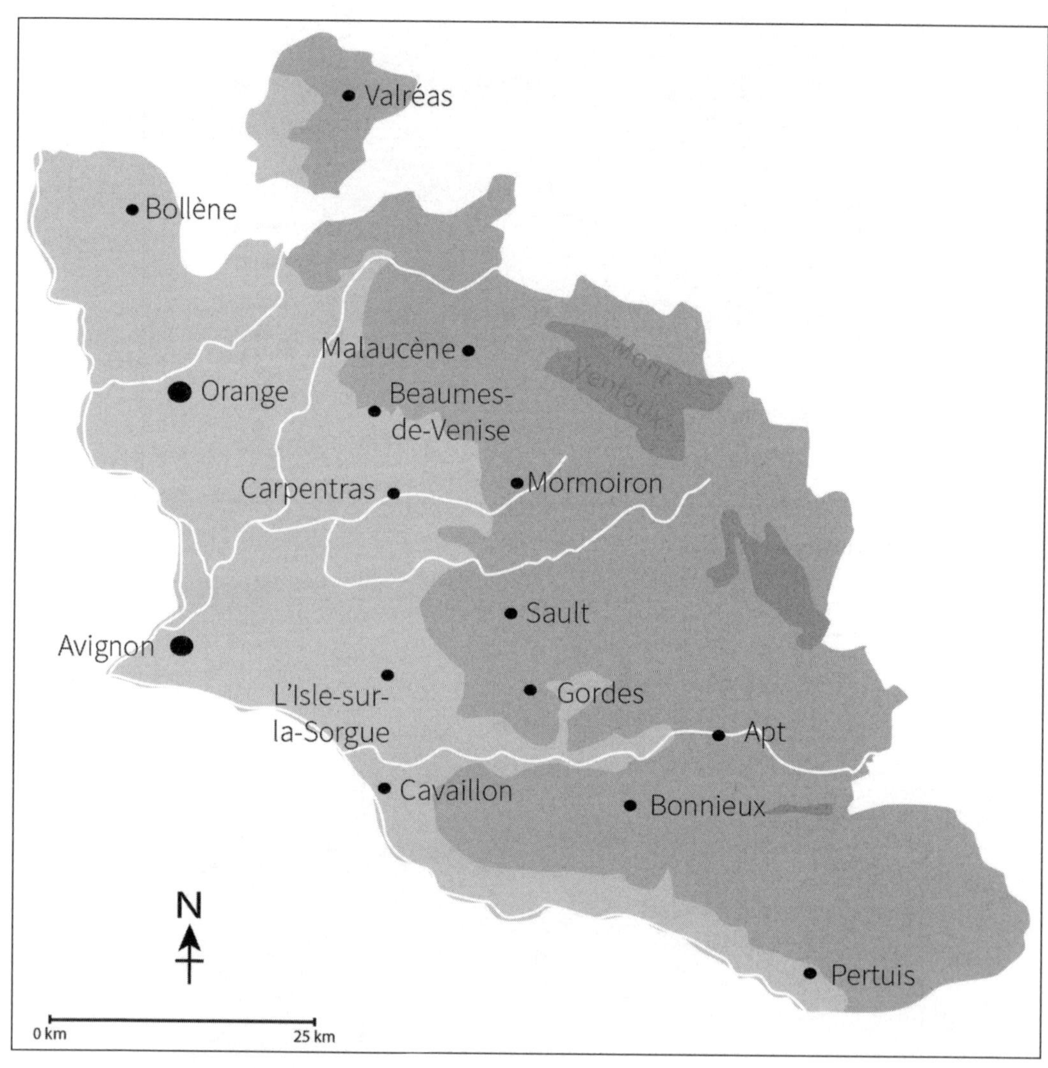

Department of the Vaucluse.

MAPS

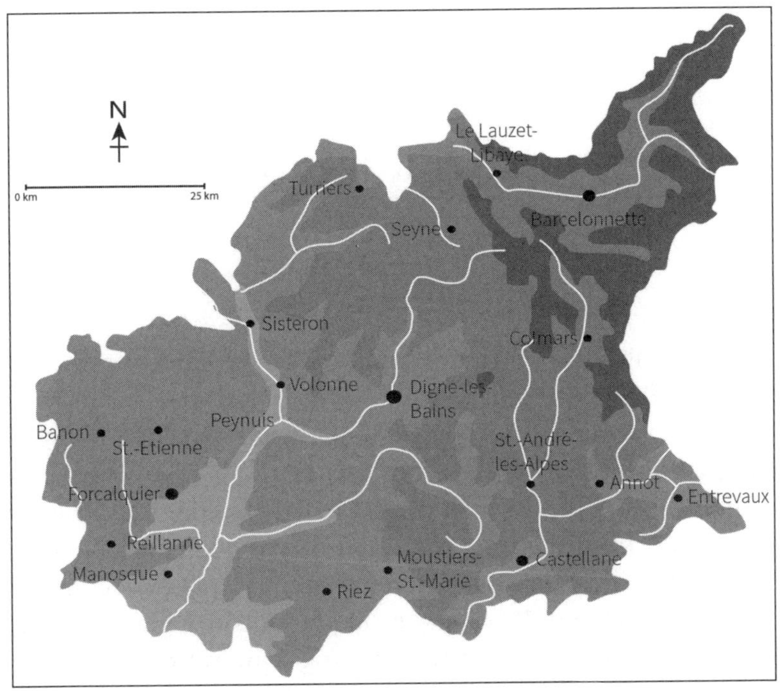

Department of the Alpes-de-Haute-Provence (previously the Basses-Alpes).

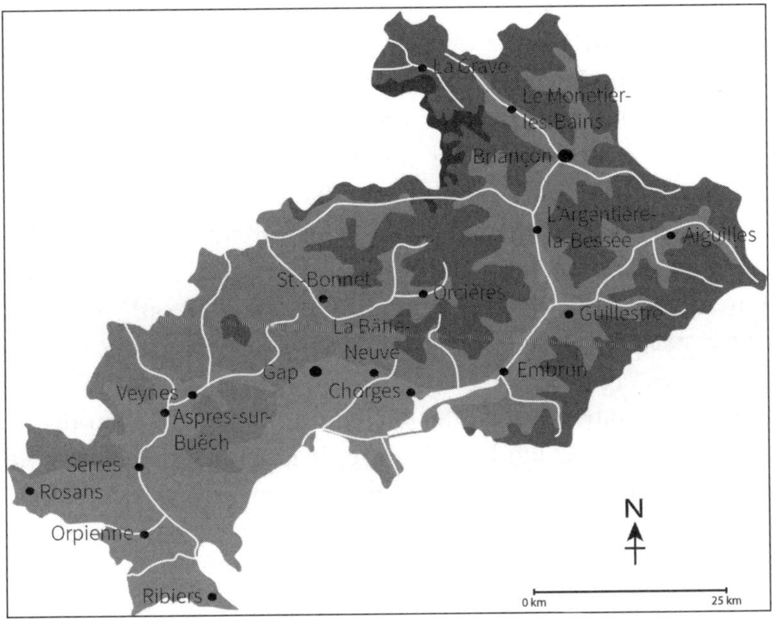

Department of the Hautes-Alpes.

Introduction

Putain is probably the most frequently used profanity in the French language. Literally, it means 'whore' but it can also mean so much more. On a Provençal summer's day, it is typically muttered in conjunction with *chaleur*, the word for 'heat'. It is a white, blinding heat which blisters the varnish on the benches along the Promenade, melts the resin from the pine trees and drives people indoors at high noon. Some relief can be found in the shade of a plane tree, preferably near a fountain in the village square, and fanned by a gentle sea breeze. Then there is the mistral, a chilly, annoying wind which blows from the interior, leaving umbrella pines permanently bent southward. Autumn leaves swirl in the alleyways and dust diffuses through the windows and doors. *Putain de Mistral!*

In the words of Noël Coward, 'Only mad dogs and Englishmen go out in the midday sun.' So, quite sensibly, the streets are empty between noon and three in the French Provençal village. The grizzled men, who have done nothing all morning but watch the passing parade, have gone indoors, and the flat bench on Avenue General Leclerc, which is their special preserve, is vacant. It is siesta time, the shops are shut and ancient shutters have been pulled closed with that familiar squeak, followed by a metallic clank. The only sound which disturbs a sweaty summer sleep is the incessant chirping of invisible crickets called *cigales*.

For the past sixteen years, the enchanting village of Plan-de-la-Tour has been the muse which beguiles me. It is a cluster of dun-coloured dwellings, bordered by vineyards, in a hidden valley, just inland from the Gulf of Saint-Tropez. As a writer of history, I pay more attention than most to a small monument at a crossroads on the edge of the village on which it is written '*Ici tombé Charles Ollivier, 15 août 1944*' (Here fell Charles Ollivier, 15 August 1944). It is the only reminder of the Second World War in the village, apart from the recent addition of a plaque commemorating Jean Vatinet, the local school teacher turned resistance leader.

Right alongside the *terrasse* of the Bar de la Poste, seated on a folding bistro chair, I pass an old dear wearing a purple blouse with a Gatsby-era hat and a captivating smile. Madame Reine and I have nodded to each other many times before. Today, her *'Bonjour'* is particularly friendly so I stop to introduce myself. 'Do you know how old I am?' is the next thing she says. 'Ninety-eight.' Now in the French language, that's a big number and difficult to comprehend. *Quatre vingt dix huit* literally means four twenties, ten and eight. I thought I had misunderstood, but I had not. (That was six years ago, and Reine, the queen of Plan-de-la-Tour, would ultimately reach the age of a hundred and four.)

Not one to miss an opportunity to question a person of this vintage about their life and times, I called on my very best French. 'I suppose you were here during the war,' I began. 'Both wars,' she answered, 'the 14–18 war and the last one.' Pointing to the pastel-coloured shutters behind her, she said, 'I have lived here in this house all ninety-eight years of my life.'

Thinking that I am a journalist, Madame Reine reminds me that her family name is Ollivier, spelled with a double 'L' (*deux 'L'*). I ask if she was related to Charles Ollivier who was shot on the corner, not 200 metres from where we are sitting. 'This village is full of Olliviers, monsieur.' Already, the conversation is becoming guarded but my curiosity is unsatisfied. I had always imagined that Charles Ollivier had come down from the hills with his comrades to eject the Germans from the village and had perhaps pressed them too closely. But Madame Reine puts a finger to her lips and says, *'C'est une énigme.'*

Plan-de-la-Tour was one of the first inland villages to be liberated from the sea on D-Day (*Jour-J*), and Reine witnessed the trucks and tanks rolling past on this very same street. 'They could not get enough of the little cups of coffee we handed to them,' Reine remembers as if it were yesterday. I neglected to ask whether or not it was *ersatz* coffee – or the real thing, which was unobtainable at the time.

Next, she mentions that her husband was exiled in Italy during the war. He may have been a prisoner of war, or he may have been deported and interned as an undesirable. Maybe he was one of those who volunteered for relief work, the *relève*, or conscripted for the

STO (Service du Travail Obligatoire) whereby young people, called up according to their school-leaving year, were forced to do manual labour for the occupier, and was by definition 'obligatory'. Some were sent to Germany under the STO, but one did have the option of going underground. Few French people actively resisted, most simply waited for better days, and, of course, there were those who openly collaborated.

It emerges that Reine followed her husband to Italy of her own accord. Travelling by bicycle, by train and by her wits, she put her life and reputation on the line. '*Nous étions forts,*' she explains clasping her wrinkled old hands together, 'We were strong, my husband and I.' 'How strong is your marriage?' she wanted to know from me. But what I was keen to find out was: did her husband go along willingly to work in Italy? Did she herself play a role in the Resistance? Who were the collaborators in the village and what happened to them?

I dare not ask Madame Reine where she fitted into the milieu, but I have noticed a frosty relationship between her and another old lady in the village. In these parts a blood feud can go on for generations, and it seems there is a *brouille* (quarrel) between the two. From other curious outsiders I have heard vague whispers about wartime allegiances. Could it be that it is the lovable Reine who was the one who did nothing, or even collaborated while her husband was away working for the Germans? And was it Lily, who is the same age as Reine but not at all approachable, who was the resistant? After all, it is she who rides in the leading Jeep during the liberation day parade, and is present at many of the ceremonies which take place at the war memorial, the *monument aux morts.*

Every town and village celebrates its own special day of liberation as well as its martyrs, and virtually every village has its symbol of the resistance. In Villecroze it is Roger Maurice who was shot on 21 August 1944 by a panicked stray German – some days after the town had been liberated. While he had taken no part in resistance activity, Maurice has been elevated to the status of a hero who died for France. He is commemorated in a street name and on the *monument aux morts*, as are those who died as deportees. Every August in Provence, the liberation is celebrated with parades, re-enactments and the usual speeches. Around every corner there is a plaque or monument commemorating a drama which played out there seventy-five years ago or more.

The cult of the martyrs and heroes started as the events were happening, and the faithful continue this tradition of remembrance at countless shrines to the *héros de la Résistance* and *lieux de mémoire* (places of memory). It is a movable feast for the history connoisseur, but in fact these are places of sorrow and pity. The commemoration of the dead has gone beyond simple remembrance. Some interpret it as symbolizing an idealized vision of rural resistance in the collective memory. Perhaps unintentionally, it is a reminder of what the Germans did.

The wartime history of Provence has been prodigiously recorded thanks to the work of Henri Michel who had been a history teacher in Toulon before the war, and participated in the liberation. He oversaw the production of a chronology of every single act of resistance. His was the first doctoral thesis devoted to the Resistance. The objective of this 'historical positivism gone mad' was said to be 'the re-establishment of a truth which puts each person in their just place' for the edification of the next generation.[1] Jean-Marie Guillon is one of the next-generation scholars who has extensively researched the activities and composition of the Resistance in the Var Department.[2]

Much of the history of the French Resistance ultimately relies on the oral evidence of veterans, and, as Robert Gilda points out, only a narrow spectrum of accounts, testimonies and memoirs, mainly from the decision-making insiders, saw the light of day. He goes as far as to say that the so-called interview has the benefit of freshness and can recreate 'atmosphere' but when it comes to detail it is useless.[3]

As one researcher in the Var discovered to her dismay, villagers would not talk about their individual experiences, and constantly referred to major events which took place in Toulon and other faraway places. Village collective memory adopted external experiences to allow pride in their past. Veterans have the tendency to tell their story in a way in which they would like to be remembered. The so-called myth of the French Resistance and its place in the national consciousness has been attributed to this reconstructing of social memory.

An untainted primary source which gives a valuable insight into the everyday life in the Maquis is the diary of an Armée Secrète leader by the name of Gleb Sivirine, better known by his *nom de guerre, Vallier*.[4] Much use was also made of the memoirs written by ex-SOE (Special Operations Executive) agents directly after the war, although they would often overplay their role.

The history of the Allied invasion itself is well covered from an operational perspective but none with such fine prose as the work of

Jacques Robichon, translated from the French in *The Second D-Day*. I have drawn liberally from Jean-Loup Gassend's colossal book, *Operation Dragoon: Autopsy of a Battle: The Allied Liberation of the French Riviera August–September 1944* which is a combination of archaeology and archival sources.

Much of the information regarding executions of French civilians and resistants is obtained from the website of the Association Pour un Maitron des Fusillés et Exécutés (PMFE) which is linked to the Pantheon-Sorbonne University, also known as Paris 1. Around a hundred historians from all over France collaborated in writing the biographies of those victims massacred between 1940 and 1944.[5] Notations are only inserted where direct quotes are made from a published source, or where a statement is controversial or conflicting.

Where so many of the 'facts' are actually folklore, it is futile to build a scaffolding of footnotes. But history is simply a story we tell about the past; or as Napoleon put it, history is 'but a fable agreed upon'. Anecdotal stories are taken with a pinch of salt and partisan histories should be read against the grain. Seldom has internal and external criticism as taught in 'Historical Method 101' been so useful, but it is not infallible.

For a French perspective on the occupation, there is no shortage of literature, or primary documents and film which stir up the muddy waters of collaboration. Although some may have wanted to erase the four 'dark years' years from the pages of history, it is in fact the most intensively researched period in French historiography. All that was necessary to bring a soupçon of this subject to the English reader was some translation work. My lavish use of French words and phrases is more for the benefit of my fellow Francophiles, and for creating a sense of place, than out of vanity.

The Time and Place

As history transcends political and natural borders, it can best be said that this book is geographically located in the bottom right-hand corner of the Hexagon of France. Officially, the Provence-Alpes-Côte d'Azur (PACA) region consists of six departments extending from the River Rhône to the Italian border, and from the Mediterranean to the high Alps. The name 'Provence' comes from the time when it was part of *Provincia Nostra* (Our Province), the first Roman province in Gaul.

The term Côte d'Azur is used interchangeably with 'French Riviera'. It is also an area which has no clearly defined boundaries. Some say that it runs between Toulon and Nice, others that it extends from Cassis to Menton. The grand old city of Nice, at that time the fourth biggest in France, is the capital of the Alpes-Maritimes. From the wide pedestrian walkway along the beachfront, named Promenade des Anglais after the English who conceived it, the smoky peaks of the Alps are visible in the background. When it was founded by the ancient Greeks, it was originally called Nike, (spelled in various ways) after the Greek goddess of victory.

Travelling west from Nice, just past the Côte d'azur airport, one crosses the River Var, but the Var Department does not start here, and the river itself does not flow through the department of the same name. Menton, Nice, Antibes, Juan-les-Pins and Cannes, the old aristocrats of the French Riviera, all fall into the Department of the Alpes-Maritimes. Even in wartime, the city of Cannes presented itself as the '*Ville des fleurs et des sports élégants*' and was preferred over Nice by the very rich.

It was in Antibes where the so-called 'lost generation' of the inter-war years gained a reputation for their drink-fuelled, and sometimes decadent, antics. Just as the dark days of the German occupation were known as *les années noires* (the dark years), the crazy decades of sunshine and freedom which preceded them could be called *les années folles* (the crazy years). The life and soul of this time and place is epitomized by Scott and Zelda Fitzgerald who in 1924 moved from New York to the 'hot, sweet south of France' where they could 'live on practically nothing a year'. With their marriage and finances under strain, following the publication of *The Great Gatsby*, Fitzgerald rented a villa in Juan-les-Pins in 1926 and began working on *Tender Is the Night*, which would take him seven years to finish.

The 1929 stock market crash brought about a change in mood. Because of the Great Depression, there was a backlash against foreigners. Jews were blamed for taking French jobs, and in 1932, the persecution began. Yet writers and artists continued to seek inspiration in the South of France, and in 1939 while writing *All Quiet on the Western Front,* Erich Remarque visted Antibes as part of Marlene Dietrich's entourage. While Remarque drank to forget, Marlene indulged in sex without gender concerns on the rocks and out on the bay. French women did not have the right to vote in 1939, and it was rare for a woman to drive a car, but on the Riviera at least, sexual fluidity was fashionable.

In total contrast to the Côte d'Azur is the cesspit of Marseille, the capital of the Bouches-du-Rhône Department. As the name implies, this is where the River Rhône, a major highway of commerce, flows into the sea. The name of the high street, La Canebière, comes from the Latin word *cannabis*, dating back to when Marseille was a source of hemp baskets and rope. Despite being linked to Marseille by close transport and institutional ties, Aix-en-Provence is a centre of art and culture. Farther east, at Cassis, the series of long narrow inlets and steep cliffs, the *calanques* (pronounced ca-lonk) are not at all ideal for a large-scale amphibious landing. The same can be said for the marshland to the west of Marseille, known as the Camargue.

It was the coastline of the Var Department, particularly the fishing ports of Saint-Tropez, Sainte-Maxime, and Saint-Raphaël which would be at the centre of the amphibious invasion. Immediately adjoining Saint-Raphaël is the ancient city of Fréjus which, in Roman times, was a naval base called Forum Julii. This is where the broken fleet of Mark Antony and Cleopatra limped into port after the battle of Actium in 31 BC. Evidence of the Roman occupation, which lasted 600 years, is everywhere to be seen in Provence. There are theatres, bridges, aqueducts, and between Les Issambres and Saint-Aygulf, the walls of a Gallo-Roman fish farm still hold firm under the water.

In the 1930s, the gulf of Saint-Tropez was frequented by Anaïs Nin, the French-born *libertine*. Her father lived in Saint-Raphaël, and it was from here that she wrote letters, sometimes erotic, sometimes in a drunken state, to Henry Miller, discussing everything from their dreams and fears to their favourite literature, to the imminent reappearance of Henry's wife, June. These nomadic artists stood out from the local villagers who seldom travelled beyond the confines of their parishes.

The fishing village of Saint-Tropez with its ocre- and saffron-coloured, four-storey houses was still relatively undiscovered when 'Colette', one of the most beloved of French writers of all time, purchased her cottage on a hillside overlooking the sea. What spoiled her paradise was the arrival of the crowds who jammed the streets with their Bugattis, and campers who pitched their tents on 'her' pristine beach. By the mid-1930s, it was only at dawn that she could swim in the Baie des Canoubiers without being pestered for an autograph or being affronted by German nudists.

Inland from the invasion beaches is the Massif des Maures, a mountain range about fifty kilometres long and fifteen kilometres across at its widest point. Some say that the name 'Maures' comes from the word 'Moor' because pirates from North Africa used to hide out in these rugged hills. More recently, the Maquis found these 75,000 hectares of rugged woodland to be a convenient base for their operations. Farther inland, the Argens River valley separates the Massif des Maures from the Provence Alps to the north, forming a fertile plain, about eighty kilometres long, between Toulon and Saint-Raphaël. Le Muy sits in this plain which is why it was chosen as the landing zone for the airborne invasion of 15 August 1944.

In much of Provence, the vegetation is typified by aromatic shrubs and trees such as lavender, sage, rosemary, wild thyme, laurel, mimosa and juniper. In the spring especially, it is as though a giant potpourri has been let loose in the atmosphere, while in winter, it is the turn of the mimosas to bloom. The term 'Maquis' was initially derived from the hardy scrubland of the region, and the French expression *prendre le maquis* means to take to the bush, or go underground.

The Vaucluse Department is strewn with world heritage sites. Avignon is the seat of the préfecture and, for a brief period in history, it was the official seat of the Roman Catholic papacy. Gordes is a walled village stuck onto a hillside and is rated one of the most beautiful, or *plus beaux*, villages of France. At the foot of Mont Ventoux, the 'windy mountain', is the village of Sault where lavender farming and cycling tourism drive the economy. The commercial centre of the Luberon region is a town called Apt. A system of canals fed by the Sorgue, Durance and the Rhône has given the Vaucluse Department the status of being the breadbasket of the region.

What was previously called the Basses-Alpes, is now the Department of Alpes-de-Haute-Provence. In the lower reaches of this region, the vegetation is typically Mediterranean with oak and olive trees, lavender, and aromatic plants such as thyme, rosemary and sage. As the altitude rises, it becomes more Alpine in nature. Most of the activity takes place along the Durance River which has its source in the Alps near Briançon and meets the Rhône at Avignon. The Verdon River is a tributary of the Durance, best known for its spectacular canyon, the Gorges du Verdon, and the Lac de Sainte-Croix with its turquoise water. The main road artery in this department is the Route de Napoleon passing through Castellane, Digne-les-Bains and Sisteron, the route taken by Napoleon in 1815 on his return from exile.

During the inter-war years, the lives and traditions of the peasants and the villagers in the Alpine region were not much changed from Napoleon's time. In this harsh climate, the scenic beauty of the mountains went unnoticed; the peasants knew only poverty, sickness and death. A not-unheard-of sentiment in these parts was that it was better to die young than live to see one's entire family die from disease, war, farm accidents and suicide. Life was wretched, and death didn't amount to much.

In contrast to the sophisticated lifestyle of the Côte d'Azur, the peasant farmers and inhabitants of backward Alpine villages in the Department of the Hautes-Alpes led stunted lives in which leisure played no part. The short summer season was a frenzy of tilling the shallow soil, cutting hay and making cheese. The villages 'hidden deep in the valley beneath the mountains high above' bring to mind Edith Piaff's 1945 hit song, *Les Trois Cloches* about the three junctures in a man's life: his birth, his marriage and his passing – all heralded by the same lonely church bell.

PART I

Chapter 1

Humiliation

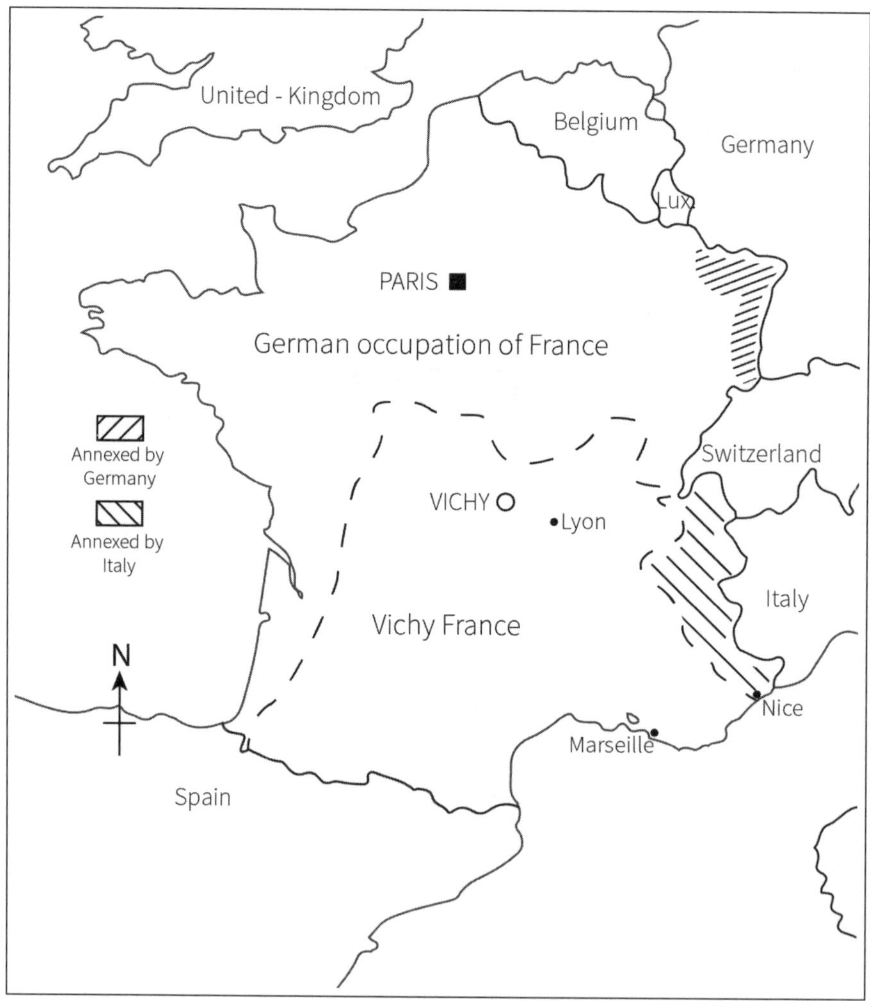

Demarcation line between Occupied Chrance and Vichy France.

HUMILIATION

When the bell tolls in a Provençal village the melancholy chimes are reassuring rather than alarming. But on 3 September 1939 the ringing was urgent and prolonged as it announced the declaration of war. This ought to have been the season for celebration as the worst of the heat is over and the grapes are reaching their prime. Families come together to help with *les vendanges*, the harvesting, and every community has its *fête* or celebration. As the wine goes into the barrels, a sense of relief is blended with anticipation. The pressure is off until Sainte-Catherine's day which is when the olives are ready for pressing.

The French nation was in turmoil, but no one was too surprised: they had been waiting for the storm to break. The 'war to end all wars' had ended little over twenty years before, and every family still mourned for someone whose name is inscribed on the *monument aux morts*. Now they put their faith in the strength of their border defences, the Maginot Line. The French army with their obsolete equipment was rapidly mobilized and sent to the north where nothing happened for eight months. This was '*la drôle de guerre*' (literally the funny war but better translated as the phoney war). Disproving the perception that they have no sense of humour, the Germans called it the '*sitzkrieg*', the sitting war, as opposed to the '*blitzkrieg*'. Life in Provence virtually returned to normal with the return of tourists for the Easter break.

When the Germans finally did invade France, the Allies managed to hold them back for just seven weeks. The German victory shocked everyone in its speed and efficiency. In 1916 the Germans had attacked Verdun for ten months without success. Now they took Verdun in little more than a day. On 10 June 1940 Marshal Philippe Pétain, hero of the First World War, surrendered and announced over the radio that he had asked for an armistice.

The nation was largely shocked and disgusted. More than a million and a half French soldiers were taken prisoner. Returning soldiers told their friends and family '*On nous a vendu*' (we were sold out).[1] Understandably, the masculinity of these men whose fathers had fought so bravely in the trenches had been impugned. It destroyed the nation's morale and self-esteem, which would necessitate the fabrication of a myth, proclaiming that the French liberated themselves – albeit with some help from the Allies.[2]

Like the conflict in the north, the Franco-Italian war got off to a slow start with a few clashes along the border in June 1940. Cross-border artillery and air bombardments were mostly ineffective. After two days of relatively heavy fighting on 23 and 24 June, the communes of Sospel, Fontan, Castellar, Briel and Menton fell into the hands of the Italians. Some called it the 'gelato war' because it lasted about as long as it took to eat an ice-cream. Forty Frenchmen were killed and the formidable Ligne Alpine was surrendered.

While the bulk of the British army had been salvaged at Dunkirk, small groups of French soldiers tried to reach England on their own. Citizens of Paris and other cities in the north fled blindly. In Provence the Route Nationale 7 (RN 7) to Nice and Italy was clogged with vehicles of every sort. Train stations were scenes of panic, and carriages were packed to overflowing. Antoine Saint-Exupéry, the pioneering French pilot, and author of *The Little Prince*, wrote that from the air, it looked like some giant had kicked open a huge anthill. In what became known as *l'exode*, the exodus, an estimated one-sixth of the population took to the roads, fleeing in front of the advancing Germans. Between six and ten million fled their homes, seeking refuge in the south. Many would remain there for the duration as it became difficult to cross back over the Demarcation line.

France was now divided by the Demarcation line into an occupied zone and unoccupied zone. In places the line arbitrarily divided villages. The northern and western part of the country, including the entire Atlantic coast, was occupied by Germany, and the rest – 45 per cent of the land and a third of the population – was ostensibly self-governed. Provence fell into the unoccupied zone, officially called l'État Français, but better known as 'Vichy France'. Caught somewhere between neutral state and German puppet, it has been the subject of endless studies as political historians have attempted to define its role, in particular to what degree Vichy was its own master.

The insignificant town of Vichy was selected as the capital after a short spell in Claremont-Ferrand. Vichy was centrally located and, being a spa town, had numerous hotels to house bureaucrats and politicians. Marshal Pétain, who incidentally owned a villa on the coast at Villeneuve-Loubert, was installed as the head of state. Despite preaching family values, Pétain had been a womanizer. Now aged 84, he was still in rude health.

The Vichy government worked at creating a powerful personality cult around Pétain. For example, it was obligatory for every place of business to display a portrait of him in the shop window. One bookshop owner took his life in his hands by placing a *vendu* (sold) sign above the portrait. Pétain's popularity prevailed even after the Vichy government was on the wane. Effectively, all power was in the hands of the prime minister, a 57-year-old lawyer with a peasant background, named Pierre Laval. His was the swarthy, evil face of the state, distinguished by thick lips and bulbous eyes.

The Vichy government blamed liberalism and decadence for having lost the war. During radio broadcasts, individualistic and hedonistic values were condemned as being morally degenerate. An ordinance in Cannes prohibited women from promenading along the beach in revealing attire, including bathing suits and culottes. Knee-length, two-piece bathing suits were made compulsory for men and women in Nice, and police did try to enforce the law. Women of ill repute (*femmes de mauvaise vie*) were interned or sentenced to hard labour. 'Morally disreputable' women included those who engaged in adultery while their husbands were prisoners of war.

Although the Vichyites tried to rationalize that working with the Germans was the only logical thing to do, and that a certain amount of autonomy was better than none, it went against everything the French Republic held dear. The trade unions were dissolved and the economy became centrally controlled to maximize production of war material. Communists were hunted down, as were Freemasons, Jews and Gypsies. Referred to as 'the scum of the earth', such people became second-class citizens and were deprived of their rights and their property.

Being mainly Catholic and conservative, the older generation and a large section of the rural population loved Pétain, and initially supported the Vichy government, despite its fascist character. Conservatives saw the Vichy government as the defender against anarchy, chaos and revolution. They found the Germans occupiers to be disciplined, 'so correct and polite'. The unmanly appearance of the French troops was compared with the youth and vigour of the conquering Germans – the 'young war gods'.[3]

For the most part, judges and magistrates collaborated enthusiastically, applying the oppressive laws without quibble. Even the church and préfectures did not dissent. Vichy police were prepared to help the Germans to round up Jews, kill resistance members and arrest those trying to escape compulsory labour service. Only a small minority of principled French people refused to cooperate with the forces of evil. The United States maintained an embassy in Vichy France until November 1942.

One of the early resisters, and co-founder of the 'Combat' movement, Henri Frenay, escaped from a PoW camp in Alsace and made his way to his mother's house in Sainte-Maxime. 'In the southern zone', he observed, 'the great majority of the population welcomed the armistice with an infinite relief and the Republic disappeared on 10 July to general indifference.' It was here that Frenay first imagined an organized resistance although 'passionately attached to the work of Marshal Pétain'.[4] In Sainte-Maxime, Rue Henri Frenay runs up from the beach to intersect with Avenue Berthie Albrecht – named after one of his disciples.

Typically, it was among the communists and less-fortunate where the Resistance found their allies. People such as this would hand over their last centime and give up their kitchen floor to accommodate fugitives of the regime. Of course, resistance against the puppet regime and the occupying forces grew stronger when it became clear that Germany was losing the war. Odette Sansom, an agent of the British SOE (Special Operations Executive) wrote contemptuously of the wealthy people who descended on Cannes:

> In dusty Delage and de Soto, Monsieur, Madame and les enfants had come twittering and twitching from the north to storm the hotels of the south. A suite overlooking the sea? One could pay. One had had terrible experiences which one wanted to forget. The war was a great foolishness and, please, one did not wish to mention it. Winston Churchill was an imbecile, who, because he refused to accept the fact of defeat, was bringing ruin on all of France. Here in Cannes, one could find that tranquility to which one's diamonds and debentures surely entitled one.[5]

If, as he would later claim at his treason trial, Pétain was the 'shield' of France, General Charles de Gaulle was the 'sword'. At first, few knew of de Gaulle's existence but through the voice of 'Free France' broadcast from London, he became a symbol of resistance. In dribs and drabs French volunteers fled their country and joined the Forces Françaises Libres (FFL) reinforcing the French colonial troops. Most of the overseas French colonies were originally under Vichy control, but with the Allied invasion of North Africa one colony after another was liberated.

Under the terms of the armistice of 1940, the Vichy regime was permitted to keep a small military force, including the entire French fleet, which was harboured in the port of Toulon in the unoccupied zone. A seminal event in the history of the war in Provence occurred on 27 November 1942. The Germans decided to take possession of the French fleet, and descended on the harbour at 4 a.m. Having already made provisions for such an eventuality, the French Navy scuttled around ninety ships to prevent them from falling into German hands. By self-sabotage seventy-seven vessels were sunk, some of the bigger ships billowed smoke for days, and oil polluted the harbour for years. Germany now possessed a deep-water port in the Mediterranean.

One surface ship and several submarines, including the *Protée* and *Casabianca*, ignored orders to scuttle and managed to reach Algiers, Barcelona and other safe havens. Tragically, the *Protée* disappeared just before Christmas 1943, together with the crew of seventy, plus three British agents. The submarine had been on patrol off Marseille and hit a mine. Quite by accident, the wreck was discovered in the harbour mouth in 1995 and was declared a war memorial. The *Casabianca*, however, completed many missions infiltrating and retrieving agents on the 'Riviera run'.

General Charles de Gaulle heavily criticized the Vichy admirals for not ordering the fleet to escape to Algiers. Thus ended any semblance of Vichy independence, Pétain became a figurehead, and the Germans tightened their grip on Provence. When he was told that Hitler was going to occupy the whole of France, Pierre Laval's only comment was, 'Those Jews on the Riviera are in for a nasty surprise.'[6]

At the same time as the German intrusion into Vichy France, the Italians expanded their presence in the eastern part of Provence. They had been there since 1940, and had already annexed the town of Menton near the Italian border. Nice and Corsica were next in line since they had once been part of Italy. In Nice, Avenue de la Victoire became Avenue Mussolini. Despite being a Vichyite, the mayor, Jean Médecin, did himself credit by refusing to change the name of the Promenade des Anglais. In the old part of the city especially, there was a large Italian population, and despite their arrogance, the Italians were mostly Catholics and had a language and culture not dissimilar to that of the French.

Disparagingly referred to as 'Macaronis', the Italian soldiers did not appear at all warlike with their excessive use of strong perfume and their mandolins. Even the elite 'Alpini' soldiers, with feathers in their hats, were friendly enough. Conversely, the Blackshirt Militia and secret police known as l'Ovra (Organizzazione per la Vigilanza e la Repressione dell'Antifascismo) were as brutal as the Gestapo. Their first targets were Italian dissidents in exile but next on their agenda was the French Resistance, especially those of the communist variety.

Standing out among the many detention centres which were run by the Italian Carabinieri and their secret police, l'Ovra, was Villa Lynwood on the western slope of the hill at Cimiez outside Nice. As soon as she could, after the liberation, the old woman who owned the villa, Mrs Benjamin Ellis, returned from Liverpool to find her Rolls Royce still in the garage but without seats, engine or tyres. On the stairway leading down to the cellar was a notice which read: 'Abandon hope all ye who enter here.' Down below, there was a contraption named 'the giro' to which prisoners were shackled by their hands and feet and then spun around. One particular item of graffiti on the walls read: 'Theo Wolff, writer, 75 years.' Theodor Wolff was a newspaper editor from Berlin, arrested while trying to get to the United States, and eventually sent back to Germany to die. Older men in particular, struggled to keep body and mind together.

Under Vichy law, anyone deemed a threat to national security was liable to be interned without any formalities and held without trial. A man named Louis Piétri was arrested when the train station in Antibes was invaded by l'Ovra and 'Blackshirts'. Interned at Salel Barracks, in Sospel, he was informed during interrogation that he and the other Antibois owed their internment to a request from the Mayor of Antibes, the highly respected Jules Grec, and others whom he names, including two priests. They learned that they had been declared 'undesirables' and 'likely to disturb the public order of the city Antibes'.

Some British and Americans civilians who had been resident in Monaco were also interned but were well treated, and even had their beds made for them, the rationale being that they might soon be trading places with their captors. More than a thousand Britons and Americans had been living on the Riviera in 1939 but most has been evacuated at the last minute. Thoughts of resistance burned fiercely in the hearts and minds of inmates. During the purge which followed the liberation, Louis Piétri would take an awful revenge on his perceived enemies in Antibes.

A part of life under the occupation was the curfew or *couvre-feu* in French. People had to be off the streets by 8 p.m. Of course, not everyone complied. Where the army of occupation was at risk of attack, the curfew was more stringent. Patrolling the streets at night, the Italian soldiers called out '*La luce*' if they saw light behind the blackout curtains, whereas the Germans were inclined to shoot at anything that moved. Young boys who threw stones at Italian soldiers would never dare do the same to the Germans.

Although the Italian occupation brought oppression and privation, there was no great fear as there would be under the jackboot of the Boche. When the Italians changed allegiance on 8 September 1943, their troops left under the scornful watch of the French citizens. The taunt went like this: 'They came proud and handsome with their feathers in their hats. They left vanquished and beaten, *la plume au cul* (feathers up their backside).'

At first, there was jubilation, people dancing in the street to accordion music, but it was short-lived. Two days later the Germans arrived, and the Gestapo immediately got to work, starting at the train station. Of course, the Jewish population had been under no illusions and the wise went into hiding in caves, barns and garages deep into the back country. Many joined the Italian soldiers in their attempt to cross back into Italy on foot through the mountains, the soldiers abandoning uniforms and weapons as they left. Tons of weapons were thrown into the sea, from where young patriots attempted to retrieve them. Like the exodus from Egypt, the fugitives set off wearing city shoes, carrying suitcases, struggling on narrow mountain trails flanked by treacherous precipices, cold and hungry. Italian soldiers were also on the route, some seemed to be alone without their officers and without uniforms. Others helped carry luggage, or took children in their arms.[7] On reaching Cuneo in Italy, the SS were waiting to take them into captivity or force them into labour. The Jews would wind up in the death camps sooner or later.

The Germans proceeded to invest the whole of Provence, disarming and interning some 330,000 Italian soldiers. Another 23,000 fled to Switzerland. How quickly the tables had turned. The préfect of the Alpes-Maritimes issued a warning that all Italian soldiers belonging to the former army of occupation now had illegal status and to shelter them in any way was an act of complicity which would elicit the harshest punishment, even death.

Wanting to win the hearts and minds of the French population, the German propaganda machine worked overtime. Cultural collaboration was facilitated through German Institutes where German classics such as Goethe were translated into French, and language courses were so popular they were oversubscribed. Children became aware of the growing tension among the adults and avoided the friendly overtures of even the most fatherly of German types. The occupied villages simmered with rumours and fears. A new language developed in which the term 'black market' cropped up continually, and the word '*milice*' (militia) was whispered by adults in anxious tones.

The Vichy militia, the Milice Française, was a paramilitary force approximately 30,000 strong, including part-time members and the youth wing, the *Avant-Garde*. Fascist in the extreme, the Milice was created by Pierre Laval himself for the purpose of combating the Resistance and was commanded by one Joseph Darnand. Some volunteered for the Milice in order to avoid forced labour, some were criminals and some were true patriots believing that they were doing their duty to France. Priding themselves in their discipline, their chief enemies were 'Jewish leprosy', 'Bolshevism' and 'pagan freemasonry', not to mention 'Gaullism'.

The elite of the Milice was the Franc-Garde, or Free Guard, which was the only unit to wear the uniform of blue trousers, khaki shirt, black tie and beret. Like the Maquis, they were organized into *mains, dizaines, trentaines, centaines* and *cohortes*. A *main* (meaning a hand) consisted of four *franc-gardes* and a *chef-de-main*.[8]

Whereas members of the regular Vichy Army (Army of the Armistice) mostly defected to the Maquis after being disbanded in November 1942, the Milice continued to collaborate, although enthusiasm waned noticeably when things started going badly for their masters. Much hated by most Frenchmen, *miliciens* and their families were pariahs in the community and legitimate targets for assassination. A reward of 10,000 francs was payable for killing a collaborator and one tract read: 'From today, every member of the Milice must be thought of as a mad dog and treated as such. Fire on the Milice.'[9]

The call did not go unheeded. Members of the Milice were gunned down in cafés and other public places. Following one assassination in March 1944, a full-on shootout occurred in Rue de France in Nice, resulting in two dead policemen and two dead resistants. The lone survivor was sentenced to death by a Milice court martial and executed by a gendarme firing squad. On 28 November 1943, Joseph Darnand held a meeting in Nice and gave an hour-long speech to an audience consisting mainly of *miliciens*. He evoked the sacrifices they had made, including thirty-three dead and twenty-five seriously wounded since April. Insisting that their deaths should not go unavenged, he made a call for volunteers to fight in what was effectively a civil war.[10]

In June 1942, the much-loathed Pierre Laval enacted the *relève* – relief work – whereby French workers were encouraged to volunteer to work in Germany and thereby secure the release of prisoners of war. Some of these 'volunteers' ended up serving in the Wehrmacht. Perhaps the Vichy regime's biggest mistake was the introduction of compulsory work service, the Service du Travail Obligatoire (STO). Begun in March 1943, this conscription of forced labour was the best recruiting tool which the Resistance could have wished for. Initially, only men aged between 20 and 22 were eligible, with exemptions for farmers, miners, students and policemen. Within a year, eligibility had been expanded to men and childless women aged 18 to 45. A *réfractaire* was one who hid or went underground to avoid the STO or the *relève*. Not all STO dodgers could be called *maquisards* – hiding is not the same as fighting.

An underground publicity pamphlet urged people to resist the STO, proclaiming that a worker for Germany is a soldier for Hitler. 'The women won't let you go, the railway workers won't let you go,' it read. 'The whole nation and all the *résistance* movements are with you. Do not sign, do not go. Defend your liberty. We will help you, together we will win.'[11]

When the Germans took control of the whole of Provence, they brought with them a multitude of even more sinister forces. The many instruments for instilling fear included the Geheime Feldpolizei (GFP), Geheime Staatspolizei (Secret State Police, or Gestapo), Sicherheitsdiens (SD), Sicherheitspolizei (SiPo-SD) and various police units, who will collectively be referred to as the Gestapo for the sake of simplicity. A rivalry existed between the Gestapo and the Abwehr, or military intelligence, who were slightly less brutal, but also less effective.

A special unit of French auxiliaries in the German Army, the 8th Company, 3rd Regiment of the Brandenburg Division, was used to hunt down those escaping the STO, the *réfractaires*. In one of their typical operations, a group of eighty Brandenburgers, assisted by Gestapo, arrived at Banon in the Vaucluse during the night of 4 December 1943. They raided homes and rudimentary camps in the Lure Mountains. A few youths were transported back to Hyères and Bandol, where they were interrogated and tortured before being deported into the 'night and fog'. It was the policy of the Nazis to conceal the fate of certain prisoners. In terms of a special decree, political prisoners were to disappear into the night and fog or *nacht und nebel* or *nuit et brouillard* in French.[12]

The Chantiers de la Jeunesse Française was yet another unwelcome infringement on the lives of residents in the Vichy state. Although it was promoted as a type of military service, it was simply another form of forced labour. All men of a military age were liable to be called up at a moment's notice by way of a letter delivered by the *facteur*, the postman. In Provence, woodcutting was the main activity but the *vendanges*, the grape harvesting, would come as a welcome change. The unlucky ones ended up breaking rocks in a quarry, like prisoners, or being offered up to the Germans as cannon fodder.

Propaganda posters portrayed the Chantiers de la Jeunesse as a healthy, masculine way of life, close to nature. In the forests and the mountains, young men were deprived of news and easily indoctrinated. Marius Vitout of Le Lavandou recounts that he was treated like an animal, and fed on nothing but chickpeas and aubergine jam. A few like Marius, with the help of a sympathetic railwayman, managed to escape while being transported to Germany, and then remained hidden with the Resistance. As many as 16,000 teenagers who were drafted into Chantiers de la Jeunesse ended up in Germany.[13]

Menfolk were largely missing from the farms and villages, many being held as prisoners of war, and others abducted, deported or sent for compulsory work service. Women had always done more than their fair share of the farm work, but now they also had to run the businesses, *boucheries* and *boulangeries*. Doctors and surgeons were also absent, which had dire consequences for the very young and elderly.

Unlike other regions of France, the Mediterranean coast is not known for the diversity of its food production. Wine and olive oil is produced on a commercial scale, while in back gardens one finds figs and pomegranates. Up in the hills, chestnuts were free for the taking during autumn, and could be made into flour or purée. No other department in the whole of France was as badly off for food as the Var. The farms of 'upper' Provence and the fertile plains of the rivers Sorgue, Rhône and Durance, helped feed the coastal towns.[14]

Left uncultivated, the land became degraded, plants and trees withered and the coast was littered with mines which made fishing from the rocks dangerous. Very few permits were issued for fishing boats and fuel shortages crippled what was left of the industry. One had to queue up at the harbour to buy a share of the diminished catch. Sardines were the primary catch before the Germans disallowed deep sea fishing which had been the backbone of the economy. It was also necessary to queue around the block for one's daily loaf. Landowners were likely to be a little more self-sufficient.

During wartime, those who departed least from the subsistence rural economy were best able to care for their families. Producing subsistence quantities of olives, wine, table grapes, figs, and honey was wiser than growing fields of lavender or trying to distribute truckloads of asparagus. Wheat is a marginal crop in these shallow soils but it was wise to grow a few hectares as a form of disaster insurance. Even with a small backyard, one could keep a cow, fatten a pig and grow a few vegetables.

Monoculture, which in peacetime could make an area prosperous from the wine or olive oil trade, became a curse during the occupation. The food ration for residents of Marseille was lower in calories than in Paris for example. The butter ration was smaller here than almost anywhere else. In France as a whole, life was harder in the cities than it was in the countryside, but in parts of Provence it was the other way around.

What the Germans needed for their war machine they simply took. They did not hesitate to rip out and melt down church bells and statues. Requisitions, known to the French as *les ravitaillements*, ranged from paper to petrol. Particularly hard in the brutal winter of 1943/4 was the pillaging of coal and wood. The German Army requisitioned as much leather as they could get their hands on to make boots for their soldiers. Horses and other livestock were required to fulfil needs of the occupying German forces and trainloads were sent to Germany or Italy. France had become the 'milk cow' of the oppressor. The result was, of course, a shortage of almost everything that in turn brought about a system of rationing.

Farm produce had to be handed over, though many farmers were accused of hoarding or selling on the black market, or parallel market, as the Germans preferred to call it. Trains laden with French coal could be seen crossing the country, bound for Germany and Italy. Railway workers had the opportunity of syphoning some off for the black market. On 10 March 1943 a large crowd in the town of Romans-sur-Isère stopped a train leaving the station with food for Germany. Food protests and strikes, organized by the underground, were a regular occurrence. Women were at the forefront of these demonstrations, as they had been during the French Revolution. 'For bread and for liberty' was their rallying cry. Hunger gives rise to rage.

Demonstrations against the food situation became displays of patriotism associated with 14 July 1944 (the national holiday). The Resistance promoted the strikes by way of leaflets, broadcasts and newspapers. Patriotic demonstrations took place in fourteen locations in Provence, but the most spectacular, with several thousand demonstrators, was in Hyères. Children suffered from malnutrition and an adult man could lose a third of his bodyweight. When it came to the *Fête des Mères* (Mother's Day), the government's propaganda poster of a joyous mother lifting up her child was caricatured by the Communist Party with a poster of its own in which a mother holds up her starvng child, crying out for help.

Ships from the North African colonies, a source of wheat and olive oil, no longer docked in the port of Nice. Bread quality plummeted and would spoil after a day. Boiled potatoes took the place of bread on some school menus. During the Italian occupation, pasta was relatively plentiful but that source dried up after 1943. Worried relatives in more productive regions of France sent packages of food but these seldom reached their destination. Only postcards were allowed to cross the Demarcation line, making it necessary for food parcels to be smuggled by ingenious means.

Rationing regulated virtually all consumer goods, including clothing, tobacco and soap. Most importantly, though, it controlled food. Cheese, eggs, meat, milk, butter, fats, oil, bread, wine, potatoes, fish – all were controlled by rationing. Citizens had to register with their local suppliers. A ration card determined how much of a type of food a person was allotted each week. Ration cards were needed for almost every commodity, even clothes. Tobacco was reserved only for men, and women sometimes resorted to exchanging their food ration cards for cigarettes. Sympathetic clerks at the town hall might forge ration cards so that mothers could buy a little extra concentrated milk for their babies although special categories of ration cards did exist for pregnant or nursing mothers.

The population was divided into categories based on age, gender and other needs but patently, rationing could not meet demand, so people had to look elsewhere. The black market renewed urban–rural links, as city folk cultivated ties with their families in the country. Children from the Var in particular were sent to stay with their country cousins in the greener pastures of the Vaucluse, Basses-Alpes and Hautes-Alpes. Even though the marketing of farm produce was centrally controlled, farmers made the most of the demand and generally they prospered.

Dressing well became a form of resistance for city women. Whatever the shortages, they were determined to retain some chic. Soon after she arrived back in London from her villa in Saint-Jean-Cap-Ferrat, the Australian-born Lady Enid Furness told a journalist about the hardships of life in occupied France. Her particular concern was the demise of fun and fashion on the Riviera, although she and her family were immune from the hunger. 'There is a shortage of everything ... everything,' she said:

> Where it is possible to buy clothes, you must give two old dresses for a new one, as well as pay an exorbitant price. There's no warmth or quality to the material. All the lovely Lyons velvets, beautiful French woollens and heavy silks have vanished totally – they've gone to Germany.[15]

Although it helped to be rich, one did not want to be seen to be living better than one's neighbour. At meal times, housewives closed their kitchen doors so they wouldn't be betrayed by the smell of lard sizzling in the pot, or the piece of prohibited meat, or the cake made with illegal flour. Denunciations, mostly anonymous, were all too common. Jealousy over food was often the cause so it was wise to be discreet. A distinction was made between those who profited excessively from the misery of the community, and those who merely tried to make ends meet.

While working for the SOE, Odette Sansom experienced first-hand the hardships of daily life for the ordinary people of Cannes under the occupation. 'Away from the sleek hotels, the cut-glass scent bottles and the shaven armpits of the Croisette [Boulevard de la Croisette], life for the people of Cannes was hard and hungry.' There was no milk at all. The 'National' soap was useless. Potatoes cost 5/- a pound, an egg 3/-, a lemon half a crown. Coffee could be bought at £3/10 a half kilo, butter at £6. A chicken cost from £4/10 to £5 according to weight. 'Fish, lavish in the forbidden sea, was a mere £2 a kilo, and the virtue of one's daughter was the price of a packet of cigarettes.'[16]

Although locally produced, olive oil was controlled by the authorities and could only be bought on the black market for about 1,500 francs per litre. By comparison, a litre of wine cost 15 francs. The black market price of a kilogram of rabbit meat was 350 to 450 francs. Wild rabbits abounded in these parts but having turned in their weapons, hunters had to resort to trapping. Squirrels, mice and even foxes ended up in the stew.

Everyone had their own recipes for disguising the taste. According to *Système D* – the French *se débrouiller*, meaning to manage or get by – it was each to his own method, *chacun sa méthode*. When coffee beans ran out, *ersatz* coffee was made with roasted acorns or chickpeas. Liquorices and boiled pumpkins were used to replace sugar. A reduction of grapes made a sweet, sticky mess called *raisiné* which served as jam and sugar. The national loaf (bread) was augmented with sawdust and rats droppings The challenges of feeding a family are encapsulated in the reminiscences of a young mother and resistant from La Garde, near Toulon:

> As time passes, rations diminish. We must stand in long lines to get what is rightfully ours, more wood or coal for heating. We put on nightcaps and layers of clothes to keep warm. There is no more petrol. On the roof of the few cars travelling, large gasifiers [gazogène units to convert charcoal to wood gas] are installed. The bicycle is our mode of travel. Rare and valuable goods are traded in the market, organized by unscrupulous smugglers at exorbitant prices. In summary, we are hungry; we are cold, especially when one is poor. Some traders show great humanity. Bakers, when they can, add some bread for the more needy … My main concern is to ensure food for my little girl. I often find myself with mothers who crave a little extra for a baby, a child, a grandmother. So I travel many kilometres on my bike to find enough to eat. The black market is king. Prices are doubled or tripled and sometimes more … Black marketeers are known as BOFs because of the things in which they trade (*beurre, oeufs, fromage*).[17]

By default, the bicycle earned the title 'king of the road'. There was even a black market specifically for bicycles and bicycle parts because these were rationed. The German Army had priority over the limited fuel supplies, so they set a limit on how many cars were allowed on the roads. Motor vehicles virtually became public property as they might be requisitioned by either side. On country roads, and even in the cities, there was a virtual absence of traffic.

The *Pocket Guide to France*, which was issued to Allied troops, emphasized the frugal and thrifty character of the French people, leading the reader to believe that this is what enabled them to survive the ravages of the occupation. Being economical was supposedly part of the national character, as was respect for the traditionally important values of civilized man, 'by the French people's good taste; by their interest in quality, not quantity; and by the lively energy of their minds. The French are intelligent, have mostly had a sensible education, without frills, they are industrious, shrewd, and frugal'.[18]

Even the most loyal Pétain supporters eventually realized that their daily hardships were due to collaboration with Germany, and general sentiment turned against the collaborationist Vichy state. Resentment festered, when the German commander at Ramatuelle demanded that the *maire*, the mayor, supply eighty men every week for compulsory labour. His letter was polite but with a threatening undertone. Everywhere on the coast, local labourers were forced to cut down their own trees for defensive works or for replanting where enemy gliders might land.[19]

Working conditions were severe, and the STO drove many a young man into the fold of the Resistance, while food shortages caused ordinary French people to engage in some form of public protest. Terrorized by the Milice, most people were too afraid to openly support the Maquis. Fortuné Ferrier was too young to take up arms, having been born in 1927, but was nevertheless conflicted: 'The Resistance tended towards the Haut-Var. I did not join the Maquis because I was afraid for my family, they would have taken my sister or my father hostage. It was very difficult to know who was right, if it was right or wrong.'[20] The Third Reich was supposed to last a thousand years, and like most others, he had a family to feed.

Newspapers and radio were controlled by the Germans, and Vichy radio was stuffy and boring, as well as being dishonest. To be informed one had to listen to Swiss Radio or the BBC – if one's wireless set had the ability to pick it up. Needless to say, it was forbidden to listen, and if caught tuning in, one could be accused of espionage so the volume would be turned right down and it became routine procedure to change the frequency dial after listening to the BBC in case an enemy came knocking at the door to check one's radio set.

A new sense of patriotism was fostered through messages of revolution in the underground press, and the holding of flag-raising ceremonies and parades on national holidays. At first, the Resistance manifested itself in small acts of passive disobedience, through symbolism and subtle gestures. On public holidays particularly Armistice Day, the *Tricolore* would be hung from telephone lines alongside the Stars and Stripes and the Union Jack. Daring young activists stuffed pamphlets through letterboxes and wrote '*A bas le gouvernement de Vichy*' (Down with Vichy) and other slogans on buildings. Following an appeal to patriots over the BBC in 1941, the walls of Marseille were covered with the 'V' for *victoire*. Even these petty protests could be punishable by death or deportation.

The village of Villecroze in the Moyen-Var was relatively isolated from the war, and the most important act of resistance occurred on Easter Monday 1943 when someone wrote '*Vive la Republique*' on the bust of Marianne. Members of the Milice and Italian soldiers from Salernes arrived to remove the statue but a crowd gathered and prevented it from being taken away. This mini-revolt is still at the core of Villecroze folklore today.

Resistance meant more than just an attitude: it meant carrying out an act. In 1941, this was mostly limited to propaganda in the form of newspapers or tracts. In Digne-les-Bains, a young hairdresser called Simone Pellissier laid a wreath at the *mounment aux morts* during a demonstration. For this, she was given a taste of the infamous Montluc Prison in Lyon.

At first it seemed futile to resist but by 1943 the German Army had begun to experience setbacks and no longer seemed invincible. Stalingrad and El Alamein were two major battles that turned the tide. This new optimism, together with the privations and persecutions perpetrated by the Vichy regime, galvanized the spirit of resistance. As the fortunes of war changed so too did the prospects of those who collaborated. Those who had unwisely picked the wrong side were now labelled *collabo* or *traître*.[21]

Extreme precautions had to be taken to prevent traitors from infiltrating a network. Making the initial contact was particularly perilous.

Prospective recruits would be sent from pillar to post using passwords, signals and subtle interrogation. Without an introduction, it might take days of such subterfuge before being accepted into the fold. Even toward the end, the vast majority of the adult population did not get involved in any way. The average French citizen did no more than try to scrape together the next meal; everyone just waited. They waited for better days: *on attend des jours meilleurs*. Support from outside would be needed to fan the flames.

Chapter 2

Humanity

With the fall of France, a tide of humanity poured into the coastal cities trying to escape German onslaught. Some believed that the Vichy state offered a safe haven. In addition to civilian refugees, there were men wanting to join armies in exile. Charles de Gaulle's famous appeal in June 1940 played a role, although few people were aware of it at first. Evoking the powerful support of the United States and the resilience of Britain, he invited all able-bodied men to join him in London:

> Believe me, I who am speaking to you with full knowledge of the facts, and who tells you that nothing is lost for France. The same means that overcame us can bring us victory one day. For France is not alone! She is not alone! She is not alone! She has a vast Empire behind her. (Charles de Gaulle, L'Appel du 18 juin)

In the very beginning, when Poland was overrun, thousands of trained Polish troops got out through Eastern Europe to join the Polish Army in exile. Others made their way to France wanting to join the Polish Army there, but had to keep moving south to be extracted from places like Biarritz on the Atlantic coast, or even farther south on the Mediterranean coast. Some stayed to fight as part of the French Resistance, and would find themselves in conflict with the tens of thousands of their fellow countrymen serving in the Wehrmacht. Pilots in particular were needed in England, and would be recruited by Camille Rayon in Chatham's Bar across from the station in Juan-les-Pins. As we will see, Rayon went from restaurateur to renowned resistance leader, and today the yacht harbour at Antibes is named Port Camille Rayon.

Escape networks organized a chain of *passeurs* (guides) and safe houses from Holland through Belgium and France to help airmen, and even leftovers from the Dunkirk debacle, reach England. At the same time, they would be landing SOE agents, stores, supplies and quantities of cash to oil the wheels of the resistance movements. It could be said that the most valuable work of the secret services was not sabotage or intelligence-gathering, but rather morale-building and salvaging of human cargo, or 'parcels' as they were known in the trade.

Large consignments were smuggled out at night on fishing boats which anchored in small coves or *calanques* near Cassis and La Ciotat. The preferred transport was an inconspicuous small fishing or trading boat called a felucca. With both engines and sails, the felucca was less visible than a steamboat. The Polish captain of the *Seawolf* had French colours painted on the hull, and on the so-called 'Riviera-run' he would pass between the islands of Ibiza and Majorca, before aiming for the lighthouse at Cap d'Antibes, which could be seen twenty-five kilometres out to sea.

High-speed motor launches operated between Corsica and some of the popular tourist beaches at Agay, Fréjus, Pampelonne and Le Lavandou. In the case of high-value consignments, submarines were used. Of course, insertions were also made by parachute or by Lysander light aircraft. On rare occasions extractions were made by four-engined bomber aircraft from rough and remote airstrips.

One of the first organizations helping people get out of Europe was the Emergency Rescue Committee whose Marseille representative was an American journalist named Varian Fry. Together with a small group of volunteers he set up Le Centre Américain de Secours and helped thousands (mainly Jews) fleeing the Nazis. Among Fry's closest associates were Americans Miriam Davenport, a former art student at the Sorbonne, and the Chicago heiress Mary Jayne Gold, a lover of the arts and the 'good life'. A self-described 'upper middle class Wasp', Gold had been one of those fleeing before the German Army on the congested roads of France. The American trio remained friends and reminisced fondly about their time in Marseille.

Part of this circle was a former French legionnaire by the name of Raymond Couraud. He too drifted south after the fall of France, having already won a Croix de Guerre at the age of twenty. In Marseille, he became involved in the smuggling of goods and people, and through these activities he also became involved with Mary Jayne Gold. In 1941, he escaped to England and became a fully fledged member of the SOE and ended the war as second-in-command of the 2nd (French) Squadron of the SAS.

Marseille was also the nucleus of the Pat O'Leary organization. As one of the best-known and most successful escape organizations, the 'Pat Line' smuggled aircrews and other fugitives out through the South of France. Pat O'Leary was the operational name of a Belgian army doctor, born Albert-Marie Guérisse, the founder of this nationwide network, which was run with military precision and discipline. Indications are that the fun-loving young French couriers were wary of this man they called 'The Belgian'. Those who worked in the rescue business were driven by military, rather than political, motives but they were amateurs nevertheless.

Evaders were accompanied by a succession of *passeurs* on perilous train journeys from the north via Lyon or Toulouse. Wearing civilian clothes and using false papers, they played dumb in the presence of French-speaking passengers who might denounce them. For every courageous citizen that formed a link in the escape chain there were scores of gendarmes, train conductors and fellow travellers who would blow the whistle on an Allied escapee. In fact, any 'parcel' could turn out to be an enemy infiltrator. A permit had to be presented at the many checkpoints, and crossing the Demarcation line in a southerly direction was particularly hazardous. Once in Marseille, fugitives would be taken into hiding before being evacuated by sea or guided across the Pyrenees into Spain.

A co-founder of the 'Pat Line', Captain Ian Garrow, like so many other Polish, French, Canadian and British soldiers, escaped the blitzkrieg and ended up in Marseille. The 51st Highland Division, to which Garrow was attached, suffered particularly heavy losses trying to hold back the Wehrmacht in June 1940, and for them there was no Dunkirk. Garrow was described as charming, tall, dark-haired, strongly built and clean-shaven. Although born in South Africa, he was raised in Glasgow and spoke French with a Scottish accent. On New Year's Eve at the end of 1940, there were a number of Scots celebrating Hogmanay in a bar at the Vieux-Port of Marseille. At midnight they sang 'God Save the King', and the owner gave them drinks on the house.

A colourful and cosmopolitan group of friends was drawn into the 'Pat' network. Among the multitude of Parisians who joined the southward exodus was Eileen Forbes, an American artist married to a successful painter named Francis Trailleux. All kinds of refugees were given shelter in their home, the Château Noir near Aix-en-Provence, which had once been home to the artist Paul Cézanne, right opposite Mont Sainte-Victoire.

Whereas Eileen Forbes Trailleux was achingly attractive, her friend and fellow worker in the Underground, Elisabeth Haden-Guest, was told by her mother, 'You are not beautiful, nor are you pretty, but you have charm, good teeth and good legs. You may make it.'[1] Born Louise Ruth Wolpert, 'Elisabeth' was of Russian-German extract, and her first husband, Peter Haden-Guest, was a ballet dancer, the son of a British MP. Forsaking the life of an aristocrat for her communist ideals, she was both princess and peasant – by her own choice.

In 1940 Elisabeth was separated from her husband and living in a small hotel in Marseille with hideous green walls, the same hotel as Ian Garrow, opposite a police station, near the Anglican church. Her 3-year-old son, Anthony, was left in the care of Eileen and Francis Trailleux at Château Noir. Eileen is reputed to have said that her friend, Elisabeth, was unfit to be a mother and unfit for intelligence work. Americans were quite legitimate in France prior to Pearl Harbor, and Haden-Guest pretended she was American, insisting on speaking English and attracting attention wherever she went.

Jean Foucarde, yet another French soldier trying to get to England, was recruited into the 'Pat' network'. Between missions across the Demarcation line, he looked after young Anthony at a house owned by his parents, but rented to old family friends who threatened to denounce him. In early July 1941, Jean Foucarde, Elisabeth Haden-Guest, Ian Garrow and three other members of the little cell were arrested. But they were lucky. One of their number, Nadine Pastrée, was from a very influential Marseille family, on good terms with the authorities, and was quickly released. Elisabeth was the daughter-in-law of a British MP, and a bit of an oddity. In addition to that, the French police who arrested them seemed to have had divided loyalties.

Elisabeth Haden-Guest was soon back in England and spent the rest of the war at her third husband's Devon estate. Captain Garrow arrived home in early 1943 and was awarded the DSO. His comrades had managed to spring him from a prison in the Dordogne by smuggling in a German guard's uniform. The home of the Pastré family, the Château de Montredon, was turned it into a refuge for artists, many of whom were Jewish, until the Germans requisitioned it for their own use. Jean Foucard sensibly disappeared into rural Lot and Garonne and worked as a farm labourer until the Americans arrived and snapped him up as a translator. Eileen Trailleux grew old gracefully in rural Aix-en-Provence, painting, gardening and taking in stray people.

Le Petit Poucet, a discreet bar at 23 Boulevard Dugommier, just off La Canebière, the historic high street of Marseille, became a regular rendezvous point for *passeurs* from the north. The owner and his wife were included in the wave of arrests of March and April 1943 that virtually destroyed the Pat O'Leary line. Another stalwart, Louis Nouveau, returned from Buchenwald to his fifth-floor apartment at 28a Quai de Rive Neuve, which still overlooks the Vieux-Port. Pat O'Leary himself was eventually caught and survived a series of concentration camps. If one organizer or agent was arrested, the entire cell was compromised. In the end, approximately fifty members of the 'Pat Line' were betrayed. The chief suspect was a smooth-talking, unscrupulous double agent, identified as Sergeant Harold Cole.

A Gestapo agent named Ernst Dunker had garnered the information which led to the spate of arrests in Marseille. All his information on the underground networks in the southern zone was held in the Flora file – so named after Thérèse Floiras, the first person arrested in a series of arrests during March and April of 1943. Her name and address had been found in the mailbox of the 'Pat' network at Le Petit Poucet. Ernst Dunker was just beginning his reign of terror.

Countless good people, with extraordinary moral fibre, were executed or disappeared into the void. Ted Coppin (*Olivier*) had worked in his parent's yachting business in Cannes before the war. He and his courier, Yvonne Experton (*Gisèle*), were arrested in what was known as *l'affaire Flora* on 23 April 1943 at the Hôtel Sainte-Marie, which is still there in the heart of the city. After a horrifying ordeal, Experton eventually came back from Ravensbrück but Coppin disappeared without a trace and was eventually declared dead. When the SOE gave up the search, Coppin's father continued looking for his son in the chaos of postwar Germany.

*

Large amounts of money were needed to pay for safe houses, documents, salaries and bribes. Ultimately, the necessary cash was supplied by MI9, the British secret intelligence service in charge of escapes from enemy territory.

The escape networks also worked closely with the SOE in London. Nancy Wake, one of the most renowned female agents, joined the SOE under her maiden name but in the early days in Marseille she was known by her married name, Nancy Fiocca. Sometimes referred to as *l'Australienne de Marseille*, Wake was born in New Zealand but grew up in Australia. Like many Australians she set off to see the world at a young age and, based in London, she often travelled to the continent.

In the summer of 1936, Nancy met her husband, Henri, in Juan-les-Pins. He was a wealthy French businessman who had a reputation as a playboy. Together they led a sophisticated life with dinner parties in their apartment with a view of the Vieux-Port of Marseille. Being a foreigner and female, Nancy had more freedom of movement than most, and guided groups of escapees over the Pyrenees into Spain. But she did more than just take evaders under her wing: she played an integral part in the running of the organization.

When the Gestapo, who called her 'The White Mouse', began to close in on her in May 1943, Nancy made the crossing to Spain, and then to England where she trained as a full-blown SOE operative. Her husband promised to follow but was arrested by the Gestapo and died, some say executed, in Saint-Pierre Prison in Marseille. She did not receive the news until the liberation.

Someone who trained with Nancy described her as 'a real Australian bombshell', with tremendous vitality and flashing eyes. Everything she did she did well. On 29 April 1944, aged 31, Nancy Wake, now codenamed *Hélène*, and another SOE operative, Major John Farmer, were parachuted into the Auvergne Region in central France to set up the circuit FREELANCE. According to legend, her parachute got stuck in a tree, and by way of a greeting, her contact on the ground, Henri Tardivat, said he wished all trees could bear such beautiful fruit. She retorted, 'Don't give me that French shit.'[2] Her use of strong language is not in question.

Some of the stories about Nancy's exploits as an SOE agent are outrageous. In articles, books and films, it has been claimed that she was the leader of a 7,000-strong resistance group, that she personally killed countless Germans, one of them with her bare hands using a technique taught by the SOE. Slightly more plausible is the story that, in order to transmit a radio message, she rode a bicycle on a round trip of about 500 kilometres through the German-occupied countryside. When she was asked what she was most proud of doing during the war, she would say 'the bike ride ... When I got off that damned bike I felt as if I had a fire between my legs. I couldn't stand up. I couldn't sit down, I couldn't walk.'[3]

By acting the giddy Frenchwoman, not in the least bit interested in the war, Nancy used her sexuality to deceive the Germans. Henri Tardivat, the resistance fighter who met her on arrival, confirmed that: 'She is the most feminine woman I know, until the fighting starts. Then, she is like five men.' Nancy herself said: 'When we were fighting, we were fighting. When we weren't, we were having a jolly good time. I never was afraid; I was too busy to be afraid.' In one often-told story, Nancy ordered the execution of a female spy and was quite willing to carry it out herself.

*

Thanks to the excellent forging capabilities of the Special Operations Executive their agents were able to move freely and withstand scrutiny. However, their French accents had to be perfect. In an interview, Francis Cammaerts mentioned that *miliciens* were more likely to identify strange accents and false papers than the average German. Robert Boiteux, a British agent with four years of schooling in France, who survived two missions, one in Lyon and one in Marseille, criticized the security of his native French counterparts. 'The French talk too much,' he said.[4]

Because they operated outside the protection of the Geneva Convention, which set out rules for the treatment of prisoners of war, undercover agents were considered unlawful combatants and could expect torture, deportation and death. In the field agents were permitted to make their own decisions, and their first objective would be to become implanted in French society, blend into the community with a false identity, and an entire background story would be invented.

F Section of the SOE, with its headquarters on Baker Street in London, nearly always named its networks or circuits after a profession, such as CLERGYMAN, SALESMAN, PHYSICIAN, JOCKEY, FREELANCE, GARDENER and HISTORIAN. Every circuit, or *réseau*, operated in a watertight compartment. They operated independently, but geographically their territory overlapped. Agents were given a fieldname or operational name to protect their families and confuse the enemy. Recruits came from as far afield as Mauritius and Seychelles, both francophone islands in the Indian Ocean. While language and operational skills were a prerequisite, it was the character of the man or woman, subjectively assessed by their instructors, which was deemed to be the most important element.

Whereas F Section was ostensibly non-political, the RF Section and BCRA (Bureau Central Renseignements et d'Action) were linked to de Gaulle's France Libre organization and mainly recruited from French exiles. BCRA agents were older than might be expected with 60 per cent being over the age of fifty. De Gaulle would have liked all secret operations on French soil to be under his control, and tensions existed between all the intelligence services, even more so when the Americans entered the arena.

In his introduction to *Forgotten Voices of The Secret War*, Sebastian Faulkes wrote that the SOE was 'distrusted at home, betrayed abroad, leaky, rash, frequently – and fatally – in breach of its own basic security rules'. Yet, the quality of the men and women far outshone the failings of the organization: 'Here is sacrifice; here is raw, selfless, bloody-minded courage, not always wisely applied, but applied, as the French would say, *à l'outrance* [to the death].'[5]

*

Perhaps the first British agent to surface in the Bay of Antibes was Captain Peter Churchill, bringing two radio operators on board the submarine HMS *Unbroken* on 21 April 1941. Although he was no relation to Winston, he would one day have to namedrop for his survival. At Cambridge, he had been an all-rounder sportsman and was proficient in a number of languages. On this occasion he did not stay long, but he would be back. Today on the Pointe de l'Ilette in Antibes there is a plaque commemorating this mission. A total of seventeen nautical operations (insertions and extractions) took place on this coast during 1942.

The OLIVE circuit was one of the first SOE networks operating in southeastern France, and its founder, Francis Basin, was one of the first recruits in F Section. Baisin arrived in Perpignan on 20 September 1941 and went on to establish a number of cells throughout the Bouches-du-Rhône, Var, Basses-Alpes and Alpes-Maritimes. Basing himself at a villa outside Cannes on the route de Fréjus, not far from where he was born, he was in contact with André Girard, head of the CARTE network and worked with the American agent Virginia Hall (*Marie*), in Lyon. It was she who provided him with the false papers to escape from Montluc

Prison and get back to England after he was again arrested by French police in Cannes on 18 August 1942.

Another close contact of Basin's was Dr Élie Lévy (aka Louis of Antibes) who was in his late forties and lived a comfortable life with his wife and two teenage daughters. As a leading member of resistance movements like Liberation and Combat as well as the Communist Party, Lévy's outgoing nature and contacts with members of disparate groups eventually led to his arrest. He would later die on a forced march between Nazi death camps.

Coinciding with Basin's departure from the field was the reappearance of Captain Peter Churchill on the night of 27/28 August 1942. In the field, Churchill was known as either *Michel* or *Raul,* and used the fake identity of a travelling salesman named Pierre Chambrun. He was tasked with creating a network called SPINDLE, building on the work of Francis Basin, but most importantly he was to act as liaison between the SOE headquarters in Baker Street and the CARTE network, the oldest and biggest network in the southeast.

Since the early years, André Girard (*Carte*) and his second-in-command, Henri Frager (*Louba*), had been building the CARTE network centred around Cannes, Antibes and Nice but they operated as far afield as Arles, Aix-en-Provence, Marseille, Montpellier, Toulouse, Clermont-Ferrand, Annecy and Lyon. It has been said that CARTE was careless, amateurish, delusional, too large, too idealistic, dangerously insecure and had no practical value. However, the British were convinced by *Carte* that he was the one who would be able to rally the 100,000 men of the Armistice Army to their cause.

Nicholas Bodington (*Professor*), the first head of the SOE F Section, was sent to evaluate the CARTE network, landing at Cap d'Antibes on 30 July 1942, together with a number of other agents. Two months later he returned to England with glowing reports. Peter Churchill, however, was not taken in by his self-aggrandizement, and in March 1943, after working together for many months, reported that André Girard (*Carte*) was out of control with temper and power. 'His head was firmly anchored in the clouds,' and the organization was characterized by megalomania and imprudence. As it turned out, the Armistice Army was disbanded and the promised links never materialized.[6]

Arriving together with Nicolas Bodington, Henri Frager and Harry Despaigne on the *Seadog* was Yvonne Rudellat (*Jacqueline*), the first female SOE-trained agent to set foot in France. She was too old to qualify as a parachutist so she was landed by sea on a rocky stretch of coast in the Gulf of Juan, a few kilometres east of Cannes. Her onward journey shows how the whole of France could be infiltrated from the south. From Cannes she travelled by train, across the Demarcation line to Lyon and on to Paris. She died of typhus in Bergen-Belsen, shortly after the young diarist, Anne Frank, died there in February or March 1945.[7]

The provision of radio equipment and trained operators was an SOE priority. Wireless operators had to be constantly on the move since the Gestapo had cars with radio-detection equipment. By means of triangulation, they had the ability to locate where a signal was coming from. It was safer to use the BBC which broadcast messages on the daily programme called '*Les Français parlent aux Français*' (The French speak to the French) on Radio Londres. Seemingly nonsensical phrases such as 'The hour is redolent with fragrance, and bells are ringing over the river' meant something to the right people.

The radioman Captain Harry Despaigne was described by his assessors as 'a curious and enigmatic personality' and a 'dark horse'. He was a burly but soft-spoken man, over 1.8 metres tall, well-built and with a military moustache.[8] Although London-born, he had French-speaking parents and he himself spoke English with a slight French accent. Despaigne's orders were to work for Peter Churchill but there was a clash of personalities. It seems that Despaigne was too serious while Churchill was too frivolous. Having witnessed the train wreck happening in slow motion, which was the CARTE network, he decided to make his own way home, over the Pyrenees into Spain and on to London.

Here, a passing mention may be made of a radioman named Denis Rake who first came ashore at Juan-les-Pins and stayed with Dr Lévy before moving north. On his second mission in 1944 he worked with Nancy Wake. Rake's childhood and theatrical background is intriguing. His SOE assessors described him as a 'trifle effeminate'. He didn't like big bangs and was dependent on sleeping pills. He carried out two missions to France and in the documentary *Le Chagrin et la Pitié* he tells of intimate encounters with a German officer among others. Apparently homosexuals made excellent agents because they were accustomed to living double lives.

The most unlikely people made the best agents. Sidney Jones (*Felix*) was 40 years old and had been Elizabeth Arden's representative in France before joining the SOE. His assessors described him as 'an excellent man in every way'. Of British nationality but born in Paris, he had made his way to England after his Austrian wife, Rosemary, was arrested for 'propaganda work' which earned her the death sentence. Jones returned to France in late 1942 and set up the INVENTOR circuit in Marseille.

It was on his second mission, in 1943, that Jones was betrayed by one Roger Bardet who had been caught and turned by one of the Abwehr's most notorious agents, Feldwebel (Sergeant) Hugo Bleicher. Acting on Bardet's information, Bleicher caused the destruction of numerous cells, and we shall hear more of him. Jones revealed nothing and managed to warn Frager about the double agent in their midst. Jones was in bed when Hugo Bleicher came to arrest him. 'It's a pity,' he said calmly 'it's such a nice day.' Even Bleicher was impressed by his courage. It is not known for certain when or how Jones died. He travelled the same route as so many SOE people, through Fresnes Prison to Mauthausen where it is believed he was executed.

A fellow passenger on the felucca which brought Sidney Jones to the South of France was John Goldsmith who was in his early thirties, and on his first mission. Born and schooled in Paris, Goldsmith spoke French with a distinct Parisian accent and knew all the slang. When it came to humans, he did not suffer fools. Animals were his passion and, in later life as a racehorse trainer, he trained over 400 winners and was once narrowly beaten in the Grand National. He enjoyed a good laugh and a good party: any success had to be celebrated.[9]

Sensibly, Goldsmith requested to be sent to the South of France on his first mission as the Vichy state was less dangerous than the occupied part of France, and he needed to acclimatize. While staying in the home of Paulo Leonetti, a former deputy mayor of Antibes, Goldsmith worked on getting a tan so as to blend in better with the local population. Leonetti was now practising as a hairdresser and came into contact with all kinds of people. He claimed that he got his best information while styling the hair of the girls who worked at the local brothel. Using the cover identity and backstory of a slick black-marketeer named Jean Delannoy, Goldsmith travelled by bicycle to Nice, Antibes and Cannes where he gave classes in sabotage.

Goldsmith was once asked to assist in smuggling a *personnage important* out of the country. This turned out to be General Henri Giraud, a popular but prickly military leader who had recently escaped from a German prison. Filled with his own importance, he was given the codename *Kingpin*. Goldsmith was summoned to meet him in Lyon, which, like Paris, had a more sinister atmosphere than the Riviera. After much negotiating and changing of plans, General Giraud and his two sons were taken to Gibraltar on the submarine, HMS *Seraph* on 5 November 1943.

Up until this point, General Giraud had been looked after by a French *réseau* called ALLIANCE, the commander of which was a young woman from a good family in Marseille. Marie-Madeleine Fourcade, codenamed *Hérisson* or *Hedgehog*, had lived in Shanghai as a young girl and had studied music. The name given to the network by the Germans was 'Noah's Ark' because all its agents were named after animals. A colleague described Foucarde as having 'an elephant's memory, a snake's prudence, a weasel's instinct, the perseverance of a mole, and she may be as wicked as a panther'. Her greatest asset, however, was that no one suspected that a woman could be in charge an organization with 3,000 agents.[10]

For some time, Foucarde hid the fact she was a woman from headquarters in London. In her 1968 memoire, *L'Arche de Noé*, Fourcade described how she was captured in Aix-en-Provence then escaped and was taken by plane to England. Six months later, in 1943, she returned to France and was captured a second time. Her escape on this occasion was accomplished by stripping almost naked and squeezing her petite body between the bars of the cell window. Ultimately, more than 400 members of the ALLIANCE organization died in concentration camps or were killed by Nazi firing squads.

A little-known but resourceful network known as F2 was started in Toulouse by former Polish intelligence officers who, rather than escaping France, used their own initiative to form one of the first cells of the Resistance. Without any financial backing, they built their own radio sets to communicate with London. Gathering Polish and French volunteers, they expanded across the entire Hexagon into Italy and North Africa. The leader of F2 in the Marseille–Toulon–Nice sector was a former naval officer, Count Jacques Marie Charles Trolley de Prévaux. In 1943, he and his wife, Charlotte, better known as Lotka, were living in a villa among the pines at Pramousquier beach near Le Lavandou. Jacques de Prévaux had recently been dismissed from his post with the French Navy at Toulon because of his Gaullist tendencies. The charismatic count, was a hero of the First World War, and with his intimate knowledge of naval matters, the information which he supplied to British Intelligence was of such value that they awarded him the Distinguished Service Order (DSO) in 1943.

Of Polish-Jewish descent, Charlotte Leitnner de Prévaux was born in New York. She had green eyes and red (some say golden) hair, and was a chic Parisian model when she met the count in 1933. He was a married man, and his parents objected, but after a passionate affair lasting seven years, they finally made it legal. The couple's resistance activities led to their arrest by the Gestapo in Marseille on 29 March 1944. Over the course of the next few months, they faced unspeakable horrors at Montluc Prison in Lyon, and were murdered on 19 August.

Jacques and Charlotte Prévaux were among the 109 prisoners who were shot at Bron Airfield, ten kilometres east of Lyon, where there is now a commercial airport. At the Nuremburg Trials it was revealed that on 14 August 1944 Allied planes had bombed the Bron Airfield, and from 16 to 22 August the Germans had employed civilians and prisoners from Montluc to fill the bomb craters. At the end of each day, when the work was finished, the civilian labourers went away; but the prisoners were shot on the spot and their bodies stacked in half-filled craters.[11]

Lotka was so badly mutilated that she was only identifiable by her long red hair. Her husband had had the opportunity of being evacuated to England in 1942, but he declined because the pregnant Lotka would have had to have been left behind. The child, Aude, was born in 1943, and was raised by her aunt. It was not until 1966 as a 23-year-old student that she learned from a chance encounter with an old librarian that she was the child of this legendary couple – even though there are streets in Paris and Toulon that bear the name Prévaux. A tribute by the *Compagnons de la Libération* reads: 'United in the action of resistance, united in the trial of the prisons, they found themselves still united in their sacrifice …'[12]

Also among those shot on the airfield at Bron, a week before the liberation of Lyon, was another member of the F2 *réseau*. Gaston Pascalis, together with his wife, Mathilde and their three children, had made their home in Cavalière where life revolved around family, animals and sports. Carrying on the work of Jacques de Prévaux, Gaston Pascalis, aged 48, was betrayed and arrested in Nice. A week later, Gestapo officers accompanied him back to Cavalière to search his house. He managed to signal to Mathilde that she was not a suspect and should not reveal anything. Although he was very young at the time, the youngest child, Éric, remembers that his father could not take him in his arms because he was handcuffed.[13] Although he was most likely buried in Bron with the other victims, his body was never identified.

La Roche Escudelier, a small outcrop a hundred metres off the rocky, deserted coast was an ideal spot for infiltration and extraction by submarine, known in the business as *le tube*. After a good run of seven successful operations from La Roche Escudelier, on the night of 26/27 November 1943, the Germans acted on a traitor's tip-off. A group of seventeen people, one of whom was Monique Giraud, the daughter of General Giraud, was about to embark on the submarine, *La Perle*. The Germans had laid an ambush and a resistance fighter named Alphonse Alsfasser, (alias Leon Granger) held them off until his last bullet, sacrificing himself to allow others to escape. He was buried in the cemetery at Ramatuelle.

Monique Giraud and about a dozen others were able to escape into the moonless night but two others of the party were captured, one of whom, Pierre Israel (alias Pierre Mortier) was executed at Les Baumettes in Marseille in June 1944. Mortier was a Jewish industrialist from the north who had sought refuge in Sainte-Maxime when France surrendered. As a delegate of the Maquis des Maures, he had recently visited Algiers to request weapons.

*

In the South of France, much of the clandestine traffic by sea and air came and went via Algeria where various secret services had their headquarters. To get there often meant travelling via Toulouse, and then on foot to Barcelona, which took eight or nine days and involved crossing the 'forbidden zone' in the Pyrenees. When John Goldsmith inevitably fell out with Girard, the capricious leader of CARTE, he returned to England via Spain and Algeria, taking a delegation of French Army officers with him. On his second mission he would be based in Toulouse, from where he travelled as far as Paris and Nice and, against all odds, he returned for a third time in 1944 to fight again alongside the Maquis during the final running battles in Provence as we shall see.

Despite the professionalism of some highly trained agents, the leadership of CARTE continued to put the network in jeopardy. The radio messages which Girard composed were verbose and unprofessional, and he insisted that they be transmitted exactly as written. One of the radiomen who had been brought to Antibes by Peter Churchill on the submarine *Unbroken* was a Lithuanian Jew, Isidore Newman. Newman did things by the book, and in the spats which ensued, Peter Churchill sided with Girard, causing an acrimonious parting.

Peter Churchill was finally assigned a radioman named Adolphe Rabinowitz (*Arnaud*), a young Russian-Egyptian Jew, who has been described as 'a giant of a man' with a 'lurid vocabulary'. Together with their more refined courier, Odette Sansom (*Lise*), a close-knit nucleus was formed. Odette arrived by felucca in October 1942, and thus began one of the most romantic chapters in the annals of the SOE. On seeing Odette for the first time, Peter noted that she had 'a mop of light brown hair, swept back to reveal a rounded forehead, down to a pair of discerning eyes, there emanated an aura of challenge that was only intensified by the determined set of her chin, below a somewhat colourless face'.[14]

Sansom's orders were to go to Auxerre in Burgundy after first picking up papers that would enable her to cross the Demarcation line. However, Peter Churchill took a liking to her and coopted her as his courier for the SPINDLE circuit based in Cannes. She was hesitant at first, because it was safer to work alone. Her first mission was to take a suitcase to Marseille, a city which was not the place for a novice. The accommodation organized for her was in a brothel for German soldiers in Rue Paradis, the same street where the Gestapo headquarters was situated. Brothels were deliberately used by those needing a place to lie low, since no questions were asked, whereas the Gestapo and police were inclined to inspect the registers of ordinary hotels. Nevertheless, it was an education for Odette, a married mother of two, who never used bad language other than the word *Zut!*

When the Germans and the Italians intensified their presence on Côte d'Azur in November 1942, Peter Churchill and Odette Sansom, together with their radio operator, Adolphe Rabinowitz, moved far north to Saint-Jorioz, nine kilometres from Annecy, overlooking the lake, which was the next best thing to the Riviera. Shortly thereafter, Churchill was recalled to London for a briefing, but he would return forthwith.

For a while now, CARTE had been doomed. A briefcase containing hundreds of names and addresses of potential members fell into Abwehr hands. The hapless agent responsible was one André Marsac, second in command to Girard. The briefcase was stolen while Marsac slept on the train, and the list was passed on to Hugo Bleicher. Marsac was arrested while drinking coffee in the spring sunshine at a café on the Champs Elysées. Bleicher then cunningly bided his time, allowing more people to fall into his trap. Posing as 'Colonel Henri', Bleicher first played a cat and mouse game with Odette, claiming that he wanted to defect.

A warning came from the SOE that 'Colonel Henri' was not to be trusted, and about forty people on the list were warned to lie low. A newly arrived agent, Francis Cammaerts (*Roger*), who was also staying in Saint-Jorioz at the time, took heed and moved south. Odette realized that it was clearly time to leave the area, but decided to wait for Peter Churchill to return from his trip to England. After meeting him at the drop zone in the middle of the night, Odette took Peter to their safe house, the Hôtel de la Poste in Saint-Jorioz. Churchill was asleep when Hugo Bleicher, together with Italian troops, raided the hotel on 16 April 1943. There was no point in putting up a fight, and Odette calmly packed some essentials, ensuring that Peter had two warm coats. Odette had always been prepared for this eventuality. Her clothing was of a quality especially chosen so that it would withstand prison conditions.

It was Odette who came up with the idea of using Peter's surname and supposed kinship with the British prime minister as a bargaining chip. She also claimed to be Peter's wife and invented a reason why it wasn't common knowledge. 'It's only a wartime measure,' Odette assured Peter, but his response was, 'If I ever get the chance I shall ask you if you'd care to make it a lifetime measure.'[15]

Before being sent to concentration camps in Germany, Peter and Odette were held in isolated torment for over a year in Fresnes Prison, twelve kilometres from the centre of Paris, near present-day Orly airport. At any one time, Fresnes held an assortment of 3,000 *morts vivants*, or living dead. Some who could not stand it any longer put an end to it all by hanging themselves from the electric-light bracket against the wall. Their corpses would be carted off on the soup trolley. Prison rations were barely enough to sustain life. Only if one survived the beatings, torture, typhoid and dysentery did one face the prospect of an executioner's bullet.

In his book, *The Spirit in the Cage*, Peter Churchill wrote of the uncertainty, the gnawing fear, the aloneness and the courage of the condemned men and women.[16]

Bizarrely, once he had caught them, Hugo Bleicher did his best to see that Churchill and Sansom were well treated. It was he who arranged for them to spend time together, and also allowed Parisian friends to send food parcels. His powers were very limited however, as the Gestapo were now in charge and there was no love lost between the Gestapo and the Abwehr, who considered themselves gentlemen rather than bullies. Bleicher came from a good home on the shores of Lake Constance and aspired to be a concert pianist. Well into his forties, he was recruited into the Abwehr because of his knowledge of French and Spanish but never rose above the rank of feldwebel (sergeant) as much as he may have liked to.

Bleicher loved all things French – including his mistress Mathilde-Lily Carré (*la Chatte*). In her memoir, *J'ai été la Chatte* (I was the Cat) Carré claims to have been a resistant but was turned by Bleicher into a double agent after feeling 'the icy breath of death' in a prison cell. Hugo Bleicher never personally shot or tortured anyone, which may explain why he escaped the hangman, although he was arrested and put on trial. In 1954, he published his memoirs, *Colonel Henri's Story,* and made contact with Peter Churchill around that time, but was rebuffed.

Odette ended up in Ravensbrück and Peter spent the rest of the war in various camps where he received better treatment than most of the other inmates due to his being an officer and a 'relative' of Winston Churchill. In 1947, Peter and Odette were married at the Kensington Registry office in London. Their marriage made the headlines, and the film, *Odette* (1950), romanticized their story. For a while they were national idols, and were together for ten years.

Several former colleagues, including Francis Basin and André Girard, publicly attacked Peter and Odette Churchill for being portrayed as heroes. For his part, Girard has gone down in history as being a well-meaning buffoon. The controversy resurfaced in 1966 with the publication of M. R. D. Foot's *SOE in France*, in which Foot, himself a former SAS soldier and PoW, implied that Churchill and Odette had lived a life of luxury on SOE's money and accomplished little of military value. Legal action followed and Churchill accepted a settlement and an apology. Future editions of *SOE in France* were revised accordingly.

*

About fifty-three out of the 500 SOE agents infiltrated into France were women, ten were captured, and three of those survived. By comparison, 700 women served in the American OSS (Office of Strategic Services) overseas but few were field operators. Much has been written about the main actors in the SOE, personal memoirs abound, but much of it is legend. Vera Atkins, who was uniquely placed to know all the facts, was even scathing of M. R. D. Foot's book, *SOE in France*. 'Some consider it the bible,' she once told an historian. 'It's about as accurate as the bible.'[17]

The intention was for the SOE to be 'a spanner in the works' of the enemy's war machine and sap his morale by keeping him in a perpetual state of insecurity. SOE agents were generally called 'saboteurs', however, as has been seen, the role of F Section in Provence involved mainly intelligence and liaison work. They were the stone in the enemy's boot, not the stone which hit him on the head. It was the uniformed military special operators like the Inter-Allied 'Jedburgh' teams, Groupes de Contre-Sabotage de la Marine Française, SAS and OSS operational groups who engaged in open combat, either on their own or in cooperation with the Maquis.

SOE agents of the F Section (like their French counterparts in the BCRA) were considered to be a permanent presence on the ground, as opposed to the paramilitary groups who specialized in short missions. A full chapter will be devoted to these special force operations which preceded Operation Dragoon. Despite the tensions and differences between them, the French underground networks and special operations of all the Allied nations were united in their determination to root out the invader from French soil.

Chapter 3

Menace

A painful and visible symptom of the occupation was the presence of German (or Italian) troops on the streets of almost every city and town in France. Off the beaten track, one might only have to endure the sight of the Boche when they were on the move. But like any colonial administrators, their tentacles reached into the furthest corners of the territory. Owing to its particular geography, and strategic importance for the defence of Fortress Europe, the people of Provence were subjected to greater tyranny than was the case in deepest France, or *France profonde*. At the peak of their presence, in June 1944, more than a million German troops were stationed in France, and under the terms of the peace treaty, the French had to pay all the costs of their upkeep – and more.

In theory, the Germans stayed out of Provence until November 1942, but Italy wasted no time in taking back what they considered to be their rightful territory. In a railway carraige in the forest of Compiègne, the French were forced to sign a humiliating armistice on 22 June 1940, and when Germany agreed to the formation of an independent state, Vichy, in the south, Benito Mussolini quickly invaded from the east. The French troops held out easily enough until forced by Hitler to sign a ceasefire on 24 June. The occupation of Menton was a propaganda bonanza. Mussolini bragged that the 'Pearl of France', which was rightfully theirs, had been returned to Italy. Part of the armistice agreement was that Italy would occupy only the territory it had captured when the ceasefire came into effect.

Residents of Menton evacuated the town, in buses and trucks, leaving their homes and heirlooms behind, thinking it would be only for a short while. The refugees journeyed in a series of convoys first to Antibes and Juan-les-Pins. Almost 90 per cent of them ended up in Pau in the Pyrenees in southwest France. Italians flocked in, and a process of Italianization began. The lira became the accepted currency, the French language was forbidden, and in school the children sang a new national anthem. Street names were changed and Menton itself became Mentone.

When the Germans violated the Demarcation line in November 1942 by taking Toulon, and the Italians increased their foothold in the southeast of France, the people of Menton hardly noticed the new influx, except that the new fascist residents greeted the Alpini with open arms when they marched through town. As time went by, and Germans replaced the Italians, more residents were displaced. Seafront buildings were considered to be critical to military operations and residents were evicted from their homes. By the time it was liberated, Menton was a ghost town and the residents had lost virtually all their possessions.

Monaco was, and still is, a sovereign state, the smallest in Europe, apart from the Vatican. Mussolini planned to take over Monte Carlo as well but Prince Louis managed to keep it relatively neutral and independent, although the Italians did come in and round up undesirables, including all the English and American nationals. But the casino remained open and the street cafés were still lively. Even then it was the epitome of affluence.

Neutrality was maintained mostly because the Reich needed financial access to the outside world and Monaco was ideal for this purpose. Nazis registered companies so as to trade in American and French stocks. Along with Spain, Monaco acted as an intermediary for Nazi Germany and a conduit for their propaganda. Monaco never experienced the hunger that was prevalent throughout occupied Europe, but toward the end there were food shortages because of broken rail linkages.

As of 8 September 1943, the Germans were fully in charge and at the time of the Allied invasion of southern France, the defence of the Alpes-Maritimes was entrusted to the 148th Reserve Division under General Otto Fretter-Pico, headquartered at Grasse. It was a combination of tired old men and young boys, most of them non-Germans, which occupied the Alpes-Maritimes. The old men who guarded the Italian border were jokingly called 'customs agents'. The division was understrength, and the vast majority were essentially Polish *Volksdeutch* or *Osttruppen* (ethnic Germans or eastern troops) from Upper Silesia which was part of the German Reich in 1944. Some had enlisted of their own free will but others were former prisoners of war. The officers, and at least one battalion of young Bavarians, were proper Germans.

For a young German soldier, who might otherwise have been on the Russian front, the French Riviera was a dream posting. The 18-year-old

Udo Taubmann arrived in Nice in March 1944, the trip lasted six days and every train got bombed on the way. Food rations deteriorated as time went on – the Russian front got priority. Duties consisted of laying mines, guarding bridges and occupying bunkers on the coastal road near Cannes. Training courses were never-ending. When there were no mines left, they just hung up warning signs. 'Sometimes we waved at the girls when they were picking rose blossoms as we marched by. I also swam in the Mediterranean Sea when we had a bit of time off … Those were good times down there in the salt water.'[1]

Guard duty involved protecting sensitive infrastructure from sabotage. For the same reason, foreigners were denied access to the coast and even ordinary citizens were encouraged to leave the coastal cities. Bicycles were banned from the Promenade des Anglais and concrete barricades three metres high were erected, allowing only pedestrian access. Eventually the Promenade was completely off limits to civilians. Young, bare-chested soldiers dug trenches, laid barbed wire and mined the beach. As the military section of the Caucade cemetery in Nice grew larger, a regular duty of the occupation troops was attendance at funerals.

While the Italians occupied the Côte d'Azur between November 1942 and September 1943, they accomplished little with their limited resources. The big guns which they installed were old French and Italian artillery pieces, as well as naval guns from ships scuttled in Toulon harbour. Now, with German efficiency, the new occupiers set about strengthening the Mediterranean Wall. Working alongside the soldiers were German civilians from the Todt Organization as well as the Reichsarbeitsdienst (RAD, Reich Labour Service) in which every good young German was expected to serve a six-month stint. Being an auxiliary organization of the Wehrmacht, the RAD was used on the Eastern Front as infantry. With varying degrees of willingness, motivated by the carrot and the stick, French STO conscripts also contributed to the disfigurement of the Riviera.

Country folk were accustomed to using wood sparingly. The usual fuel burned in stoves was *petits bois*, small branches of live oak, slightly wet so as not to burn too quickly. The trimmings from pruned grape vines were used for cooking in warmer weather. The army of occupation, however, was a rapacious consumer of timber as a substitute for coal and for construction of defensive works. Wood was also transformed into charcoal-based 'gazogène' for fuelling motor vehicles. Private owners and the forestry authorities had no choice but to cut down vast tracts of forest. Sometimes, the Germans started fires to flush out résistance fighters, and Allied bombing also destroyed thousands of hectares of woodland. At the time, someone speculated that it would take a hundred years for all the trees to grow back.

When Field Marshal Erwin Rommel carried out his second inspection of part of the *Südwall* – the Southern or Mediterranean Wall – on 2 May 1944, all he saw was Toulon and Hyères where the preparations were the most advanced, but he was far from impressed. Redoubling their efforts, the Germans began to build bunkers, casemates and pillboxes on the charming beachfront promenades. Ingeniously, the Germans disguised their blockhouses to look like shops and other innocent structures. On the beach at Fréjus and Saint-Raphaël, and in the delta of the Argens River, brightly coloured refreshment stands and cabanas concealed weapons of all shapes and sizes.

Along with mock defences, at La Nartelle, there was a fortified wall, three metres high and nearly two metres wide along the length of the beach. Neither aerial strikes nor a heavy naval bombardment would be able to inflict more than a few scars on this ugly concrete structure. A similar wall ran along the beachfront between Mandelieu and Cannes, where shiploads of sand and cement had to pass through the submarine nets in the port for this work to be completed.

Rommel's visit had precipitated a flood of orders for local contractors and labourers. Building activity reached a crescendo during the first three weeks of July 1944. East of the Rhône, from Marseille to Nice, there were now about 600 individual blockhouses equipped with an array of guns. A number of flak units were sited between Sainte-Maxime and Menton.

That most recognizable of all landmarks in Nice, the castle on the hill between the old town and the port, was fortified with scant regard to its historical significance. It was turned into a minefield with concrete bunkers and artillery emplacements, interlinked with trenches and tunnels. Mortars were positioned so that they could rain down bombs on the city itself when the Allies came. Trees were cut down to improve fields of fire. Even more outrageous was the demolition of the Casino de la Jetée, an iconic structure built over the sea in classic Belle Époque style. The 4,000 tons of iron in its steel girders were used for tank barricades.

Steel and wooden stakes, dubbed 'Rommel's Asparagus', were planted on the beaches and in the fields as far inland as Draguignan.

At La Croix-Valmer, a beautiful forest was dismembered for anti-glider posts, and at Ramatuelle all the parasol pines behind the Pampelonne beach were cut down to open up a field of fire for German machine guns. This callous destruction of trees disfigured the Gulf of Saint-Tropez. At La Foux, where there is now a Géant Casino supermarket, there were once thirty magnificent parasol pines lining a horseracing track. The trees had been the pride and joy of the community for generations, but were now obstructing the field of fire of a battery sited on a slight rise overlooking Port Cogolin. No amount of pleading by the community could change the mind of the German commander, and one afternoon in June, during siesta time, a huge explosion shattered the peace as the trees were dynamited.[2]

Villas and bastides were demolished along a thirty-kilometre stretch around Hyéres for the same reason. At Cavalière alone, fifty houses closest to the sea were flattened. A party of German soldiers would arrive with a bucket of paint and smear a black cross on the door as a way of telling the owners that their home would soon be non-existent. Many more houses at strategic points were evacuated and converted into blockhouses. Invariably, all the details and specifications were passed on to the Allied intelligence services by resentful French workers.

French men between the ages of 16 and 60, and childless women under the age of 45, were conscripted to work on construction sites, and as a result, other areas of economic life became paralyzed. Informal exemptions were made for fishermen, as well as waiters and waitresses serving German officers. It was not long before an industry sprang up fabricating false documents certifying employment in these capacities. Although the hours were long and gruelling, and the wages low, working on the Mediterranean Wall was preferable to being sent to Germany under the STO. Daylight savings time was kept in force year-round, thereby adding two hours to the work day. Wages were supposed to be frozen but certain industries paid 'black' wages or contrived long overtime at double rates.

Fear of deportation or execution was used in conjunction with friendly overtures to keep the French under control. In 1944 a notice in *Le Petit Var* offered a reward for reporting sightings of shot-down enemy aircraft or parachutists. A few weeks later, the same newspaper announced that anyone helping or sheltering the enemy would be inviting execution. First it was the carrot and then the stick.

In contrast to the contempt with which the citizens of Poland, Czechoslovakia and Yugoslavia were regarded by their occupiers, the French were treated with a distant respect.

In return, the French also recognized their occupiers as people. On the beach, it was impossible to tell German swimmers from French ones. Strangely, as time wore on they became almost immune to the German presence, at least in public, although the brutality of the occupation was intensifying. The alien presence seemed so permanent that, in public places where daily life went on, it grew invisible. It was as if an unspoken agreement existed among ordinary people, to pretend that the occupier, and even the war itself, did not exist.

The show went on with stars like Maurice Chevalier, Josephine Baker and Edith Piaf performing for affluent audiences on the Riviera. For a while, cabarets were filled with Wehrmacht and Gestapo officers who purchased pink wines and perfumes from Grasse for their *frauleins* back home. Evidently, German men were shocked at how much makeup the French girls wore in the big cities.

With their love of regulations, the Boche imposed fines for not crossing the road at the proper crossings, and cyclists were stopped for riding three abreast. While children quickly learned which Germans were approachable for sweets, and which were not, adults showed their hostility by shrouding themselves with silence, refusing to acknowledge them. Lady Enid Furness, who remained in her villa at Cap Ferrat under Vichy rule until arrest was imminent, told a reporter on arrival in London: 'I saw a young woman with a baby on a bus. A German soldier got in, sat down alongside her, and began to play with the baby. The mother turned her back on him, shifting the child hastily away to the other side.'[3]

Jean Guéhenno, a prominent literary figure, wrote an essay in 1943 entitled 'To the German I pass in the Street' in which he advised his fellow Frenchmen to ignore the oppressor, to deny them the warmth of a human exchange. Although he did concede that even among the Germans, there were all kinds of people, just as there were among the French. He noticed one German soldier in particular, an old man whom he passed every day, and recognized his loneliness and humanity.

The plump, middle-aged soldiers who quietly carried out their occupation duties in the South of France got to know the local shopkeepers and barmaids and a live-and-let-live relationship was established. Among the many nicknames they acquired was 'Fridolin', after a musical comedy character. Another was 'Frisé' which means 'curly', a sarcastic reference to their close-cropped skulls. People went to Mass as usual, and if the Italian or German soldiers wanted to attend, they could not be refused. When Father Celestin Buisson, the priest in charge of the seventh-century church near the port in Sainte-Maxime saw the fervour with which these men prayed and sang, he decided that war is a 'colossal stupidity'.

This growing acceptance of the oppressor in their midst did not go unnoticed by the more militant resisters. The indiscretion of their womenfolk, in particular, was a festering wound. Sexual complicity crossed a line that economic collaboration did not. A pamphlet which was picked up by the authorities in Place Victor Hugo in Toulon on 29 April 1943 issued a stark warning to women who fraternized with the occupier. Clearly, the *épuration*, the purge, which took place after the liberation was not a spontaneous thing:

> There is one insulting prostitution which deeply hurts our patriotic feelings. Without doubt, it is generally those women of ill repute [*des femmes de mauviaise vie*] who provide these visitations [*fréquentations*] but there are also, unfortunately, women could have more recently been classed in a category of 'honourable persons'. This promiscuity cannot remain unpunished. It is an outrage to our soldiers who are fighting on African soil. It is offensive to our prisoners and our deportees, it defiles everyone. These women must know that they are being watched and they should make arrangements to flee with their lovers when the hour of liberation arrives. By staying here, they will not escape punishment.[4]

The notice went on to warn the owners of nightclubs which catered to Germans, as well as the orchestras and women who entertained them there, that they would lose their licences and face other measures in due course. The pamphlet was transcribed by the Director of Police in Toulon, and sent to the préfet of the Var in Draguignan without any adverse comment attached.

Ordinary people, caught between the Resistance and the occupier, were afraid to say what was on their minds or be associated with known dissidents for fear of being compromised or denounced. The wartime experience of a French countrywoman in an isolated hamlet, high up in the Alps above Briançon was one of distrust, hypocrisy and small-minded jealousies, as well as close community. Although the Germans seldom stopped in the village, their influence was perpetuated by the mayor and his puppet-master, the sous-préfet, the state's representative in the region. Unlike the previous war, time went by without anyone being really involved – no prisoners, nobody missing in action. 'Since the peasants did not have opinions about anything,' the countrywoman wrote, 'and had always followed the mayor like sheep,' they stuck to the side of caution. 'When a few Germans came by, they all but licked their boots. It was the reign of fear and silence.'[5]

As far as the Germans themselves were concerned, their troops were well-disciplined and in good order. The commander of the 19th Army was proud of the 'positive relations' which existed and in his mind the response of the population was one of 'friendliness and good sense', while keeping a dignified distance. German troops were under strict orders to respect women and civilian property. To help keep the men in line, official brothels were set up in the Hôtel Métropole in Nice and the Hôtel de Paris in Cannes. Marseille has always been famous for its houses of ill repute.

The Germans were said to be always 'correct' in their behaviour toward women, especially those of a higher social class. More cynical observers, like John Goldsmith, remarked that it was not because of any inherent goodness but rather because of the Teutonic respect for authority. The men would behave as they were told by their superiors, and the prevailing policy was to behave correctly and normally. If the order of the day was to run amok, they would have done so with the same efficiency. Both the French and German authorities seem to have taken rape most seriously when bourgeois women were involved.

Working-class women were more likely to have contact with soldiers in the workplace. Germans frequented cafés and hotels throughout France and it was often the barmaids, waitresses or cleaning women in these institutions who were reported to have sexual relationships with German soldiers. Single mothers were also more likely to enter into a relationship for the perks that were on offer. It has been hypothesized that the reason why women accused of 'horizontal collaboration' were treated harshly after the liberation was not so much the act of sleeping with the enemy, but rather the benefits which they got from it.

German soldiers stationed in France eagerly anticipated dalliances with French women, knowing that there was an absence of young French men. Little did they know that they were called *saucisses* (sausages) by the French, especially when referring to the act of horizontal collaboration. For a girl to be seen in the company of a German soldier was scandalous and elicited angry stares. Relationships between French women and German men tended to flourish in large urban areas where there were high concentrations of German soldiers. This provided not only the necessary opportunity, but also anonymity. German soldiers were often pleasant, well brought-up and even anti-Nazi.

The Italian troops were incorrigible where women were concerned, and even 14-year-olds were not safe.[6] It has not been ascertained how many babies were born to Italian fathers but it is estimated that the German Army left behind 200,000 babies who would forever be branded as sons or daughters of the Boche. Someone caustically commented: 'Certain people don't hesitate to lift a glass with the Germans at the Central Café. The bellies of some girls are bulging outward, a product of the amorous passions of young soldiers.'[7]

Collaborators came in many guises but none were more hated than those who proudly wore the uniforms and wide berets of the Milice. These not-so-young thugs were part of the community they now terrorized. They were in a better position to know the allegiances of their fellow citizens and eavesdrop on them. Armed *miliciens* permanently patrolled the Nice railway station as the Gestapo trusted them more than they did the French police. However, being criminally inclined, they were more likely to profit from their positions than professional policemen or soldiers. Some members of the Milice were from good families, and politically they included Pétainists, fascists, right-wingers or anti-communists.

One of the most brutal German military units of all those employed in France in the fight against the Resistance was composed of French volunteers. The 8th Company, 3rd Regiment of the 242nd (Brandenburg) Division was especially formed to infiltrate communities (out of uniform) and carry out anti-partisan operations. The officers and non-commissioned officers were German; the footsoldiers, who spoke faultless French with a Provençal or Parisian accent, were mostly very young, and included criminals and ex-*miliciens*. Attached to the

19th Army, the 8th Company had its first headquarters in Marseille but later moved to the Vaucluse.

Today, some military types consider the Brandenburger commandos to have been the elite of German special forces. The unit was the brainchild of Hauptmann (Captain) Theodor von Hippel who had learned the art of guerilla warfare under General Paul von Lettow-Vorbeck, during the East African campaign of the First World War. Typically, they were fluent in foreign languages and deployed as small commando units to penetrate into enemy territory and sow confusion. A few of the survivors joined the Foreign Legion and went to fight in Indochina or, using their skills in disguise and evasion, simply disappeared.

*

Even before the Germans officially occupied the south of France, there were Gestapo agents to be seen everywhere in their felt hats and suits with padded shoulders but who were obliged to restrain themselves in the early days. The Marseille office at 425 Rue Paradis was one of the seventeen Gestapo regional offices in France. Scattered outposts or 'antennas' reported to Rue Paradis. In Provence, these *antennen* were located in Nîmes, Avignon, Toulon, Digne, Draguignan, Nice, Cannes, Brignoles, Aix-en-Provence, Monte-Carlo, Orange, Hyères and Briançon, ensuring coverage over the whole southeast.

Among the first Nazis to arrive in Nice after the German takeover was SS Hauptsturmführer Alois Brunner, a specialist in hunting down the Jews of Europe. Brunner, a 31-year-old Austrian captain, was charged with overseeing the final solution of the Jewish problem in the Alpes-Maritimes, and reported to Adolf Eichmann. Described as a puny little man without any expression, Brunner established his offices at the Hôtel Excelsior on Avenue Durante, not far from the Nice train station. Within those walls, the most frightful atrocities were carried out. The building with its beautiful Belle Époque architecture is still in existence today.

The Gestapo, with a permanent staff of fifteen, operated out of the Hôtel Hermitage in Cimiez, on the outskirts of Nice. An annexe, used for 'intense interrogations', was located a kilometre away at Villa Trianon. A network of informers, consisting of barmen, barbers and brothel-keepers worked on commission. When the office of the Gestapo asked for forty female informers and interpreters, they received 300 applications.

During the first two years of the war, Jewish refugees from all over Europe, including Germany and Austria, were arriving in Nice, Cannes and other towns of the Riviera where the Italians were still in control. Cramming the sidewalk cafés and the parks, trying to look like they were on holiday, one observer remarked that they were the ones wearing black clothes that looked too big for them, their possessions having been reduced to diamonds sewn into the lining of their coats. Cannes was the preferred refuge for those who could afford it.

In the Alpes-Maritimes, a census was taken in 1941 with the aim of identifying Jews who had immigrated since 1936. In Cannes, only 128 were registered, whereas the mayor estimated that there were at least 4,000 in his municipality. For some, these represented extra mouths to feed, and even the exorbitant black market prices were blamed on the Jews.

Access to the land of liberty, equality and fraternity was not automatic. Even those fleeing extermination had to have a visa. Milan was a meeting place for Jews who had travelled from Germany and Austria. Some tried to cross through the Alps, and others handed over their jewellery to pay for a clandestine crossing into France. San Remo and other ports were considered stepping stones to the new world. The mainstream, but fascist newspaper, the *Petit Niçois*, proclaimed that there should no more be a place for these parasitic foreigners.

Once in Nice, all immigrants had to report to the police station with assurances that they had the means to support themselves during their stay. One synagogue was custodian of a bundle of notes which was then passed from family to destitute family for the purpose of proving that they would not be a burden on the state. The advantages of being in cities such as Nice, Cannes or Marseille were that they were big enough to become invisible and were close to Spain which remained a possible escape route. In fascist circles, the South of France was referred to as *chez le Juif*, the home of the Jews.

Although there may have been loyalty among old friends, there is documented evidence of how the people of Avignon denounced the Jews and painted anti-Semitic graffiti and smashed windows in Rue de la République. In Saint-Tropez it was proposed to prevent Jews from staying for longer than two months, so as not to 'contaminate' the resort town with their wealth. In Nice, the Promenade des Anglais was now only open to Aryan walkers, thus ensuring enough space on the public benches.

Except where it suited them, the Vichy authorities prohibited Jews from practising as doctors, dentists, lawyers, professors, teachers, journalists and in other professions of influence. Exceptions were made for those who were at least fifth-generation French. Enrolment of Jewish students at universities was capped at 3 per cent. Jewish-owned businesses and farms in Provence, including the famous Châteauneuf-du-Pape vineyards, were confiscated and 'Aryanized'. Five villas in Cannes and Beausoleil belonging to Edouard de Rothschild were confiscated.

French Jews had been living under threat of deportation since the massive round-ups in Paris in July 1942, but Marseille came in for special treatment between 22 January and 24 January 1943. During the round-up, conducted by French police under the supervision of SS officers, almost 2,000 Jews were arrested. They were sent first to les Baumettes Prison in Marseille, then to Fréjus, before being crammed into trains bound for the extermination camps. Ultimately, around 5,000 Jews from Marseille and surrounding areas were murdered.

In particular, the 1st Arrondissement at the Vieux-Port was considered by the Germans to be a 'terrorist nest' full of foreign bandits who ambushed them in the narrow streets. On orders from Heindrich Himmler, the Vichy police chief, René Bousquet, willingly carried out the demolition of the neighbourhood. It is even said that he was in favour of wiping the entire city of Marseille off the map. To the Germans, the city was 'the cancer of Europe'. At least 1,494 houses on fourteen hectares of land in the *quartier* Saint-Jean were dynamited, displacing 30,000 people.[8]

In implementing the 'Final Solution', the chief of the Gestapo's Jewish Office in Paris, SS Captain Theodore Dannecker, made a personal inspection of the camps in the south and was disappointed by the small number of Jews interned in places like Camp des Milles at Aix-en-Provence which had become became a transit camp (*centre de rassemblement*) from where 2,000 Jews were deported to Auschwitz. Continuing on to Nice, Dannecker authorized a round-up of Jews, beginning at 2 a.m. on 26 August 1943, and lasting a number of days.

In their sinister black Citroëns, the Sicherheitspolizei/Sicherheitsdienst (SiPo/SD), generically known as the Geheime Staatspolizei, or Gestapo, would suddenly block off a street and stop anyone who looked slightly Jewish. Unlucky individuals were thrown into the back of the *'panier à salade'* (salad basket) or Black Maria. Men were subjected to 'medical examinations' and those who were circumcized were assumed to be Jewish regardless of one's identity documents. 'Specialists' in judging facial features decided a person's fate in an instant. Jews were accosted at their hotels or on the beach and brought to the Excelsior where they faced torture for information about family members.

Two or three times a week, in groups of about sixty, a consignment of human beings would be herded to the station, a few hundred metres up the street, lined with spectators. But it had been a disappointing catch for the Germans, partly because the BBC had broadcast a warning, and many Jews were hidden by friends or just disappeared. Furthermore, sentiment had turned against Vichy as the public came to realize that Jews were not the cause of their misery.

After the initial haul, the Gestapo had to rely on informers who were paid up to 5,000 francs for denouncing a Jew. Hotel registers would be scrutinized by gendarmes and Gestapo but French police often refused to arrest Jews. In restaurants and hotel lobbies, informers would try to blend in while listening into conversations. Religious gatherings provided them with unmatched opportunities to turn in people of a particular faith. In order to speed up deportations, the Gestapo used sub-contractors from the underworld, but these were often more interested in extorting valuables than making arrests. In addition to these auxiliaries, there were those who had absolutely no authority. Known as 'fake Gestapo', they raided the homes of wealthy Jews purely for the purpose of plunder and for the official reward.

As far as persecution of the Jews is concerned, the period under Italian occupation from November 1942 to September 1943 has been referred to as the 'Italian Respite' or 'Italian Interlude'. Because Mussolini planned on annexing Nice, he tried not to antagonize the citizens. Pamphlets were distributed by the Italians claiming that they had no hostile intensions on their side. It is said that the Jewish population in Nice 'flourished' and grew from 13,000 at the end of 1942, to 30,000 in September 1943.[9] Whereas some in the Italian military may have spoken out against the persecution of the Jews, and sometimes intervened on their behalf, they did not block the 'final solution' as has sometimes been asserted.

Contrary to received history, things did not go well for the Jews in Nice under the 'protection' of the Italian Zone. According to a local historian, 'the Italian presence was not as soft as all that'.[10] The Italians arrested 1,366 Jews as opposed to the 1,229 arrested by the Nazis. It is likely, however, that many of these did not possess French citizenship. According to another source, 4,200 people of all nationalities were deported from the Alpes-Maritimes; only 590 or 14 per cent returned, and of the Jews, only 3 per cent survived.

Even children were aware of the misfortune which had overtaken their Jewish neighbours. Memories of babies being ripped out of their mother's arms would never be erased. Situated not far from the present-day Stade de France and Charles de Gaulle airport, Drancy was the final staging point for Jews en route to places like Saarbrücken, Neuebrenn, Mauthausen, Natzweiler and Dachau. Unable to envisage an Auschwitz, the children in Drancy internment camp referred to their final destination as 'Pitchipoi', a nonsense, imaginary place.

After being rounded up by the SS on 17 March 1944, Jean Kahn, a Jew from Capentras was taken first to the Gestapo in Avignon, on Boulevard Saint-Ruff, where he was booked by a young blond woman speaking perfect French. Very politely, she asked for his identity, the address of his wife and civil status. Next, he and his companions, including a British family, were delivered to Sainte-Anne Prison in Avignon, where they were received at the gate by a young-looking man, about 35 years old, wearing a light-coloured suit. Kahn realized it was Charles Palmieri the 'Jew-Hunter' whom he had previously seen in the Carpentras area. Later he would recognize Palmieri in photographs from his trial.[11]

Charles Palmieri, a former petty criminal from of the Marseille underworld was affiliated to the Avignon Branch of the Gestapo. He ran an operation called Bureau Merle which claimed to be a commercial enterprise, but was dedicated to hunting Jews. In addition to the commission for each Jew they delivered, Palmieri and his gang also extracted huge ransoms as well as jewellery from the victims. As a sideline, he provided information to Ernest Dunker on the movements of the Maquis in the Var.

With the 'round, pink face of a doll', Palmieri has been described as being greedy, unscrupulous and cold, exploiting the vulnerability of the Jews whom he hated with a vengeance. When a crying mother pleaded, 'What do you want with my baby?' Palmieri replied, 'Sausage meat.'[12] In June 1944, he was transferred to the Gestapo headquarters at Villa Montfleury in Cannes.

By 1944, Alois Brunner had closed down the Excelsior and returned to Drancy in Paris. The Nice operation had not been one of his success stories. In the end, he escaped justice and was given refuge in Syria where he was employed to advise the security police on torture and repression techniques developed by the Nazis. The Israeli intelligence services tried to kill him but only succeeded in taking out an eye and four fingers with two different parcel bombs. The Simon Wiesenthal Center believes that he died in Syria in 2010.

Some *Niçois* are ashamed at how little was done to rebel against their oppressors but in fact they had a better record of protecting their Jewish citizens than did the Parisians. Countless heroes and heroines helped in their small ways, but one individual, Angelo Donati, a Jewish banker, used his wealth and influence to great effect. Working together with a Catholic priest, Father Marie-Benoît, he organized the evacuation of thousands, many of them to the small town of Saint-Martin-Vésubie on the Italian border.

No less courageous were the spontaneous acts by individuals like the Marseille school teacher responsible for saving Pierre Vidal-Naquet – today a prominent historian. On hearing that Pierre's parents had been arrested by the Gestapo at their home, the teacher organized a group of fellow pupils to track the boy down and prevent him from returning home. Stanley Hoffman, who became a political scientist at Harvard, wrote of how his history teacher in Nice dried his tears when his best friend was deported, and gave false papers to his mother so that they could flee a Gestapo-infested city. 'This man wipes out all the bad moments, and the humiliations, and the terrors. He and his wife were not resistance heroes, but if there was an average Frenchman, it was this man.'[13]

Among the numerous Jewish organizations which gave assistance by smuggling children into Switzerland or by providing counterfeit documents, there was also an armed Jewish Resistance, the Armée Juive, which was formed in Toulouse in 1940, but also operated in Nice and Lyon. Those who denounced Jews, or persecuted them, were hunted down by their hit squads whose members took oaths in Hebrew. One of their successes in Nice was the assassination of an informer named Georges Karakaeff or simply 'Kara'. After making advances to a pretty young girl, who happened to be a member of the Underground, he was lured to a deserted spot, where a man stepped forward and shot him three times.

*

In Saint-Tropez, the Kriegsmarine, the German Navy, which was responsible for the coastal defences, was housed in various buildings around the port, including Hôtel de Paris which was opened in 1931 and attracted the who's who of the world of art, literature and intelligentsia. The hotel restaurant continued to serve its famous Grand Marnier soufflé to its demanding new clientele. After the Germans checked out, it became a popular watering hole for American officers who would have found the amenities surprisingly plush after what they might have read in the official guidebook:

> Don't expect plumbing in French hotels, railway stations and homes to be like modern American plumbing. It isn't. The French would appreciate an up-to-date American bathroom, with all the gadgets, but have never been able to afford it. After all, maybe your granddad wasn't brought up with one either, and he managed to survive.[14]

Juliette Paglia was 19 years old and a receptionist at the biggest hotel in Sainte-Maxime, the Hôtel des Palmiers. The property was divided into two sections, one being requisitioned by the Germans whose store of food was stolen at every opportunity, but according to Julia, they were always 'correct'. Virtually next door, the church near the port was used to store ammunition, and if it had been hit by a stray bomb, there would have been nothing left of the old quarter. For six months, Father Celestin Buisson was obliged to hold his church services in a room in the municipal casino which has been a landmark on the beachfront since 1923.

In La Garde and Toulon, German officers ensconced themselves in the most beautiful houses. School buildings were allotted to the rank and file. Alternative accommodation had to be found for classrooms and the number of lessons reduced. Families were not necessarily thrown out of their houses, but they had to share space with their unwelcome guests. For the child living in Saint-Étienne du Grès in the Bouches-du-Rhône Department, it was an uncomfortable arrangement. The soldiers in grey-green uniforms slept in the house. They strutted through the halls, their boots creaking over the Provençal tiles. They travelled about incessantly, on foot, in trucks, in horse carts driven by their 'Mongolian' mercenaries. The blond soldiers, often bare-chested, coped badly with the dry Provençal heat.[15]

Because Germany's best troops were needed on the Eastern Front or on the Atlantic Wall, those manning the defences in southern France were often older men or foreign conscripts. These *Osttruppen* consisted of Poles, Russians, Azerbaijanis, Armenians and Czechs. As occupying troops they were adequate, but were usually happy to surrender with bright, sometimes toothless smiles after the fighting started. Typically, these units were stiffened with ethnic German officers and a sprinkling of fanatical young Aryans.

At the time of the invasion, the German 19th Army, a part of Army Group G, was responsible for all of Provence. General Johannes Blaskowitz, commanding Army Group G, and General Friedrich Wiese, heading the 19th Army, were the principal German military commanders responsible for the *Südwall*. Already short of manpower and equipment, the strength of Army Group G steadily waned as unit after unit was ordered to the Normandy area. A number of anti-aircraft units which had protected the bridges over the Rhône, and the anti-tank companies of four infantry divisions, went north during June and July 1944. By 15 August, Blaskowitz had lost two-thirds of his armoured reserve and about a quarter of his infantry divisions. One source estimates the German strength on Dragoon D-Day at approximately 53,670 troops, with an effective combat strength of 41,175.[16]

The Luftwaffe was also at a low ebb with less than 300 aircraft of all descriptions in the area of operation. One of the busiest groups was the fighter group, Jagdgruppe 200, based at Aix les Milles and Avignon. Once a dirt strip with a hangar, Avignon Ost is now the city's airport. Besides defending against daily bombing raids, they also carried out attacks on concentrations of 'terrorists'. The Kriegsmarine was in charge of the coastal batteries but with a long coastline to defend, from Spain to Italy, they were very thinly spread. The only 'warships' which were of any use were a few high-speed patrol boats and torpedo boats based at Antibes.

By early August 1944, it was common knowledge that southern France would be the next Allied target, and all units of Army Group G were ordered to remain in place and defend the coast at any price. With the prospect of facing a formidable invasion force and with the growing sabotage and harassment by the Resistance, the German high command was getting anxious. Although suffering from a shortage of fuel, vehicles, batteries for the radios, even guns and ammunition, the (mostly foreign) foot soldiers were living in ignorant bliss, cooling off in the sea, watching the 'airshow' over the Gulf of Fréjus, totally relaxed, and happy not to be on the Russian Front.[17]

Chapter 4

Defiance

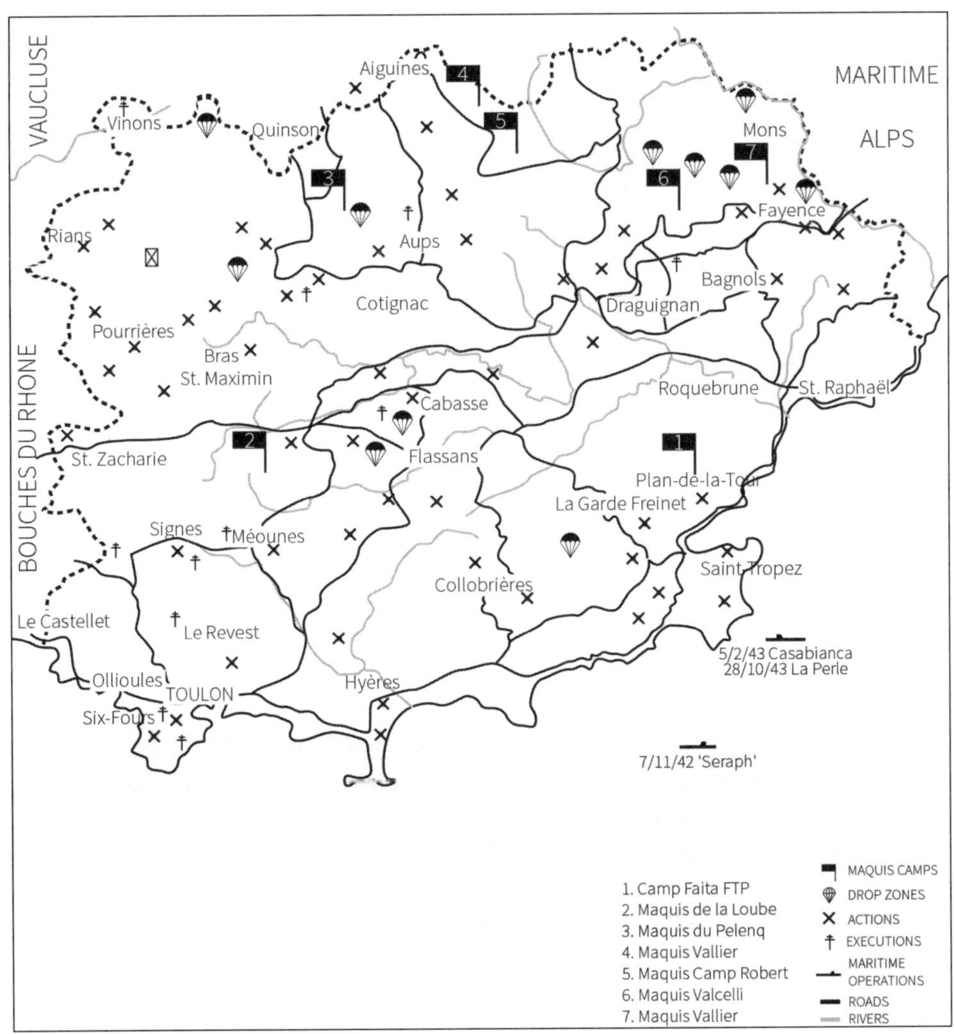

Resistance activities in the Var.

It can be said that France was at that time in a state of civil war, but the great struggle going on below the surface between the members of the Resistance and the Gestapo had very little effect on ordinary lives. Rumour and the grapevine told of clashes, of arrests and reprisals, and the dreaded red posters announced the shooting of hostages, but most people just obeyed the regulations and went about their business.

Just as there were many ways of coping with the occupation, there were many levels of collaboration and resistance. There was a fluid spectrum along which one could oscillate from hero to villain. One option was *attentisme* – a passive waiting on events –but even *attentiste* might have been 'functional resisters' by omission. Likewise, there were 'functional collaborators' who could have spoken out but did not. The 'eloquence of silence' could also be interpreted as a form of resistance. A tiny minority were driven to take up arms.

With time, the flame of resistance would burn fiercely in the southeast of France, but at first it only flickered and smouldered. Passive resistance only gradually gave way to something more active. Because of the number of refugees there, Marseille led the way. Small, localized groups banded together and set about acts of sabotage, intelligence-gathering and helping escaped prisoners of war. The rescue of Jews, Allied airmen and other fugitives became a real and effective form of resistance. It was not even necessary to be armed, and few were. Only as a last resort would one leave home to camp in the mountains and forests. While women were indispensible as couriers and *passeurs*, the Maquis bands consisted almost entirely of men. Many Italian soldiers who found themselves in a tight spot with the sudden change of sides decided to take to the hills and join up with the Maquis, and a number of Jews decided to become the hunter rather than the hunted.

At grassroots level, a group of six close friends made up a *sizaine,* and five *sizaines* made up a *trentaine.* Each person only knew the identities of the five others in his *sizaine* as well as the head of his *trentaine*. On arriving at a Maquis camp, one early volunteer expected to find an army, but only a group of four men were there to welcome him. These four men, he later found out, were worth an army in term of courage and determination. Their only weapons were some old Lebels – a Fench rifle which first entered service in 1886 – and shotguns.

Partisan groups could be of any size, have any political ideals and any sort of paramilitary organization. Their leaders could be carpenters or colonels in the regular army. In the cities, resisters typically did normal jobs in the day and slept at home. The first distinction can therefore be made between the *Résistance légaux* and the *Résistance illégaux*. The *légaux* lived incognito among the population and went about their daily lives, providing a support service to the *illégaux* who were known to the authorities and consequently had to live in the forests and mountains. Alternatively, one may view the Resistance as a political underground movement and the different groups of Maquis as their military counterparts.

As some historians have pointed out, there was not just one Resistance but many different resistances. Resistance simply meant refusing to accept the German occupation and a willingness to do something about it. It is more accurate to refer to the 'resistance in France' as opposed to the 'French Resistance'. Furthermore, a significant number of resistants in France were not French. Some of the most fanatical fighters were Spanish, Polish and Italians cut off from their homes. British and American special operators played a significant role but warrant a chapter of their own.

Resistance was more urban than rural, some movements were communist, some were pro-de Gaulle (Gaullist), but being vehemently anti-fascist, it was the communists who were the driving force. Perhaps only 2 per cent of the adult population ever actively resisted, although the French have always propagated the narrative of a nationwide, collective Resistance. From small intimate groups of families and friends they grew into a wide variety of organized movements, which a few courageous leaders tried to transform into a more effective whole.

Through the efforts of legendary resistance leader, Jean Moulin, and a few others, the Conseil National de la Résistance (CNR) was formed on 27 May 1943, and its founding principle was the decision to follow General de Gaulle. Jean Moulin was de Gaulle's personal representative, and was tasked with bringing all the notoriously quarrelsome factions together under one umbrella. Although essentially an administrator, this former préfet was destined to become one of the most charismatic and romantic figures of France's wartime history.

Throughout France, there are boulevards, avenues, town squares, esplanades, crossroads and institutions which bear the name of Jean Moulin. In the Alpes-Maritimes alone, there are at least four monuments dedicated to him, as well as three schools and more than a dozen streets.

In Draguignan there is a Lycée Jean Moulin and even in little Plan-de-la-Tour his name is fittingly given to a hidden alley.

Moulin was a man of the south: his family's residence was at Saint-Andiol near Salon-de-Provence. He also knew Marseille well, having spent six months there in 1941. At the Hôtel Moderne near the Vieux-Port Moulin had meetings and drank pastis with Henri Frenay and other leaders in the south. Posing as an art dealer, he made frequent visits to Antibes and Nice where he had a 'gallery' at 22 Rue de France. An accomplished artist in his own right, he hung his own artwork on the walls. In the apartment above, he held meetings and forged his organization called Combat. At the time, few people knew his true identity and only much later would they come to realize that the charismatic art dealer known as *Max* or *Rex* was in fact Jean Moulin.

After a meeting with de Gaulle in London, Moulin parachuted into the department of the Bouches-du-Rhône, near Eygalières in the Alpilles Mountains on the night of 1/2 January 1942. A haunting sculpture of a parachutist today marks the spot where he and his two companions landed, near Salon-de-Provence. Later based in Lyon, France's second city, Moulin continued with his work until someone betrayed him to Klaus Barbie, known as 'The Butcher of Lyon'. During interrogation he suffered unspeakable tortures: hot needles were stuck under his nails. While in transit, in July 1943, he committed suicide rather than talk.[1]

The motive for his betrayal may have been political or financial, and there was more than one suspect, but shortly before his death in 1991, Barbie himself named Raymond Aubrac, as the culprit. Until then, Raymond Aubrac had been revered as a hero of the Resistance, but now had to spend the rest of his life trying to clear his name. Klaus Barbie is said to have been directly responsible for up to 14,000 deaths. He fled to South America but was brought back to France to face trial in 1983.

Raymond Aubrac, a staunch communist, once made an audacious escape from captivity with the help of his pregnant wife, Lucie, and lived to the age of 97. Both Raymond and Lucie Aubrac wrote extensively of their experiences, but their wartime record has been somewhat tarnished. Aubrac was appointed as the Regional Commissioner of the Republic in Marseille after the liberation and was in charge of prosecuting collaborators. Some writers have even attacked Jean Moulin's legacy, but he remains the most exalted figure of the French Resistance. An iconic image portrays him wearing a fedora hat and a scarf covering up a scar on his neck, the result of a suicide attempt during a spell in a German prison. One controversial theory is that it was an OSS agent with a dubious heritage, one Fred Brown, who unintentionally led to the arrest of Moulin following a meeting between the two in Avignon.

Virtually a dozen different organizations were active in the south, and each one of these could consist of a number of sub-groups. Chief among them was the Francs-Tireurs et Partisans Français (FTPF), usually shortened to just FTP. Loosely translated, Francs-Tireurs et Partisans means the 'Free Shooters' or 'Irregular Riflemen'. The name has its roots in the rifle clubs or citizen forces dating back to the nineteenth century. It was now the military wing of the French Communist Party. Exiled Spanish republicans and anti-fascists from almost all other countries of Europe filled their ranks. Many, but not all, members were committed communists. They had political commissars and called each other 'comrade'. British and American commanders were wary of them, so it is no wonder that the FTP were last in line when it came to the fierce competition for weapons drops.[2]

The Mouvements Unis de la Résistance (MUR) translated as Unified Movements of the Resistance, grew out of three early resistance movements thanks to the efforts of Jean Moulin. One of the original component organizations, Combat, was co-founded by Berty Albrecht, a fearless anti-fascist campaigner and resistance organizer who eventually hanged herself in a Gestapo prison. Having been born in Marseille, there are a multitude of streets, schools and colleges across Provence named after her. The MUR was Gaullist by persuasion, and being more structured than any other local Maquis, they provided training, false identification papers, medical services and had an underground press. Its armed wing was called Armée secrète (AS) and in contrast to its main rivals, it had a policy of 'wait and see' until the time was ripe.

With a much lower profile than the other two, but having some influence in the south was the Organization de Résistance de l'Armée (ORA), created soon after the German invasion of the Free Zone in November 1942. It consisted of former French military personnel and ex-prisoners of war, but being recently converted from Vichyism, they were viewed with suspicion. François Mitterand (aka François Moreland), a former Vichyite and future president of France, was one of the founders. With the weapons taken from the Vichy army, they were initially better armed than most, and being professionals, the French secret service, the BCRA, was more inclined to work with them. The strategy of the ORA was to build up an underground army and remain hidden until the Allies made an appearance. Politically, they were not friends of Charles de Gaulle, but they nevertheless agreed to work together with the Forces Françaises de l'Intérieur (FFI), the umbrella organization which was controlled from outside the country.[3]

As opposed to a resistance 'movement' such as the FTP or Combat, a network or *réseau* was linked to the SOE, OSS or BCRA in the outside world, and had a military objective. They were small, specialized and secret. The leadership of resistance movements came from the same prewar governing elites although they were the younger generation. The foot soldiers in the *réseaux* were typically from the lower strata of society.

Women were the lifeblood of the Resistance. Evoking the appearance of the ideal housewife, women were able to move about more freely than men, who were likely to be stopped and asked why they were not working in the STO. Within the *réseaux*, new occupations came about, such as the *courier*, *passeur* and *agent de liaison*. A *passeur*, also known as a *convoyeur*, was someone who guided downed airmen and other evaders along lines of escape, and was quite likely to be female.

Marcelle Zunino, the young mother from La Garde near Toulon was a *courier*: 'Our first rule is prudence. I know some members of our group only by their pseudonyms, mine is *Renée*. The second rule is discretion. Even to my family I say nothing of my activities. One must be silent because the dangers are everywhere, and denunciations, sometimes anonymous, lead to the cells of the Gestapo where the worst horrors are suffered. Then imprisonment or deportation.'[4]

Employing feminine wiles or playing the damsel in distress helped many an *agent de liaison* get out of a tight spot. On a mission to Marseille, Jacqueline Lautier was stopped at the Pont du Var at the western end of Nice, close to where the airport is today. The bridge had recently been bombed and the train could not depart as usual from the Nice central station. With her false identity card, and secret documents in her bag, she feared the worst. However, knowing that she could rely of the gallantry of the French policemen, she walked straight up to the blockade and asked them to help her load her luggage on the train.[5]

As a *passeur* for the aforementioned Pat O'Leary Line, Denise Sainson (*Dalila*) helped Allied airmen escape to North Africa via Perpignan and Spain. She sheltered dozens of escapees, and once had four Americans staying in her apartment above a bicycle shop at 7 Rue Barralis in Nice.

She fed them and found them civilian clothes. Because they couldn't stand being cooped up, she would take them out for walks, just down the road to the Hôtel Palais de la Méditerrané which still stands front and centre on the Promenade des Anglais.

Lucie Aubrac writes about the resistance experience as being inseparable from her roles of wife and mother. During her second pregnancy she helped her husband escape from prison by posing as an aggrieved girlfriend. Even women who stayed at home could be seen to be resisting. There is a story about a resistance fighter who, while staying in a woman's home, woke up to find her ironing his clothes. 'There is no need for you to put yourself out like this on my accord,' he protested. 'I'm not doing it for you', she said, 'I'm doing it for France.'

Hélène Deschamps (*Anick*) was unique in that she was recruited locally into the OSS on the word of known resistance leaders, and given on-the-job training. Although born in China and raised in Senegal, Madagascar and Réunion, Hélène Deschamps returned to Aix-en-Provence in her teens where she became involved in resistance activities. It was the political bickering among the disparate partisan groups that led her to work for the Americans as part of the first OSS circuit in France. Set up in July 1943 to report on enemy dispositions prior to D-Day, PENNYFARTHING operated in Montpellier, Avignon, Marseille and Pertuis in the Luberon.

During the momentous month of August 1944, Deschamps travelled to Saint-Tropez, crossing paths with a group of FTP *maquisards* who accused her of being a Nazi agent, and were quite prepared to shoot her out of hand. Clearly, some FTPs were gangsters, more political than patriotic, and considered the OSS to be the vanguard of an imperialist regime.[6]

Having started the war in opposition to the Allies, the communists changed sides in June 1941 when the Germans invaded Russia. Then they began the struggle for internal power in France. The SOE agent John Goldsmith also found communist resistance groups the most difficult to deal with: 'It is little wonder that they trusted no one and found few who would trust them.'[7] It was the inaccurate portrayal of the lives of SOE agents in popular culture which inspired Goldsmith to write his book, *Accidental Agent*, in 1971 but one narrative which he felt needed correcting was 'the apparent universal comradeship of resistance fighters throughout France and their undivided loyalty to General de Gaulle'.[8]

OSS Captain Geoffrey Jones parachuted into DZ (drop or dropping zone) *Prisonnier* at La Roque Esclapon in the Var on 10 August 1944. At the nearby perched village of Mons, reached by a rugged track, he joined forces with the FTP Maquis *Valcelli*, led by Joseph Manzone, said to be an able and enthusiastic communist. Jones had great respect for his Maquis comrades: 'Our outfit was made up of a wonderful group of people, for whom, I guess, I was the catalyst. These were the Frenchmen who honestly produced results for their country. These are the kind of people that are worth respecting, and the hell with the ones who were busy denouncing each other in order to get political power.'[9]

Nonetheless, these *maquisards* 'were carried away with the idea of being communists and seemed to think that it was romantic just to live on the mountaintop and call each other Comrade'. They had a political commissar for each of their three battalions. When he took about twenty of them into a small action, and the guns started going off, Jones looked around and all but two had disappeared, but he put it down to lack of training – not lack of courage.[10]

One morning, Jones was honoured with a parade where the Maquis drew themselves up and sang 'L'Internationale' and 'La Marseillaise'. The age-old 'Internationale', so loved by communists, socialists, anarchists and resistance fighters of all persuasions, was originally written in French and the first two lines proclaim: *Debout, les damnés de la terre, debout, les forçats de la faim,* (Stand up, damned of the earth, stand up, prisoners of starvation). These words gave courage to many a condemned prisoner, as did the singing of the national anthem, 'La Marseillaise' and 'Le Chant des Partisans'. Popular songs that echoed within prison walls included the recent hit 'Le closher de mon coeur' and the evergreen 'Il pleut sur la route'.

When Peter Churchill was in the Fresnes Prison, a 15-year-old boy, a staunch communist and resistance fighter was in the cell below him, awaiting execution. Unlike Churchill who turned to God in his hour of need, communists generally had the courage of their atheist convictions and 'behaved magnificently in prison and went to their deaths like heroes'.[11]

The Nazis had no qualms about executing such young boys (or girls). In the Alpine town of Besançon, and throughout France, the name of Henri Fertet is immortalized as the result of a letter which he wrote to his parents on the morning of his execution on 26 September 1943. After apologizing for the pain which the letter would bring and saying goodbye individually to family and friends, bequeathing them his book collection, he wrote: *'Adieu, la mort m'appelle, je ne veux ni bandeau ni être attaché. Je vous embrasse tous. C'est quand même dur de mourir.'* (Goodbye forever, death is calling me, I don't want a blindfold or to be tied. I kiss you all. All the same, it's hard to die.)[12]

Another young hero of the Resistance, Guy Môquet, was 17 years old when he was executed on 2 October 1941 for distributing communist material. The terms of endearment with which he addressed his parents and little brother in his last letter make for difficult reading: *'Ma petite maman chérie, mon tout petit frère adoré, mon petit papa aimé.'* The opening line reads, 'I'm going to die!'[13] The name of Guy Môquet became renowned in the Resistance after the letter was published in an underground newspaper. One of the detachments of the Maquis de Maures was immediately named after him. To this day, the story of Guy Môquet is taught in schools, and a station on the Paris Metro is named after him.

The two main camps of the Maquis de Maures were called Camp Faïta and Camp Robert in honour of two early martyrs, Vincent Faïta and Jean Robert, guillotined in Nîmes. In December 1942, Camp Faïta was founded at Cargues between La Garde Freinet and Gonfaron. Members of Camp Faïta would become known as 1ère Compagnie FTPF de Provence, offshoots or detachments of which diffused new blood into various other groups as far afield as Marseille.

A leading expert on the Maquis in the Var, Jean-Marie Guillon, sings the praises of the Maquis des Maures, later known as the Brigade des Maures: 'These are ultimate fighters. They are, in their youth, the best representatives of the generation of the Resistance. They symbolize what the communist resistance wants to be in the eyes of others, its partners and the public: Courageous to the point of heroism and sacrifice of life.'[14]

In the early days, the coast of the Var was known for having the most dynamic resistance in the whole of Provence. This band of *maquisards* operated along the coast from Sainte-Maxime to Le Lavandou. Minor acts of sabotage included the destruction of a telephone line at La Foux and the electrical transformer at Saint-Pons-les-Mûres, which powered a torpedo factory. When their activities started to attract too much attention from the Germans, a splinter group moved to the northern slopes of the Massif des Maures near La Garde Freinet, above Vidauban, while others moved farther north to the Basses-Alpes. These bases also provided refuge for any youngster hiding from the Gestapo, Milice, L'Ovra or the STO.

The founders of the Maquis des Maures were unlikely warriors. Jean Despas was a refugee from Paris now living in Saint-Tropez. Marko Célébonovitch (Čelebonović in Serbian), the son of an eminent Belgrade lawyer, had studied law and economics in England, but was now living on a farm near Saint-Tropez where he indulged his passion for painting and sculpture. Both his wife and daughter played an active role in the struggle. Alix Macario from Cogolin, has been described as an anti-fascist through and through, *pur et dur.* He had fought with the Spanish Republicans until he was wounded, and brought back some knowledge of guerrilla warfare. From their first headquarters on a remote farm at Forêt Domaniale du Dom, near Le Lavandou, their activities involved the distribution of pamphlets and painting of graffiti on buildings around Saint-Tropez.[15]

At that time there was a small local railway which ran along the coast all the way to Saint-Tropez. New recruits for the Maquis des Maures were met at the station in Sainte-Maxime or at the less-populated La Nartelle siding. The procedure when one got off the train was to whistle a particular tune and to hold a string in one's hand. The recruit would approach someone holding a piece of string, and ask: 'What time is it?' 'It's midnight' was the correct response.[16] Anna Casu, originally from Grasse, was in her late twenties when together with her husband and her brother she joined the Maquis des Maures in Sainte-Maxime. On a farm, on the Plan-de-la-Tour road, she hid young people called up for the STO until they could be linked up with the Maquis.[17]

Although most members were farmers and forestry workers, the Maquis des Maures included a few students, artisans and traders. In September 1943, its ranks were swelled by about 135 former Italian soldiers as well as deserters from the German Army (mainly Armenians). A community of anti-fascist Italians who had moved to the South of France in the 1920s and 1930s were some of the earliest members. The Landini family, which had been forced out of their native Tuscany, became active in the Communist Party and its armed wing, the FTPF. Brothers Roger and Louis led the first attack on a German train on the line between Saint-Raphaël and Cannes while the 16-year-old Léon stood guard. The family would eventually be devastated by arrests, deportation and torture.

Radicalization of the Resistance began in 1943, and an article in an FTP newspaper declared: 'Kill the German to purify our territory, kill him because he kills our people … Kill those who denounce, those who have aided the enemy … Kill the policeman who has in any way contributed to the arrest of patriots … Kill the *miliciens*, exterminate them … strike them down like mad dogs … destroy them as you would vermin.'[18]

With liberation almost assured, 1944 ushered in a second generation of *maquisards* who were slightly more professional, better equipped, and more inclined to cooperate with one another. A bespectacled school teacher from Plan-de-la-Tour, Jean Vatinet (*Celtic*), a member of MUR, was instrumental in bringing together various factions to form the Maquis de la Brigade des Maures, which in turn was incorporated into the FFI. The Brigade des Maures was efficiently organized into four sectors which would each have different tasks on D-Day.

Plan-de-la-Tour was bereft of young men, approximately thirty-five of whom were now in PoW camps in Germany. Jean Vatinet decided that the families of these men had given enough, so he mainly recruited his fighters from the neighbouring village of Grimaud. Some have said that in Plan-de-la-Tour there were no collaborators at all. If there were traitors in their midst, they would have been rooted out.[19] In fact, both Jean Vatinet and his wife, Eléonore, were teachers and fervent patriots.

Among the so-called *légaux* members of the Resistance were the teenagers who were able to stay at home and move freely in their communities. They provided the liaison with the *Résistance illégaux*, carrying messages and supplies. The Maquis des Maures arose from the local community and was supported by a large part of the population. Even after being dispersed into small groups, they continued to exist in the relatively densely populated areas of Sainte-Maxime and Cogolin. Conversely, in the Haut-Var, the Maquis were more of an external creation consisting of younger men, sometimes impetuous, many of them from the coastal cities like Toulon and Cannes. These groups were forced to keep on the move.[20] The winter of 1943/4 is remembered as being one of the coldest ever. As conditions worsened, even the hardiest *maquisards* were forced from their mountain hideouts to seek shelter on farms or in remote villages.

An ominous sign that the year ahead would be a brutal one for the people of Provence was the killing of nine young *marquisards* and an old shepherd at Limate Farm near Signes on Sunday, 2 January 1944.

The *fusillés* – a much-used word in those times, meaning those who were shot – were members of 1ère Compagnie FTPF de Provence, who had recently moved from the Saint-Tropez area. During the autumn, hunted by the Germans, the group moved farther inland and higher into the hills of the Massif des Maures around La Garde Freinet where icy winds blew, and men were reduced to eating boiled leaves of vines and brambles. Finally forced to split up, the group, calling themselves the Guy Môquet or 'Marat detachment', moved on foot and with mules to Signes where they believed that they would have a balcony seat for the Allied *débarqement* (disembarkation).

Arriving in Signes during the cold and wet autumn of 1943, the Guy Môquet contingent based themselves at Limate Farm in a secluded valley, four kilometres south of the town. In the early days, their armament had consisted of a few rusty revolvers and bolt-action rifles from the First World War, but thanks to some deserters from the Italian Army, they were now better equipped. After Italy exited the war, almost 200 Italians were scattered on farms around La Garde Freinet, Le Luc and Gonfarnon. Most stayed only a few days but some fought to the end.

Signes, twenty kilometres inland from Toulon as the crow flies, was fated to become a favourite place of execution for the Germans, but up until this time it had been a peaceful, isolated plain, surrounded by pine-covered hills. The population of around a thousand, mainly farmers, had swelled since the bombing of the submarine base in the Toulon harbour on 24 November 1943. Houses had been flattened, electricity and water were cut off, and frightened residents who did not have relatives to stay with in a safer location, preferred to take their chances in this green valley.

An American aircraft had been shot down during the bombing raid over Toulon on 24 November 1943. At least one of the crew survived and was snatched to safety by the Maquis. Perhaps it was as a result of the ensuing manhunt that their camp was brought to the attention of the Germans. As usual, there were also one or two traitors among the townspeople. Soon after the arrival of the American airman (or airmen), the mayor sent an anonymous letter to the préfecture of the Var in Draguignan, mentioning the presence of 'foreigners' in the area.

The populations of small villages in the Var were mostly Catholic, right wing, conservative and often pro-Petain, and it is said that the people of Signes were patriots who had fought for their country in the First World War and also during the disastrous opening days of this war. They supplied the Maquis with whatever they needed. These young *soldats de l'ombre*, soldiers of the shadows, felt no need to hide: some even attended dances held at the Hôtel des Acacias to relieve the monotony of life in the forest.

As with many 'anti-terrorist' operations, the raid was carried out by Frenchmen of the 8th Company, 3rd Regiment of the 242nd (Brandenburg) Division. When the detachment of about seventy-five 'German' troops arrived at Limate farm at about 9.30 a.m. on a Sunday morning, there were 11 *maquisards* in camp, five having just departed on a mission. At the first sign of trouble, the group leader, 22-year-old Pierre Valcelli (*René*) threw all documents into the fire. Two or three managed to flee but the rest fought like demons.

The firefight lasted for forty-five minutes (some said two hours). It is unknown how many, if any, were killed or wounded before the *maquisards* ran out of ammunition, smashed their weapons and surrendered. After being forced to dig their own graves, half a metre deep and seven metres long, they were riddled with bullets at close range. Nine fighters and a 67-year-old shepherd were killed in this, the first of three massacres at Signes.

When villagers approached the farm on 5 January, the shallow grave was easily found: body parts were sticking out of it. One body had thirty-three wounds from bayonets and bullets. Heads were crushed in, the shepherd had been shot in the abdomen and left to die. The other victims were young men aged between 21 and 23, a fireman from Paris, a ski instructor, a tailor from Sainte-Maxime and two Italian soldiers. A gendarme tried to take photographs of the corpses but his camera and film were confiscated by the Germans. Emotions ran high when the bodies were brought down to the cemetery for burial. Underground newspapers, which proliferated in almost every community, helped spread the horrific news.

A week later, on 9 January, two foreign *marquisards* from the same detachment, Ludovic Basset and Jules Sansonnetti, who were returning from La Garde Freinet, were arrested at the Hôtel des Acacias and deported, never to return. It was clearly time to leave the Var, and the survivors of the 1ère Cie de Provence FTPF began withdrawing to Barrême, twenty kilometres northwest of Castellane in the Basses-Alpes. Proving that they still had a long reach, the communists assassinated two high-ranking German officers from the Todt Organization at Le Thoronet on 8 February; and three months later the son of the tobacconist in Signes was executed for having led the Brandenburgers to Limate Farm where today a lonely monument stands in the middle of a meadow.[21]

It was in February 1944, that the FTP, MUR/AS and the ORA united under the banner of the Forces Françaises de l'Intérieur (FFI) which had its headquarters in London. Up until the time of the invasion, when every *maquisard* aspired to wear an FFI armband or *brassard*, they still identified strongly with their separate, original organizations, and not all local leaders were thrilled by the amalgamation. A trusted Gaullist, General Pierre Koenig, was appointed overall commander of the FFI, based in London. The leader of the FFI in the R2 Region was Robert Rossi (*Levallois*), a dashing military pilot. Rossi would be arrested by the Gestapo in Marseille on 16 July and executed at Signes two days later, as we shall see.

Colonel Phillipe Beyne was a career army officer commanding the Maquis Ventoux which operated in the Basses-Alpes (now Alpes-de-Haute-Provence) and in the sparsely populated northern part of the Vaucluse Department, on the border of the Drôme. With his large force of 150 to 200 men, Beyne was going against the principles of guerrilla warfare. Having captured a German truck packed full of arms and ammunition in October 1942, his men were well armed. In February 1944, their headquarters was located in Séderon, a small town in the Drôme, and various companies were camped in and around the abandoned hamlet of Izon-la-Bruisse.[22]

On the evening of 21 February 1944, members of the SS and the Brandenburgers from Digne and Sisteron surrounded the village of Sèderon, roughed up the inhabitants and looted houses. Then, guided by two turncoats, who until two days previously had been with the Maquis, the motorized column moved to Izon-la-Bruisse. In the early dawn of 22 February, with the ground covered in a thin layer of snow, the pickets were overrun and the seventy-four *maquisards* occupying the school were caught by surprise.

The informants pointed out the section chief, *Mistral*, who was immediately executed, while the rest were driven to Eygalayes, four kilometres down the valley, despite the efforts of other *maquisards* who descended from the mountains to try to free their comrades. When they arrived at the Monteau camp the captives were lined up against a wall and relieved of their money, their watches and rings. At about 1 p.m. the massacre began. Four by four, the partisans were led behind a farm building and shot. Miraculously one man, Rolland Perrin, escaped. As he arrived at the corner of the farm building and saw the corpses stretched out in the snow, he realized that he had nothing to lose. A friend, who had been shot but was still alive, shouted out encouragement and the cry gave him wings.

Although this atrocity took place in the Drôme, most of the victims came from the Vaucluse; some survivors hid out on a farm near Le Barroux, at the foot of Mont Ventoux, to lick their wounds. Of the thirty-five murdered *maquisards*, four were Italians, one German and one Romanian. At least five were Jewish. On their way back to Séderon, the soldiers arrested four unlucky local men on the road at a place called Vallaury de Barret. Only two returned home. In the state-controlled media the massacre was reported as a successful operation in which 'a terrorist camp was wiped out'.[23]

<h1 style="text-align:center">Chapter 5</h1>

<h1 style="text-align:center">Evasion</h1>

For a history of everyday life – *histoire de la vie quotidienne* – of the Maquis in Provence, there can be few more valuable, less tainted sources than the diary of Gleb Sivirine, better known as *le Lieutenant Vallier*, who was the leader of one of the most important and well-disciplined groups in the Var, the Armée Secrète (AS). Born in the Ukraine, his family moved to France when he was eight. Having been a mathematics teacher, he was clearly a thinking man. His diary mentions having conversations about the concept of infinity as he and other *maquisards* whiled away the hours in the wilderness.

During his first few weeks in the forest, while it was all still a novelty, *Vallier* did not relish the thought of returning to civilian life. On his nineteenth day in the Maquis he wrote: 'Here I am the captain of the ship, the only master on board after God, I'm the doctor, I decide all things, whatever they are, and they are varied, and very unexpected. Caring for the physical and moral health of people who are so different, is not an easy task, but it is an experience that will surely enrich me.'[1]

The novelty soon wore off, however. He complained about there being too many chiefs, too many contradictory orders, too much misunderstanding and too many broken promises. Once, after almost six months of living like a hunted animal, he wondered whether or not it was all worth it. Death could be waiting around every corner. On one patrol, *Vallier* and friends came across a Boche in a camouflaged position, but 'the character is too greedy' and tried to shoot all three at once. 'We hear the bullets whistling above or beside us, and in the open air and God knows where! He shoots at least 20 bursts of 4, 5 or 6 bullets and I still do not understand how we are all alive. Beside us we see chips of flying stone and cut branches above our heads.'[2]

Nothing forges friendships like shared danger and hardship, and one of *Vallier's* closest companions, someone he relied on, was a Corsican named Dominique. Quite a lot older than the average *maquisard*, Dominique was a tough but reliable character, 'always moving, and especially eager to go to war against someone'. When he started telling a story about some or other collaborator, everyone laughed, because they already knew the ending. Nevertheless, when the inevitable conclusion came, be it by machine gun or grenade, everyone burst out laughing. Like the archetypal Corsican, he had a terrible temper which could even shock himself at times. It is no wonder he was a fugitive from the police.

Dominique's name appears consistently in *Vallier's* diary until the day he is *mort au combat*, as we will see. Among his best men overall were Max and Marcel. With Marcel he could discuss anything that came to mind. Max was still young (22, while Marcel was ten years older). At one point they spoke about religion, and *Vallier* realized that they had already discussed it lot among themselves. 'Marcel denies everything and Max is very religious. I gave a few words about my attitude. My respect for the morals held at the core of every religion, not an absolute belief in the dogma and ritual practices.'[3]

Among the bad apples was one Edmond Bertrand, who was described as a loudmouth and the worst character whom *Vallier* had ever seen 'in a region which is fertile with examples of this kind'. Once during a small skirmish, Bertrand ran away, taking with him documents, identity cards and all the tobacco that there was. *Vallier* scornfully speculated that if he had been taken by the Germans, they would have known the exact location of the camp within an hour.

Then there was *Vallier's* oldest *maquisard*, Marius Honorat, an 80-year-old farmer from the Draguignan area who had sheltered an agent (a radio operator) in contact with the Allies. When he was denounced by a *milicien* and sought by the Gestapo, he found refuge with the Maquis. Honorat was always volunteering for missions, and *Vallier* didn't like to turn him down for fear of aggravating the cantankerous old fellow.

'We always encounter strange characters,' wrote *Vallier* of the *drôles de types de personnages*. It was as though they were characters in a novel. An obnoxious politician in Aiguines, the closest village to the Maquis camp for a time, had recently established a printing business, and intended publishing a fictionalized story of recent events. The Maquis *Vallier* would have the starring role in the book, if after the landings, they would occupy Aiguines and help the politician get re-elected. *Vallier's* response was, 'On that day I will probably have much more important work than to install the new councillors of Aiguines.' The politician admitted that he had bought the printing business for his future poetic and literary works '*car je suis un homme de lettres, mon lieutenant, un véritable homme de lettres*' (because I am a writer, my lieutenant, a true man of letters).[4]

By contrast, Dr Angelin German, recently qualified as a gynecologist, was described by *Vallier* as 'a very nice guy'. He arrived at the AS camp on 9 June 1944 along with two nurses, and for the first time the fighters had the comfort of knowing they would be properly treated if wounded. The doctor, or *Le Toubib* (The Medic) as he was known, moved between camps and had a secret clinic at a place called Riou, between Lorgues and Salernes. He would be instrumental in choosing the site of the Rhône American cemetery in Draguignan and was also part of the forensic team which opened the mass grave at Signes in September 1944. *Le Toubib* was a resident of Flayosc all his life, serving four consecutive terms as mayor between 1971 and 1989. In addition to his role as a politician, he delivered more than 15,000 babies during his career.[5]

More than anything, the life a *soldat de l'ombre* is remembered as being one of constant movement. Using a tactic which they called *goutte de mercure* (drop of mercury), the Maquis would scatter when disturbed, and reform later. It was not healthy to stay in one place too long. Camps were very often sited on abandoned farms with the farmhouse serving as the command post. A house too well camouflaged was not ideal because it did not allow for enough warning of unwanted visitors. It was also not good for morale if one had to stay hidden all day, unable to make a noise or 'do manoeuvres'.

More often than not, these camps were in remote locations, high up in the mountains. Whereas most normal people in the Var lived at altitudes of 400 metres, the Maquis base at a farm called Louquiers, near Mons in the eastern part of the Var, was situated at 950 metres above sea level. The view in all directions was 'amazing'. The whole side of the Alps was visible and the many mariners among them never tired of watching Nice and Cannes, the Lérins Islands and the peninsula of Saint-Tropez. However, *Vallier* decided it was time to leave this place once his men were properly armed and equipped. With all the parachute drops at La Roque Esclapon, the area was getting too busy for his liking.

From Mons, it was a two-day walk to the Canjuers Plains where several Maquis groups would roam for the next four months. There were some shepherd huts, and the only other people on the mountain were woodcutters and beekeepers, although the town of Aiguines and the Verdon River were not far away. On the other side of the Verdon, the Germans were running a logging operation.

For carrying their food, weapons, and ammunition, *Vallier's* men made bags using fishnet and empty potato sacks with parachute straps which soon cut into their shoulders. Apart from their weapons and ammunition (250 rounds per man when available), *maquisards* carried little more than their bedding and a change of clothing. As in all things *Vallier* carried more than his share of the load:

> I keep a sleeping bag, 2 shirts, 2 shorts, enough to wash, medications, (more for others than for me) and ammunition. Socks too, obviously. And one luxury: paper, my two books and my pen. During this time I have really got used to writing, and that's the only time I can give myself for intellectual life, so to speak. My working life is so full that if I started to read I could not find time to write. So I do not read. (2 or 3 people have a few books).[6]

Camp life went through a period of relaxation to allow the men to rest after the journey but then it was time to get back to work. Long training walks (more than twenty kilometres) were not easy for everyone, and there were many who struggled. This was a worry because they might get rid of their ammunition rather than carting it with them 'as soon as they feel the danger at their heels'. *Vallier* planned to test his men to see who could 'really walk'. The ones who could not keep up would be left behind on farms. On a training march to the summit, which was at 1,577 metres, they could see Mont Ventoux, a view which evoked strong emotions.

Being at such a high altitude, one was more exposed to the elements. One night, during a strong mistral wind, the guard took shelter in a shepherd's hut and failed to notice the arrival of the 'big boss', the head of the Resistance in the Var, Louis Picoche. The irate Picoche asked where he could find the *Vallier* camp. After giving directions, the guard added that if he wanted a more efficient guard he should invite the resistants who slept at home every night to join them on the mountain.

Some tried sleeping in a cave but it was terribly humid so, in groups of three or four, they made small cabins for shelter. The days would still be spent outside, in the shade of a blanket stretched out between two trees. On the first day of spring, 1 May 1944, *Vallier* mentioned that he wore only short trousers, belt and a watch. He even had a wet towel on his head for protection from the overly hot sun. 'We are at about 1,400 metres and it is basically the first day of hot weather since we got here. Usually it is very nice from 8 am to 11 a.m., after which the wind picks up and it literally freezes after sunset. At this point, there is almost no wind, just a breath and my team is shirtless.'[7]

Whether moving camp or on a training march, hiking became a necessary part of life. For *Vallier* himself, it was a most enjoyable activity, much the same as *tourisme pédestre*. Crossing mountains 'along stony paths and amid tufts of lavender, thyme and heather in the fragrant atmosphere' or down to the Verdon River on a well-known trail, he was doing what he loved. He swore that after the war he would follow the entire course of the roaring Verdon River. In one of nature's great beauty spots, the young men enjoyed riding the rapids, or playing the fool diving off the rocks. The river was also handy for doing the laundry.

In these remote villages of the Var, there was true solidarity with the local population, despite the risk that the presence of the Maquis could bring. Unlike in the cities, denunciations were rare. Everyone did their bit, from the baker who provided bread, to the town clerk who gave false documents, the postman, the mayor, the teacher or the priest. As for the peasants, they would give what they could in the way of food. The ordinary citizen in these desperate times would hide and assist Allied airmen who parachuted into their world.

Even though their presence could attract a violent reaction from the Germans, some of these townsfolk took a special interest in their local Maquis and did all they could to protect it. As fighting in the region became more commonplace, so the *maquisards* were treated with more caution and respect. Once when *Vallier* went down to Aiguines with the car to pick up some supplies, he was amused to see the fear and respect which the locals held for him: 'They are trying to be on my good side without going too far so as to be compromised, yet proud at the same time to know the "Lieutenant". I am beginning to be known in the region, if not in the Var, now!' As far as Draguignan and Toulon, people spoke about Lieutenant *Vallier*, leader of the Résistance in the Haut-Var.

At this point he decided that he would change his name and forever after be known by his *nom de guerre – Vallier*.[8]

At times, *Vallier* drove around on the main roads with a Cross of Lorraine flag flapping in the wind and 'FFI' in huge letters on the windshield of his petrol-driven car. When arriving at a junction in the road, the occupants of the car would prepare their weapons and perhaps experience a 'tiny heart attack' waiting to see whether or not there was a roadblock, but then continue as if nothing happened. *Arrive qu'arrive* (whatever happens happens).

Vallier's diary tells of a perpetual struggle against carelessness, laziness and discouragement. There was also the occasional serious breach of discipline. Three men, armed to the teeth – *armés jusqu'aux dents* – went down to Aiguines and Les Salles where they ransacked a farm and stole money. *Vallier* sent a patrol to search for the three 'drunken characters' and found them asleep at 11 p.m. The next day, Max and Dominique helped *Vallier* return the stolen goods and established a tribunal. The three accused narrowly escaped a firing squad as they would be needed for the coming battle.

It was necessary to remind the *maquisards* that admission to the underground movement was 'a voluntary service in the army of Free France, with all the rights, but above all, the duties of a true soldier'. *Vallier* warned his men that deserters would be treated like army deserters – given a court martial and receive 'the only pronounceable sentence against traitors'. Ironically, the German Army did not consider the Resistance to be legitimate soldiers and they would not be treated according to the rules of the Geneva Convention. If captured, they would invariably be executed as 'terrorists'.

One day, *Vallier* and some of his men drove into Compssur-Artuby, high up above Draguignan, where there were two or three *miliciens* who needed to be taught a lesson, and also a tobacco shop where he intended to commandeer whatever was smokable, plus a truck to take the loot home. *Vallier* went to get the *milicien* while Yo did the truck and Alain commandeered seventy-five packs of tobacco and twenty-two cigars, 'almost a fortune!' Earlier in the year, gendarmes at Barjols had killed an FTP *maquisard* during a tobacco-requisitioning operation, but on this occasion, *Vallier* had the cash and paid the tobacconist the 896 francs he owed her. She could not believe her eyes. '*Mais alors, vous êtes presque amable,*' she stammered (But then, you're almost kind). *Vallier* replied in his most dignified manner that they were neither thieves nor pillagers.[9]

As soon as the truck was ready, they picked up the two guards they had dropped off at the entrance to the village and drove down the road. The truck then stopped and the *milicien* was marched off at gunpoint, convinced that he was going to be executed. 'Kill him!' Yo shouted and fired a shot into the air. The poor collaborator collapsed and could not speak, then got a few slaps for good measure. The lesson would serve him personally, but most importantly, it would serve as a warning to others. When it came to dealing with poor farmers, *Vallier* hated begging for food, and found it easier when he was asking on behalf of somebody else. For the supply of bread and some other supplies, the FFI had standing agreements in place, but on occasion *Vallier* had to ask farmers for food. An account was kept of everything. There was a difference between stealing and requisitioning, however; considering that the press was controlled by the authorities at this time, it is not surprising that when the Maquis helped themselves to supplies they were referred to as 'armed bandits'.

Generally the food was wholesome and abundant, but not too varied. 'Alas! fresh vegetables do not abound in the country but we found two cabbages, two leeks and a nice squash. Eggs are more easily found.' The wild boar, or *sangliers*, which are very common in these woods, were a primary source of meat, and the hunt itself was much enjoyed. Below are just two extracts from *Vallier's* diary which reveal two extremes in the daily struggle for food:

8 March 1944
Shortly after the operation, we had an intake of new recruits.
But this time it was not the 'class of 44' or returnees from
Germany. They were seven good cows, a little lean, that the
owner of the farm sent us so we kept them to do the grass
growing around the house … we have 10 or 20 litres of milk
per day, half a litre per man, what a bargain!

17 April 1944
Since April 1, the supply of bread has been very difficult. When
fresh bread arrived it was clearly insufficient. This week,
we have received 55 kg for 8 days, i.e. about 7 kg per day

and as we are 38, it is less than 200 grams for each man.
Compared to the promised ration of 400 grams, this is still
a big difference and it is quite painful.

*

While it may be true that an army marches on its stomach, guns and explosives were also basic requirements. These would be dropped by parachute. As far as some groups were concerned, it was too little too late, but in reality tons of large, cylindrical, sheet-metal containers were dropped throughout the mountainous areas of Provence. In what is known as the 'roof of the Var', the busiest drop zones were between Brovès, Mons, Bargemon, Seillans and Comps-sur-Artuby. The task of collecting, storing and distributing the supplies, which included cash and scarce goods like penicillin, was initially carried out by the Section Atterrissage et Parachutage (SAP), the Landings and Parachute Section.

The SAP was responsible for selecting drop zones, and for organizing the reception, storage, and distribution of weapons and explosives. With regional and departmental structures, SAP controlled hundreds of localities where agents and supplies could be landed or dropped. Clandestine drop zones were sometimes identified by way of a Michelin map, and the RAF would first do a reconnaissance flight, but there were also a handful of established drop zones.

The Maquis of the Ventoux counted as the best equipped, best trained, and most active in the Department of Vaucluse. Colonel Philippe Beyne, with his deputy, Maxime Fischer, commanded about a thousand men on both sides of the Rhône River. The man in charge of the SAP in this area was Commandant Camille Rayon (*Archiduc*), alias Pierre-Michel, or just P-M. Built like a boxer, Rayon was a 29-year-old former restaurateur from Antibes. In Algiers he had met SOE Major John Goldsmith, known to him as 'Jean', who then returned with him to France as his liaison officer. While he is not well known outside of Provence, Goldsmith considered him one of the most remarkable resistance leaders in France.

Another well-known drop zone was on the Plateau of Dina, above Puget-Théniers where the Route de Grenoble (R202) heads west through Digne. The man in charge, Gabriel Mazier, was hard pressed to pick up the precious loads before they fell into the hands of the FTP, Vichy forces, or other scavengers. On the night of 3 April, six members of the Gestapo arrived in Puget-Théniers and forced a member of the resistance group to lead them onto the plateau where they sized the weapons. Not only were the weapons lost, the unfortunate guide was tortured to death at Villa Trianon, the Gestapo HQ in Nice.

One month later, the Boche again came to Puget-Théniers looking for a weapons store. It appears that they might have been tipped off by an FTP member who had only recently come into the village asking for a share of the weapons for his group. When these were refused, he had mysteriously disappeared. Mazier and four of his men were guarding the store on a nearby farm when the soldiers arrived, tyres screeching. By hurling grenades most managed to escape, although one *maquisard* was killed by his own grenade, and Mazier was wounded. Eight villagers were rounded up to be shot; fortunately a German-speaking gendarme was able to save their lives, and the hostages were taken away for STO work duty instead.

In a parachute drop, the standard planeload consisted of twelve to fifteen containers, the contents of which varied according to the need. A mixed consignment might include six Bren guns with 1,000 rounds, thirty-six rifles with 150 rounds, twenty-seven Sten guns, five pistols, fifty grenades, eighteen pounds of plastic explosives, 156 field dressings, 6,600 9mm rounds, 3,168 .303 rounds, and forty empty magazines. Bazookas and six-pounder anti-tank guns could also be dropped for special purposes. In some accounts, mention is made of boxes of boots being brought in.

The US Army Air Forces prided themselves in being ahead of their time in providing 'next-day delivery' but purportedly only about half of the supply missions flown were successful. Francis Cammaerts, leader of the JOCKEY circuit, complained about poor service from SOE's Algerian headquarters, codenamed *Massingham*. Bad packing apparently resulted in the loss of one-fifth of supplies. John Goldsmith countered:

> All I can say is that Cammaerts seems to have been singularly unfortunate. All the supplies I asked for were delivered on time, and if the RAF was doing the job, they landed more or less in the right spot. American pilots were more erratic, for they liked to operate at about 3,000 feet, took only one look at the spot and sent their loads on their way with the pious hope that they would land somewhere near the target.[10]

On more than one occasion, containers were sent crashing through the roofs of houses in the town centre of Apt. Using animal-drawn wagons and trucks, the containers would be carted away whole or first unpacked, and stored in some friendly farmer's store or perhaps in a cave until needed. It would have been foolish for the reception committee to keep anything at home, even the parachute silk, as it could mean the death sentence if their house was searched. At Vins-sur-Caramy, between Brignoles and Le Luc, four members of the SAP were arrested in the process of retrieving supplies which had gone astray. The four included Jean Mazzone and his two sons. The Germans followed them to the site of an arms cache in a cave and there they were shot on 29 July 1944. On the original, hand-engraved headstone, it is written: 'This cave served as a hiding place for the parachuted arms. The executioners with their bloody hands, made it a mass grave, and alas, they were the only witnesses. For these atrocious crimes, the blood of these patriots cries out for vengeance.'

As of 10 March 1944, before moving to the Canjuers plateau, *Vallier* complained that he still could not arm a third of his men and hated to think of what would happen in the event of an attack. He knew that there was a supply drop coming in the next day and expected to have to fight for his fair share. There was no need to worry, however, because on 13 March he wrote:

> In the morning we had a task to get arms and ammunition sufficient to arm all my men and this afternoon I made the distribution to each. Now I really have soldiers under me, and if the opportunity presents itself, I do not intend to refuse a fight, if there is a serious chance of victory. Obviously, I'm not crazy enough to attack 200 opponents, but up to 50, that does not scare me.[11]

Vallier's men were now well armed, but the same could not be said for the Brigade des Maures. The leaders on the Saint-Tropez peninsular, Marko Célébonovitch, Alix Macario, Jean Despas, René Girard, Marc Rainaut and the Battaglia brothers had forged a cohesive unit that contained elements of the FTP, the ORA, and the AS but this group seems to have been at the back of the queue when it came to weapons drops. Some twenty-six drop zones existed in the Var Department, but since 6 June, only eight deliveries were successful, and of these, two occurred after 15 August – too late to be of much use. Part of the problem was that there was a shortage of transport from Algeria.

A common criticism of the resistance fighters is that they lacked discipline or were filled with excessive zeal. OSS and SOE agents mention the lack of training as their main concern. 'These people worried us nearly as much as the Germans,' said OSS Lieutenant William Macomber, who was 24 at the time. 'They were all youngsters itching for a chance to blaze away with their Stens, and their enthusiasm, plus the notoriously light trigger-pull of the Sten, made us nervous.'[12]

Goldsmith did mention the poor quality of the Sten guns which had been delivered to the Maquis of the Ventoux. Too many of them were unfinished and had to be worked on by Pierre-Michel's gunsmiths before they were issued. The Sten sub-machine gun was mass-produced from a metal mould for 15/- to 30/- apiece. With one moving part, it was designed to use captured 9mm ammunition. It was wildly inaccurate but effective at close quarters.

While still camped near Mons, soon after having received their new weapons, one of *Vallier's* men had a fatal accident with one of these unsophisticated guns. Nineteen-year-old Georges Maranincchi was returning from an operation when *Vallier* heard a gunshot and had an immediate premonition of disaster, an icy feeling running down his spine. 'Little Georges fell like a log.' Reflexes came into play, the shirt was unfastened, and there was a small round hole straight into the heart from where the blood was spurting like a fountain. Death was instant.

Georges had been warned not to bump the Sten gun, which was very sensitive, but it happened anyway. 'Stupid accident, stupid, stupid, entirely the fault of the kid,' *Vallier* wrote, 'but the fact remains that it shakes you strangely (*drôlement*).' The boy was buried high up on the plateau, in a pine forest, during a hailstorm: 'It was a moving ceremony, military honours were performed by comrades, the flag was at half mast, and absolution was given by Max since Georges was a practising Catholic and I wanted him to be buried according to his beliefs.'[13]

*

René Char was a child of Provence. Born in the idyllic Vaucluse village of l'Isle-sur-la-Sorgue and schooled in Avignon, he later worked in Cavaillon. Codenamed *Alexandre*, he joined the Section Atterrissage et Parachutage at the earliest opportunity, and became the man in charge of the Durance drop zone based at Céreste north of Pertuis in the Vaucluse. His 1946 collection of wartime writings, *Feuillets d'Hypnos*, is a combination of poetry, prose, philosophy and history. When called away to Algiers in July 1944, Char hid his notebook in the wall of an abandoned building used by the Maquis. Recovering the manuscript in 1945, he prepared it for publication making only slight edits to the austere, obscure, but honest verses. Subsequently, Char moved in the same circles as Pablo Picasso and the philosopher Albert Camus, and his name became known throughout France. Hypnos is the Greek god of sleep, and Char's fragmentary texts are evocative of the sleepless and brutal nature of life in the Resistance: 'In the past when I went to bed the idea of a temporary death in the arms of sleep was a comfort to me; today I go to sleep just to live for a few hours.' But the nightmares did not go away: 'We have taken stock, over every inch of our bodies, of the pain the torturer may one day exact; then, with a heavy heart, have gone out to face him.'

One of Char's closest comrades was Roger Bernard, a young man from Pertuis. On 22 June 1944, the Brandenburgers took control of Céreste, where the SAP was based, just north of Cucuron. When Bernard unsuspectingly walked into the town, he was stopped and searched. It is said that he was carrying a revolver and wearing American shoes. Consequently, he was shot at the abandoned railway siding of Viens, in the district of Saint-Martin-de-Castillon. For René Char, the loss was especially hard to bear because Roger Bernard was a promising poet. The requiem which Char wrote for his friend reveals an obsession with death: '*Je vais vivre. Je vis! Je vis sur l'éternelle joie vivante de mourir.*' (I am going to live. I live! I live on the eternal living joy of dying.)

Perhaps what was haunting René Char in his dreams was the fiery crash of a Wellington bomber on a drop zone called *Abatteur*, near the hamlet of Chavon, which was in his area of control. A parachute drop was being expected and the reception committee had lit their beacons. A bombing raid was taking place over Valence that night, and one of the RAF bombers, probably hit by flak, desperately sought a place to land. Seeing the beacons and mistaking them for a Resistance landing strip, the pilot decided to take a chance. At 2 a.m. on 10 May 1944, the *maquisards* saw the plane fly over, disappear and then come back at low altitude, and at full throttle, only to watch it crash into the valley below, now named La Combe de l'Avion, The Valley of the Aeroplane.

At dawn the carbonized remains of the crew were found. The heat had melted the identity tags of all but the rear gunner, Eric Howell. The *maquisards* were shaken when they realized that Howell was 22 years old, the same age as themselves. The pilot, John Huggler was 29, and the navigator, Harry Lane, was 28. The last two crewmembers, Neville Green and Walter Jackson, were both 21 years old. René Char conducted the funeral, and today there is a memorial, made from the welded wreckage, which marks the remote crash site, fringed with lavender and wild thyme.

*

In preparation for the invasion of southern France, the priority of guerrilla groups was to hinder enemy movements on all roads and railways. Sabotage gave the Boche a terrible headache, and railway workers were particularly well placed to create havoc. The Maquis' claim to sabotage fame in the Var is the blowing of a railway bridge at Carnoules in the summer of 1943 on the main line between Nice and Toulon, causing rolling stock to be derailed. Nevertheless, the marshalling yards at Carnoules continued to be a target for the US Fifteenth Air Force for another year. On one raid, in the absence of both flak and fighters with clear weather, only 35 per cent of the bombs landed within 400 metres of the briefed aiming point. On the wall of the Carnoules train station, there is a plaque to the memory of the twenty-eight SNCF (railway) employees who were killed in the town, many from Allied bombing, and many of them women.

The Maquis *Vallier*, being relatively quiet on the operations side, was at first content with the knowledge that in conjunction with FTP, they had tied up a force of about 1,000 enemy troops plus all their equipment, armoured vehicles and sometimes aircraft. Eventually *Vallier* would become frustrated and envious of what was happening a few kilometres to the north, on the other side of the Verdon. The Maquis in the Basses-Alpes were carrying out a series of sabotage operations, 'while we [*Vallier* and his men] who have weapons and we ask only to serve, we are reduced to the most perfect inaction'. If the landing did not happen soon, he was of a mind to move on.[14]

Other groups, like the FTP at Camp Robert, were more mobile and active. They occasionally scattered in small detachments to carry out sabotage, deal with collaborators, and collect supplies. Their operations covered a wide area on the edge of Haut-Var, between Vinon-sur-Verdon in the West, Carcès in the south and Ampus in the east. The most intense period of action was in mid-July. This translation of the writing of Jean-Marie Guillon oozes admiration for the FTP:

> Boldness, initiative, spontaneity of action and sometimes recklessness, characterized this activity that bore the mark of an enthusiastic and uncompromising youth, where the love of a challenge and an element of sport was combined with the feeling of being at the vanguard of politics and patriotism. They did not hesitate to criticize those who, in their eyes, passively awaited the liberation.[15]

In July 1944, just one month before the Allied landings, *Vallier* was still locked in bitter rivalry with his FTP counterpart, Dominique Thomas. Nevertheless, on one occasion, the two groups got together to share ideas, and carried out joint training exercises. It was *Vallier* who initiated the exercise and who had the most to offer in military terms, but when it was over, about a dozen of his men decided to defect to the FTP camp. Their motivation was partly political – two or three were committed communists – but the others probably preferred the less disciplined lifestyle of the FTP.

Vallier did not try to influence their decision and feigned indifference, but to his diary he gave away his feelings of resentment: *'il n'a guère gagné que des nullités'* (all they got was the 'nobodies'). In a later entry, he noted with satisfaction that the FTP had told him that these defectors were counted among their best men. Now, less than a month before the landings, *Vallier* expressed his concerns about future cooperation with the communists. 'Currently we fight side by side for the same purpose,' he wrote, 'but how will it be after the war?' All their actions were governed by political goals, such as the future communist domination throughout the Haut-Var. Moreover, in Aups, their leader already called himself *commissaire du peuple*, 'commissar of the people'.[16]

In line with his instructions, *Vallier's* main goal was to maintain a strong force of well-trained and -equipped men to be ready for D-Day (*Jour-J*), although he would not easily have passed up a tempting target. Once, when one of his sentries came running to inform *Vallier* that a German truck was approaching the camp, it was almost a disappointment when it turned out to be a 'friendly'. Just in case, the men took the warning seriously and followed the drill. Clearly, morale was high but action was lacking – at least for some.

*

Until 1944, the Champsaur Valley, situated between Grenoble and Gap in the Hautes-Alpes, had been quite peaceful. A few small bands of *maquisards* were scattered around Méoullions, Champoléon and Saint-Jean where the church was the nucleus of resistance. The clergyman, Abbé Robin (*Ludovic*) was responsible for distributing food and weapons which he hid under his floorboards. Another priest, Père Louis Poutrain, had recently been deported; his brother, the 36-year-old Pierre Poutrain, now led the group, taking a huge load on his shoulders, both physically and spiritually. Unlike the communists of the FTP and the scientifically minded *Vallier*, the Maquis of the Champsaur were deeply religious. Their daily routine went as follows: rise early in the morning, pray, raise the flag, military training, sport, then kitchen and other chores. In the afternoon it was military training or foraging. The blissful evenings were spent in prayer and fellowship.

By all accounts, Pierre Poutrain was an exceptional man, and much loved by everyone, always on the move. It was a huge blow, therefore, when he was arrested in a safe house where he was taking a much-needed rest. After almost three weeks of interrogation, on the afternoon of 19 June 1944, a German officer came into the cell with a list in hand and shouted, 'Poutrain, Humetz, Balmens, Mourenas, Meyer'. Outside there was a van waiting, and, with a Gestapo car leading the way, the convoy sped off to a farm on the outskirts of Gap. As they were led off into a green meadow, Pierre Poutrain passed the terrified farmer's wife, and said, 'Pray for us, it's the end.' Pierre himself never stopped praying: 'He was always in conversation with God,' said his brother Louis. Surprisingly, the Gestapo let him keep his rosary. It was taken from his cold, stiff fingers and given to his wife.

Another leader of the Maquis in the Champsaur was Paul-Marie Radius, a young professional officer, originally from Brittany. Like Pierre Poutrain, he was a wanted man, and was arrested when the bus in which he was travelling was stopped at a roadblock. He was on a mission to obtain medicine for one of his men. He too was tortured for three weeks in the Gestapo headquarters, Villa Mayoli, and then shot, together with another prisoner, on the evening of 10 July at Moulin du Pré on the banks of the Luye, just south of Gap.

One week later, on 17 July 1944, members of the same Maquis carried out an abortive attempt to free a comrade who was being transported to Villa Mayoli in Gap for torture by the Gestapo. An ambush was sprung at the hamlet of Laye north of Gap on the Route de Napoleon, but a nervy *maquisard* opned fire too soon. German reinforcements also turned up unexpectedly. The young and inexperienced fighters fought hard, ignoring their rule of 'hit and run', resulting in four killed in action. Seven farmhouses were burned in retribution. Although mortified by the loss, FFI leaders and SOE operatives were highly critical of the operation.

Overlooking the wheatfields of the Champsaur Valley towards the high peaks of the Alps, a cenotaph towers over the hamlet of Laye. It is the manifestation of heaven on earth. At the place where he fell on 17 July, there is a smaller monument to Amédée Para, an 18-year-old Boy Scout, originally from Marseille. In Gap there is an active Scout troop, as well as a street, named after him.

Following the D-Day landings of 6 June 1944, the Maquis were emboldened to carry out more daring ambushes and sabotage. Every train leaving Marseille for Lyon after D-Day was derailed at least once during its journey. If there was going to be an invasion in the south, the Wehrmacht had to maintain links with Berlin and other key cities. Manning defences all along the Mediterranean from Italy to Spain, the Germans were stretched to the limit. As the ranks of the Resistance swelled with new, mostly unarmed recruits, they presented a tempting target. More than one bastion of resistance had the audacity to declare an independent republic. These were the dynamics that triggered a series of vicious 'anti-terrorist' operations during the next phase of the war in Provence.

Chapter 6

Duplicity

On the morning of 6 June 1944, as soon as the news was heard on the radio in the far-off village of Artignosc, a *maquisard* named Max came running into the *Vallier* camp, stammering with breathlessness and emotion: '*Mon Lieutenant, mon Lieutenant, ils ont débarqué dans le Nord.*' (Lieutenant, Lieutenant, they have landed in the north). The feeling which prevailed among the Maquis was one of relief, followed by reckless exuberance. Those who had been sitting on the sidelines now clamoured to be on the right side of history.

At the time of the D-Day landings in Normandy, General de Gaulle made an appeal over the BBC calling on the Resistance for a general insurrection, a *levée en masse*. His exact words were: '*Pour les fils de France, où qu'ils soient, quels qu'ils soient, le devoir simple et sacré est de combattre l'ennemi par tous les moyens dont ils disposent.*' (For the sons of France, wherever they are, whatever they may be, the simple and sacred duty is to fight the enemy by all the means at their disposal.) At the same time, the Allies announced a general mobilization order. Unfortunately, this precipitated a false start, *a faux depart*, with tragic consequences.

Paradoxically, on 10 June, the military chief of the FFI in London, General Koenig, ordered the cancellation of these mobilization orders by telegram: '*Freiner au maximum activités de guérilla ... Rompez partout contact dans mesure du possible pour permettre phase réorganisation. Evitez gros rassemblements. Constituez petits groupes isolés.*' (Put the brake on maximum guerrilla activity. Break any contact as far as possible to allow reorganization phase. Avoid large gatherings, constitute small isolated groups.)[1] Volunteers who were unarmed were supposed to be sent home, but some leaders considered it psychologically damaging, and, besides, civil servants, workers at the Toulon arsenal and gendarmes from across Provence could not just report back for work.

Koenig's counter-command came too late to prevent a wave of premature uprisings; the consequences would be severe. When the Maquis of the Ventoux, whose ranks had already been thinned in February, learned of the Normandy landings, they immediately prepared for battle. Sixty to seventy *maquisards* went to Vaison-la-Romain, woke the printers, and printed posters calling the people to arms. Everything that represented Vichy in the town was torn down and the people were ecstatic. Restaurants and bars opened their doors to the *maquisards*. Although roadblocks had been set up, a Boche accompanied by a civilian drove into town and both were shot down. The inevitable reprisal came on 10 June when a column of between 1,200 and 1,500 Germans arrived in Vaison-la-Romain. One group, known as the Maquis Vasio, had been formed here and put up a good fight. They had promised the mayor that they would not fight in the town but a major battle ensued involving an aircraft and a bombardment from artillery sited at the village of Plan-de-Dieu. At 9.30 p.m. the inhabitants were herded into the huge Place de Montfort, in the centre of Vaison-la-Romain and threatened with machine guns. According to the resistance leader, sixty Germans were killed, which is a gross exaggeration. French losses were fourteen fighters and three civilians.[2]

Two days after the Normandy landings, on 8 June, the FFI had also taken control of the village of Valréas in the Vaucluse and set up roadblocks at the entrances to the town. In order to 'clean out this nest of terrorists', the Germans again assembled a host of 1,200 men, including the 8th Company, 3rd Regiment of the Brandenburg Division, accompanied by various auxiliaries and security police. The column of tanks, armoured vehicles and trucks invested the town at noon on 12 June 1944.

After executing thirteen people in the neighbouring town of Taulignan in the Drôme, the Germans rampaged through the streets of Valréas, looting, smashing doors and windows and burning houses. An officer ordered the mayor, Jules Niel, to have the inhabitants gather in the Place de la Mairie. As the Nazi ranted and raved, an interpreter with a perfect Parisian accent translated his every word. The twenty-seven captured *maquisards*, plus another twenty-seven randomly selected civilian men were lined up in front of a wall. The mayor tried to intervene, but managed to save only two. Slowly and deliberately, in stages, the firing squad carried out its work, with an officer delivering the coup de grâce. Some Frenchmen sang 'La Marseillaise' or the 'Internationale'. The cry of *chérie* (darling) was also heard above the din as men called out to their wives. At one stage, the executioners took a break and went into the nearby hotel for a drink.

By evening, about fifty bodies lay in front of the wall. A German officer carefully counted them and ordered that they must not be touched until the next day. Regardless, during the night, Red Cross nurses and other volunteers came to examine the pile of bodies. Five men were found to be still alive. They were taken to hospital, and to make up the numbers, five bodies of *maquisards* killed elsewhere during the day were placed in the pile.

One of the wounded men died during the night, but the other four lived to bear witness. One man who defied death was Émile Bouchet. He had previously been arrested for 'communist activities', having sung the 'Internationale' at a banquet. On his release, he continued to risk his life by harbouring Jews from Lyon. There is some uncertainty about the final death toll, but ultimately fifty-three coffins had to be ordered. On the long list of martyrs are the brothers Fernand and François Devès, aged 21 and 18 respectively. The oldest victim was 75, the youngest seventeen.

All of the atrocities which took place in Provence in the wake of D-Day pale into insignificance when compared to the murder of 642 men, women and children in the village of Oradour-sur-Glane in the Limousin on 10 June 1944. This unprecedented brutality was carried out by a battalion of the 2nd SS Panzer Division Das Reich which was en route from Toulouse to Normandy. Supposedly in retaliation for partisan activity in the area, the panzergrenadiers began by gathering the men in barns where they were machine-gunned in the legs, and, as they lay writhing on the ground, they were covered with petrol and burned to death. The women and children were locked up in the church which was then set alight. The village of Oradour-sur-Glane was left completely untouched, and today it is a memorial to the countless forgotten atrocities, such as those which took place in Provence.

Almost as though their efforts were coordinated countrywide, the Germans struck yet again that same day, 10 June, this time at a 'terrorist' camp in the Var. Since May, a group of resistants had been based at a farm called Le Coutronne near Plan-d'Aups (not to be confused with Aups in the Haute-Var). Plan-d'Aups is inland from Toulon in the Sainte-Baume Mountains.

Here the Maquis were accumulating a substantial arms cache while new recruits poured in. After being welcomed into the fold, they would be directed to a second camp farther up above the road. Parachute cloth hanging between the trees served as tents. There were approximately 200 men in total – fourteen *pompiers* (firemen) arrived in one batch – but many were still unarmed. The camp was just beginning to get organized when, on 10 June 1944, the Germans attacked in force.

Lookouts had not been properly posted and the camp was taken by surprise. All those who had no weapons were ordered to make a run for it. The battle raged above and below the road because the two camps were attacked simultaneously. As the ammunition ran out, *maquisards* smashed their weapons against trees then fled through the woods down a valley leading to Saint-Zacharie. Some of the casualties were taken from there by car to the hospital in Aubagne, bluffing their way through German roadblocks en route. From the doctor there they heard that the Germans had lost forty-seven troops, while the Maquis lost eleven.

Among those who got away was a British SOE operative, Captain (later Major) Robert Boiteux (*Nicholas*) who was chief of the GARDENER network. Slightly wounded, he found his way back to Marseille where he joined in the street fighting during the uprising there. A former Bond Street hairdresser, gold prospector and boxing champion of Kenya, Boiteux was in his mid-thirties, and being short and dark, blended in with the people of the South. On this, his second mission, he was told that he would be linking up with a Maquis of a thousand men, but found it consisted of no more than forty.[3] Even with the assistance of the SOE or OSS, the Maquis were never strong enough to take on the Germans in a conventional battle, and wherever large groups were concentrated trouble would be sure to arrive.

Also motivated by the landings in the north, a large group of FFI recruits gathered on the Siou Blanc plateau to await the invasion of southern France, which was thought to be imminent. Containers of weapons were being parachuted by the Allies and it is said that there were 400 fighters scattered throughout this mountainous region. Eight *maquisards* from Toulon, aged between 18 and 24, were arrested at Roboeuf farm, then transported to Le Castellet, near Toulon, and executed the following day, 17 June 1944.

As the days grew longer and warmer, the Resistance also grew in confidence. They would now ambush small, isolated convoys, and establish safe perimeters within a ring of villages for drop zones, or even 'fortified bastions' with felled trees and barricades blocking the access roads. The gendarmes sometimes worked with the Maquis in these areas and doctors set up field hospitals. Slowly, Vichy and German authority was eroded. The higher up in the mountains the bigger the groups of resistance fighters.

In the Ubaye Valley, thirty kilometres northwest of Barcelonette, toward Larche, Colonel Jacques Lécuyer, a leader of the ORA whose *nom de guerre* was *Sapin* (Pine Tree), declared a liberated zone – the 'Independent Republic of Ubaye'. Among those who pitched up to support were the two top men in the southeast, Colonel Francis Cammaerts, leader of the JOCKEY circuit, and Colonel Henri Zeller, a professional military officer and FFI commander of regions R1 and R2. The area was of strategic importance for controlling the road to Italy.

In response to Cammaerts' request for weapons, a consignment of a hundred containers arrived on the night of 11/12 June but it came too late to be distributed, and the 'uprising' was quickly crushed by a German armoured column. Major Alistair Kerr Hay (*Edgar*) of Inter-Allied Mission MICHEL, tried to hold a narrow pass called Pas de Grégoire, ten kilometres from Barcelonette, on 13 June. He was a 32-year-old married man from Edinburgh, an accountant in civilian life. Next to him at the roadblock was another member of team MICHEL, a Jewish medic named Henri Rosencher who tells how Alistair Hay managed to immobilize a German tank with a PIAT anti-tank missile. When they jumped up to celebrate, Hay was hit in the neck by a machine-gun burst, severing an artery. All were 'overwhelmed by the fall of this giant' and he is now buried in the Mazargues War Cemetery in Marseille.

That night the order was given to disperse, and *Sapin's* band moved south through the mountains to Colmars.[4] The Maquis had paid heavily for their audacity. *Sapin's* decision to revert to open warfare, coupled with the lack of air support, led to recriminations all round. Against the wishes of Robert Rossi, Cammaerts and Zeller told their men to stand down and now made their way to the Vercors where another, more serious uprising was underway. As a result of the intrigue and infighting, Mission MICHEL lost their focus and the remaining four would all eventually fall into the hands of the Gestapo. Henri Rosencher, was the only survivor of Mission MICHEL. After being captured on the Vercors, tortured at Montluc Prison and deported to Dachau, he returned to find that his family had been wiped out. Rosencher later qualified as a doctor and published his wartime memoir, *Le sel, la cendre, la flamme* (*Salt, Ash, Flame*) in 2000.

In reaction to criticism that he had been inactive while comrades were fighting for survival in the Vercors, Colonel Jacques Lécuyer's ORA temporarily occupied the village of Guillaumes in the northern Alpes-Maritimes between Barcelonnette and Castellane. Two battalions of Reserve Division 148 were sent to squash this small uprising threatening the German lines of communication. This time the Boche met with disaster. On 18 July, the column ran into an ambush near Thorame-Basse and the lead truck exploded as the first shots were fired. It seems that bullets severed a high-tension cable which fell onto a truck loaded with fuel and ammunition. At least nine were killed in the explosion.

*

A liberated zone of sorts was established in the village of Aups, a most agreeable corner of the Haut-Var, a summer retreat where black truffles proliferate in the shade of ancient chestnuts and oaks. The weather is a few degrees cooler than at the coast and life proceeds at a leisurely pace. Passing out of the medieval gates of the village, one continues climbing to the Canjuers plain which is a vast limestone plateau extending to the Gorge du Verdon and the Basses-Alpes. The name, Canjuers, is derived from Campus Julii after Julius Ceasar who camped here even before his conquest of Gaul. It is still a military training ground today.

Two big groups of Maquis were based around Aups, which is an indication of its relative security. It was here, at Camp Robert, that the communist FTP printed their underground paper *Le Cri du Haut-Var*. Also in this area was the Maquis *Vallier* of the Armée Secrète who by late spring were the largest Maquis in the Var. For a time, life was good for the *maquisards* in Aups and the high-lying villages of Les Salles, Aiguines and Régusse. They enjoyed strong support from the local population and often gathered at the Restaurant Authieu in the village.

The peace and quiet of the Haut-Var was soon to be shattered by the Germans, who had long been gathering intelligence, and planning an expedition to subdue the terrorist strongholds on the Plains of Canjuers. On the evening of 7 June 1944, the day after the Normandy landings, a German motorcyclist and a truck full of French gendarmes accompanied by the Gestapo arrived at the entrance of the village while FTP *maquisards* from Camp Robert happened to be rounding up collaborators. Shots were fired from sub-machine guns and grenades were thrown, resulting in two German dead, including the motorcyclist, and three wounded. Taking two hostages with them, the Germans withdrew. But Aups was now a target for reprisals.

The Germans preferred it when their French lackeys did their dirty work, and tried to involve the préfecture, gendarmes and Milice. In the end, it was the Milice who took charge of the crackdown. On 12 June, 300 to 400 *miliciens* from as far away as Marseille took over the village of Aups where they began rounding up men to build fortifications in Saint-Raphaël. At that point, two unsuspecting *maquisards* from the Vallier group happened to drive into town to collect supplies, but were stopped at a roadblock near the northern entrance to Aups. A gun was found in their vehicle and the two men, Ernest Millet and François Duchâtel, were shot on the side of the road. Duchâtel was a former gendarme, and in addition to the monument marking the spot where he fell, his name has been given to a square in the centre of Aups and, in 2018, to a new barracks for the gendarmerie in La Valette du Var. For *Vallier*, this loss was personal: Millet had been a close friend, and the fact that it was the Milice who were responsible, made him furious. It would be almost a week before *Vallier* could write about it:

> Ernest was killed by a bullet in the face, and Duchâtel, after exhausting his revolver ammunition, was killed standing at attention. The militiamen left the body outside in the sun all day with a sign saying, 'Thus die traitors to France', and we want that there is no hatred between French! Once I wanted only fight against the Germans – but the night I learned this, I swore vengeance for Ernest and Duchâtel.[5]

In the round-up of 12 June, the owner of the Restaurant Authieu in Aups was arrested but many other FTP *maquisards* managed to escape the village; 120 of them arrived at the *Vallier* camp a day or two later with no food or ammunition. One of the more competent *maquisards* among this group was a woman, Marie-Jeanne Mazza (*Marianne*), but judging by the surprise expressed by *Vallier*, female fighters were a rarity.

At the funeral two days later, a large section of the population gathered. So many new recruits were forthcoming for both the AS Maquis and FTP, that those who were unarmed had to be sent home. Among them were a few *faux maquisards* who infiltrated the camps and reported back to their German masters. They were believed to be Brandenburgers, as this was their usual tactic. Two women also appeared at this time who turned out to be agents of the Gestapo. One was a 22-year-old telephonist, the other was an older woman. The one woman tried to escape and was shot in the leg. Under interrogation she confessed to being a spy for the Gestapo in Draguignan, and had been on her way to summon them or the Milice. *Vallier* set himself a time limit of eight hours to consider the death sentence. At 5 o'clock in the evening he formed the firing squad commanded by Pierrot and Dominique, his two section chiefs, and explained that what they were doing was not an act of vengeance, but of justice and he wanted everyone impeccably dressed and dignified.

The women were told that they were to be executed as traitors to France for working with the Germans. They were brave enough, but some of the *maquisards* were 'quite affected by the performance'. Vallier himself admitted that he was 'very pale and quite emotional – not by the fact of their death, but by the responsibility for deciding on the death of two living people'.[6]

*

Folklore of the Maquis is strewn with stories of executions of suspected traitors, both men and women. When John Goldsmith, the SOE agent working with the Maquis Ventoux, wrote about having to take the life of a woman accused of being a collaborator, he was writing twenty-five years after the fact, and he was at pains to point out that it made sense at the time. But that did not make it easier:

> I pushed the muzzle of my pistol against the nape of her neck, just below the bun, shut my eyes and pulled the trigger, pushing as I did so. The woman fell face forward in front of me shuddering and jerking. Then she lay quite, quite still and I vomited in the bushes beside the path.[7]

At the same time, Pierre-Michel (*Archiduc*) took the daughter a short distance away into the forest and shot her. He was unmoved, saying: '*Cela fait deux vaches de moins*' (that makes two cows less). There is no way of confirming the veracity of this account, as Goldsmith never mentioned any dates. He did, however, mention that the executions were as a direct consequence of the betrayal and subsequent slaughter of a group of *maquisards*. He felt that he was partly to blame as he had vouched for the traitor, an agent called *Noël* whom he had met in Algiers and who had now changed allegiance.

As it happens, there was a double agent called *Noël* (Maurice Seignon de Possel Deydier) who alerted the Gestapo to the presence of 400 members of l'Armée Secrète who were gathered in the mountains, just south of the River Durance, in the Bouches-du-Rhône. Ensuring that in every department the Maquis was punished for gathering in large numbers, more than a thousand German troops, including Brandenburgers and Reichsarbeitsdienst (RAD), supported by the Luftwaffe, ran rampant through the villages of Lambesc, La Roque-d'Anthéron and Charleval, the last two communities being the worst affected.

Throughout the district, a total of sixty two *maquisards* were either killed in action or captured and executed on 12 June 1944. The next day, on a farm called Fenouillet, twenty-eight more resistants were made to kneel down with their hands tied behind their backs and then shot. Ten of these were from Lambesc and surrounds, the rest had been transported up from prisons in Marseille. On top of all the other massacres that took place between 10 and 16 June 1944, this was a black week for Provence.

To mark this, the bloodiest raid in Provence, a large monument was erected on the Plateau of Manivert, alongside the Chapelle Sainte-Anne in the commune of Lambesc. A plaque on a rock facing the monument reads: 'On this monument are engraved the names of the 272 resistants of our region, victims of Nazi barbarism. Their memory is honoured in this place, every June 12 by the remembrance of the sacrifice of 62 of them fallen in these hills on June 12, 1944.'

*

Shockwaves of the D-Day landings in Normandy were also being felt in the Alpes-Maritimes and in the Basses-Alpes. On 6 June, at a crossroads near Saint-Julien-du-Verdon, the Maquis ambushed a number of German vehicles, killing seven, one of whom was a high-ranking officer, the second-in-command of the Digne Gestapo. During the next few days, the Germans hunted down the 'terrorists' in the mountains, searching the surrounding villages, shooting, arresting and deporting people at will. As the insurgency intensified, another Gestapo officer was caught, tried and executed by the Maquis in Castellane. On the 9th, two Germans were pulled off a train at Pignes, taken to Saint-André-les-Alpes, and executed.

By way of retribution, the Gestapo in Nice decided to carry out a mass execution in the same village in which their own people had been ambushed. Thirteen young prospective recruits for the Maquis Férion, including four who were still at school, were loaded onto a truck and driven into the mountains. On reaching a place called Bar-Sur-Loup, two of the boys, originally from Antibes, were taken out and shot in retaliation for some bombing which had taken place there.

The convoy rolled on, and at around 5 a.m. on 11 June 1944, they arrived at the entrance to Saint-Julien-du-Verdon (Lac de Castillion did not yet exist). The German soldiers opened the back and said to the prisoners, 'You're free!' As they got down and walked off a short distance, the Germans opened up with their sub-machine guns. Nine died on the spot, or from the coups de grâce. The bodies were left where they lay. Two others, found barely alive a little farther away at the edge of a thicket, managed to relate what happened before they expired.

Next day, the Castellane gendarmerie arrived at the scene and began to identify the bodies caked in dirt and blood. One of the bodies remained unidentified until 1994. Children from the village pulled a cart with the dead to the cemetery where the bodies were washed, and a lock of hair cut to give to the families. Fugitives avoiding the STO came down from the mountains and dug the eleven graves. The young victims, students at Lycée Masséna, had gone off without telling their parents, but the last letters of two of the boys are in the public domain.

Roger Demonceaux wrote: 'Because of the intrigues of the Milice, the Gestapo and the German troops, I was forced to join my comrades of the Maquis. I regret to have disobeyed you and to make you feel sad, but I am aware that today the time has come for everyone to fight for our country. Don't worry about me, I will be careful.' Believing that he would be home soon, Césaire Aubé wrote to his gendarme father in Nice, just before leaving for Mount Férion: 'I write these few words to say goodbye and not goodbye. While I write this letter, you can believe that I feel a lot of pain but accept it with courage. You Dad, you will understand better, you went to war when you were my age. Do not judge me too harshly because duty calls me, and one day you'll be proud of me.'[8] A few days later, on 16 June, near Allemagne-en-Provence in the Basses-Alpes, a German column, including a detachment of Brandenburgers, arrested a group of young people from the Var seeking to join the FTP Maquis. The Germans were there to carry out reprisals for the assassination of two collaborators in Vinon-sur-Verdon on 7 June. The young people were first made to watch the execution of nine people in the Place d'Allemagne before being led to a site called Ravin des Bayles near Saint-Martin-de-Bromes where they were massacred just before midday.

Fifteen bodies were found; fourteen were identified. Most had come from Brignoles and the surrounding villages of Le Val, Montfort and Carcès in the Var. Two or three were former Italian soldiers. There was also a group of friends from the same soccer team, one as young as 16, determined to join the Maquis together. The group had gathered in Cotignac to take the bus to Riez. They were unarmed and the circumstances of their arrest are unclear but, undoubtedly, there was treachery involved.

*

At a time when it was a risky proposition to make a show of strength, on 1 July 1944, *Vallier* organized a parade at the war memorial in the town of Aiguines to honour the fallen in the Great War, as well as the recent casualties like Millet and Duchâtel. Without advance notice, *Vallier* went into Aiguines to inform the people of the parade. Two sections, uniformly dressed, formed up outside the village. One was commanded by Pierrot and the other by Dominique, and with *Vallier* at the head, they sang and marched flawlessly through the village. At the raising of the colours, during the minute of silence, they could hear the sobs of Madame Dûchatel and her two young daughters, Isabelle and Monique Next stop was Les Salles, five kilometres down the road, which was particularly sympathetic to the Resistance. When they arrived the whole village was already gathered in the street, the women were in tears. After the ceremony, the citizens welcomed all forty-four of them into the town hall. Everyone brought something – eggs, bread, cheese, and of course, wine. The feast ended with songs of home, *des chansons de chez nous*, and a *crème* offered by *les demoiselles* of Les Salles. Had *Vallier* not controlled the consumption of wine, the return journey might have been a challenge.

For both the AS and FTP Maquis in the Haute-Var, 22 July 1944 was a black day. The Gestapo with their auxiliaries arrived from Brignoles at 6 a.m. to mount another attack on the village of Aups. A garage which was used by the FTP Maquis for repairing their vehicles, and adjoining houses were blown up. A vehicle belonging to the AS *Vallier* camp was also ambushed, two of its occupants were killed and two others wounded.[9]

Vallier had a premonition of disaster and did not have to wait long to hear the news. Dominique and Étienne were dead and two others had been wounded. For five minutes *Vallier* deliberated on what to do: he had to go for the wounded but did not want to risk the lives of more men. In the end he took six men, sufficiently armed. Fortunately, the Germans were no longer there, and the *maquisards* were able to mourn their comrades. Étienne had been killed instantly by a bullet to the head, while Dominique was torn by several bursts and had wounds from grenade shrapnel. The bodies were left in Aups and everyone drove home in silence. Dominique had left twelve hours earlier, full of confidence and joy, so sure of not being affected in this war, even though he had come through the most perilous situations.[10] The danger had not yet passed when *Vallier* and fifteen men went back into the village the next day to do the honours at the funeral. There they learned that Germans and the Frenchmen wearing Waffen-SS uniforms were attacking the FTP camp and that they were all around Aups. *Vallier* left immediately and it was just as well because five minutes after the funeral a column of at least 300 Germans marched through town.

A 17-year-old girl named Rosette Cioffi had been mortally wounded in the thigh outside the town hall and died next day in Draguignan. Some say that she was an *agent de liaison* who was shot while trying to warn the fighters. Others say she was an innocent bystander. Some say she sang 'La Marseillaise' on her deathbed, others say her last words were, 'I know I will be avenged.'[11] Perhaps because of her feminine youth, she has been incorporated into village culture as a hero of the Resistance. Streets are named after her and she is commemorated on a plaque in the main square. A shopkeeper from Aups, 47-year-old Louis Gautier, was also killed while trying to flee and there is a small square named after him.

The whole AS camp was now broken up into small sections and moved to new locations in the forest. As has been mentioned, the FTP camp at the farm La Tardie also came under attack, and fell back in disorganization on the AS camp. As always, in a difficult situation, the various factions were split, and leadership squabbles surfaced. One group went to the Quinson area while some Camp Robert members joined up with the FTP in the Basses-Alpes where an even worse calamity would occur. Aups and the Plains of Canjuers would be calm now until August. The eye of the storm had simply moved north.

Chapter 7

Despair

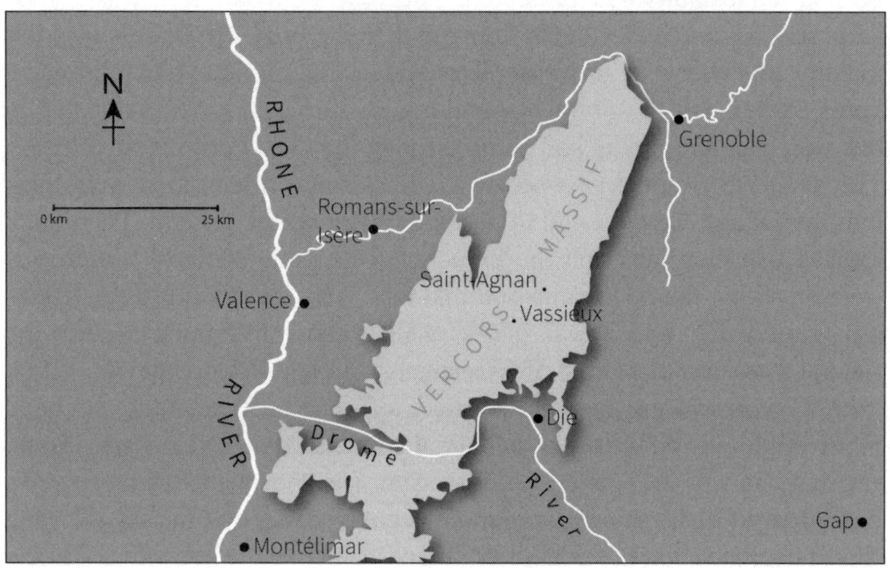

The Vercors Plateau.

As Peter Churchill was being extracted from France on the night of 23/24 March 1943, for a brief consultation in London, a new SOE agent by the name of Francis Cammaerts (*Roger*) climbed down from the still-running Lysander. The turnaround time was a mere three minutes, and there was no time for small talk. According to Churchill, he greeted Cammaerts with a 'Welcome friend, there's a car waiting', and then 'Good Luck'.[1] In the version given by Cammaerts, Churchill's only words were a warning to always have paper with him when he went to the toilet because it was a scarce commodity in France.[2] In the eight hours of recorded interviews held by the Imperial War Museum Cammaerts shares a few such insights into everyday life, as well as a colonel's grasp of the political and military imperatives.[3]

98

Cammaerts had originally been sent to organize DONKEYMAN, an offshoot of the CARTE circuit, operating in the upper Rhône Valley. But after witnessing the lack of discipline and resulting spate of arrests, he decided to form his own *réseau* in southeastern France, called JOCKEY. For a while Cammaerts was based in Cannes, getting the feel of life under the occupation. From Avignon to the high Alps, in what was known as the R2 sector, he organized and trained many different groups of resistants, built up communications and organized reception committees for arms drops.

The liaison and radio operator for the JOCKEY circuit was Cecily Lefort, a London-born woman of Scottish blood, who had been married to a French doctor and living in Brittany since she was twenty-four. It was considered prudent to be part of the uniformed forces before being deployed so as to be under the dubious protection of the Geneva Convention. Cecily, codenamed *Alice*, was in the Women's Auxiliary Air Force (WAAF) before she was trained by the SOE and flown in by Lysander on 16 June 1943. She was betrayed and arrested while meeting a contact in Montélimar in the Drôme in September 1943; she died in the gas chamber at Ravensbrück aged forty-four.

After a short visit to London, Cammaerts returned to France in April 1944 but the Lysander developed engine trouble and caught fire. Cammaerts and the crew of four bailed out at 3,000 metres over the Drôme Department, and were rescued by a Madame Girardin, who served omelettes, wine and coffee before alerting the Resistance. While the aircrew was shepherded home to England via Spain, Cammaerts continued his journey by bicycle. In an interview for a BBC documentary in the year 2000, he said, 'The most important element was the French housewife who fed us, clothed us and kept us cheerful.'[4]

For much of the time Cammaerts had his centre of operations in Seyne-les-Alpes, a fair-sized town in the Basses-Alpes. Although Seyne is situated between the busy towns of Digne and Gap, it is off the main thoroughfares in a secluded valley. From here, *Roger* travelled on winding roads to the outposts of his domain, encompassing Briançon, Avignon, Grenoble and Lyon, Marseille, Cannes and Nice. His main reason for travelling south from Seyne was to ensure that everything was in place to secure the Route de Napoleon, up the Rhône Valley, when the Allied invasion came. Sadly, he received only contempt from the American commander who benefited in the end.

Nicknamed *grands pieds* (big feet), Cammaerts was six foot four (1.93 metres), a disadvantage in his line of work as he stood out in a crowd. Among his *maquisards* he was known as *le grand diable Anglais* (the big English devil). Being half Belgian and half English, he spoke fluent French with a deep resonance in his voice. With his degree in English and History from Cambridge, he made an inspiring teacher and headmaster. A man of great principle, the experience of the First World War had turned him into to a conscientious objector and he was sent to work the land in Lincolnshire. In 1942, at the age of 26, after his brother, Pieter, was killed serving in the RAF, he was headhunted by the SOE. One of his assessors on the officer's course described him as 'rather lacking in dash, not suitable as a leader'. Ironically, of all the F Section SOE agents, he was perhaps the most effective.

Cecily Lefort's replacement as courier for Cammaerts was one Christine Granville, born Krystyna Skarbek. Of Polish aristocracy, she spoke multiple languages, although her English was fractured. Codenamed *Pauline*, and carrying false papers proclaiming her to be Jacqueline Armand, she was parachuted onto the Vercors Massif, a so-called plateau straddling the departments of Isère and Drôme on the night of 6/7 July 1944. For the first two weeks she toured the JOCKEY circuit, seeing firsthand the state of disarray among the various groups. In one of her earliest reports, she enthused: 'I am very happy with my work. *Roger* is a magnificent person … they treat him as the only neutral person … the unity in the whole of the South of France depends on him.'[5]

*

By the end of July, there had been a breakthrough in Normandy, and the German Army was also retreating in Italy and Russia. It would have dawned on many of the occupation troops that France was lost. At times like this, they vented their anger and frustration on the ordinary population as well as the Resistance. With Army Group G dispatching unit after unit northward to Normandy and concentrating much of its remaining strength along the coast, the FFI had taken control over large areas of southern France, posing serious threats to German lines of communication, especially in the Rhône Valley around Grenoble in the region of the Rhône-Alpes. As a result, Army Group G deemed it necessary to take drastic steps to clean up an area known as the Vercors Massif.

Southwest of Grenoble in the Drôme Department, the Vercors Massif is a mountain with a number of basins surrounded by forested ridges and sheer rock cliffs but known as the Vercors 'Plateau', possibly because of the flat valley floor. Access to the hamlets and villages on the plateau is by way of narrow, winding roads carved out of the rock. The area had long been a safe haven for the Maquis, and since the Normandy landings, a FFI force of up to 4,000 men and women had gathered there and established a liberated 'republic' with its own laws, finances and flag. German traffic along the highways of the Rhône Valley came under repeated attack but all attempts to retaliate came to naught as the access roads to this mountain fortress were blocked. Any plan of attack would have to include aircraft.

After the Normandy landings, the leadership of the Vercors had sent urgent messages begging for men and supplies (including tobacco) and warning of 'merciless retaliation' but the response from SPOC (Special Projects Operations Centre) had been muted. Now having been the target of bombing and reprisals for some time, the Resistance sent a stream of messages to Algiers asking for heavy weapons. It therefore seemed like a gift from the heavens when on 25 June 1944, a drop of 420 containers floated down onto the plateau. The contents included more than 1,000 small arms (Bren guns, Sten guns and .30 calibre rifles), as well as thirty-four bazookas but no mortars or much-needed heavy weapons. Some reassuring messages were also transmitted.

Upon receiving word that the Vercors population had begun their insurrection, the SOE agents and OSS teams nearby hurried to the plateau to organize more weapons drops and assist in any way they could. As will be explained in the next chapter, the OSS fielded three-man teams called 'Jedburghs' and fifteen-man teams called operational groups (OGs). As opposed to the SOE agents, these were trained, uniformed members of the military. Their missions were typically given female names. The French BCRA, as we have seen, was more akin to the SOE, while the Inter-Allied (IA) teams could be any combination of the above. All were represented on the Vercors, and Francis Cammaerts found himself to be the senior Allied liaison officer. A record of this period was preserved by a Parisian cameraman whose film footage was turned into a 1948 documentary called *Au cœur de l'orage*.

The latest consignment of arms served to boost morale of the Vercors inhabitants and raised the hope that paratroopers would soon arrive en masse. This hope was not entirely unfounded since five or more teams of special operators had been dispatched to the area in a matter of days. These were OG JUSTINE, Jedburgh teams VEGANIN, DODGE and CHLOROFORM, as well as BCRA mission PAQUEBOT and two Inter-Allied missions (SOE, OSS and BCRA) both baptized EUCALYPTUS. The second EUCALYPTUS was carrying eleven passengers including a surgeon for the Maquis. The senior British officers, Major Desmond Longe of the EUCALYPTUS team, and the leader of VEGANIN, Major Neil Marten, butted heads badly about the wisdom of congregating in such numbers and VEGANIN left the area before the battle commenced.[6]

Mission PAQUEBOT, led by Captain Jean Tournissa, had arrived on the plateau during the night of 6/7 July, bringing Christine Granville with them. Their task was to make a landing strip for Douglas C-47 Skytrains (RAF designation 'Dakotas') on the plateau. Tournissa immediately mobilized a force of nearly 400 *maquisards*, civilian volunteers, and young farmers, and began clearing a strip 1,050 metres long and 140 metres wide. A week earlier, on 29 June, the fifteen-man American team, OG JUSTINE, had flown in from Blida, an airfield south of Algiers. Believing that these uniformed commandos were an advance party of an army of paratroopers, people of the Vercors gave them a warm welcome.

Commanded by first lieutenants Vernon G. Hoppers and Chester L. Myers, the OG mission was to carry out guerrilla warfare against the German lines of communication in the region, but first they had to provide training in the use of the newly arrived weapons. At Saint-Martin, where they were based, there are photographs of them mingling with the population and attending parades. According to an OSS source, the group carried out two ambushes on 2 July and 7 July, but local sources mention only one ambush on 10 July.[7] Hoppers and Myers led their heavily armed group together with about thirty *maquisards* to lay an ambush at the Col-de-la-Croix-Haute, southeast of the plateau, on Route 75, five kilometres from Lalley. When the first truck entered the ambush it was stopped by a bazooka, and finished off with a Browning automatic rifle (BAR) and Bren guns. From the heights on the side of the road, gammon bombs were thrown into the backs of the open trucks. The troops debussed and returned fire from a few hundred metres away, wounding one *maquisard* who was captured and shot in the village square, ignoring his plea that he was a combatant.

At 9.30 on the morning of Bastille Day, 14 July, two groups of American bombers flew over the Vercors Massif and released hundreds of containers suspended by red, white and blue parachutes. In terms of aircraft and tons of weapons, it was double the size of the 25 June delivery. Henri Rosencher, the Jewish medic who was part of the ill-fated Mission MICHEL, documented his deep emotions:

> The sky was filled with a hundred Allied planes glittering in the sunlight sowing hundreds of parachutes which burst open in the blue sky like the corolla of white flowers, descending joyously and carrying around 1,200 containers. It was a magnificent fête! The planes dipped their wings in salute, the sky full of them! It was more beautiful than a fireworks show! It was an imposing spectacle, enchanting and elating! Among the maquisards, the enthusiasm was indescribable.[8]

As the last B-17 began its run, it was attacked by enemy fighters which then began strafing the teams collecting the arms. At first, everyone thought they were Allied planes 'but as they dived towards the landing strip, the dreaded swastika was plainly visible. They dived to about eight metres on the open plain where everyone was standing and opened fire at point-blank range'.[9]

Not only did the enemy planes prevent immediate recovery of the weapons, but they continued all day strafing and bombing the principal towns, breaking up the parades and ceremonies planned for Bastille Day. Clearly, the *maquisards* had learned how to handle their weapons because, according to the report by Major Desmond Longe, five German fighters were seen to come down. This may well have been an exaggeration, but Bren gunners positioned on the Col-de-Rousset, a high point overlooking the plateau, were credited with one or two. One of the Fw 190s came down at Châteauneuf-de-Galaure, west of Grenoble, where its pilot was taken prisoner by the Maquis. Some say that it was hit by gunners in one of the B-17 bombers.

On 21 July, a cold and cloudy day, the Germans attacked with a force of gliderborne paratroopers near Vassieux-en-Vercors. In the first wave, seven gliders landed in the meadows, taking the resistants completely by surprise. At 10 a.m. a second wave of fourteen gliders arrived, carrying

140 men – each glider carried ten men including the pilot. This time the FFI were ready for them and more than one glider was hit. In 2012 the remains of four Germans were excavated from a crash site near Montjoux, thirty kilometres south of the Vercors.[10]

In this operation, which the Germans called 'Bettina', the attackers included a number of *Gebirgsjäger* (Austrian mountain troops) and *Fallschirmjäger* (paratroopers). Some witnesses have said that the worst atrocities were committed by the *Osttruppen*, referred to as 'Mongols' by the French; others are convinced that some of the worst culprits were *miliciens* or Frenchmen in German uniforms. Members of the Gestapo were assigned to the various battle groups for the purpose of interrogating prisoners. They clashed with the Wehrmacht who had issued a special directive to the effect that when fighting 'terrorists', one should act with 'force and decision' but that the German soldier 'must keep his legendary discipline and must honour his reputation as a correct and chivalrous fighter'. [11]

On the afternoon of the 21st, a strong counterattack was made with 400 men, including the OSS commandos who added considerably to the firepower, but it was not enough. Supported by light mortars and Bren guns, the French were about to gain the upper hand when Lieutenant Hoppers, the commander of JUSTINE, ordered a withdrawal, Lieutenant Myers being out of action after an emergency appendectomy. Hoppers was later accused of having lost his nerve at the critical moment. At this stage, morale was good, but anger was growing when it became apparent that no Allied reinforcements would be forthcoming. After numerous messages were sent requesting air support, Eugène Chavant, the beleaguered civilian leader sent a famous signal to SPOC, accusing them of being 'criminals and cowards' for having forsaken the people of the Vercors.

Things started looking up on 22 July. The German paratroopers had dug in and occupied farmhouses but were trapped at Vassieux. Lacking supplies and ammunition, they just managed to hold on to their positions. German ground forces trying get up to the plateau were ambushed in the mountain passes. A second glider lift had to be cancelled due to bad weather. But then, on the 23rd, reinforcements started arriving, and the *maquisards* were unable to break up this new assault.

That day, 23 July, the dashing Lieutenant Abel Chabal, led another hopeless counterattack. Chabal sent a last message: 'I am almost completely encircled. We prepare for a Sidi-Brahim. *Vive la France!*'[12] (Sidi-Brahim is a reference to a battle which took place in 1845, where the French in Algeria fought to the last round against a superior force of Berbers. Refusing all calls to surrender, they resorted to a bayonet charge and only a handful got out alive.)

Eventually, on the evening of 23 July, a final message was sent to London saying that the defences had been penetrated, and the order was given to disperse. Those *maquisards* who were unable to escape through the cordon were hunted down by German patrols and executed on the spot. In the towns and villages the Germans began an orgy of destruction and killing. Civilians, women, and the wounded were not spared. Some of the younger victims included Suzanne Berthet, an 8-year-old girl, Alice Giraud, who was only a little older, and Lucien Emery, a child who had presented flowers to the American parachutists. The entire Martin family, including 16-year-old Alice, were murdered in their home on 21 July. The villagers were prevented from burying the bodies, and for days they lay rotting in the sun. Many of the victims were later reinterred in the nécropole de la Résistance at Vassieux-en-Vercors. Monuments and cemeteries are to be seen everywhere in the Vercors. One memorial which seems designed to evoke anger is the Mur des Fusillés in La Chapelle-en-Vercors, a stone wall in a courtyard where sixteen young men of the village were lined up and shot on 25 July.

As the Germans closed in from the north, the wounded *maquisards* had first been evacuated from the plateau in a bus, two trucks and a car, down the winding road to the town of Die. The doctors, however, thought they would be safer back up on the plateau in the Grotte de la Luire which is well hidden by folage and is accessed by a narrow footpath from the village of Saint-Agnan. Carting their equipment with them, they set up an aid post among the jumbled rocks on the floor of the damp cave.

When they discovered the Grotte de la Luire on 27 July, the German NCO ordered everyone out, and those being carried on stretchers were executed when they reached the bottom of the path. Altogether 25 wounded *maquisard*s were shot either on the spot or later on the side of the road near the village of Rousset, ten kilometres away. The 26-year-old Lieutenant Francis Billon of BCRA Mission PAQUEBOT, who had broken his leg while parachuting in, was one of the seven people murdered at Rousset on 28 July. Lieutenant Myers of OG JUSTINE, had also been in the field hospital recovering from an appendix operation, and witnessed the wounded *maquisards* being killed without mercy. Surprisingly, he was spared.

Two doctors and a priest were taken to Grenoble and shot in a mass execution on 10 August. Seven nurses were held at Montluc Prison in Lyon then deported to Ravensbrück where the 25-year-old Odette Malossane died in the spring of 1945.

Guided by a Frenchman, the British members of EUCALYPTUS escaped via Chamonix into Switzerland. The three remaining members of PAQUEBOT got through to Romans-sur-Isère in the Department of the Drôme. OG JUSTINE spent eleven days in the woods above Saint-Marcellin, surviving on raw potatoes and morsels of cheese, and squeezing moss to extract water. Aided by the Maquis, the OG, together with eleven downed airmen, then moved north and hid out in the Belledonne Mountains until 24 August, by which time American forces had taken Grenoble. There they learned that the largest force ever deployed against the Resistance – 8,000 to 12,000 men – had been sent to destroy them, and that the Germans thought that it was an American battalion they were up against rather than just the fifteen-man operational group.[13]

After many days and nights of living in the forest, with little more than dandelions for food, the first civilians ventured back to Vassieux-en-Vercors: the sights which confronted them might not be believed if photographs did not exist. Some men had been beheaded, a number had been castrated and others hung upside down. At La Murre, two men were found hanged from one tree. One of them had both eyes and his tongue cut out. The other had one foot resting on the ground so that death would arrive when it was no longer possible to stand. By his position, it seemed that a German had to jump on his back to make him collapse.

In the hamlet of du Château, a 12-year-old girl named Arlette Blanc was found still alive, stuck in the rubble of her home. Beside her were the bodies of her mother, two sisters Jacqueline (7), Danielle (4) and a little brother Maurice (18 months). One by one they had succumbed to their injuries after many hours of calling out for help. Arlette could do nothing, her legs caught between two beams. On Thursday, 27 July, the priest heard her fading cries and she was freed, but she had leg injuries and gangrene had set in. Carried in a wheelbarrow four kilometres to the house of Madame Achard in Saint-Agnan, she was washed and looked after, and seemed to be on the mend. Her story has been immortalized in French folklore: 'I asked two Germans for water but they went away laughing at me,' Arlette told the priest who had only recently officiated at her first communion. 'Someone must write to Papa, he lives at 24 Rue Joseph Bouchayer, in Grenoble.' On Sunday she ate something and then complained of stomach pains. The pain quickly spread. 'I did not think that so much suffering was necessary to die,' she cried. 'I am going to die and my Papa is not here. I know I'm going to die. Where will they bury me?' She was buried in a corner of the garden. On a small cross marking the grave it was written, 'Here rests Arlette Blanc, died 31 July 1944 aged 12. Pray for her.'[14] Arlette's father, André Blanc, who lived in Grenoble, had sent his wife and children to Vassieux for their safety. Mercifully, he died in Germany and was later reburied in the National Cemetery at Vassieux with all eleven members of his family.

The butcher's bill cannot be determined with absolute certainty. Early estimates put the number at 639 FFI and 201 civilians killed but later research indicates a lower figure of 332 resistance fighters and 131 civilians killed on the plateau, but to this must be added approximately a hundred FFI killed or executed away from the Vercors. This would increase the French casualty figure to around five hundred and seventy. On the German side the official report listed sixty-five killed and eighteen missing.

Forty civilians were deported, including the nurses from the hospital. Several villages were laid waste: 573 houses were burned. On 5 August, after an operation lasting fifteen days, the Germans finally left the area.[15] But the suffering of the Vercors population was not over. After several weeks of avoiding German patrols, the survivors were in very poor health. Some moved away but others lived through the winter months with minimal food, shelter or clothes. There was an outbreak of scabies and boils, among other things, and medical facilities were unavailable and unaffordable. Despite calls by the authorities to come to terms with these war crimes, the mental scars have never healed.

For the time being, the Germans had secured the Rhône Valley, but the Resistance was not destroyed as is often asserted: they simply reverted to their guerrilla activities, biding their time. When news of the catastrophe spread, some resistance leaders like Camille Rayon (*Archiduc*), and his advisor, John Goldsmith, were critical of the poorly timed uprising as well as being saddened by the waste of brave lives.

But the false dawn on the Vercors was not seen by all as a total disaster. As Colonel Zeller, the FFI regional commander for the south-east, was travelling to Apt to be picked up by Lysander, he had time to reflect on the bigger picture: on the railway lines connecting Briançon, Grenoble, Livron and Aix-en-Provence no train ran; no isolated German vehicle could travel the highways; no control existed outside of the garrison towns, from which the enemy only emerged in force, and even these columns were attacked by an unseen enemy. The German soldier was bewildered and demoralized. 'We know him,' wrote Zeller, 'we steal his mail.' Evidently, he looked with fear on the mountains, forests, and narrow valleys 'from which any moment a thunderbolt can crash. He awaits the arrival of the Allied soldiers like a deliverance'.[16]

The concept of a 'redoubt' garrisoned by the local population, with or without a stiffening of airborne troops, which could hold an area of French soil until the invading armies overran it, was highly attractive, but it was contrary to all principles of irregular warfare. For the guerrilla, the general rule is that mobility means victory and stability spells defeat. In the case of the Vercors defence, a tragedy was unavoidable due to the fact that more than half of the defenders were local men who fought valiantly, but vainly, to protect their families.

*

At the time of Vercors, there was so much pain everywhere that nobody can be blamed for trying to shut it out for a little while, and it is no secret that Christine Granville and Francis Cammaerts became lovers. It may be remembered that Granville had parachuted onto the Vercors plateau to join the JOCKEY circuit on 6 July 1944 as a radio operator and courier. This was not her first mission: she had previously been on operations in Poland, and had had a number of narrow escapes. Cammaerts was Colonel Zeller's second-in-command, and *chef* of the JOCKEY circuit.

Before and during the battle of the Vercors, Cammaerts and Granville had been constantly on the wireless asking SPOC for heavy weapons and more personnel to defend the plateau. As senior SOE operatives, they had no expectation of surviving the enemy onslaught. On the same day as the massive weapons drop by the US Air Force, the two were staying in the hamlet of Saint-Agnan which came under attack by the Luftwaffe, and Cammaerts confessed:

> The night of the 14th [Bastille Day], Christine and I spent
> the night together in a burning hotel in St Agnan. It was the

> first time we'd made love. We were absolutely certain we
> were going to die the next day; it was all over, this was the
> end – the hotel was on fire, bombs were falling, troops were
> gathering on the side of the mountain … we simply went
> into each other's arms.[17]

In the morning, they were standing at the window, and a fighter with a bomb slung beneath it flew straight at them. They could see the pilot's face. 'If he releases it now, we've had it,' Cammaerts said, and on the word 'now' the bomb was released. It skidded across the roof and buried itself in the ground behind the hotel. Christine gripped his hand and laughed, 'They don't want us to die!'[18]

When the order came to disperse, just before the cordon tightened, the pair managed to slip away. On her own, Christine now undertook a journey into the Alps where she hoped to be able to convince a contingent of Polish conscripts in the Wehrmacht to defect to the Resistance. Cammaerts returned to his home base in Seyne-les-Alpes, thirty kilometres north of Digne in the Basses Alpes, and continued with his liaison work.

By the time of the invasion, Cammaerts had spent more than a year in France and was highly regarded. His longevity can be attributed to his ultra-cautiousness, never spending more than one or two nights in the same place, and telling no one of his movements. Newcomers to the R2 sector would sooner or later meet up with the man named *Roger* for a briefing, and depending on conditions on the ground, plans might be changed.

On 9 August 1944, a new mission called TOPLINK, intended for operations in the Alpes-Maritimes and the Var, parachuted into the DZ *Assurance*, six kilometres west of Seyne. The two-man mission consisted of Alexander 'Xan' Fielding, codenamed *Cathédral*, and Captain Julian Lezard, a large-bodied, liberal-minded South African whose unconventional character has been colourfully painted by his friend, Xan Fielding.

Although still a captain at the age of 40, 'Lizzy' Lezard had seen more varied service than most colonels. He had volunteered for a number of paramilitary missions in almost every 'private army' then operating in the Middle East. As each one of his commanding officers, who had taken him on simply as court jester, soon discovered, 'his irreverent wit and unpractical jokes merely served to conceal a quality of which he seemed positively ashamed – namely, courage'.[19]

In the 1930s, Lezard had been a top tennis player, captaining Cambridge and the South African Davis Cup team as well as competing at Wimbledon. He did some basic parachute training with the SAS and was 42 years old when he went to France with Xan Fielding. Lezard's codename was *Eglise* (church), which was appropriate since he was second-in-command to *Cathédral*, although he joked that it should have been *Synagogue* since he was partly Jewish.

The insertion of the two agents did not go well. Two attempts had to be aborted because the pilot could not pick up the weak torchlights which identified the DZ. On the third attempt they were dropped from a high altitude, and strong winds blew them two kilometres off course onto a rocky outcrop. Having only had minimal parachute training, Lezard braced both his legs on landing and was lucky to get away with only two fractured vertebrae. Left in the care of a Maquis doctor, he now looked forward to spending time at the gaming tables in Monte Carlo once this 'invasion business was over'.[20]

The focus of the mission was the upcoming invasion, and the members of the TOPLINK team – Xan Fielding and Christian Sorensen – travelled with Cammaerts to *Archiduc's* camp near Apt to meet with some of de Gaulle's representatives who were flying in. The driver of the Red Cross truck in which they were traveling was Claude Renoir, the youngest son of the painter. On their return journey, on 13 August, they were stopped at a roadblock between Digne and Seyne. Fielding had been brought up in Nice, where his grandparents had property, but his French was a bit rusty. It seems his accent, the false documents and identity did not stand up to interrogation. Although they remained calm and stuck to their stories, they were carted off to the Villa Marie-Louise on the outskirts of Digne, for questioning. A firing squad was a certainty.

That Cammaerts and his colleagues escaped the firing squad was entirely due to the courageous intervention of Christine Granville. On getting word from Claude Renoir, who had not been arrested, Christine cycled forty hilly kilometres to Digne where Cammaerts, Fielding and Sorensen were being held. In order to make sure that she was at the right place, Christine skulked outside the prison singing a popular song which she knew Cammaerts would recognize. On hearing a faint voice coming from within the walls, she walked in to negotiate for his release.

She did not hide the fact that she was a British agent, and managed to convince one of his captors that she was the niece of General Bernard Montgomery, and that the Allies, soon to arrive, would not take kindly to the mistreatment of her 'husband'. Finally, a large bribe of SOE money was paid over, and the three were released just hours before they were to be executed. Had her plan backfired, Granville herself would have suffered a terrible fate.

As one contemporary admirer explains, 'I would have believed anything Christine told me, and done anything she asked.' Christine Granville was clearly a person of outstanding courage with exceptional charms. One of her SOE assessors described her as 'a very smart looking girl, simply dressed and aristocratic. She is a flaming Polish patriot, she made an excellent impression and I really believe we have a prize'. Xan Fielding, one of the three SOE men who owed her their lives, provides us with a priceless vignette:

> Not that she in any way resembled the classical conception of a female spy, even though she had the glamorous figure that is conventionally associated with one; this she preferred to camouflage in an austere blouse and skirt which, with her short, carelessly combed dark hair and the complete absence of make-up on her delicately featured face, gave her the appearance of an athletic art student.[21]

Volumes more could be written about this true heroine but no less than four full-length biographies of her life have already been published, and some say that she was the inspiration for at least one of Ian Fleming's characters in his James Bond novels. Tragically, she was stabbed to death in 1952 in London by a man whose advances she had rejected. Xan Fielding never forgot his debt of gratitude, and dedicated his 1954 book, *Hide and Seek: The Story of a Wartime Agent* to her memory.

Cammaerts attained the rank of lieutenant-colonel and was decorated with the DSO, Légion d'Honneur, Croix de Guerre and the American Medal of Freedom. With the advent of peace, he returned to his wife, Nan, and to his work in education. During his career, he created and ran an international exchange for schools, then established teachers' training colleges in Kenya and Botswana, before returning to England to head a teachers' training college there. He and Nan retired to a small farm in the

Drôme, among members of his former circuit. Later they moved to the Hérault, where Nan died in 2002 and Francis followed five years later at the age of ninety.

The 'bother' of SOE agents falling in love was apparently a British thing. The French would 'just copulate and that is that', so said the Romanian-born Vera Atkins, one of the legendry staff members at the SOE's Baker Street headquarters.[22] Her observation is seconded by an Anglo-Saxon sociologist who spent time in a village in the Vaucluse and found that the French believe that since the sexual urge is a natural part of our existence, little may be gained from fighting against it. 'It is like all inevitable aspects of life; since nothing can be done about them, they might as well be accepted.'[23]

Agents were advised to avoid relationships, and, according to John Goldsmith, those who did not heed this advice were far more likely to be distracted. Yet he himself had a girlfriend in Toulouse during his second mission, under the alias Jean Delannoy. After a while he took the girl partly into his confidence, revealing that he had a wife in England and a whole other identity. The girl accepted it; 'To me you are just Jean Delannoy,' she said, 'he is the man I love, if he does not return from his travels one day, I will be suffering no more than thousands of women in France who wait in hope.' As for his wife, the man who returned to her would be no different from the one who left her. John Goldsmith and Jean Delannoy were two different people.[24]

Chapter 8

Audacity

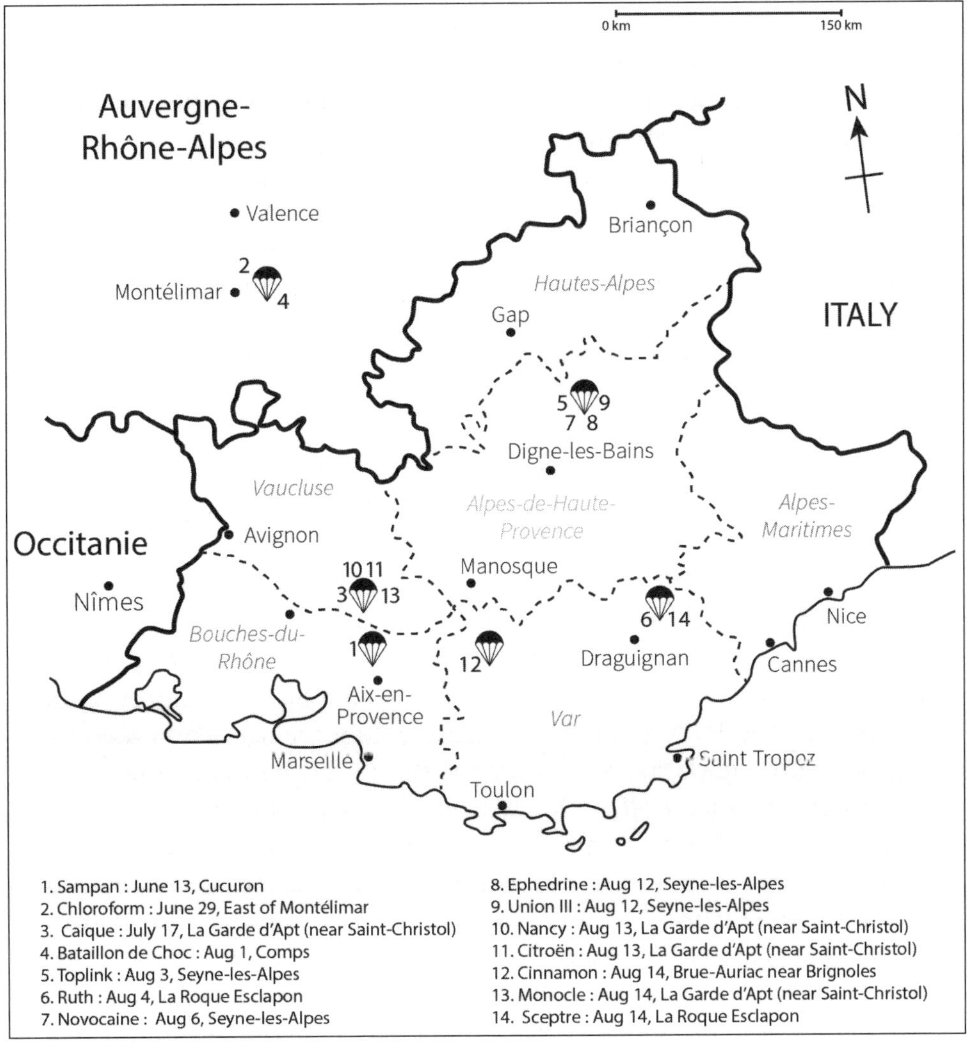

1. Sampan : June 13, Cucuron
2. Chloroform : June 29, East of Montélimar
3. Caique : July 17, La Garde d'Apt (near Saint-Christol)
4. Bataillon de Choc : Aug 1, Comps
5. Toplink : Aug 3, Seyne-les-Alpes
6. Ruth : Aug 4, La Roque Esclapon
7. Novocaine : Aug 6, Seyne-les-Alpes
8. Ephedrine : Aug 12, Seyne-les-Alpes
9. Union III : Aug 12, Seyne-les-Alpes
10. Nancy : Aug 13, La Garde d'Apt (near Saint-Christol)
11. Citroën : Aug 13, La Garde d'Apt (near Saint-Christol)
12. Cinnamon : Aug 14, Brue-Auriac near Brignoles
13. Monocle : Aug 14, La Garde d'Apt (near Saint-Christol)
14. Sceptre : Aug 14, La Roque Esclapon

Allied special operations in Provence.

Allied special operations in the invasion zone encompassed a multitude of different organizations. Since the Americans entered the war in Europe at a relatively late stage, it stands to reason that the British Special Operations Executive had agents on the ground in France long before the American Office of Strategic Services came onto the scene. Some would say that the important, and dangerous, groundwork had already been done prior to 1944. Not surprisingly, there was some professional jealousy between the different organizations. The British and the Americans often disagreed bitterly while General Koenig, the FFI leader in London, would have liked full control of both the SOE and OSS in France. Communist resistance groups mistrusted the OSS whom they considered to be the agents of de Gaulle. Equally, the OSS was wary of the communists.[1]

An animal of a slightly different hue was the Special Operations (SO). These Inter-Allied Missions (IAMs) were in direct support of Allied operations, without any nationalistic agendas, they therefore came under the control of Allied commanders.[2] Special Forces Headquarters (SFHQ) and the Special Project Operations Center (SPOC) were based in Algiers. *Massingham* was the name given by the SOE to this nerve centre of the Mediterranean theatre where the OSS and the Bureau Central Rensiegnements et d'Action (BCRA) had their headquarters. Agents put final touches to their training at Club des Pins, a group of villas in a secluded area about twenty kilometres west of Algiers.

For practical as well as political purposes, SFHQ decided to create Inter-Allied units representing Britain, the United States and France, or more specifically, the SOE, OSS and the BCRA. While Inter-Allied missions were of short duration, the British-controlled F Section had more permanent agents who were tasked with building *réseaux*, networks or circuits. The BCRA was the French intelligence service headed by Major André Dewavrin, alias *Colonel Passy,* and had been operating independently since 1940 – mainly in small groups or alone.

Larger groups of French marines – Groupes de Contre-Sabotage de la Marine Française – were sent in prior to the invasion of Provence to prevent the Germans from destroying infrastructure in what were known as 'Counter-Scorch' missions. Mission SAMPAN was responsible for preventing sabotage to the Toulon harbour. Mission GÉDÉON, which was to reinforce SAMPAN, landed at Brue-Auriac on 12 August, only three days before the invasion. The leader of GÉDÉON, Jean Ayral, was to die in the fighting to liberate Toulon. A third French Navy commando team, CAÏQUE, was sent to Marseille to try and salvage the port infrastructure there. Among the more obscure parachute operations in the Drôme, were the two fifteen-man 'sticks' of commandos from the 1er Bataillon de Choc (shock troops) which landed in the Comps area, east of Montélimar on 31 July and 1 August 1944. Having been four years in exile, and based in Algiers, one of the commandos, who could have landed on his feet, preferred to roll as he hit the ground and taste the grass and the soil of his homeland. There was a strong wind and the leader, Lieutenant Corley, knocked his head against a low wall and was rendered comatose. Officer Cadet (l'Aspirant) Raymond Muelle took charge of the operation and led the Maquis in the liberation of Grenoble.

The Jedburghs were specifically three-man Inter-Allied teams, the name arbitrarily derived from the codename of the first such mission. In the South of France, their goal was to turn the Resistance into an effective fighting force. While they did join with the Maquis to harass and destroy enemy lines of communication and supplies, they often found themselves trying to dampen the exuberance of the Resistance rather than trying to incite them. The instructions to the special operations teams were to confine themselves to guerrilla activities and avoid pitched battles or open warfare. 'Surprise, kill, and vanish' was the Jedburgh maxim.

While the Jeburghs are perhaps the best-known branch of the OSS, there were also larger combat units known as operational groups (OGs) who are considered to be the forerunners of the Green Berets, the US Special Forces. The OGs, usually composed of men from particular American ethnic groups – dependent on the ethnicity of the target country – were organized to fight in groups of about fifteen as this was the capacity of the C-47 aircraft. The SAS, OGs, and some Jedburgh teams wore uniform so as to be more easily identified by the Resistance, and it was good for morale all round.

Operating with the Maquis in the hills, and also in the towns, under the noses of the Germans, the special operations teams were there to encourage rather than command. Although no SAS units were deployed to the R2 sector, there were eighteen or more SAS missions in the rest of France, taking the fight behind German lines in their modified Jeeps. Whether an operative was in uniform or in civilian clothes, he was likely to be summarily executed if caught. Hitler's Commando

Order – *Kommandobefehl* – made up in clarity for what it lacked in brevity. Just this one paragraph of Hitler's diatribe would have been enough to get the message across:

> I order, therefore: From now on all men operating against German troops in so-called commando raids in Europe or in Africa, are to be annihilated to the last man. This is to be carried out whether they be soldiers in uniform, or saboteurs, with or without arms; and whether fighting or seeking to escape; and it is equally immaterial whether they come into action from ships and aircraft, or whether they land by parachute. Even if these individuals on discovery make obvious their intention of giving themselves up as prisoners, no pardon is on any account to be given.[3]

Under no circumstances were 'commandos' to be treated under the rules of the Geneva Convention. It was forbidden to hold them in PoW camps, even as a temporary measure. They were to be shot immediately, unless they could be handed over to the SD for interrogation, in which case, they should be shot immediately after all the information had been extracted. This order did not apply to the treatment of soldiers taken prisoner in the course of normal operations, or in major landings or airborne operations. Neither did it apply to airmen seeking to save their lives by parachute.

One OG in Italy did fall victim to Hitler's Commando Order. Codenamed GINNY II, the operational group of fifteen OSS men of Italian heritage was discovered on 24 March 1944, in a barn near the village of Carpineggio. General Anton Dostler ordered their execution. The Americans were all wearing military uniforms and insignia of rank, as was proven when their bodies were exhumed from their mass grave. At his trial, Dostler claimed that he was acting on the orders of Field Marshal Albert Kesselring but he was still convicted of carrying out an unlawful order. Other German officers tried to prevent the execution, but it was carried out anyway. Dostler was captured on the last day of the war and on 1 December 1945 it was his turn to face a firing squad.

Operational groups were strictly military, unlike other special operations and intelligence organizations such as the SOE. The role of the OGs was much like that of the smaller two- or three-man teams, as they also carried out guerrilla operations far behind enemy lines, working with indigenous resistance groups. They were also very similar to the SAS in terms of size of the units and their function, but not in terms of their command, their equipment or language skills. The composition of the OG depended on the country in which they were operating. Team members would have knowledge of the language, culture and geography of the target country. All members were American nationals but represented many ethnic groups including Norwegian, French, Greek and Italian.

Jedburghs and OGs were held back until the last minute because SPOC was not sure that there would be any invasion, but during the first two weeks of August 1944, special operations intensified throughout the southeast in the R2 sector. Although not all of these were deployed in Provence, their tasks were directly or indirectly devoted to paving the way for the coming invasion. Inland, road and rail links had to be cut to isolate the landing zone, and the time was nearly ripe to instigate a general uprising among the Maquis.

By August 1944, in addition to the 'Jeds' and the other special operations people, approximately 1,100 Americans were active in OG units throughout Europe. By the end of the war, there may have been up to 2,000 members of OSS operational groups in the field. In total, eighty-seven OGs were sent to France in August 1944 and eighty-six more in September. Partly as a cover and partly to reflect the size of the unit, the name was changed to 2671st Special Reconnaissance Battalion.

Despite the often-heard criticism of 'too little too late', some US Seventh Army commanders believed that the OSS had never been more active or effective than in the South of France. They were credited with collecting information on the composition of the German troops, location of ammunition dumps, length and breadth of the landing beaches, depth of the water and position of every pillbox. This must have been done by the earliest missions because most of the Jedburghs who were sent here in July and August 1944 accomplished little. It has already been alluded to that the OSS and the Jedburghs parachuted into areas where the Resistance was already thriving, largely thanks to the F Section of the SOE.

The Central Intelligence Agency (CIA) of today grew out of the OSS, and the title of a book by Robin Winks, *Cloak and Gown*, suggests that a college degree was more useful than a dagger. OSS agents operating behind enemy lines were backed by the best brains that could be assembled in the world of academia. The research and analysis branch, numbering about 900 researchers, was known as the 'bad eyes brigade' because a disproportionate number wore glasses. The operators themselves were educated men, being those most likely to have command of a foreign language and of the geography of foreign places. The ideal recruit was said to be 'a PhD who can win a bar fight'. Yale and Harvard contributed the highest proportion of recruits relative to their graduating class size.

The selection process was designed to find the unconventional mavericks who could accomplish their missions on their own in enemy territory. It was the un-submissive troublemakers who succeeded rather than the high-flyers accustomed to being at the top of the class. Psychological tests attempted to identify individuals who were unconventional and unafraid of authority. The performance report of one prospective agent stated that 'the subject is not a fool but gives a good impression of one'.

Unlike the F Section agents, Jedburghs had to already be in the military. Before being sent to Britain, the Jedburgh recruits went through selection and training in the Catoctin Mountains of Maryland, near Washington DC, adjacent to the present-day presidential retreat of Camp David. Course material covered intelligence-gathering and reporting techniques, enemy identification, weapons instruction (including enemy weapons), demolition and sabotage, fieldcraft, scouting, reconnaissance, mapping and 'morale operations'.[4]

Among the first Jedburgh teams sent from Algiers to the South of France was the unhappy team VEGANIN which jumped into the Isère near Beaurepaire, south of Lyon, on 9 June 1944. In command was a hard-headed Englishman, Major Harry Neil Marten. The radio operator, Sergeant Dennis Gardner, never got to use his finely honed skills. His parachute didn't open due to a malfunction of his static line. On hearing of Gardner's death, SPOC sent a replacement radioman with team DODGE, and on 24 June the Jedburgs, together with their AS-aligned *maquisards*, hiked sixty kilometres cross-country to the Vercors, to lend a hand to the forces already gathered there.

As a result of resistance activity in the valley below the Vercors, the Germans had been terrorizing villages in search of 'terrorists'. Finding no trace, they resorted to burning, raping and pillaging. On their arrival, VEGANIN found the AS and FTP at each other's throats, and hostility toward the Maquis in general. According to the French member, Captain Gaston Vuchot, the FTP had no appreciation for military authority, spending their time thieving and foraging, showing no interest in fighting. Even the better leaders looked after their own interests. 'Their sense of honour was completely absent.' Clearly, these communist fighters had no wish to cooperate with anyone associated with de Gaulle.

Jedburgh mission CITROËN dropped into the Vaucluse Department near Apt on the night of 13/14 August 1944. Having only twenty-four hours on the ground before Dragoon D-Day was clearly not enough time to get to know their surroundings, let alone organize the local resistance. This was the opinion strongly expressed by two of the team members in an interview for the Imperial War Museum's oral history project.[5]

In command of CITROËN was Captain John E. St Clair Smallwood, a well-educated Englishman. The native French-speaker was Captain René-Clément Alcée, a French Foreign Legion officer who would later be killed in the Algerian War. Sergeant F. A. 'Fred' Bailey, a Cockney by birth, was the wireless operator. All were equally keen for action. Had they not all got on well together, substitutions would have been permitted. Captain Smallwood was rather laid-back and a bit of a maverick. He had nothing good to say about his SOE assessors, who in turn had nothing good to say about him, although he was very athletic and excelled in the physical training.

Bailey had trained as a wireless operator in the Royal Armoured Corps but found them to be more concerned about getting leave than getting into the action, so when in 1943 a circular came round asking for volunteers for special duties, he did not hesitate. Wireless skills were honed at Henley-on-Thames, and like most other SOE agents he did his parachute training at RAF Ringway near Manchester. Special training was conducted at the SOE facility at Milton Hall outside Peterborough as well as other locations in Scotland, England and North Africa.

For their final preparations, the team had gone to Algiers where they were accommodated in a former French officer training facility, set in a nectarine orchard. To round off their training Smallwood led his team on a 104-kilometre walk through the mountains in the Algerian summer.

As the mission drew closer, the Jeds learned about the topography of the target area. At the special operations HQ they met the female wireless officers, whose job it was to remain in contact with the agents. Plans were delayed for reasons unknown to the team members who were 'champing at the bit', but eventually they passed through the busy Blida aerodrome.

As the American B-24 Liberator crossed over the coast of France on the night of 13/14 August, some distant flak was encountered and the team was dropped from a great height, slightly off target, among the lavender bushes. The radioman was equipped with two radio sets as they could be easily damaged during the landing. Other equipment carried by Bailey included a sidearm and an American M-2 folding-stock carbine. Standard British battledress was worn with no insignia. In training, the men had been told that if someone was arrested, they should try to hold out for forty-eight hours to allow the others to take evasive action. Bailey didn't allow himself to think of such an eventuality.

At the industrious Drop Zone *Armature*, near La Garde d'Apt, the parachutists were first met by a Spaniard who had not one word of French, causing the Allied operators to wonder if they had not been dropped into the wrong country. It seems that the Maquis were interested only in collecting the supplies, which were scattered over a wide area, and would not have tolerated any interference with the running of their operations. Bailey griped that the Maquis were unreliable and never showed up on time for meetings, while Captain Smallwood referred to them as the 'Third Eleven', the implication being that the first two teams had been wiped out.[6]

The visitors were taken to the village of Sault to meet the leader of the Resistance in the Mont Ventoux area, Commandant Beyne and his assistant, Max Fischer. Undoubtedly, they would have come across *Archiduc* and Major John Goldsmith, who was the SOE advisor in this area. Together with two companies of Maquis, they were assigned to cover the right or northern bank of the Durance River. This was a sector which would lie in the path of the retreating Germans, and team CITROËN would be ideally placed to act as scouts for the American forces.

Installed in a farmhouse at La Bastide-des-Jourdans, midway between Manosque and Pertuis close to the border with the Var, CITROËN waited for news of the invasion. After a few days, the command post was moved to an empty house next to the police station in Pertuis where they remained until the Americans arrived on 20 August, five days after the landings. Bailey mentions that a few demoralized Germans were locked in the cells of the police station while the crowd outside was baying for their blood. One German officer asked that he be shot rather than be handed over to the mob. Smallwood alluded to an incident where he authorized the execution of three German hostages when requested to do so by a Maquis leader. 'And so I made myself a war criminal,' he admitted.[7]

When the Americans entered the town, they were plied with alcohol, as always, but as far as Bailey was concerned they were already drunk, and ready to shoot anyone. As a radio operator, Bailey was considered too valuable to risk going into combat. He remained at the command post transmitting messages which mainly concerned enemy troop movements. The other two, together with the Maquis, were involved in some skirmishes. Scouting ahead, Captain John Smallwood and his men entered Avignon an hour before the Americans. Stopping only for lunch, they pushed on a little too hastily and ran into an ambush at Courthézon, not far from Châteauneuf-du-Pape, the renowned wine estate in the Côtes du Rhône wine region.

During the advance, these irregular troops would simply phone ahead to the next village to find out if there was an enemy presence there, but as Smallwood patrolled out of Pertuis to Cadenet in his Citroën motor vehicle, with his loyal Russian-German bodyguard riding shotgun on the mudguard, they ran into an armoured German rearguard blocking the road. The sequence of events is confused, but it seems that as the tanks came rumbling down the street, the Jeds beat a hasty retreat; then a leader of the Pertuis resistance, Gilbert Gay, climbed onto one of the Tiger tanks and slipped a 'Gammon' grenade through the visor, killing the entire crew. Shortly after getting back to Pertuis, Smallwood and an American colonel found Gilbert Gay at the Bar de la Poste. The colonel unpinned his decorations from his own jacket and awarded them to the *maquisard*.[8] Both he and Smallwood would later be formally recognized with a Croix de Guerre. In an interview recorded in 1990, Smallwood mentioned nothing about this incident. 'I have very little to say about operations there,' he stated, 'very little happened.'[9]

*

Jedburgh Team NOVOCAINE was inserted at Seyne-les-Alpes on the night of 6/7 August 1944 and was working with 150 young and hardy *maquisards*, mostly controlling roadblocks and mountain outposts. Many were mountaineers and proficient skiers, wearing the floppy berets of the Chasseurs Alpins, a unit which was formed in the eighteenth century to guard the pass against an Italian invasion. As fit as the Jedburghs might have been, they could not always keep pace with the *chasseurs* on the march. While safely camped at Vallouise, they operated on the road between Briançon and the Montgenèvre Pass in order to prevent the enemy from escaping into Italy. Ultimately, they set their sights on liberating Briançon.

OG NANCY, consisting entirely of Italian Americans, fifteen men in all, arrived in Provence on 13 August 1944. Although they landed at DZ *Armature* near La Garde d'Apt and Saint-Christol, about twenty-five kilometres to the northeast of the town of Apt in the Vaucluse Department, their ultimate destination was Briançon, 400 kilometres to the northeast in the Alps, on the French–Italian border in the vicinity of the Montgenèvre Pass. Most of the members of NANCY suffered cuts and bruises from the rough landing, but nothing serious. The reception committee consisted of only a few *maquisards* and they had made no provision for moving the equipment. Somehow, almost all of the OG's rations disappeared at this stage. For a day or two the team remained in the Maquis camp where some downed US airmen were awaiting extraction.

After a little haggling with the Maquis, the OG, with three guides, set off at night in a wood-burning truck, sleeping bags and rucksacks lining the sides while the men crowded in the centre prepared to fire through cracks. It was a highly uncomfortable, but at the same time exciting trip. At first flat tyres and lost guides jinxed them, but the truck continued on, often along main roads under the noses of German patrols and garrisons, without being stopped. At Sisteron, the guides bribed the local gendarmes to let them cross the Durance. From there to Guillestre it became a parade of wine and roses. It was D-Day (15 August 1944) and the radio was calling upon southern France to rise up and oust the Germans. The presence of fifteen Americans this far north a few hours after the invasion created a tremendous impression. At Seyne, they unexpectedly met Christine Granville, and, according to the leader of the OG, Captain Arnold Lorbeer, 'the stories of her womanly charms had not been exaggerated'.[10]

Early on in their mission, NANCY was joined by thirty gendarmes who had deserted from the German garrison at Briançon. Instead of heading for Vallouise, where the other special operations teams had congregated, they then headed farther east to Cervières at the foot of the Col-d'Izoard, which features regularly on the route of the Tour de France and Giro d'Italia. From this base, the OG carried out a few uneventful operations with partisans on the Italian side of the border. Arnold Lorbeer had the distinction of leading a second mission – OG SPOKANE – which parachuted into the Italian Alps in March 1945. Operational group NANCY and other special operations in the Hautes-Alpes will again come to the fore apropos the liberation of Gap and Briançon.

*

Just as the Vercors uprising was being snuffed out, another operational group was infiltrating 160 kilometres to the north. On 1 August 1944, OG UNION II parachuted into Les Saisies between Lake Annecy and Mont Blanc in the Haute-Savoie. The team consisted of John Coolidge, a captain with the Army Air Corps, and five US marines under Major Peter Ortiz. A Free French officer, Joseph 'Jo-Jo' Arcelin, accompanied the team, and had papers identifying him as a US marine although he spoke not a word of English. On this his second mission to France, Ortiz was tasked with preventing the enemy from destroying key installations in the aftermath of the landings.[11]

Each member of UNION II was in a different aircraft when the seventy-eight B-17s took off from England carrying supplies for the Maquis. One parachutist, Sergeant Charles R. Perry USMC from Needham, Massachusetts, plummeted to the ground when his parachute malfunctioned. Gunnery Sergeant Robert La Salle was also injured and took no farther part in the mission. When jumping from 120 metres, there is no time to open one's reserve 'chute.

At the burial the next day, Ortiz wore full service dress with all his ribbons, and even the *maquisards* under the command of Jean Bulle were smartly turned out. Local women made an American flag to be placed with the body. In the middle of the drop zone, already littered with discarded supply containers, the grave was covered with stones and flowers, and neatly fenced with newly made pine railings. A massive cross made of pine logs, squared in the Alpine style, stood at the head. Perry's mother decided to leave her son's body where it was, with the promise that the site would be taken care of by the people of France in perpetuity, but he now rests in the Rhône American Cemetery in Draguignan.

Having trained the Maquis in the use of their newly acquired weapons, UNION II moved south to the town of Centron where, by mischance, they ran into a convoy carrying several hundred German troops. Under a hail of bullets, the members became separated. As Ortiz and two others, Jack Risler and John Bodnar, fought from house to house, the villagers implored them to give themselves up to avoid the annihilation of their town. Well aware of what had happened at the Vercors a few weeks previously, Ortiz decided to surrender on condition that the civilians be left unharmed. (Ortiz spoke German, as well as French and Arabic.) In one fabulous account, an old Frenchwoman tried to shield him with her body, but he gently pushed her aside and walked toward the enemy holding a white flag, with bullets kicking up dust at his feet.[12]

Born to an American mother and French father, but with Spanish roots, Pierre Julien Ortiz grew up in southern California, and, craving adventure, served five years in the French Foreign Legion, attaining the rank of sergeant. By the time the United States entered the Second World War, Ortiz had fought for France against the invading Germans in 1940, and had spent time in a German PoW camp, but managed to get back to the United States. On enlisting in the US Marines, his instructors soon realized that this was no ordinary recruit, due to extent of his knowledge of military matters and language skills, not to mention the medals he already wore on his chest. He was given a commission and sent to parachute training although he had already made 154 jumps with the Legion.

With his experience in the Legion, Ortiz was ideally qualified to operate behind enemy lines in North Africa, and was first deployed in Tunisia where he worked in cooperation with the SOE. In January 1944 he parachuted into the Haute-Savoie region of southeastern France as part of Special Operations mission UNION. Legend has it that on this operation Ortiz overheard a group of German officers in a café in Lyon badmouthing either him or the Marine Corps, or the United States. In one version, he left the place and then came back in his Marine Corps uniform, dispatching them with a brace of .45 Colt automatic pistols. Another version of the story has it that, at gunpoint, the Germans were made to drink a toast to the President of the United States and to the Marine Corps but were left otherwise unmolested.[13] The story is made more plausible when linked to the rumour that Ortiz 'practically lived on Benzedrine'.[14]

When Ortiz laid down his weapons in Centron, he had no illusions about his chances of survival, but it seems that the Germans were impressed to discover that their battalion had been held off by only three Americans, and treated them as prisoners of war and not as spies. Back in California after the war, Ortiz acted in a few films while continuing to serve in the military until reaching retirement with the rank of lieutenant colonel. In addition to two Navy Crosses and two Purple Hearts, he had an assortment of French decorations plus a British OBE. At his funeral at Arlington Cemetery in 1988, there were representatives of the British and French governments present. On the fiftieth anniversary of the events in Alpine village of Centron, the town square was renamed Place du Colonel Peter Ortiz in an impressive ceremony. In attendance were former members of the local Maquis, and former members of UNION II, as well as Mrs Ortiz and their son, Colonel Peter Ortiz (Jnr) USMC.

*

During the liberation celebration at Digne, both Francis Cammaerts and Xan Fielding, freed from Gestapo headquarters only three days before, revisited the scene of their brush with death. In nearby Sisteron, Cammaerts and Christine Granville paid a visit to Brigadier General Frederick B. Butler's headquarters but received a frosty reception – possibly because of their dishevelled appearance. Cammaerts offered to provide information regarding the dispositions of FFI fighters in the hills to the north, and to liaise with them. Without even taking his eyes off the map on the wall, Butler replied: 'I'm not in the least bit interested in private armies or bandits.'[15] At the US Seventh Army headquarters, on the other hand, Cammaerts was received with courtesy, and Lieutenant General Alexander 'Sandy' Patch assigned him to de Lattre's Army B, west of the Rhône. Christine Granville went off to Italy to work with the Polish PoWs there.

On the same night that the CITROËN team landed in the Vaucluse, Jedburgh team CINNAMON parachuted into DZ *Fantôme* near Brue-Auriac in the Var Department. Robert Boiteux of the GARDENER circuit was on the ground to welcome the one British and two French members but found that two of them had broken limbs. A French doctor at first refused to treat them, pleading that the Germans would shoot him. Boiteux took out his gun and said, 'Either you get shot later or I shoot you right now.'[16] One of the Jeds did link up with the Maquis of Saint-Jean-du-Puy near Trets – between Aix-en-Provence and Brignoles – but the scope of this mission has been described as 'minor'.

A similar fate befell Jedburgh Team SCEPTER which consisted of two Americans, Lieutenant Walter C. Hannah and radio operator, Master Sergeant Howard Palmer, led by Captain François Franceschi. Landing on DZ *Prisonnier* at La Roque Esclapon, twenty kilometres northeast of Draguignan, the plan was to join up with the Organization de Résistance de l'Armée (ORA), in the Alpes-Maritimes. However, there was no reception committee, Palmer sprained his knee and the captain broke a leg. Their mission thwarted, the team holed up in the village of Mons. Although by road the closest village to the DZ, apart from La Roque Esclapon itself, is Comps-sur-Artuby, the village of Mons was closer to all the action and could be reached on rough tracks.

DZ *Prisonnier* was better suited for supply drops than human cargo because it is a small rock-covered plateau bordered on one side by a sharp precipice and on the other by a high cliff. Although the name La Roque Esclapon comes from *La roche éclatée*, which means shattered or exploded rock, the village of this name is situated in a lush, pasture-covered basin, given over to dairy farming. The actual drop zone was situated on the valley rim, on the mountain known as Mont du Malay at an altitude of about 1,400 metres. It was a busy place in the days and nights leading up to the invasion.

Jedburgh team MONOCLE, which landed at DZ *Armature* in the Vaucluse on the night of 13/14 August 1944, did not sit around waiting for the US Army to arrive. Lieutenant Ray Foster and Sergeant Robert, both from Minneapolis, were caught up in a plan to try and free Major Cyrus Manierre of team DODGE who had been stopped in a Milice roadblock on 3 August near Grenoble while still wearing his US Army dogtags. Ultimately, team MONOCLE did not get involved but the Resistance did mount an unsuccessful attack on the prison in Lyon. When he was handed over to the Germans Manierre managed to convince them that he was a downed airman, and they sent him to Stalug Luft I, a PoW camp for the air forces. Although at first they did not recognize each other, Cyrus's brother, Bill, also happened to be in Stalug Luft I, and the Germans made a big thing of reuniting the two brothers.

*

Indeed, the OSS OG JUSTINE had arrived on the Vercors at the end of June, but most other OGs dispatched to the south in August arrived too late to make any real impact. Nevertheless, it made a huge impression on the enemy when they realized that they were now being harassed, not only by ragtag *maquisards*, but also by American commandos in full uniform. Mission RUTH was the only OG which landed directly in the invasion zone – at DZ *Prisonnier*. Landing on 4 August 1944, two members were injured and had to be left in the care of the locals.

In addition to strengthening the Resistance and transmitting intelligence to Algiers, mission RUTH was to prevent the movement of the enemy along the Route de Napoléon between the coast and Sisteron on the River Durance. Their area of operations would therefore be around Gap, Sisteron and Digne-les-Bains in the Alpes-de-Haute-Provence and northern Var. It was a two-day trek from the DZ to the Maquis camp at Saint-Jurs, a short distance north of the touristic village of Moustiers-Saint-Marie. Carrying their heavy equipment, the group followed a rugged cross-country route during the day and stuck to the roads at night.

On their backs, the men carried the following items: carbine with ammunition, canteen, toilet paper, sewing kit, .45 pistol with three magazines, packet of salt or salt pills, two pairs of socks, pocket knife, matches in waterproof case, gloves (optional), six grenades, medical kit, athletic supporter, notebook and ever-sharp pencil, razor, soap, towel, toothbrush, toothpowder, comb, cigarettes, sleeping bag, entrenching tool, two rolls tape, nine pounds of prepared charges, gasmask and container, grease paint, watch, compass, rations, cough drops, field cap, escape kit and flashlight.[17]

The Americans could not help but notice the scarcity of food and coffee, although alcohol seemed to be plentiful. A bottle or two of wine typically turned up at meal times, be it breakfast, lunch or dinner. From time to time special operations teams would receive a supply drop containing such treats as powdered coffee and chocolate, or, even more importantly, mail. Milk was obtainable but had to be boiled before use. Water was also not always safe to drink, but every village in Provence had a fountain, gravity-fed by a river or a spring, some dating back to Roman times.

Over the next few days, OG RUTH blew up four bridges but SPOC soon decided that this was counterproductive and ordered them to concentrate on ambushes. Lieutenant Carl Strand therefore moved with four men into the Les Mées area, west of Digne, while Lieutenant Mills Brandes took the others to set up ambushes along the Route de Napoléon. In his observations of the American 'commandos', one *maquisard* from Saint-Jurs scoffed: 'They had nothing to do because everything had been demolished that deserved to be. For a long time, they were living in their three tents, 500 metres from us, in what was a small holiday camp.'[18]

*

Captain Geoffrey Jones (*York*) and Capitaine de Corvette Leon-Pierre Allain (*Lougre*) parachuted into DZ *Prisonnier* at La Roque Esclapon, in the early hours of 11 August 1944. Both were injured on landing in a ravine. Jones gashed his left leg and was badly bruised. Allain mangled his right ankle and had to be injected with morphine and carried out on the back of a mule. Allain's mission had been to take charge of the anti-sabotage teams at Toulon but because of his injury he decided to team up with Jones. In any event, all the action was happening around them.

Being a Special Operations operative as opposed to regular OSS, Jones was not in uniform; he wore an old blue suit to blend in with locals, grew his hair long with a substantial moustache, and generally looked scruffy. His identity card said that he was a mute, suited only for farm labour and had therefore been exempted from military service. SPOC almost decided not to send him because he knew too much about the planned invasion and his capture would have been disastrous. Before he joined the OSS, Jones had been attached to an airborne field artillery unit and since June had been training and organizing recruits at Blida airfield near Algiers. Shortly before he left for France, he was promoted to captain to give him more influence. Originally, his mission was to lend his artillery expertise to the Maquis on the Vercors plateau, but fortunately for him, it was cancelled. His new mission was to destroy the radar station at Cap Dramont. Having spent part of his youth in Fréjus, he would have known the area well. As it turned out, he did not get to Dramont in time, but rather devoted his energies to the clearing of the glider landing zones.

Essentially, Geoffrey Jones had been sent to France as a replacement for Jean Maurice Muthular d'Errecalde (*Lucas*), an OSS agent who, as we will see, was arrested in Saint-Tropez and executed together with François Pelletier of the BCRA. In fact, the two were still alive and in captivity when Jones arrived on French soil but SPOC would not learn about their death until after the liberation. Nevertheless, when d'Errecalde failed to return to Algiers as planned, SPOC decided to send the 24-year-old Geoffrey Jones.

*

Half a dozen Jedburgh teams and operational groups had been dropped into the invasion zone during August but by the middle of September 1944, they and all other special operations in southeastern France had

128

been withdrawn to Grenoble which became a sort of international HQ. In the cafés where the Jedburgh teams congregated and mingled with the public, politics was the main topic of conversation. The progress of the war was not as important to them as who would govern now that the Germans were gone. For some, the Vichy period was now a source of embarrassment, although others have said that the transition happened quite naturally with no embarrassment. Overnight, the marshal's portrait was taken down and replaced with that of General de Gaulle. It was like turning the page of a book to proceed with the next chapter.

With no war left to fight, the men and women of the SOE and OSS were at a loose end. Wherever two or three of these 'human time bombs' were gathered together after their deactivation, they would be looking for a fight. Whether it was for the enjoyment, or over some perceived insult from a competing group, they threw themselves into any scrap which broke out between soldiers. One by one, or team by team, operators trickled into Paris and then back to Milton Hall, their original depot. Having lost their sense of purpose, many of these adrenaline addicts ran wild or sank into depression and obscurity, but most agreed that their war had been fun. Some, whose killer instinct had been properly awakened, continued to ply their trade in the Far East.

In Lyon, a dinner was held at a long table in a restaurant. One extra place-setting and an empty chair represented absent comrades. Some now took on the task of finding out what had happened to those colleagues who had vanished into the night and fog. The SOE sent 470 men and women to France, and 118 of them did not return. Approximately 265 Jedburgs were deployed to France, fifteen were killed in action or died of wounds, two were killed in parachute malfunctions and one was killed by a *maquisard's* accidental discharge.[19] Among the 355 members of OSS operational groups in France, ten were killed, forty wounded and four were missing or captured.

Chapter 9

Courage

One needs look no farther than the Rhône American Cemetery in Draguignan, where countless names of air force personnel are inscribed on panels dedicated to the missing, and on the white crosses, row upon row, to see that this was an air war as much as any other kind. Building up to the invasion, there were 5,000 Allied planes based in the Mediterranean Theatre, including 3,000 flying from Corsica and Sardinia, mostly belonging to the American Twelfth and Fifteenth Air Forces. From their bases in Italy, Mediterranean Allied Air Forces (MAAF) flew bombing missions over southern France, targeting transport infrastructure to isolate the invasion zone. Bridges over the River Rhône at Arles, Avignon and Tarascon were a priority, and Toulon harbour was hit with monotonous regularity.

Bombs went astray, and on 27 May 1944, 525 civilians were killed in Avignon by American bombs. Fortunately, the ruins of the ancient Pont d'Avignon, made famous by the children's song, came to no harm. The city's beautiful boulevards, however, were piles of rubble, and families had to squeeze together to make room for distant cousins whose homes had been vaporized. People could not understand why the Allies were so relentless and wondered why the Tarascon Bridge, destroyed on 12 August, was so hard to hit.

During this period of intensive bombing of the infrastructure in the Rhône Valley, members of OG ALICE, based in the Drôme, happened to see American bombers accidently destroy a part of the town of Crest, killing thirty-eight civilians and wounding a hundred others. Three American planes were supposedly seen to be hit by ground fire but the crews were snatched to safety by the Maquis. The two officers in charge of the OG went into the town, visited the hospital and explained that the bombing was a mistake, which supposedly helped to quell ill feelings.

Most of the later bombing was done by the four-engined B-24 Liberator or 'Liberaider', as it was fondly called. Daytime reconnaissance missions were flown by the twin-hull Lockheed P-38 and F-5 Lightnings. The Mustang P-51 fighters did escort duties, and later provided close support for the troops on the ground. The dangers which they faced came from flak batteries along the coast as well as the Luftwaffe fighter groups which would be scrambled to intercept the raiders, and in the earlier years they posed a formidable threat.

At one time, the Luftwaffe occupied almost all of the civil and military aerodromes on the Côte d'Azur. Not all were operational – some were used for training purposes. Ju 87 'Stuka' pilots learned their dive-bombing techniques at the Base Aéronautique Navale (BAN) Saint-Raphaël. Messerschmitt Bf 109s flew out of Orange, about twenty kilometres north of Avignon. Salon-de-Provence was a base for Heinkel He 111 bombers, and at Aix Les Milles was a squadron of Focke-Wulf Fw 190s.

By the time Siegfried Freytag came to be based at Les Milles, near Aix-en-Provence in January 1944, he was Gruppenkommandeur of Jagdgeschwader 77 (JG 77 or Fighter Wing 77) and had shot down almost a hundred Allied aircraft. Having reached the century mark on 13 June 1944, most of his victories were won over Malta, but in the South of France he had little success, possibly because he had recently been shot down and also injured in Italy when his airfield came under attack. In August 1944, the group was based at Orange on the River Rhône, focusing its attention on the invasion of Provence.

As one of Germany's most decorated young fighter aces, Freytag was eventually called to the defence of the Motherland and scored his 102nd and final victory over Holland. When the war came to an end, he was still alive but his whole family had perished. Finding a home in the French Foreign Legion, he served for eighteen years as a foot soldier, retiring with the rank of corporal. His final years were spent at the Domaine du Capitaine Danjou near Puyloubier, a 220-hectare wine estate worked by old or disabled legionnaires. On the back label of their wine bottles is a line from the Legion's code of honour: *Tu n'abandonnes jamais les tiens, ni au combat, ni dans la vie* (You never abandon your own, not in combat, nor in life).

Another top pilot from JG 77, Eduard Isken, shot down seven planes over southern France in July and August 1944, but he was luckier than most of his comrades who would drink themselves silly every day, out of sheer joy of surviving another day. Oberleutnant, or First Lieutenant, Ziegfried 'Wumm' Lemke of JG 2 was one who lived to see the end of the war, by which time he had flown 325 combat missions and racked up seventy victories, including twenty-five Spitfires, eight P-47s, six P-51s and numerous bombers. Young and inexperienced Allied pilots stood no chance against seasoned veterans such as these, even when flying the sublime Spitfire.

Ziegfried Lemke had only just been posted to the South of France and had eleven kills to his name, when on 27 January 1944 he added three more. On that chilly morning, eight Spitfires from the 4th Fighter Squadron, 52nd Fighter Group of the US Twelfth Air Force flew a reconnaissance sweep from Calvi, Corsica. About ten kilometres inland from Hyères, they saw two Bf 109s taking off from an airfield at Grande Bastide. Lieutenants Ottaway Cornwell and Harold Beedle dived to attack, leaving two others flying top cover. Unfortunately, they failed to notice two other German aircraft, already airborne, which pounced before the covering Spitfires had a chance to react.

Cornwell and Beedle (both Texans) were seen to crash into the side of a mountain near Pierrefeu-du-Var, while a third pilot, Lyle Kater a 23-year-old from St Louis, Missouri, made a run for home but was shot down over the sea near the Îles d'Hyères. Seventy years later, while looking for mushrooms on a wooded hillside in the Var, an amateur historian stumbled upon the wreckage of a Spitfire, still with its camouflage paintjob, and the skeletal remains of the pilot. The American-made parachute buckles and the frames of the aviator sunglasses suggested that the aircraft belonged to one of the two US fighter squadrons equipped with Spitfires.[1]

Dental records and DNA identified the pilot as First Lieutenant Ottaway Cornwell. The three pilots shot down by Ziegfried Lemke with such ruthless efficiency on 27 January 1944 are remembered on the Tablets of the Missing in Draguignan and Florence. Ottway Cornwell will now have a rosette next his name, indicating that he has been accounted for. Although he had no children, he was married. In August 2018 the relatives, including Ziegfried Lemke's son, were present at an emotional ceremony in the Draguignan Cemetery where the American pilot now rests.

From time to time, when a plane fell from the sky, parachutes would open, but many who went down over the sea were never recovered. After a raid on the U-boat base at Toulon on 29 April 1944, a flak-damaged B-24 of the 450th Bomb Group, piloted by Oscar J. Anderson, ditched seventy-five miles off the coast of Provence. All ten crewmembers made it into the two life rafts but the navigator, Lieutenant Preston McKart, had broken his back and died slowly. It was traumatic for the other crewmembers when they tipped him overboard but they did what they could to make it a dignified send-off. They drifted for three days before being rescued by a German floatplane. The injured were treated at a German hospital in Toulon where Corporal Bill Gernhauser, the ball turret gunner, had his leg amputated.

If one had to choose a place to bale out over occupied Europe, a good option would have been in the mountainous regions of Provence. Not only was there a strong presence of resistance fighters in these backwoods, it was also not too difficult to reach Switzerland, Italy or the Mediterranean. Flyers who were shot down in northern France usually tried to make their way to Spain, travelling by road and rail, putting their trust in their false identity papers and the reliability of their guides or *convoyeurs*. Ordinary people, as well as committed resistants, risked everything to keep the downed airmen out of the clutches of the Germans, although there were still those prepared to betray the presence of an Anglo-American intruder.

Along the coastline it was all but impossible to evade capture. When hit by flak on 25 May 1944 the pilot of a B-24 jammed the controls to steer away from a built-up area, crashing into the parasol pines between Cannes and La Bocca. As the crew floated to earth, they were shot at, but were luckier than the crew of *Lucky Lady* which exploded in a ball of flame over Agay and crashed into the red rocks of the Esterels. The pilot got out alive, but died from burns three months later. On 27 May, a B-24 with a half-naked woman and the name *Miss-I-Hope* painted onto the nose, crashed into the Bay of Agay with the loss of six lives. The wreck is today an attraction for divers.

When an airman made a successful escape from enemy territory, once back at base, he would make an 'Escape Statement' in which French place names were often incorrectly spelled and information regarding the fate of other crewmembers was not always accurate. Thanks to the copious documentation which was generated by both the American and German bureaucracy following the shooting-down or disappearance of an aircraft, the survival experiences of aircrews on the run in Provence can be pieced together.

On the day of the terrible civilian casualties in southern France, 27 May 1944, a B-24 Liberator of 461st Bombardment Group, Fifteenth Air Force, took off from Torretta airfield in Italy bound for Salon-de-Provence. As it crossed the coastline at Antibes, it was hit by flak, knocking out two engines. After jettisoning the bombs, the pilot, Lieutenant Gerald J. Maroney of the Bronx, New York, headed for Switzerland but abandoned that plan when the entire right wing caught fire and the plane started to rapidly lose altitude. First the navigator and gunners baled out, then the bombardier and co-pilot. The captain remained in his seat until all the crew were clear. By the time he baled, the plane was 400 feet above the ground; he landed twenty metres from wreckage which was found on the mountain at Aiglun twenty kilometres north of Grasse near the remote hamlets of Le Mas and Les Sausses in the Alpes-Maritimes.[2]

The German report on the incident stated that 'the entire area is full of terrorists' which meant that the chances of a downed Allied pilot making it home after baling out over the hills north of Grasse were extremely favourable. Three crewmembers had been injured and were captured immediately. A fourth, Benjamin Norrid, was rescued by the FFI but their camp at Puget-Thénier, northeast of Castellane, was attacked on 25 July and he too became a PoW. The remaining six split up and made good their escape.

The co-pilot, Lieutenant (later Captain) Winston Lawrence, was assisted by a British agent and was able to keep in permanent contact with Algiers. He was also able to make contact with the rest of the crew, who hid out in the village of Les Sausses, near Saint-Jeannet on the River Var, where they were looked after by a Joseph Pommier for three months. On their departure, the men gave Monsieur Pommier a signed chit to enable him to claim for their keep for eighty-nine days. After hearing about the landings in the Department of the Var, on 21 August, Winston Lawrence assembled everyone and they made their way without incident to Saint-Tropez.[3]

Lieutenant Earl Rodenburg, the co-pilot of a B-17, baled out over the Southern Alps on 26 May 1944 when a fire broke out on board. Two other members of this crew also baled out. One was killed as a result of his parachute getting tangled while the other met up with Italian partisans and a British special operations team. It transpires that the pilot flew the plane, named *Bataan Avenger*, to Corsica with his head out of the window as he couldn't see through the smoke, and only after landing discovered that some of the crew had stayed with the plane. Rodenburg landed on a steep hillside near Breil-sur-Roya, inland from Menton, and was immediately picked up by woodcutters.

For two weeks Rodenburg was hidden by the manager of a restaurant at the railway station, Georgette Rosa, who then placed him in the hands of the Maquis. Guided first to Nice and then north into the Basses-Alpes, contact was made with other downed airmen, including Winston Lawrence who mentioned it in his missing aircrew report. Three months later, the Maquis camp near Castellane was attacked and Rodenburg was captured.[4]

An epic aerial battle took place over Provence on 12 July 1944 when a total of 499 bombers and 114 escorts were sent to bomb rail yards and bridges across southern France. Particularly hard hit was the 767th Squadron of the 461st Bomb Group based at Toretta in southern Italy. Their target that day was Nîmes station. Cover was provided by nineteen Lightning P-38 dual-fuselage fighters and twelve Mustang P-51 fighters. Ready to intercept them was a score of Messerschmitt Bf 109s and a half-dozen Messerschmitt Bf 110 twin-engined fighter-bombers.

The first of six B-24s to be shot down or badly damaged over Provence on the morning of 12 July 1944 was piloted by Lieutenant Robert Sanders. Near Bras, en route to Nîmes, the plane was attacked by two Bf 109s, probably from Jagdgruppe 200 (Fighter Group 200) based at Aix-en-Provence. Fires started on the flight deck and in bomb bays of the aircraft. Alarm bells went off and the order to bale out was heard over interphone. Sanders baled out through the nose wheel door about fifteen seconds before the plane exploded and crashed about ten kilometres south east of 'Seillons' (Seillons-Source-d'Argens near Brignoles). The plane was seen to hit the side of a mountain, 150 metres from the 'highway' suggesting that this was probably the main RN 7. According to local sources, the exact location of the wreck was at Saint-Martin des Pallières in the Saint-Maximin district.[5]

A German patrol on the highway immediately started pursuing. Sanders ran up the mountain and concealed himself in a thicket from where he watched the Germans pick up the parachute harness and Mae West. Continuing over the mountain, he encountered two Frenchmen who took him to small stream in a nearby wood. They advised him to remain there while they fetched bread, ham, tea, wine and some very strong white liquor, as well as civilian clothing and a revolver. Later that night, Sanders was taken further through the mountains to join up with three other members of his crew. The French people reported that they buried three men from the front section of plane: one was identified as Second Lieutenant W. J. Graham, the navigator, and the other two were believed to be the pilot, First Lieutenant Richard Fawcett from Massachusetts, and co-pilot, Second Lieutenant Frank Densted. Sergeant Leonard Johnson from Berkeley, California, was too badly wounded to bale out. He, together with Sergeants Joseph Benetich, and Walter Gladkowski (also from Massachusetts), are now buried in the Rhône American Cemetery in Draguignan.[6]

A second Liberator, was shot down at 10.50 a.m. between Seillons and Ollières, presumably by the same two Messerschmitts which annihilated Sanders's plane. Although the B-24 disintegrated in the air, the entire crew were seen to bale out. The pilot, Chester A. Ray (Jnr), from Detroit, was badly burned, but he and the tail gunner, Thomas Moss, landed safely and were cared for by the locals until they could be evacuated from Apt. According to local sources, some American airmen were hidden in the wine cellar of the cooperative in the village of Bras, about ten kilometres from the crash site.[7]

Three badly injured crewmembers landed on the domaine de Boulon, less than a kilometre south of the RN 7. A doctor attended to them but their injuries were severe, and at their request they were transported to Saint-Maximin and placed in the care of the Germans. Second Lieutenant Merrill Spring of East Aurora in upstate New York later died in captivity despite his father having received a letter from him in a PoW camp saying that he had had a foot amputated but was recovering.

Although Chester A. Ray reported that his co-pilot, Lieutenant Richard Dargie, of Saint Malden Massachusetts, was shot on the ground, photographs taken by the Maquis show his battered body wrapped in a parachute as they buried him. It appears that the Bf 109 pilot had machine-gunned him in cold blood while he was in the air. Two other crewmembers, Arnold Ducatman of New York and Arthur Morgan of Dunwoody, Georgia, plummeted to earth with burning parachutes, having been fired at during their descent. Their initial resting place was in the village cemetery at Olliers.[8]

The third B-24 to be shot down that day crashed north of Aix-en-Provence near Pertuis at La Roque-d'Anthéron at 11.05 a.m. The entire crew parachuted safely but some ended up in the hands of the Germans. Then at 11.30 a.m., a fourth plane came down near La Tour-d'Aigues, north of Pertuis in the Luberon. Sergeant Lupe Montana did not bale out, and the pilot, Captain Robert Swanzy, was machine-gunned while descending by parachute. Both were buried in the cemetery at La Tour-d'Aigues and later repatriated to their hometowns in the United States.[9]

To crown it all, an aircraft named *Dwatted Wabbit* piloted by the youngest officer in the group, Lieutenant William A. Barnes (Jnr) from New Jersey, tried to ditch in the sea off Toulon but the entire crew of ten was lost. The fifth and sixth stricken aircraft were badly damaged but managed to make it to Corsica and Spain respectively. This must have been the Luftwaffe's final fling in the South of France because as air raids intensified in the days before the invasion, bomber pilots invariably reported 'no flak, no fighters'.

Thanks to ordinary French men and women, young and old, many of the survivors were soon safely back at their base in Italy. One family in the Var cared for Lieutenant Robert Sanders and three others of his crew in a deserted farmhouse for a total of 24 days, refusing to accept any money. On 5 August, transport was arranged in a civilian wood-burning vehicle to take the four Americans around a hundred kilometres north of Seillons to another camp in mountains, about twenty kilometres east of Apt. Then, at 3 a.m. on 11 August they were taken fifteen kilometres from the camp to a landing strip in a clearing, under the noses of a German garrison in the nearby town. Finally, on 12 August, the escapees, evacuees and other VIPs were flown in a DC-3 (the civilian equivalent of the C-47) with a British crew, back to Italy.

So many downed airmen were gathered at a farm called ferme des Espagnols near La Garde d'Apt awaiting extraction, that they were known as the 'American Maquis'. In their escape statements, the camp commander, identified as 'Pierre Michel', got special mention for supplying food, blankets, tents and cigarettes. This is clearly a reference to Commandant Cammile Rayon whose cover name was Pierre-Michel, and *nom de guerre* or codename *Archiduc*.

Just forty-eight hours previously, one of the forgotten dramas of the war had played out on this very airstrip. On the night of 9/10 August, a Dakota had landed, bringing around a dozen passengers, including Major Michael 'Bing' Crosby of Jedburgh team GRAHAM. Both he and Captain John Smallwood of CITROËN would be on hand for the liberation of Apt, and both would go on to serve with the SOE in Burma. Crosby had been on the training staff of the SOE before his deployment.

Among those scheduled to fly out was John Goldsmith, but as we shall see, he remained in the Mont Ventoux area until September. Another person waiting for extraction was Ronald Midoux who was one of the French marines who had parachuted into Cucuron on 14 June with the three others of mission SAMPAN. Now he was leaving with reams of important information about the coastal defences at Toulon. The invasion was only four days away.[10]

Some of the facts about the mission flown on the night of 9/10 August, known as Operation Nuptial, are confused. Many chroniclers have said that the pilot of the RAF C-47 Dakota was a South African. In fact, the pilot was Flight Lieutenant Bryan Rostron, and perhaps the confusion arose because he had gone to flight school in Southern Rhodesia and then learned his excellent navigation skills in South Africa. Some credit must go to the American co-pilot who was something of a legend – Flight Lieutenant James McCairns. Now based at Bari in Italy, 267 Squadron was involved in special operations across Europe, and on this occasion the point of departure was a small airfield at Cecina near Livorno. The perspective from the air is always different from that on the ground, and Rostron's long-lost memoirs are illuminating.

All went well as Rostron reached the coast and crossed the River Durance, identifying the area of the landing strip without any problem. After flashing the recognition signal with an Aldis lamp for about ten minutes without any response from the ground, the pilot began to wonder what had gone wrong. Reducing power as much as he dared, to conserve fuel, Roston circled slowly for almost an hour. It was a very clear night and he could see a German airfield in the distance toward Orange with aircraft taking off and landing, oblivious of the intruder's presence.

Headlights were eventually seen further up the mountain flashing the correct recognition signal. The reception party then marked out the strip with hand-held torches in the form of an 'L'. The Dakota landed along the leg of the 'L' toward the base of the 'L' and stopped very quickly. It was subsequently found that the strip was just '1,000 yards long and consisted of 200 yards of ploughed field, 400 yards of stubble and 400 yards of lavender bushes – not the best surface for an airfield'. To add to the problems, beyond the lavender bushes was a small wood over which they would have to fly on takeoff.[11]

The C-47 Dakota usually carried about twenty paratroopers with all their gear, and waiting on the ground were 31 American airmen hoping for a flight to freedom. For obvious reasons they didn't have any luggage so Rostron decided to try to take them all, although the surface of the strip and the height of the airfield, which meant slightly reduced power from the engines, made takeoff risky. Rostron explains: 'I went right to the end of the strip, put on full takeoff power against the brakes and a little bit of flap, released the brakes and set off along the strip. When we hit the lavender the aircraft slowed appreciably and it was obvious that we would have to be going much faster when we came to the bushes if we were going to get off.'[12]

Takeoff was aborted and the Dakota returned to the end of the strip where the passengers were told that he would try again with eight less. To their credit, the eight most senior officers got off the plane and, although he had no authority to say so, Rostron promised that he would return the following night, provided they reached Italy safely. This time the plane reached flying speed before it hit the lavender and left the ground with about a hundred yards to spare, just clipping the tops of the trees.

On arriving back at Cecina just as dawn was breaking, Rostron remembers someone taking a photograph of the escapees who were dressed in the 'most weird and wonderful clothes, mostly looking like scarecrows'. The Americans were most effusive in their thanks and the thing that had impressed them most of all was that 'we had been able to find the strip in the middle of nowhere in the middle of the night – I don't think navigation was a strongpoint in the American Air Force'[13]

True to his promise, and without asking permission, Rostron returned the following night. The Maquis were much impressed by the pilot's commitment but could not keep their rendezvous because the enemy was now alerted. From Rostron's point of view, the warning bell was the dead-straight flare path, all the lights equidistant and the same intensity: 'Obviously the Germans had heard us the night before and laid a trap, but with usual Teutonic thoroughness, had overdone the effect – no underground flare path would have been as bright or straight as that, so we put down our nose and went home as quickly as we could.'[14]

In the early days, if a lone aircraft was heard in the night sky over France, it was likely to be the RAF on a covert mission flown from Tangmere airfield near Portsmouth in England. As the war went on, these operations started from Blida in Algeria as well as from Italy and Corsica. The RAF used Wellingtons, Halifaxes and Whitleys for dropping supplies and personnel although many SOE agents were flown in by Lysander, a light aircraft which could land just about anywhere. From January 1944, the load was shared by the 801st Bomb Group of the US Eighth Air Force. Dubbed the 'Carpetbaggers' after the codename of their first mission, some called it the air arm of the OSS.

Using B-24 long-range bombers which had been specially modified and painted with a glossy black anti-searchlight paint, the Carpetbaggers flew thousands of missions over occupied Europe. Agents being inserted or extracted, whether male or female, were always referred to as 'Joes'. Parachutists exited from a hole in the fuselage where the bottom machine-gun turret was normally found, and the hole from which they dropped was called the 'Joe hole'.

*

Among the air forces using the island of Corsica as an immovable aircraft carrier, was 2/33 Squadron whose oldest and most famous pilot was Antoine Saint-Exupéry, beter known for being the aristocratic author of *The Little Prince*. Although born in Lyon, his mother, the Countess Marie de Saint-Exupéry, lived in Cabri just outside Grasse, between 1934 and 1971. Saint-Ex, as he was known to his friends, was almost as famous for being a pioneering aviator as he was a literary legend. Although his books had not yet made him wealthy, he had moved in high circles in the United States.

On the night of 31 July, two weeks prior to the invasion, he set off on his ninth reconnaissance mission to collect intelligence on German troop movements in and around the Rhône Valley. The P-38 Lightning's guns had been removed to make way for the five automatic cameras. By all accounts Saint-Exupéry was suffering from depression brought about by a multitude of problems, including physical pain from a dozen plane crashes, marital issues and financial woes. Now he was considered unfit to fly and was about to lose his wings. As Saint-Exupéry crossed the sea, he would have known this was almost certainly his last military mission. At about 9.30 a.m. he crossed the French coastline. He was never heard of again. Word of his disappearance made international headlines, and quickly spread across the literary world that 'Ex' or 'Tonio' as he was known, had been recorded as 'Pilot did not return, presumed lost'.[15]

Many theories have been advanced about what caused the crash. Some have postulated that it was a political assassination because he was intensely disliked by General Charles de Gaulle who, in a speech, implied that Saint-Exupéry was a collaborator with the Vichy regime. A German pilot – Horst Rippert, an experienced pilot with Jagdgruppe 200 – claimed to have shot him down, although there is no official record of this. According to Rippert, he heard almost immediately on American radio frequencies that Saint-Exupéry was missing, and he decided to keep quiet about it.[16] Many of Jagdgruppe 200's actions took place over the sea, and aircraft they shot down fell into the 'drink', but the pilots could still be heard calling their victories in over the radio. Afterward they filed claims, had them accredited, and those records survive. Then in 1998, a fisherman's net snagged an identity bracelet on the sea floor near the island of Riou, south of Marseille, engraved with the names of Saint-Exupéry and his wife, Consuelo. Subsequently, divers have found the wreck of what is almost certainly the aircraft Saint Exupéry flew. No bullet holes were found, and the wreckage suggested an almost vertical crash at about 500 miles an hour. The preferred hypothesis at the time was oxygen-supply failure, but suicide is now at the top of the list of possible explanations.[17]

Countess Marie Saint-Exupéry, Antoine's 69-year-old mother did not hear of her son's disappearance until two weeks later. Her family kept the news from her and it was only when she went into Grasse to see an old friend that people came up to offer her words of comfort. The countess had last seen her son before he went to America in 1940 and his escapades had brought her much worry over the years. 'Don't give up hope, my poor Marie,' said the friend who heard the news on the radio. 'Maybe Antoine's been injured or taken prisoner, anything is possible you know, we mustn't despair,' the friend continued. But a mother's intuition is powerful.[18]

All over Provence there are streets, schools and hotels named after Saint-Exupéry – as is the airport in Lyon. He is the subject of numerous films in multiple languages. In his mother's hometown of Cabris, images and figurines of 'The Little Prince' are everywhere to be seen. *The Little Prince* has been translated into more than 250 languages and is one of the best-selling books of all time.

Because one of his books, *Pilote de Guerre* or *Flight to Arras* in the English version, about the German invasion of France, was published in

France during the time of the Occupation, Saint-Exupéry incurred the wrath of de Gaulle. Ironically, the book was banned by the Vichy regime because one or two sentences were deemed to be offensive to their German masters. An underground version of the book was published in Lyon in 1943. Other writers refused to publish during the Occupation because it might seem to be an act of collaboration.

On the subject of writer-pilots, mention must be made of Joseph Kessel, one of the most famous of all French writers. Many of his novels were translated into English and more than a dozen made into film. The Prix Joseph Kessel is a literature prize, given to 'a book of a high literary value written in French'. Although he was born in Argentina, Kessel was schooled in Nice, and after extensive travels as a journalist, he made Toulon his home. In 1942 he was active in the Resistance as a member of the CARTE network on the Côte d'Azur. When things got too hot he and his nephew, Maurice Duron, crossed the Pyrenees to get to England. Sitting in a pub in England, Kessel wrote the French lyrics, from the original Russian, for the 'Chant des Partisans' which would become the anthem or call-to-arms of the French Resistance.

Kessel had also been a pilot in the Great War, and won the Croix de Guerre in both world wars. Now in his mid-forties, he was accepted into de Gaulle's Forces Aériennes Françaises Libres as a member of 342 Squadron of the Royal Air Force. The 'Lorraine' Squadron, as it was known, was made up of French nationals, one of whom was Romain Gary, another renowned and enigmatic novelist. Life was not easy for a Russian-Polish Jew, but in the late 1930s he and his doting mother moved to Nice where Romain Kacew, as he was then, made French his first language and began writing. After the liberation, Romain Gary returned to Nice but found that his mother had been dead for three years, and the letters which he had been receiving had all been written during her illness and posted after her death.

Gary is one of the elite few to have been awarded the Croix de Guerre, the Légion d'Honneur and Compagnon de la Libération. Included in the long list of his literary works, under multiple pen names, is the screenplay for *The Longest Day* (1962). Twice he was awarded the prestigious Prix Goncourt for literature, and was celebrated in Hollywood, but typically he was a troubled man. In accordance with his mother's teachings that a man must fight for only three things – a woman, honour and France – Gary challenged Clint Eastwood, whom he accused of having an affair with his wife, to a duel. The Russian was accomplished with sword and pistol, and had it materialized, it would not have been his first duel.

*

As the invasion of southern France drew closer, Allied pilots became increasingly aggressive as they searched for targets of opportunity. None was safe from an attack from the air. A fisherman named Raymond Forneron was fishing off his boat in a cove near Le Lavandou. Suddenly, he heard a roar overhead and looked up to see a wave of Thunderbolts bearing down on him, their five-pointed stars glinting in the sun. With fiendish accuracy they blasted an anti-aircraft battery on the tip of the peninsular at Cap Bénat. Rockets and bullets shrieked and whined, striking the rocks and churning up the water. Raymond saw spurts of water, made by the bullets, making a straight line toward him, punching five holes in his boat. One projectile smashed his right hand: his biggest fear was that he wouldn't be able to play *boules* again. It must be said that in these times, *boules* was a major distraction.[19]

Every day there was an aerial display for the residents of the coastal towns. It seemed that Allied planes were making a sport of bombing the coastal batteries and blockhouses from Agay and Dramont to Les Issambres and Saint-Pons-Les-Mûres near Port Grimaud. The targets, which had been identified by resistants on the ground, and passed on to the air force by Allied agents, were being knocked off one by one.[20]

Despite their thick concrete bunkers, now pockmarked and pitted, the airstrikes caused enough casualties among the German troops to fill the Saint-Tropez hospital to overflowing. Civilians, even pregnant women, were told to make their own arrangements elsewhere. Once it was realized that Saint-Tropez would be at the epicentre of the *débarquement*, the landings, civilians quickly evacuated, taking only important documents and essentials with them.

Civilians continued to be killed and injured and had their homes destroyed throughout Provence right up until D-Day. Their testimonies have a common refrain of loud noise, terror, dust, children crying and emerging from a cellar with terror-filled eyes to find death and destruction all around. On Dragoon D-Day – 15 August, which was a holiday – a large family gathering on a farm near Aix-en-Provence was interrupted in the middle of lunch by bombs falling a few hundred metres away.

Everyone ran inside with plates in hand, after which nobody felt like dessert. One school teacher in Toulon instructed the children to sing 'La Marseillaise' to drown out the sound of distant explosions.[21]

The final softening-up operation – Operation Nutmeg – began on 4 August and continued until 3.30 a.m. on D-Day. On 7 August, 300 planes attacked along a 300-kilometre line from Nice to Montpellier. The next day it was the turn of the Italian Riviera around Imperia to get pounded. On 11 August every radar station on the coast was hit. Enemy airfields were now being regularly raided to prevent their Junkers, Dorniers and Focke-Wulfs from taking off. On the night of 14 August, bombers lit up the coast from the Isles de Hyères to the Esterel heights. There was no air raid siren in Le Lavandou, the church bell did the job, but during August, nobody bothered to ring the bell because the town was in a constant state of alert.

During the months of July and August 1944, all the local newspapers, *Le Petit Var* and *Le Petit Niçois* as well as *Le Provençal* reported bomb damage and warned citizens of Marseille and Toulon to get out of town while it was still possible. On 4 August, '*très violents bombardements*' were reported at Nice and Avignon. On 7 August a number of raids were reported at Toulon, Avignon, Orange, Miramas and Arles. Thirty-eight civilians were reported killed at Avignon on 9 August, and on 15 August *Le Petit Marseillais* mentions thirty-one deaths. Even at this stage, the terms 'enemy aircraft' and 'American aggressions' were used in the Vichy French papers, but their editors would soon change their tune.

During an aerial battle which took place over Provence on 12 August 1944, at least two American fighter pilots came to grief. Lieutenants Langdon Johnson and Joseph Gordon, flying P-51 Mustangs, were escorting the bombers near Toulon when they were hit. Johnson, who had one kill to his name, crashed into the sea and is remembered on the wall for the missing at the Rhône American Cemetery in Draguignan. Joseph Gordon, a New Yorker, is buried at the Epinal American Cemetery. Both these pilots were from the famous unit named after the Tuskegee Army Air Field in Alabama, and which was comprised solely of African-American pilots.[22]

The following day, another Tuskegee airman, Lieutenant Robert O'Neill from Detroit, was strafing targets at La Ciotat when he had a mid-air collision with an enemy fighter over Saint-Jean-du-Puy near Toulon. The American was able to bale out and was picked up by the

Maquis of Trets within an hour of touching the ground. Being black, he was quite a celebrity and was kept safe until the liberation of Toulon two weeks later. On his arrival back in Italy, he was annoyed to find that his squadron colleagues had already 'divvied' up his belongings and were wearing his clothes.

The Tuskegee 'Red Tail' Fighter Group had its share of victories but another one of their number, Alexander Jefferson, also from Detroit, was shot down by ground fire on 14 August on what was his nineteenth mission. Parachuting to safety, he landed in a forest but was picked up by the Germans and spent the rest of the war in PoW camps in Poland and Germany. Having been treated by the Germans like any other Allied officer, Jefferson arrived back in New York in mid-1945 to find racism and segregation alive and well. As he walked down the gangplank in his officer's uniform, a white army sergeant on the dock, called out, 'Whites to the right, niggers to the left.' In another source, the sergeant is said to have used the word 'negro'.[23]

In the final days and hours before the invasion, the Mediterranean Allied Air Forces did their best to disguise their real targets by pounding sites from Genoa, Italy, to well past Marseille. For the flyers themselves, the change in targets simply confirmed that the invasion was imminent. The war diary of the 461st Bombardment Group of the Fifteenth Air Force, based at Toretta airfield near Cerignola in Italy, reveals that on 12 August a deception raid was carried out on gun positions south of Genoa, but on 14 August they switched to the real thing – gun positions near Fréjus.

The Fifteenth Air Force also began dropping leaflets from the water's edge to about seventy kilometres inland proclaiming, 'The front in the South of France is now a reality!' The propaganda provided the troops of the German 19th Army with a wealth of details concerning the might of the Allied forces, and the last line read: 'At this hour, the crucial question for you is to decide whether to die or to become prisoners of war.' The propaganda, aimed principally at the Armenian troops, exhorted them to 'stop fighting for Hitler and his clique … The time will soon be ripe for you to get clear of your present predicament. Be ready!'[24]

At this time, bombers of the Twefth Air Force were picking on gun positions at La Ciotat, as well as Fréjus and Saint-Tropez. Their war diary claims to have achieved 100-per cent bombing accuracy on the raid of the 14th, and in a briefing later that day, all personnel were informed of the invasion set for the morrow. Every detail was disclosed, including the points of landing, the identification of landing forces, their strength and their objectives. The diarist noted approvingly that this policy of revealing secret military operations before they took place made a big hit with the men.

Bombing raids and efforts to confuse the Germans continued even into the morning of the attack, when radar-clogging aluminium strips were dropped over the Marseille–Toulon area, followed by hundreds of booby-trapped, dummy parachutists. American PT (Patrol Torpedo) boats caused further confusion by dashing in and out of harbours. The film star Douglas Fairbanks (Jnr) carried out one such mission near Cannes where, in 1939, he had attended the first film festival. Fairbanks was one of the VIP guests who arrived on an ocean liner chartered by MGM, but war was declared before the festival got going.

When the invasion fleet sailed, it headed up the Italian coast before making a left turn in the night fog of 14 August. The few Luftwaffe spotters in the air were convinced that the destination was Genoa. People on the island of Corsica, which lies directly in the flight path from Italy to France, were awakened by a mighty roar. The air armada filled the sky from horizon to horizon, and left no further doubt that the invasion of southern France was underway. This was the culmination of weeks of anticipation, marred by an upsurge in raids, reprisals and crackdowns on the Resistance, as we shall now see.

Chapter 10

Cruelty

At the beginning of 1944, SS-Oberscharführer (Staff Sergeant) Ernst Dunker was at the peak of his career. With the help of innumerable *Sonderkommandos* – mercenaries, informers, auxiliaries and collaborators of every type – he had infiltrated almost every underground network and decapitated the leadership. Dissidents, resistants, innocents and Allied agents from all over the south passed through Gestapo headquarters at 425 Rue Paradis. Each individual facing a different calamity, be it torture, deportation or execution.

The MONK circuit was one of the last of the SOE F Section circuits still active in the lower Rhône Valley, and also one of the smallest. In charge of MONK was Captain Charles Milne Skepper, a graduate of the London School of Economics and recipient of the Rockefeller Fellowship. From an early age he had been a serious socialist and social justice campaigner and had travelled extensively. In 1939 he found himself in Shanghai and was captured by the Japanese but released in a prisoner exchange.

Charles Skepper was one of four SOE agents flown in by Lysander on 16 June 1943.[1] The other three were women: Diana Rowden, Noor Inayat Khan and Cecily Lefort (Cammaerts' wireless operator). As fate would have it, none of them survived. During the nine months he was based in Marseille, Skepper used the cover of a dealer in antiques, a trade he knew well. By all accounts, when Skepper was arrested in his Marseille apartment on 23 March, he did not give himself up without a struggle. The Gestapo then waited at the apartment for other members of the cell to show up and arrested them as well. These included his wireless operator Arthur Steele (23) and courier Eliane Plewman (*Gaby*).

Arthur Steele was the son of a British Tommy from the Great War who had married his French sweetheart from Noeux-les-Mines, where Arthur was born in 1921. Arthur had been a boy-soldier since the age of 14 and served in the artillery until joining the SOE. He set up his radio base in the hills around Barjols while Eliane Plewman travelled up and down to Roquebrune and Saint-Raphaël to meet and guide new arrivals. Born Eliane Sophie Browne-Bartroli in Marseille, Plewman spoke multiple languages and was married and living in Leicester when she was recruited into the SOE. Aged about 25, Eliane had a tiny frame and stood five foot tall, but had a huge hatred of the Nazis.

A new member for the MONK circuit had parachuted into Vinon-sur-Verdon on the night of 6/7 March 1944, and, due to bungling by the OSS and/or SOE staff, the Gestapo were waiting on the ground to meet him. Twenty-two-year-old Lieutenant Jack Sinclair was born in Rouen to a French mother, and lived for a time in Marseille where his father was a corporate executive. One of his SOE assessors remarked that he was so reserved 'one hardly knew he was there'. Sinclair was being held in Baumettes Prison and suspicion naturally fell on him for betraying the MONK network, but it later transpired that a French national had denounced them. Dunker and his assistants tried to extract information out of the SOE agents by giving powerful electric shocks between the eyes which made their faces almost unrecognizable.

Jack Sinclair was made to disappear while still in Marseille while Charles Skepper, Arthur Steele and Eliane Plewman were sucked into the tunnel which took them through Fresnes Prison into Germany where they vanished into the night and fog. Arthur Steele was among a group of prisoners at Buchenwald summoned by the camp loudspeaker to the 'Tower Block' on 9 September 1944 and not seen again. Skepper was posthumously awarded the MBE, but it is not known how he met his end.

Investigators established that Eliane Plewman, together with three other female SOE agents, Madeleine Damerment, Yolande Beekman and Noor Inayat Khan, was transferred to Dachau in September 1944. Immediately on arrival, the women were told that they were to be executed and that there was no appeal. A witness told of how they grew pale and began to weep and then asked for a priest, but were told that there was none available. Two by two, holding hands, they were taken into a wooded area outside the camp where they were made to kneel down – then shot in the back of the neck. Of course, there are no records, but the SS executioner and camp guard, Wilhelm Ruppert, was hanged in 1946 for this and other crimes.

*

During the summer of 1944, the weight of the German yoke became unbearable but the circumstances of the occupier had also become ever more precarious. Even the life of an ordinary German soldier in the South of France had become a doubtful proposition. To venture out on the roads was to invite a rocket from a P-51 Mustang or a fusillade from the forests. Gestapo agents and their informers were prime targets for assassination.

Two men pretending to be hungry and on the run were given refuge on a farm near Draguignan. They turned out to be informers and had the farmer arrested. Receiving word that the two traitors would be driving to the coast, a teenage *maquisard* named Aimé Leocard, together with his *sizaine*, set an ambush at Trans-en-Provence, between Draguignan and Le Muy. The position was not well chosen: the six simply hid in ditches on the side of the road, and waited for an hour. Unexpectedly, a truckload of German soldiers came along and opened fire, but the boys got away. The informers remained alive for a few more months, but eventually got their just reward.

Acting independently of any resistance group, Aimé Leocard sprang five patriots who were being held by the Gestapo in the Draguignan prison. He and two friends went into town and tied up and gagged the garbage collector, ripped the phone off the wall, freed the prisoners and guided them to Aups to meet up with the Maquis. For his deeds, Aimé would be awarded the Croix de Guerre, but his greatest legacy is the Souvenir Franco-Américain, a non-profit organization which he founded to keep alive the memory of those buried in the Rhône American Cemetery. Because of this work, he received recognition from President Ronald Reagan, and was made an honorary member of the 517th Parachute Infantry Regiment.[2]

An assassination unit, or *groupe d'épuration*, of the Brigade des Maures executed one of the Gestapo's star informers in Sainte-Maxime, where a series of *rafles*, or roundups, took place during July. Then, in retaliation for the death of a German soldier at Saint-Pons-les-Mûres near Port Grimaud, a German detachment from Brignoles came and took away twenty-two hostages. As they were being carted off, Alix Macario put up a poster saying that if the hostages were executed, no German soldier would return to Germany alive. Although the Brignoles garrison arbitrarily shot ten hostages on 27 July, it appears they were not the ones from Sainte-Maxime. When victims were needed for mass reprisals, Germans tended to shoot whomever was in the police cells at the time.

Resistance hit squads, known as *équipes de tueurs*, would not normally involve themselves in other activities, so as not to unnecessarily compromise themselves. They could be either men or women who might not be physically strong but required special mental powers. Among certain groups, the unwritten rule was that only French traitors and Nazis – not ordinary German soldiers – should be targeted.

Invariably, there would be consequences. In the words of John Goldsmith, 'Blowing up bridges and murdering Germans had unpleasant side-effects.' Paradoxically, when two uniformed German railway workers, mistakenly believed to be high-ranking officers, were shot down on Boulevard Tzarewitch in Nice on 28 June 1944, the sanctions were mild: stricter curfews were imposed, and access to restaurants, the beach and the cinema was restricted for a two-week period.

Then, the unintended shooting of an unteroffizier, an NCO, at a checkpoint near the village of Gattières in the back-country of Nice elicited a different response. The *maquisards* responsible vanished into the hills, but two men, Séraphin Torrin and Ange Grassi, were taken from the village and hanged from street lamps on the corner of Rue Hôtel-des-Posts and the Avenue de la Victoire, one block from Place Masséna in downtown Nice. The disfigured bodies were left hanging for a full day with notices pinned on them warning that this was the fate of terrorists. The police blocked streets with their bicycles and forced residents, including children, to walk past the grisly sight.

A chain of events was set in motion after a courier for the CIRCONFÉRENCE *réseau* was arrested at the Virex-Port of Marseille, and among the documents which fell into Gestapo hands was confirmation of a meeting at the Café des Sports on Cours Sextius in Aix-en-Provence. The Gestapo set a trap but two Underground assassins, *Pioche* (Pick) and his partner, *Hache* (Axe), decided to set an ambush of their own in a narrow alley. In the shootout, two Gestapo officers were killed and one wounded. The 24-year-old Roger Joseph Olive, alias *Hache*, was shot through the heart and had to be left behind. Being inseparable friends, *Pioche* and his band raided the morgue to retrieve the body. After the liberation, Roger Olive was given a proper burial and today there is a plaque to his memory in the street where he fell on 17 July 1944.

Head of CIRCONFÉRENCE was Louis Burdet, a former manager of the Hyde Park Hotel in London, trained by SOE's RF Section (as opposed to F Section). In more peaceful times, he became head of the Stafford

Hotel in Mayfair, a favourite haunt of former SOE agents – including Nancy Wake. The name *Pioche* appears in the accounts of more than one SOE agent. He was a charming, well-dressed killer who, after the assassination-gone-wrong, became a regular at the bicycle shop in Apt, which was used as a safe house by *Archiduc* and John Goldsmith.

In the Vaucluse, the Maquis Ventoux carried out a series of bold attacks on the German lines of communication, and no convoy, not even an armoured one, was safe on the roads around Mont Ventoux. Between 4 and 8 August, at least two German columns were ambushed by Captain Robert Bourcart's men near the village of Sault. On the first occasion, five Germans were killed, four of them officers. The reprisals were clearly measured when, on 11 August, the owner of a farm and four of his lavender cutters were shot near the hamlet of Saint-Jean-de-Sault. The farmer, Gustave Roux, was in fact a member of the SAP who ran the *Spitfire* drop zone, and his name is remembered throughout the commune of Sault.

*

The Marseille branch of the Gestapo, consisting of approximately 130 men and women plus their auxiliaries, had been hard at work. They had recently made a massive haul of senior resistance members at Oraison in the Basses-Alpes, and the cells on the 7th floor of 425 Rue Paradis, were filled to overflowing.

Having been lured into a trap with the false information that the town had been liberated by the FTP, the resistants drove into Oraison on 16 July 1944 at 5.45 p.m., confidently brandishing weapons. All exits had been blocked by a detachment of about a hundred soldiers, possibly Brandenburgers. The attending Gestapo then arrested a total of eighteen people, including two young women. One man, a Spaniard, made a run for it and was cut down. According to an official report from the Gendermarie, residents of the town remained calm while the prisoners were loaded into two trucks which set off in the direction of La Brillanne at 8 p.m.[3]

Within two days of their arrest at Oraison, the Gestapo had extracted as much information as they were going to get and eleven of the eighteen were sentenced to death after a mock trial. One of these was Louis Martin-Bret, a leading light in the Mouvements Unis de Résistance (MUR) of the Basses-Alpes. Today there is a school named after him in

Manosque. Another was a 33-year-old doctor, Leon Dulcy, a native of Avignon, where there is a sports stadium which bears his name.[4]

Among those who were already in the cells of the Gestapo was Jules Moulet, a successful businessman and resistant from Marseille, who had been arrested on 13 July. His only daughter, Simone, would always remember the last time she saw him and never forgave herself for sulking when he left for his final meeting. She had refused to give her father a goodbye kiss because he had set her some homework exercises.[5] There is a street named after him in the neighbourhood of the family home.

On 18 July 1944, twenty-six prisoners, mostly high-ranking members of the FFI, were loaded onto trucks. The human cargo included Dr André Daumas from Oraison, and Robert Rossi, an air force captain in charge of the FFI throughout the R2 area of operations. Two were brothers: Lucien and Georges Barthelemy. Their younger brother, Louis, had been shot at the time of his arrest the previous month. The social standing of these men is evident from their vocations, which include a civil engineer, a lawyer, two teachers, a professor of philosophy and a number of students.[6]

Henri Chanay (*Grand Michel*) the leader of IAM MICHEL and his colleague, Michel Lancesseur (*Victor*), both of them military officers, had also fallen into the hands of the Gestapo. The two had narrowly escaped arrest during a raid on their safe house at Vinon-sur-Verdon, south of Manosque, on 14 June. A month later they were supposed to meet with Robert Rossi at the Café Les Danaïdes in Marseille. Ernest Dunker was waiting there, expecting to arrest Rossi when the two Allied agents were deemed to be 'looking suspicious'. Rossi was picked up the next day.

From Marseille and through Aubagne, the small convoy wound its way up the Mont Sainte-Baume, then funnelled through the narrow main street of Cuges-les-Pins toward Signes. It was a hot summer's day and residents of the three-storey town houses were having their siesta with the shutters closed. After cresting the hill, about five kilometres before the road descends into the fertile valley, a rocky track leads through stunted pine and scrub into a depression about two or three hectares in size. This site was chosen not for its remoteness but rather because it was an area known to be infested with 'terrorists' and they needed to be sent a message.

There was one witness, a woodcutter from Cuges by the name of Maurice Percivalle. While following a small footpath he heard people singing 'La Marseillaise'. Intrigued, he went to investigate. The captives were digging a ditch, injured and bleeding. It was they who were singing. Suddenly he came face to face with a soldier in a German uniform, machine pistol held at the hip. They stared at each other for a couple of seconds, then in broken French and what may have been a Polish accent, accompanied with an urgent nod of the head, the woodcutter was told to '*Partir! Partir!*' and '*Kaput! Kaput!*'

It was not until 17 September 1944, some weeks after the region was liberated, that the grave was opened. German prisoners of war were brought in to carry out the gruesome task of exhuming the bodies. This time there would be photographers and a forensic pathologist on hand to keep record. Two had been shot in the head but their death was due to asphyxia. They had been buried alive. Three died from skull fractures caused by a blunt instrument. Another was death by strangulation. One was shot in the neck. One was shot in the back. Five were killed by bullets in the head, from the front. The rest had been shot multiple times in the side of the head by a machine gun. Recognition of the bodies was very difficult because lime had been poured on the faces to conceal their identity. At least three have never been identified. Although the bodies are no longer buried there, the mass grave (le Charnier de Signes) is now a national cemetery. Two rectangular plots with granite slabs mark the execution site.

Henri Chanay, the leader of MICHEL, was found to be among the twenty-six victims, but the body of his teammate, Michel Lancesseur, was never identified. The 24-year-old captain had tried to escape by digging a hole in the ceiling using a broken bottle but was betrayed by a cellmate. Some say that he lost his mind through torture and was deported, but from the Gestapo's own records, it has been concluded that Michel was tortured for a few more weeks before being murdered in this same location on 12 August. In the space of five years, the Lancesseur family would lose three sons.

*

In the Moyen-Var, a new detachment of the FTP based itself at Villecroze, not far from Aups. Numbering about twenty, they were relatively well armed with Sten guns and a Bren gun. Recently returned from the Basses-Alpes, they called themselves Détachement Battaglia in honour of Marcel Battaglia (*Vaillant*) who had just been killed near

Castellane. Two more Battaglia brothers are on the list of *Morts pour la France*. Paul was one of those who died in the attack on Limate farm near Signes on 2 January, and René died as a deportee. They were a Sainte-Maxime family, and today there is a Rue des Frères Battaglia in this seaside town. Instead of keeping a low profile as ordered by the Communist Party leaders in the region, the Battaglia group remained close to civilization and, driving around in their requisitioned vehicles, attracted the attention of the Germans. On 27 July 1944, they were surrounded and eight of their number killed. Survivors went to lick their wounds in Salernes, and were on hand to participate in the liberation of that village three weeks later.

Now the massacres were becoming almost monotonous and evermore arbitrary. On the very same day as the Battaglias were decimated, the Germans shot ten hostages who were being held in the prison at Brignoles. The oldest was 72 and the youngest 20 years of age. These were people who had been rounded up over the past few days in the municipalities of Méounes, Le Val, Cotignac, Brignoles and Barjols for minor infractions such as breaking the curfew. The execution took place in the community of Pontevès near Barjols, culminating with a funeral in Cotignac. Residents of all persuasions, as well as representatives of all resistance groups in the area, were present among the massive turnout.

*

To secure their rear, the occupying forces also turned their attention to the Haute-Var where a number of Maquis camps had been left unmolested for too long now. At the beginning of August, the Germans, enthusiastically assisted by their French auxiliaries, searched villages and burned farms in the Canjuers area, killing two *maquisards* near Tourtour. The village of Bauduen was surrounded, its inhabitants interrogated and some taken as hostages. One of them, a new recruit in the AS, gave away the location of two arms caches, but by the time a new raid was unleashed, on 6 August, the 'drop of mercury' tactic had come into effect.

At this stage, the FTP contingent decided to move Camp Robert from Aups to a place higher up in the Canjuers, near the Verdon River, in the triangle between Montpezat, Saint-Laurent and Sainte-Croix-du-Verdon. (Lake Sainte-Croix did not exist at the time.) On the high ground, there was only rock with wooded patches before the steep slope down to the river. There were about eighty men from various groups, not all under

154

one command. Some were 'defectors' from the AS. As usual there were rivalries at play, but all groups shared the objective of reclaiming their country, as well as the bonds of brotherhood and camaraderie. It gave them the feeling 'that they exceeded themselves, which is the greatest kind of self-esteem.'[7]

It was unusual for so many to be concentrated in one place, and it went against the principles of guerrilla warfare. Interestingly, the camp was also inhabited by five Americans, crewmembers of a plane which had been shot down near Rians. It has been speculated that the Maquis camp was betrayed either by a fighter who spoke under torture or by some 'suspicious' character from Draguignan – who was subsequently 'eliminated'. A reconnaissance aircraft had flown over a few days previously, and must have spotted a target worthy of a full-scale operation. When the 'Germans', about 800 in all, attacked they came from three different directions.

At the dawn of 11 August, a sharp fusillade alerted everyone. The sentries, a group of Polish deserters from the Todt Organization, were later praised by survivors for facing the enemy with great courage. The plan in the event of attack by superior forces was to run rather than fight, thereby avoiding encirclement. After an exchange of fire, everyone dispersed, every man for himself. It would have been impossible to count all the bodies scattered across the commune, but nineteen bodies were buried at Riez, which is now nestled on the edge of the Lac Sainte-Croix. Ten of these had been captured, taken first to Digne and then to Fabres near Montagnac where they were executed. It was once whispered that they were killed by crushing them under trucks, but officially it did not happen. Four bodies were later found in the town of Sainte-Croix-du-Verdon, and five in the municipality of Montpezat. The five American airmen surrendered, hoping to be treated as prisoners of war, which seems to have been the case.[8]

As it happened, *Vallier* and his men were no longer at Canjuers when the attack of 11 August took place. Smoke could be been seen coming from his old *poste de contrôle*, his command post, and *Vallier* received the reports by bush telegraph. As usual, the Brandenburgers and *miliciens* were the main culprits, and he vowed to wait for them along the road and ambush them on their return journey. To *Vallier* they were 'all the scum and dregs of soldiery' bent on persecution.

*

As to be expected, these violent spasms would intensify as the day of reckoning approached. Just three days before the Allied invasion of Provence, on 12 August, a second mass execution was carried out in the Vallon des Fusillés at Signes. In fact, it was the third mass killing at Signes if one includes the shooting which occurred at the nearby Limate farm on 2 January 1944. On this occasion, there were nine victims. Among them were at least two Allied agents, Lieutenant François Pelletier and Major Muthular d'Errecalde, an American officer affiliated with Mission MICHEL. It is believed that the one unidentified body belonged to a third Allied agent, Michel Lancesseur, also of mission MICHEL. It should be remembered that the leader of MICHEL, Henri Chanay (*Grand Michel*), had been a victim of the 18 July massacre at this exact spot.

Lieutenant François Pelletier (*Reuben*) was an agent of the Bureau Central Rensiegnements et d'Action. His main mission was to work with the resistance to prepare the way in the invasion zone by providing information about German defences from Toulon all the way to Menton. Promoted to captain in March 1944, he first established himself in Cogolin, covering the area between Saint-Tropez and Draguignan. The Maquis with which he worked had a camp near La Garde Freinet, where there is today a monument to him and OSS officer Jean M. Muthular d'Errecalde, on a crest of the mountain pass between Grimaud and Vidauban, at Col-de-Vignon. Pelletier was barely 23 years old when he was posted to the BCRA in Algiers in November 1943. His two brothers, Michel (21) and Antoine (19), were students in Paris. Their sister, Marie-Claire, was at home. Pelletier was from northern France, schooled first at Beauvais, then in Belgium. Coming from a family of farmers, he studied to become an agronomist and managed a commercial farm until joining the Resistance.

Pelletier's instructors at Club des Pins, one of the OSS training facilities in Algeria, found him to be very intelligent, hard-working and keen to learn. They wrote: 'He does not drink or smoke. He seems to have no vices.' Stubbornness was considered an asset in this line of work. Moments of leisure he spent improving his English and reading the New Testament. Shortly prior to his first mission, his handlers warned that he had little experience of life, that he was perhaps a bit too reckless and would not make a good leader. At the end of his training he was judged fit, capable and knowledgeable in the field, qualified in parachuting, map-reading, demolition – and an excellent marksman.

After two failed attempts to infiltrate by sea via Corsica, Pelletier and his radio operator, Jean Paoli, parachuted into La Motte-d'Aigues in the heart of the Luberon on the night of 7/8 March 1944. The password for the reception committee was '*Où est notre poupée?*' (Where is our doll?), the response '*Tout près d'ici*' (Near here). Pelletier's identity card carried the name of François Perron, physically distinguishing him by his amputated index finger, light brown or sandy-coloured hair, and a height of 1.8 metres.[9]

Travelling with him was his BCRA comrade, Maurice Seignon de Possel Deydier (*Noël*), who was to stay in Marseille while Pelletier and Paoli went on to the Saint-Tropez peninsula. Pelletier was accommodated in Cogolin by the Pattachini family who owned the cinema there, and later at 'Villa Jeannette' in Saint-Tropez where the cinema manager lived. Paoli stayed with the family of Jean Despas near Draguignan where he hid his transmitters in a barn.

Fernand Vié, a resident of Ramatuelle, remembers how he and a friend were recruited at the Café de l'Ormeau where they regularly drank coffee with the local *agent de liaison*. After the Normandy landings, they were told to report to Pelletier's camp near La Garde Freinet on the northern slopes of the Massif des Maures, and to take supplies with them. Bypassing Grimaud, they cycled up the steep hill to La Garde Freinet. At the Col-de-Vinon, a *maquisard* awaited them. '*Mot de passe!*' he demanded. '*La Saint Jean c'est le 24 juin,*' (St John's Day is on 24 June) Fernand responded. At the camp, Pelletier welcomed them and showed them where to hide their bicycles. About twenty more young men arrived from the surrounding villages. Fernand felt that the farm was not very secure, so he and his friend built a fortification out of rocks on a highpoint from where they looked down on the village of Plan-de-la-Tour. Some of the newcomers were so nervous that they went straight home.

Working closely with Jean Despas and Marko Célébonovitch, the leaders of the Brigade des Maures, Pelletier organized a weapons drop on 13 July, north of La Môle (where the Saint-Tropez airport is today). Some of the precious weapons were hidden in a ditch on the farm La Crotte near La Garde Freinet, but were seized by the Germans in a raid on 25 July. Needless to say, the farm was burned, but the farm owners and *maquisards* escaped into the forest. The Germans seemed more interested in the stores of brandy and *vin cuit* – wine aged in oak and cooked in a cauldron.

As head of maritime operations on the Riviera, Pelletier sometimes stayed at Cap Lardier, on the eastern point of the Bay of Cavalière, to meet and greet *clandestines* arriving by high-speed motor launch from Corsica. Communications were maintained with Algiers, Corsica and London. Important messages would be transmitted by the BBC in the evenings. If an operation was to go ahead, the announcer might say, 'Let's see the morning rise on the mountains,' and if there was danger and the mission was to be aborted, the message would be along the lines of, 'Nothing is ever lost when everything would seem hopeless.'

While on deployment, Pelletier learned about the death of his younger brother Michel, shot as a 'terrorist'. He wrote to his cousin Bernard: 'Michel died a saint, as a martyr, after giving his full measure … I feel like a little boy. It's sad, very, but splendid. And Mom and Dad have been splendid.' Even his parents had been arrested by the Gestapo but were released after a month. On 16 June, soon after the Normandy landings, François wrote to his family: 'Nothing is happening here. You all be careful during these times. I'm perfectly fine, there have been a series of quiet moments and great work, beautiful inner joys and some disappointments.'[10]

It was around this time that François Pelletier met Nicole Célébonovitch, the daughter of Marko, and it seems that he was smitten. Only a day before his arrest, he wrote to his parents that he had met this girl with a mass of brown hair and shapely figure, serious and shy but full of confidence. The images taken of her a few days after Saint-Tropez was liberated, leave no doubt that she was very feminine despite having a pistol on her belt and a cigarette in hand. Any hopes of a future together were dashed on 24 July 1944 when Pelletier was arrested by the Marseille branch of the Gestapo. Nicole lived in Saint-Tropez until her passing in 2016.

On that fine summer's day, Pelletier cycled down to the Restaurant Muscadins on Rue Général Allard near the port of Saint-Tropez. He had gone alone to meet Jean-Maurice Muthular d'Errecalde (*Lucas*), the American OSS officer who was part of the disastrous IAM MICHEL, two of whom had already fallen into the hands of the Gestapo. A fourth team member, Alistair Hay, was killed on 13 June trying to defend the 'liberated zone' around Barcelonette.

Muthular d'Errecalde had travelled from Aix-en-Provence to Saint-Tropez and was about to embark for Algiers on a high-speed motor launch carrying information on the dangerous rivalry between resistance groups in the R2 region. Colonel Lécuyer (*Sapin*) had come into conflict with Captain Robert Rossi (*Levallois*) over whether or not they should lie low or go over to the offensive. *Sapin* had on 16 June given orders for his *maquisards* to stand down while Rossi was keen to fight. Perhaps d'Errecalde had fallen out with his leader, *Grand Michel*, who had been arrested on 15 July. Now he needed to get back to Algiers to report on matters. He was also going to deliver maps of the minefields on Pampelonne beach which Pelletier had compiled.

In Saint-Tropez d'Errecalde stayed at the Hôtel Aïoli, and the next day he lunched with Pelletier at the restaurant where they were joined by a friend and fellow agent, Maurice Seignon de Possel Deydier (*Noël*). At the end of the meal, the restaurant was raided by the Gestapo, and the group was herded over to the naval offices of the Kriegsmarine at the port of Saint-Tropez. In d'Errecalde's medal citation, it is stated that he prevented his documents from falling into enemy hands but some weapons and documents were found in the garden shed where Pelletier was living. Nicole rushed to the port where she caught a last sight of François as he was being shipped off to Marseille.

Gestapo headquarters in Marseille was an office building where some of the rooms had been converted into cells. Official documents found in the offices after the liberation reveal that Pelletier underwent three interrogations, on 24, 25 and 31 July, at the hands of Ernst Dunker. Undoubtedly, Pelletier and d'Errecalde knew precise details of the coming invasion but gave away nothing of value to the enemy. Dunker's notes indicate that he got much information about Pelletier himself but nothing about his work. As previously mentioned, the farm, La Crotte at La Mourre, near La Garde Freinet, was raided on 25 July, the day after Pelletier's arrest, but by all accounts this was a coincidence.

Although of Basque descent, d'Errecalde (*Lucas*) was in fact an American, born in Lamar County, Texas, in a town called Paris (one of fifteen municipalities in the United States named Paris). He was a 34-year-old married man and had been practising as a lawyer in New York before the war. According to a fellow prisoner, d'Errecalde was particularly strong in his faith and spent most of his final days in prayer. He was hoping that being an American citizen might save him and he regretted having disposed of his uniform.

After his arrest, Pelletier's family tried all possible interventions and even enlisted the help of Cardinal Emmanuel Suhard, the Archbishop of Paris, but to no avail. While still in Algiers François had written the classic 'in the event of my death' letter to his parents. It was a long and rambling letter begging their forgiveness for having given them so much pain, asking them to understand his motivation, insisting that he could have chosen an easier path but it would not have been his path, that it would not have made him happy. Thanking his parents for a 'pure, whole, happy family life', all twenty-four years of it, the gist of it was '*Je ne regrette rien*' (I have no regrets).

In what would become known as the Valley of the Martyrs, twenty-six resistance leaders had been executed on 22 July; now on the morning of 12 August 1944, three days before salvation was due to arrive, d'Errecalde and Pelletier were taken with seven other prisoners to the same clearing in the forest. Right next to the existing mass grave, on the edge of a newly excavated pit, they were made to line up. This time there were no witnesses apart from those who did the killing.

When the bodies were exhumed a few weeks later, some were found to have their mouths open as though gasping for air, their fingers curled and torn from scratching at the earth. Pelletier and others had still been alive when buried. Pelletier's autopsy report revealed than he was wearing a white and green checked shirt and that he had been 'hideously tortured'. He was posthumously awarded the Croix de Guerre, and in Saint-Tropez, Cogolin, and La Garde Freinet there are streets named after him. Up in the north, the village square in Saint-Omer-en-Chaussée, a small farming community near Bauvais, is named after his brother, Michel, and both their names are on the *monument aux morts* in the village.

Preposterous as it may seem, it was soon discovered that François Pelletier had been betrayed by a certain double agent, known to the Gestapo by the pseudonym *Érick Dimker* or just *Érick*, and it transpires that this was none other than his friend and colleague, Maurice Seignon de Possel Deydier (*Noël*). The two had trained in Algiers together and were deployed at the same time. An adopted child from an old and respected Marseille family, *Érick* aka *Noël* was aged about thirty. Photographs show him to be a nice-looking man with a humorous, open face. Much information about this episode is contained in a report known as the 'Catilina Report', signed by Senior Sqaud Leader, SS-Oberscharführer Ernst Dunker (*Delage*). The file was found after the liberation of the city and is accessible in the Archives Nationales.[11] Dunker's work entailed reporting to his superiors in the Gestapo regarding the personages, plans, and activities of the Resistance in the Marseille region. He had more than 200 active informers on his books and had predicted the imminent Allied landing in the Var Department.

Noël or *Érick* had at his own instigation approached Dunker with offers to provide information for payment, but all that the traitor got in the end was a burst from a machine pistol once he had outlived his usefulness, since he had now become a danger to Dunker himself. The double agent did not live to see the outcome of his final betrayal because he was put against a wall on 8 August 1944 in the Baumettes district on the outskirts of Marseille. His obituary appeared in the *Populaire du Sud-Est* on 1 October 1944, portraying him as a hero who had volunteered his services for the Gaullist army in Algiers, carrying out important secret work with the resistance. Clearly, the contents of the Catilina file had not yet been examined. Under interrogation, Dunker, who was a cold-blooded killer, allegedly said that the way *Érick* operated made him sick and that he was a despicable individual.[12]

The Catilina file also contained information on another double agent, Jean Multon, an associate of the resistance hero, Jean Moulin. Multon worked with Ernst Dunker and Klaus Barbie, turning in many resistance leaders including Berty Albrecht and members of the 'Pat' escape network, before making his way to North Africa. Having installed himself as a member of de Gaulle's Free French Army he returned to France and took part in Operation Dragoon. However, his past sins were soon discovered and he would be executed at the Fort de Montrouge where numerous Gestapo collaborators and French auxiliaries would be shot between 1944 and 1949.

The SOE had sent an operative, Adolf Feingold, to Marseille in March 1944 to assassinate either Dunker or his superior, Rolf Mühler, but seems to have lost his nerve and crossed into Spain after a few days. Eventually, Ernst Dunker would also get his just reward. He was arrested in Paris with his mistress in May 1945 but was only executed in 1950. Dunker was fairly low ranking, but highly effective and ruthless. Between interrogations, he was friendly and polite, even respectful to his prisoners, sometimes bringing them coffee and cigarettes.

Like Adolf Eichmann and others of his ilk, Dunker epitomized the concept of the 'banality of evil' whereby people can do evil without being evil, and can perpetrate the most heinous acts although their hearts are not filled with malice. During the inter-war years, Dunker led a colourful life. He was fluent in French, English and Italian, having worked as a barman at Saint-Raphäel. He also worked in Milan, and in 1935 he was a waiter at the Grosvenor House Hotel in London. In 1939 he was running a milk bar in Hoboken in the United States. At his trial, Dunker unsurprisingly claimed to be simply following orders. 'We do not all have the fortune [*le bonheur*] of being French, unfortunately, I am German', he said in his closing statement. In 1954, the entire Marseille branch of the Gestapo was put on trial, most of them in absentia. Charges included criminal association, (*association de malfaiteurs*), murder, illegal arrest and confinement, looting, assault, robbery and destruction of inhabited buildings. Dunker's immediate boss, Lieutenant Paul Kompe, and the Jew hunter, Alois Brunner, were two of those sentenced to death in absentia. The Gestapo chief in Marseille between January 1943 and June 1944, Rolf Mühler, had his death sentence commuted to twenty years' hard labour. After his release in 1956 he became an insurance salesman.

PART II

Chapter 11

Reckoning

When reflecting on the planning for Operation Dragoon, historians have placed great emphasis on the fact that it nearly did not materialize at all due to differences in opinion between the Allied leaders. Winston Churchill was not at all in favour of a second landing in Europe but was eventually talked into Operation Dragoon. Some say that this is where the codename for the operation comes from. Supposedly Churchill said he was 'dragooned' into agreeing to the plan. Another theory is that the name is derived from the similar-sounding 'Draguignan' which was the location of the German headquarters about twenty-five kilometres inland, and one of the primary objectives of the operation. Once upon a time the town was called Dragonianum, and the name on the map might well have caught someone's eye.

Initially, the codename given to this second invasion of France was 'Anvil', but fearing that it had been compromised, it was changed two weeks before D-Day. It had nevertheless been a fitting name because it would bring about the crushing of German forces between the northern 'Hammer' (later Overlord) and the southern 'Anvil'. A different perspective is shown in a French propaganda poster where the FFI is the anvil on which the Nazi emblem is being crushed by the hammer of the combined Allied armies. Having learned valuable lessons from Overlord, the planning for Dragoon was meticulous and essentially faultless.

Assembling in Corsica was an armada consisting of 600 transport ships escorted by 250 warships and 2,000 aircraft. The invasion force included the battleships USS *Nevada*, USS *Texas*, USS *Arkansas*, HMS *Ramillies* and the French battleship *Lorraine*, with twenty cruisers for gunfire support and air cover from eight aircraft carriers. The main assault force from the sea was codenamed Kodak Force, while the three commando operations on the fringes were labelled Stika Force, Romeo Force and Rosie Force.

Centred on the small ports of Saint-Tropez and Saint-Raphaël, the invasion zone extended for seventy-two kilometres from Cavalière to Agay. The assault from the sea would hit the beaches of Cavalière, Rayol, Ramatuelle, Sainte-Maxime and Saint-Raphaël. From west to east, the sectors were designated Alpha, Delta and Camel, and allocated respectively to the 3rd (Rock of the Marne) Division, the 45th (Thunderbird) Division and the 36th (Texas) Division – also known as T-Patchers. Totalling approximately 150,000 men, the US Seventh Army was under the overall command of Major General Alexander Patch. The insignia of the Seventh Army was an Inca-type pyramid with seven steps leading to the top. Officially it represented the 'Pyramid of Power', but unofficially, it was said to signify the 'Seven Steps to Hell'.

The French ground forces were at least 200,000 strong, and included 90,000 French Europeans, mostly *Pieds-Noir* or colonials (literally 'Black Feet') and 110,000 *indigènes* (natives), mostly from the Maghreb but also some from Sub-Saharan Africa. All but 2 per cent of the officers were Europeans. All equipment, including 1,100 tanks, was provided courtesy of the US Army. Issues surrounding racial discrimination in the ranks and in pensions were raised in the 2006 film *Indigènes* and continue to this day. With the exception of the commandos, the French forces were to come ashore in the second wave, and additional colonial units were scheduled to arrive over the next nine days. The main objectives of the French Army B, commanded by General Jean de Lattre de Tassigny, would be Toulon and Marseille.

The flanks of the landing would be screened by three commando detachments, two of which were French and one 'Canadian'. The last-mentioned, the 1st Special Service Force (FSSF), was a combined Canadian and American unit which had originally been created for a sabotage mission in Norway, but had been deployed to Italy. While the Canadian contingent consisted of prospective paratroopers, the Americans were recruited from US Army units in the Southwest and on the Pacific coast. Preferred occupations included lumberjacks, hunters, prospectors, explorers and game wardens. Highly trained in commando skills, they were feared by their enemies, who dubbed them 'The Devil's Brigade'. Among friends, they were known as 'Forcemen'. They would be the first to land on the islands of Port Cros and Levant to clear any defences there.

As had been the modus operandi in Normandy, Operation Dragoon would kick off with an airborne operation, to be codenamed 'Rugby'. The American airborne units included the 509th Parachute Infantry Battalion, 551st Parachute Infantry Battalion, 550th Airborne Infantry Battalion and the 517th Parachute Infantry Battalion. The latter, together with its artillery and engineer support, temporarily became known as the 517th Parachute Regimental Combat Team but here they will simply be referred to as the 517th or 517th PIR. All of the airborne units together made up the 1st Airborne Task Force (FABTF) – so called because it was only half the size of a typical division. The most-often cited numbers are 5,000 American paratroopers plus approximately 2,000 members of the British 2nd Independent Parachute Brigade.[1] In command of the 1st Airborne Task Force (FABTF) was the legendary Major General Robert T. Frederick, formerly of the FSSF, who having been wounded in battle eight times, acquired the title 'last of the fighting generals'. Aged 37, he was one of the youngest generals in the US Army.

The goal of Operation Rugby would be to drop into the district of Le Muy and prevent German reinforcements from reaching the beachheads. They were to hold the ground where gliders of the 550th Infantry Battalion would land late in the afternoon. Causing mayhem and confusion behind enemy lines was the paratrooper's forte and went without saying. In this they would be assisted by the Resistance. During the breakout, the FFI would be the eyes and ears of the Allies and protect their flanks.

It was common knowledge, even to the average person on the street that the Allies intended to follow up on Operation Overlord. It has been said that Operation Dragoon was the worst-kept secret of the Second World War, but exactly where and when it would happen remained in the realms of speculation. Some did in fact predict that Napoleon's birthday – 15 August – would be the day. Invasion fever burned everywhere in Provence, the Maquis saw their numbers swell and the Wehrmacht was on full alert.

As we have seen, a new round of reprisals was perpetrated against various groups of resistants during the final weeks preceding the arrival of the Allies. This was partly due to the Germans needing to gain control over their rear, while they faced an assault from the sea. Up until now, the shadow war in Provence had been bubbling under the surface. Amateurs had been fighting an asymmetrical battle against the Gestapo and their auxiliaries, but the overwhelming power of the Allied coalition was about to descend on this corner of Provence.

An *agent de liaison* at La Garde, Marcelle Zunino, waited with feverish impatience for the message to come through: 'These are long days and endless nights … My little girl has gone to safer places, with my parents … We collect the weapons that we have.'[2] Allied planners had counted on the Resistance being ready to help and *Vallier* was prepared: 'As we approach the long-awaited moment, we push instruction as much as possible, because I would love to not get there with untrained and unprepared troops.'

Clearly, the Maquis *Vallier* had advance warning because they began their journey to the coast on 9 August. They crossed the whole Var Department, a distance of 110 kilometres, partly at night, and on foot in four days. The route took them through Flassans and Les Mayons to Collobrières where a leadership crisis arose. A former head of the FFI in the Hyères sector tried to impose himself as leader, seemingly with the support of some of the men. *Vallier* decried this 'Johnny-come-lately' as 'an ambitious politico' who wanted to capitalize on his six months of preparation. Before departing on the final leg of their trek out of the wilderness, *Vallier* decided to conduct a poll to see if he still had the support of his men. It would be a secret poll and *Vallier* asked not to be shown the ballots, passing the results straight to his commandant. It appears that even those who were grumbling voted for *Vallier*. Perhaps the discontent was due to fatigue and hunger. After arriving at what was to be their last Maquis camp at 4.30 a.m., a soup made in a washing machine, which tasted like soap was 'swallowed up at full speed, without any complaints about the taste', after which everyone except *Vallier* went to sleep'.[3]

While slipping through the German lines, one needed to be sure of one's bearings and the so-called guides argued about exactly which direction was southeast. Nevertheless, *Vallier* could boast of bringing fifty-two heavily armed men safely through, with Boches blocking all roads and only a Michelin roadmap to guide them through the woods and trails. For the first time, *Vallier* allowed himself to make plans for after the war: 'Until now, it seemed so distant and so uncertain that I forced myself not to think about it, I did not want to let myself go somewhere that could then make it hard to do an about-turn.'[4]

On 14 August 1944, *Vallier* was camped at Col-des-Fourches, a remote highpoint between Les Mayons and Collobrières, listening to the sound of aircraft overhead and explosions shaking the ground. That night, the *maquisards* slept under century-old chestnut trees on a thick layer of ferns. On the morrow, they would meet up with Free French and American forces and be given their first task. By wearing their FFI *brassards* – armbands – included in recent supply drops, they hoped to be treated as combatants as opposed to terrorists, if captured. *Vallier's* diary of life in the Maquis was coming to an end.

The eagerness with which the Resistance and the general population awaited the *débarquement* knew no bounds. The FFI, however, still encountered people who refused to shelter them, doctors who refused to treat them and priests who refused to say prayers for their dead. Despite the widespread rejection of Vichy, such daring actions could result in one's own demise. Ever since the start of the Italian campaign in 1943, the Maquis had been expecting this landing. Information was continually being received that it really was a matter of days. The young and the naive spoke constantly of 'major upcoming events', only to have their hopes and optimism sunk when nothing happened.

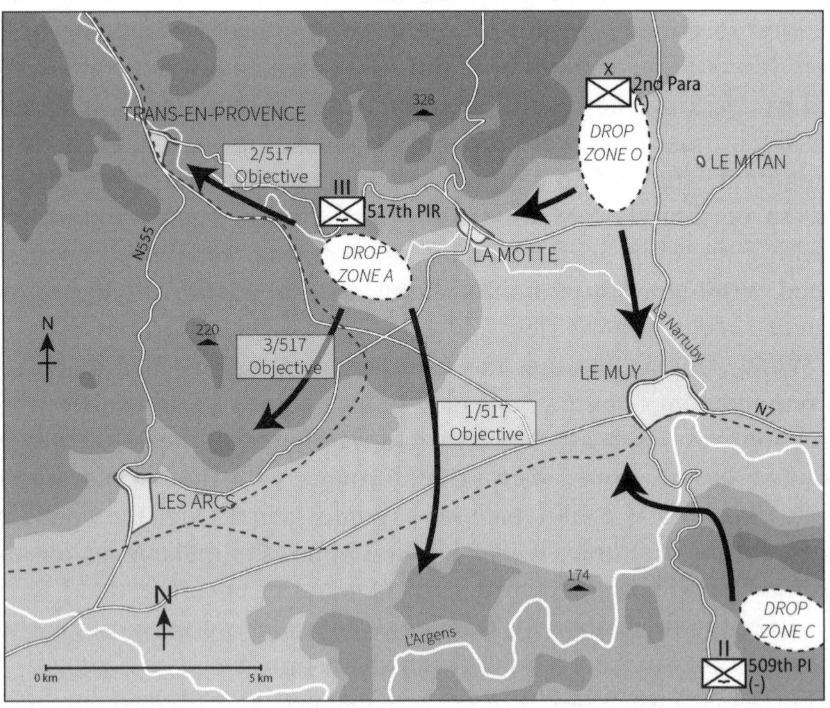

Operation Rugby designated DZs.

Due to the presence of OSS operatives, namely Captain Geoffrey Jones, key resistance leaders in the Moyen-Var had been informed of the upcoming invasion three days before Dragoon D-Day, and had immediately begun mobilizing. Commandant Jean Blanc, head of the FFI in the Les Arcs sector, informed his chief, Captain Fontès, at Draguignan who dispatched about twenty-seven gendarmes to join the Maquis of Brovès. Jean Blanc's deputy, Jean Cassou, set off to alert the FFI groups in the villages of Le Muy, La Motte and Trans-en-Provence, which were to be at the centre of events. He had instructions to prepare the landing fields for the gliders. Barbed wire and pointed stakes called 'Rommel asparagus' had been planted there, and vineyard trellises also presented a hazard. In Draguignan, as in other centres, some of the men went to help while the greedy prepared to seize political power.

The arrival of Jedburgh mission SCEPTER served to confirm that this was indeed the start of something big, although the heavier-than-usual bombing had already removed all doubt. A meeting was called of the leaders at Mons on the afternoon of 14 August. Together they could muster some 200 *maquisards,* one of whom was told by his chief to take a crate of Sten guns to Lorgues by train. From the station, they were carried by a rickety old truck to a local *boulangerie* where they were unpacked downstairs among the wood-fired bread ovens. Huddled around the radio in the bakery, the group began their vigil. That night, they heard the personal messages on the BBC indicating that the *débarquement* was on for the next day.

The Brigade des Maures had gone to ground after the arrest of Pelletier and d'Errecalde on 24 July and the raid on their base at La Garde Freinette the following day. Now that there was no doubt about the date and place of the invasion, the Maquis des Maures under Alix Macario and Marko Célébonovitch assembled in the Val d'Astier between Cogolin and La Môle, ten kilometres from Saint-Tropez. In the towns, German troops became increasingly agitated and increased their patrols, firing at anyone breaking the curfew. In Le Lavandou, Father Hélin was prevented from doing his rounds. Although active in the Resistance, he had missed the broadcast. Nevertheless, through some intuition, he had gone to bed fully clothed.

Over the airwaves came the coded phrases announcing the commencement of Operation Dragoon: *'Ici Londres ... veuillez tout d'abord écouter quelques messages personnels ... Nancy a le torticollis*

... je répète ... Nancy a le torticollis ... Le chasseur a faim ... je répète ... le chasseur est affamé ... La girafe ne porte pas de faux col ... Gaby va se coucher dans l'herbe' (This is London ... please first listen to some personal messages ... Nancy has a stiff neck ... I repeat ... Nancy has a stiff neck ... the hunter is hungry ... I repeat ... the hunter is starving ... the giraffe is not wearing a collar ... Gaby is going to lie in the grass).

Near Saint-Tropez, René Girard, could hardly catch his breath, as he had just heard the messages. Girard, an engineer by profession, had not known until now exactly where the Allies were planning to strike but his men had been on alert for the last twenty days. Nicole Célébonovitch got on her bicycle and rode like the wind down to the Renaissance Café at Place des Lices and began spreading the word to a trusted few. Suddenly everyone wanted to be in on the action and some set about making their own FFI *bassards*. One would-be-*maquisard* used mercurochrome and *bleu de méthylène* to reproduce the colours of the French flag.

Meanwhile at Mons, the Maquis were planning to knock out what they believed was a German radar installation at the nearby village of Fayence. The 'radar station' was probably just a strongpoint on the heights above Fayence, on top of a large boulder called La Roque. SPOC had considered getting Geoffrey Jones to do the job, and he was just waiting to get the go-ahead via the radio. However, because of the classified information which he was privy to, it was deemed safer to get the Maquis to do it. Jones, Allain and the gendarmes from Draguignan then set off in a pick-up truck, a *camionette*, for the invasion drop zone at La Motte and Le Muy, which is today a thirty-minute drive from Fayence.

No Germans were encountered but an American fighter-bomber dropped a bomb thirty metres from the truck. It gave Allain a funny feeling – *drôle de sensation* – to think that he might be killed by his own side. The US Navy Hellcats flew more than 500 sorties during Operation Dragoon, launched from the carriers USS *Kasaan Bay* and USS *Tulagi*.

The airborne invasion had begun, and by chance some paratroopers who had been dropped off course were landing in the hills around Fayence, Seillans, Callian, and Tourrettes. The first fellow Americans encountered by Jones were some men who were attached to the 517th Parachute Infantry Regiment (PIR). Arriving in La Motte at 5.10 a.m., Allain heard the roar of C-47s, which he recognized from parachute school, and saw white sails draped from trees, houses and high-tension wires. Others were descending from the sky by the thousands.

On the morning of 15 August, in towns and villages deep in the hinterland of Provence, people were beginning to push open their shutters to greet another scorching day. Some were preparing to attend the Assumption Day Mass. A few solitary aircraft streaked across the sky, but they were not armed with bombs and bullets. On this occasion, two million pamphlets fluttered to the ground. Up the Rhône Valley and as far north as the Durance River, the last drop was at about 8 a.m. The text was in French, German, Russian, Czechoslovakian, Polish and Armenian:

> Armies of the United Nations have landed in southern France. Their objective is to drive out the Germans and to effect a junction with the Allied forces that are advancing through Normandy. The French forces are participating in this operation. They are fighting alongside their Allied comrades at arms, on the sea, on the ground and in the air. The French Army exists again. With all its past traditions of victory, it is battling for the liberation of its homeland. Remember 1918! All Frenchmen, civilians as well as military, have their parts to play in this campaign in southern France. Your role will be explained to you. Listen to the Allied broadcasts, read the posters and leaflets, pass the word along to your neighbour. Help us to bring the conflict to an end as quickly as possible.[5]

On BBC Radio, the Supreme Allied Commander, General Eisenhower, broadcast a message to all the inhabitants of the South of France warning them to stay off the main highways and not to linger under the bridges. In the event of an air raid, people were advised to stay under a staircase, lie flat on their faces and keep away from windows. Children were to wear identification tags.

*

It was just before 2 a.m. on 15 August 1944 when the first five Dakotas flying low over the Mediterranean, were spotted just off La Ciotat, between Toulon and Marseille. This was exactly the place where the German coastal command expected the landings to occur, but they would soon realize that it was a ruse designed to keep them guessing. To add to the confusion, each of the Dakotas released sixty dummy parachutists over the wooded hillsides on the outskirts of La Ciotat. Made of rubber, and dressed like American paratroopers, they also carried time charges set to explode just as the Germans were closing in on them. In a newscast the following morning Radio Berlin condemned this trickery as something only the devious Anglo-Saxon mind could have conceived.

Meanwhile, 100 to 150 kilometres to the east of the dummy diversion, the invasion fleet was approaching the coast. In addition to all the troopships, mine-sweepers and Liberty ships, there were 250 warships, including the 18-month-old *Catoctin* which had been designated as the headquarters for the invasion forces at sea. The *Nevada* and the *Texas* turned their 14-inch guns against the beach of Sainte-Maxime, while the battleship *Arkansas* and the heavy cruiser *Tuscaloosa* concentrated their fire on the Saint-Raphaël sector where the defences were the strongest. The veteran Royal Navy battleship *Ramillies* stood off Pampelonne and Cavalière-sur-Mer. Another legendary British ship in the armada was the *Ajax*, which had been involved in the battle of the River Plate when the *Graf Spee* was scuttled.

Easily visible from Hyères on the mainland, is the group of three islands called the Îles d'Hyères. Like three sentinels, they guarded the approaches to the landing beaches as far as Cavalière-sur-Mer. Being well aware of their strategic value, the Germans had evacuated all the inhabitants, mined the beaches, and installed heavy artillery. The Îles d'Hyères had to be the first objective of the amphibious invasion, but the third and largest island of the group, Porqucrolles constituted no threat to the landing beaches, and had therefore not been included in the plans.

The amphibious assault was made by nearly 2,000 commandos of the 1st Special Service Force (FSSF). Approaching the islands in rubber boats and canoes, by 2 a.m. on 15 August, all had landed safely on Port-Cros and the Île du Levant. Total surprise was achieved by scaling steep cliffs. On the Île du Levant, a small group of about sixty Germans held off the attackers of Stika Force for sixteen hours after the first landing. It was then discovered that one of the big gun batteries covering the landing beaches was in fact a wooden dummy with pipes for guns.

On Port-Cros, the battle continued throughout the following day and into the morning of 17 August. A small garrison in one of four old stone forts refused to surrender, and it was necessary to call in the big guns of HMS *Ramillies*. Anything lighter 'bounced off like tennis balls'.

Although the islands could have been taken by attrition, nine over-eager commandos were killed or died of wounds in this phase of Operation Dragoon. Two unsuspecting enemy ships, one laden with ammunition, were picked up on radar as they came out of Toulon harbour. After a brief duel with USS *Somers*, their fiery end lit up the dawn sky.

Just off Pramousquier beach, near Rayol, east of Cavalière-sur-Mer, Colonel Georges-Régis Bouvet was preparing to take Cap Nègre. His Commandos d'Afrique had been specially selected and trained for the task of knocking out the three German 6-inch guns and the electrically operated flamethrowers that defended the position. One officer had been selected for his knowledge of this section of coast. It happened that he was the owner of a small villa at La Croix-Valmer, on the Bay of Cavalière. After they had landed at Rayol and occupied Cap Nègre, Bouvet's men would have the task of holding the coastal road at Cavalière-sur-Mer until tanks of the American 3rd Division could reach them.

While on board ship, Colonel Bouvet reminded the men of Romeo Force that they would have the honour of being the first to set foot on the French mainland and that part of their mission was to draw as many German defenders toward them as possible. In preparation for their night attack, the 700 commandos had been trained for cliff-climbing and the clearing of minefields. Only one platoon would carry out the initial attack.

Although the enemy was caught by surprise, the going was rough. A shower of grenades cascaded onto them, and one officer, Noël Texier, was knocked off the cliff, his body bouncing off the rocks and finally coming to rest on a small ledge. No one went near him. Textier himself had ordered that in such an eventuality, the wounded should be left behind. Through shell craters, and in darkness, the commandos pushed forward and scrambled to the top of the cliff where the Germans were 'running around like chickens with their heads cut off'. Apparently more of them were shot by their comrades than by the French commandos. The main body of Romeo Force, consisting of 600 commandos, came ashore about a kilometre west of where they were supposed to be, but the first battle of D-Day in Provence had been easily won. Texier is buried at Rayol-Canadel, close to where he fell, and there is a street in Le Lavandou which bears his name.

On the far right of the invasion zone, Anthéor is nestled in a small cove on the outskirts of Mandelieu-la-Napoule. The coastal road between

Cannes and Saint-Raphaël runs high above the beach and a large bridge and a strongpoint here had long been a target of the US Air Force. A group of sixty-seven French commandos was assigned to go ahead of the main landings to blow holes in the road. Designated Rosie Force, the Groupe Naval d'Assaut de Corse, under the 39-year-old Capitaine de Corvette Gerard Marche, felt privileged to be among the first to set foot on the French mainland. Almost all these men had left France to join de Gaulle in 1940.

Using inflatable boats, they began landing at 2.10 a.m. and except for a few flares, at first all was deathly quiet. According to intelligence reports, there should have been no mines in this area, but in fact, the exact spot where they had landed was a freshly planted minefield. Nevertheless, an army specialist with a mine detector was part of the group. He was the first to be blown up. Thinking that it was a grenade attack, everyone hit the ground and where men landed, the earth blew up beneath them. It seems that the mines had been connected to each other so that when one exploded a whole string would go off.

The lead officer, Christian Auboyneau, and a sailor named Jean Campana were among the first to be blown up and, against all odds, both survived. Auboyneau had both legs torn apart and his stomach ripped open, and one of his eyes torn out. Jean Campana was even worse off, with a perforated lung, kidney, a shattered arm and leg. He was urinating blood and breathing through his chest, making a rustling sound, but fortunately he suffered no haemorrhage.

The Germans went over to see the results of their handiwork and gave a bit of first aid, but then left. Some of the wounded could have been saved if the bleeding had been stopped. A lieutenant who had been shot high up in the leg lasted a couple of hours before he died through loss of blood. Quartier Maitre Chef Guidoni was shot in the throat. It was not too serious but he bled out and died five or six metres from Jean Campana.

Up above, the Germans remained concealed, holding their fire. Without a mine detector among them, the men now inched their way through the crumbling rocks and thorny underbrush of this steep cliff. Again, there were shattering explosions on all sides. Men were blown into the air. The three medics worked assiduously over the minefield with their sulpha kits and syringes of morphine, guided through the blackness by the screams and moans of the wounded.

In the pre-dawn, the roar of Dakota engines could be heard coming over the sea. The nearby coastal village of Agay was directly in the flight path of the waves of aircraft winging their way to the drop zones at Le Muy, thirty kilometres away. The aerial invasion had begun, and there was no point in the Naval Assault Group continuing with their abortive mission. The survivors were in a desperate situation, pinned to the ground in the light of the flares which had now added to their discomfort. The commander, Gerard Marche, had also been injured and wanting to keep his maps and plans out of enemy hands, tried to get back to the boats but was blown up only fifty metres from the sea. He lay still for ten agonizing minutes, then staggered on but fell down a cliff onto the rocks where his body was found the next day.

Daylight came and the Germans called out instructions for those who were not wounded to make their own way through the minefield. Lieutenant Letonturier was only fifteen metres away from the road, on his hands and knees, when he was blown up and fractured a leg. At Anthéor, the butcher's bill now stood at eleven dead and seventeen badly wounded. Those still alive would be rescued by the Americans the following day and taken to Saint-Raphaël where a field hospital had been set up.

With heavy hearts the Frenchmen were taken into captivity, leaving their wounded comrades to their own devices. The only able-bodied officer, Lucien Chaffiotte, and a few others were held at Théoule until late in the afternoon and then taken to the German headquarters in Grasse for interrogation. More than eight hours later, the Germans were still mainly concerned with finding out what the central point of the invasion was. Chaffiotte stubbornly told them, 'Port Vendres' – which is on the border of Spain.

In the heat of the day, and without water, the other twenty or so survivors were made to walk to Grasse, a distance of forty kilometres. At the height of their suffering, eight kilometres from Grasse, the men hardly noticed a peasant woman carrying a basket of vegetables pass by, nor did she seem to be taking any notice of them. Just as the woman was passing the column, one of her baskets dropped on the ground, spilling out its contents. When someone bent down to help her pick up her scattered vegetables, she whispered in his ear: 'Be prepared! There is going to be an attack in the forest to free you!'

A group of five young resistants, including the brothers Francis and Fernand Tonner from La Napoule, had set off by bicycle on the Route de

Grasse armed only with pistols. At Auribeau-sur-Siagne, the *maquisards* pretended to be fixing their bicycles then confronted the German escorts as they came round a corner. There were only three Germans, and nobody expected them to offer any resistance – but they did. One was shot, another escaped and the third hit Fernand Tonner with his rifle. Grappling on the ground, Fernand managed to grab a rock from the hands of his assailant and smashed the man's skull.

Some of the shattered French commandos refused to make a run for it, saying that for them the war was over, but about ten of the captives followed Francis Tonner into the forest, and then to Tanneron where they awaited the arrival of the Allied forces. For his exploits Fernand received an official citation from the French Navy and the Croix de Guerre. The two Tonner brothers would again come to the fore during the liberation of their hometown, La Napoule.

*

Tuesday 15 August was to be a holiday – Assumption Day – and 18-year-old Pierrette Friolet had planned to spend the day picnicking with friends on the hillside at the Pétignon estate close to what would become Drop Zone 'C'. She was with her mother at the Bar le Provençal situated on the RN 7 at the western entrance to Le Muy when they received advanced warning that the landings were going to take place the following day. Wisely they changed their plans, and about twelve friends gathered in the basement where they stayed the night of the 14th and the whole of the next day. A German command post was located just down the road at the Château de des Peyrouas (now the retirement home Les Milles Soleils).

Those who were not privy to the advance warning went about their normal business and came in for quite a shock even though the continuous droning of the air armada overhead told them that something was up. A farmer going out to fetch his cows thought it was the Germans playing 'war games'. A drunk on his way home after a long night thought he had seen the devil when he came across a paratrooper with a blackened face.

The three drop zones, designated 'A', 'O' and 'C', were situated between La Motte and Le Muy, twenty to thirty kilometres inland. The first two were fairly flat, lying between the Nartuby and Argens rivers, and close enough together so as to be almost indistinguishable from the air. Drop Zone 'C' was in the foothills of the Maures to the south of the Route Nationale 7, and was therefore rocky and steep.

Less than 50 per cent of the pathfinders managed to accomplish their tasks, but the overall mission was considered a success. Crossing the coast at Agay and arriving over the target at about 3.30 a.m., one team jumped after its sixth run-in on the target and another circled for about half an hour before it dropped its load and went home. A stick of pathfinders from the 517th Parachute Infantry Regiment landed in the woods five and a half kilometres east of DZ 'A' and just east of Le Muy where they met some resistance. As a result, they only set up their Eureka Beacon late in the day.

Some pathfinders and troopers landed in the middle of Le Muy and had to fight their way out. At her grandmother's house, at the bottom end of Rue Hoche, Pierrette's father, Justin, went to answer a knock on the door. An American paratrooper was there wanting directions, but a bullet intended for the American instead hit the 44-year-old Justin Friolet. He collapsed mortally wounded and lay outside in the hot sun all day. Forty years later, the American soldier, Leslie Garvin, made a pilgrimage from Oregon to Le Muy to visit the family of the Frenchman who was killed in his stead.

One stick of pathfinders from the 509th Parachute Infantry Battalion found themselves high up in the Esterel Mountains at Le Malpey with a prime view of the amphibious landings at Saint-Raphaël. Ten kilometres to the north, as the crow flies, another pathfinder team of the 509th landed high up in a forest at Belluny, halfway between Tanneron and Montauroux. From their vantage point they would have been able to see and hear at least some of the action which would take place on the roads in the valley below. The story of their adventures over the next few days will be told in a later chapter.

*

From Anthéor, where the French commandos landed in a minefield, to the centre of Cannes it is only twenty-six kilometres along the coastal road. With all the activity at sea and overhead, the sound of battle seemed even closer than that. At Villa Montfluery, the Gestapo headquarters in Cannes, Hans Moser and a few of his staff, together with their mistresses, sat round the dinner table until the early hours planning their escape. When news of the first landings reached him, Moser immediately began burning papers and informed his agents that they would be retreating to Nice and from there to Italy.

Pondering their fate in the cells below the villa were twelve prisoners – ten men and two women. One of the women, Conchita Biacca, was an Italian-born, dark-haired beauty; she was also pregnant. Like some of the other the prisoners, she was a member of the Underground. At least four were members of the Maquis group known as *Tartane*. Only one, Hyppolite Séguran, a farmworker from Cagnes-sur-Mer, was from these parts. They knew about the Allied landings and could hear the rumbling of the guns. Some of the prisoners were optimistic, until they heard footsteps and saw the look on the faces of the three Nazis, Hans Moser, Willy Baue and Richard Held. The latter, a studious-looking petty criminal from Alsace, was wearing civilian clothes.

After his subsequent capture and interrogation, Richard Held gave a statement describing how on Moser's instructions he escorted the 'Czech woman' to the steps of the villa on the ground floor, and told her she was free to go. Going back to the basement, Held noticed that Moser and Bauer had their service pistols in hand and suspected that the other prisoners were going to be executed. At around 8.30 p.m., everyone was ordered into one cell:

> At that moment I heard a gunshot fired in cell number 2. I turned around and saw this gunshot had been fired by Bauer on Mademoiselle Conchita, who was screaming and holding onto Bauer. She fell on the ground making Bauer bend forward. It is at that moment, and taking advantage of my movement, the last prisoner, whom I later found out was Mr Negri, managed to escape. I arrived next to Bauer as he fired a second shot into Mademoiselle Conchita who was on the floor. I then took out my pistol. Several shots were fired in the hallway, in which I heard sounds of a precipitous escape. Bauer and I rushed to the door of cell number 2, where I saw several prisoners running toward the grilled door that closed the hallway. Seeing that some of the prisoners were going to escape, I emptied the entire clip of my pistol into them, in other words, seven bullets. Bauer did the same. As for Moser, he was firing from the back of the hallway and into cell number 4. All the prisoners fell one after the other as we fired.'[6]

Richard Held speculated that he killed two of the prisoners, but then a ricochet wounded him in his foot. Stepping over the bodies, he went upstairs to bandage it. Moser and Bauer stayed behind for a few minutes to finish everyone off. By pretending to be dead, two men survived. The one named Negri ran up the stairs and out of the front door. Wild shots were fired at him by a French turncoat, the 17-year-old Paul Malaguti who was hired by the Gestapo as a driver. While Richard Held was executed for his role in the Montfluery Villa Massacre, Paul Malaguti joined the French Foreign Legion under a pseudonym and fought in Indochina. Despite his appalling past, he was pardoned and, in more recent times, played a leading role in Jean-Marie Le Pen's right-wing National Front Party.

*

Although not in any immediate danger of being overrun, the Gestapo in Nice went crazy with frustration and fear. They too knew their day of reckoning had arrived and ordered the execution of twenty-three prisoners being held in the cells. The place of execution was an empty plot of land, not far from Gestapo headquarters, in the Ariane district, on the northern periphery of Nice. The truck disgorged its human load and led by a priest, the group stumbled down toward a rock face. Somebody began singing 'La Marseillaise'. A machine gun had been set up on the opposite side of a small stream. Those who survived the first burst tried to make a run for it but were shot down by the guards. Although they had been shot many times, some were still moving or moaning and were administered a coup de grâce in the head or neck.

In what is now known as the Ariane Massacre of 15 August 1944, the victims included a 57-year-old cousin of General de Lattre de Tassigny's, a nurse, two boys of 16 and 18, and a retired officer taken as a hostage for his son who had joined the Resistance. A priest was also shot, his only crime being to bury two *maquisards*. In addition to these martyrs, there were two informers who had outlived their usefulness to the Gestapo.

Lying next to the body of one of the women, Hélène Vagliano, was a basket with a piece of bread and a pear, given to her by her mother who thought she was being moved to another prison. Hélène Vagliano was the 35-year-old daughter of a Greek shipping owner, president of the Cannes-La Napoule Golf Club. Educated at St George's School at Ascot in England, Elaine, as she was known to her English friends, spoke

French with an English accent. She led a privileged life of hiking, snow skiing and boating on the Mediterranean.[7] During the occupation, she did charity work, but was involved in the Underground, and at one stage after her arrest, she was able to whisper to her mother:

> I would never have been arrested without a denunciation. I had burned all my papers immediately after the arrest of R.C. Without that there was no proof against me. I have seen her file, she told everything, even the things that no one knew except she and I. She spoke of two letters that I had given her. It's serious, very serious, as well as the information on clandestine routes to Spain. She provided names. They did not hit her; she talked immediately. I believed she was my friend. I had such confidence in her. Oh! Mama![8]

On 29 July 1944, five *miliciens*, members of the Légions de Volontaires Français Contre le Bolchévisme, had arrested her and her parents in Cannes, stealing whatever valuables were in the house. Taken first to the Gestapo offices at the infamous Villa Montfleury, Hélène was interrogated and tortured while her family and other prisoners in neighbouring cells could hear her sobbing all night. After two days of beating and humiliation, the prisoners were transported by lorry to a prison in Grasse. From her filthy cell Mrs Vagliano could hear her child's voice saying, 'I don't know', 'Oh! Don't do that', then screams of agony. In front of ten men the torturers had undressed her completely and burnt her whole body with red-hot irons. It seems the Gestapo were trying to get details of the girl's work and make her denounce friends who were thought to be pro-Anglo.

Moving ever closer to the heart of darkness, the prisoners were all put in a closed lorry and taken to Villa Trianon, the Gestapo headquarters at Cimiez in the northern suburbs of Nice. For beds they had sacks of straw, full of fleas and vermin. No toilets, only a bucket, a small rusty tap and a basin under it for both washing and drinking. Hardly any nourishment was given except for a black liquid and sour bread.

Hélène's mother, Danaë, was released after a week but before leaving the prison, she was able to see her daughter whose arms, legs thighs, and neck looked like raw beef from the beatings. This was the last time Danaë would see her daughter: the Gestapo officer would not allow them to touch. News of the landings had reached the prisoners, and hopes soared, but at 3 p.m. that day, the soldiers came to take them away.

All of this was contained in Danaë Vagliano's sworn statement in her quest for justice: 'My daughter left our house on the 29th of July at 10.30, happy, healthy and full of the joy of living for she knew the landing would be soon. She returned to Cannes on the 30th of September in her coffin covered with the French flag.' Every resistance group in the south was represented at the funeral; men and women formed a guard of honour, keeping a vigil throughout the night. Someone sang 'Ave Maria', followed by her favourite piece by Johann Sebastian Bach, the melancholy 'Viens douce mort' (Come sweet death). Posthumously awarded the Légion d'Honneur and the title 'Heroine of France', there is also a street named after Hélène Vagliano in the heart of Cannes.

Chapter 12

Confusion

Contrary to the expectations of ordinary citizens, the first signs of their liberation on 15 August came from the sky. At approximately 4.15 a.m., the roar of aircraft flying at low altitude, and the wail of sirens woke the residents of Le Muy from their slumbers, and the clatter of machine guns fully got their attention. Between getting dressed and praying, they opened their shutters just a crack but the only thing that greeted their eyes was the thick fog that was blotting out the entire landscape. So thick, and so unusual was the fog at that time of year that people who woke before daybreak thought it was artificial. From the air, only the mountaintops could be seen sticking out through the fog layer, causing some parachutists to think that these were islands in the sea.

Bruna Aldani, nicknamed Brunette, lived in the Quartier des Ferrières, which is on the northwestern edge of Le Muy. From here there is a clear view toward La Motte and Ferme du Mitan which was soon swarming with men and machines. She was 16 at the time and never forgot the emotions which overwhelmed her when she was awoken by a cacophony of sound but her picture is blurred:

> We had already heard the American Flying Fortresses, scores of them, as they flew overhead in our region during the day. We watched them from the Ferrières, saw them come from the sea, fly over Saint-Aygulf, heading towards Draguignan. One had a feeling they followed the Route Nationale [RN 7]. As we were there, the roar went crescendo, probably because the planes were numerous and flew above us at low altitude. We all stayed in bed, feeling some anguish all the same … What was going on?[1]

American and British paratroopers were intermingled as they hit the ground in the dark and misty dawn. The first thing was to cut themselves out of their harness, and make contact with other members of their stick. The password in the first hour was 'Lafayette' and the countersign 'Democracy'. An alternative password was 'Billy' and the countersign 'The Kid'. When a British trooper could not remember the countersign when challenged, he finally came up with 'Some fookin' cowboy', or so the story goes. There are also accounts of American paratroopers firing at their British allies, having never seen uniforms such as they were wearing.

It was daylight, but still foggy, when Geoffrey Jones arrived and identified himself to Colonel Rupert Graves, commander of the 517th Parachute Infantry Regiment. Acting as liaison with FFI leaders, he helped guide disorientated paratroopers to their assembly points, including the Château Sainte-Roseline, just northeast of Les Arcs. The château had been identified during the planning stages as one such rendezvous point. Its owner at the time was the Baron de Rasque de Laval, and it is still surrounded by many acres of vineyards today. Some of the buildings date back to medieval times and the mummified remains of fourteenth-century Roseline of Villeneuve are preserved in the abbey.

For 11-year-old Jacqueline Gezilly, this was the most exciting time of her life. Her sister Michele, two years older, had shaken her awake. Dawn had not yet broken, and the night sky over their home in the Château Sainte-Roseline was filled with the rumble of engines. Their mother, the Baroness de Laval – Jacqueline and Michele were her daughters by her first marriage – was pouring drinks for two soldiers smeared with black and green paint. Unsure at first, the two girls had to be won over with chewing gum. Designated as a dressing station, the château and its courtyards started filling up with wounded paratroopers.

As the gliders began coming in, one pilot described the scene in the air as being like 'Piccadilly Circus at high noon with the traffic being directed by an insane policeman'. Flying wing to wing, several aircraft collided. One cargo-carrying glider, which was being towed too fast, broke up over the Mediterranean, fifty kilometres northeast of Bastia, sending the pilot and co-pilot (Flight Officers Robert Hardin and William Kern) plummeting to their deaths. Only Hardin's body was recovered and he is buried in his hometown of Little Rock, Arkansas. A total of eleven glider pilots, and eight men of the 550th Airborne Infantry were killed in crashes, and over a hundred were seriously injured. Many of the glider pilots were veterans of the Normandy landings.

After being informed of the exact location of the two glider landing zones, *maquisards* helped to clear obstacles. Pilots also had to contend with trees, vineyards and other gliders clogging the landing grounds. Out of the 400 or so gliders, 150 broke up on landing. It is no wonder that these machines made of steel tubing and plywood were called 'flying coffins'. Huge clouds of dust rose as gliders skidded along the ground at 120 to 140 kilometres per hour. They bounced and scraped, and lurched across the field until stopped by a solid object. Looking at the crumpled wrecks, it occurred to some that only a miracle allowed the Jeeps, guns and men to come out unscathed.

It seems that the exact number of men and machines involved in the airborne operation is anyone's guess. Regimental histories, concerned only with their own narrow experience, differ from each other. Therefore, it was decided to use the figures which are written in stone (literally) on a monument at Le Muy. There it is inscribed that the airborne invasion involved 9,700 men, 535 transport aircraft and 410 gliders escorted by fighters, as well as 221 Jeeps, and 213 pieces of artillery.

Over 100 gliders landed on the Domaine de Valbourgès, which is in the middle of the drop zone between La Motte and Trans-en-Provence on the road to Draguignan. The entire area between Le Mitan, La Motte, Trans-en-Provence, Les Serres, Glastron, Les Esclans and Le Muy became a hive of activity. Jeeps dashed to and fro, picking up the wounded and carrying them to the aid station at Saint-Roseline where Colonel Rupert Graves of the 517th PIR had his command post. Others were taken to the château at Domaine de Valbourgès, the temporary aid station and HQ of the 551st Parachute Infantry Battalion, nicknamed GOYA (Get Off Your Ass) after their regimental motto, *Aterrice y Ataque*, or Land and Attack.

Civilian souvenir hunters cycled from Draguignan to the landing fields, stripping the wrecked gliders of their valuable instrumentation. The most popular items were the wheels, compasses and identification markings on the fabric. Not more than 1,000 parachutes, both personnel and cargo types, were recovered and sent to Rome for salvage and repair. Fewer than fifty gliders out of 400 could be salvaged. Seventy-five years later some pieces of glider frames can still be found around Le Muy, one entangled in the branches of a tree.[2]

Some resistance was encountered at all the landing zones in the form of sniper fire and brief firefights that caused a number of casualties on both sides, but mostly on the side of the Germans. Half a mile south of Le Muy, a demolitions platoon with some military policemen, was attacked: one American was killed and eight others captured. At daybreak, a German patrol on motorcycles was ambushed and three were killed. Approaching Le Muy, a patrol of the 517th collided with a strong German force. One American was killed, and five others captured. The captives, all wounded, were taken to Le Muy and treated by a French doctor and a British medic. At the aid post there were also Germans who, only hours before, had been such a source of fear and were now mere human wrecks, groaning with pain and begging for water as they lay helpless.

Lieutenant Charles Hillsdale landed with his stick three or four kilometres northwest of Lorgues, where there was the usual garrison of Germans. Nevertheless, they entered the town and dropped off a wounded man at the hospital. Continuing toward Les Arcs, they sent out two patrols scouting ahead. Near Draguignan, one of these three-man patrols became entangled with a group of Germans, killing three and taking twenty-five prisoners who, despite their protests, were handed over to the FFI. The other patrol got lost and went off on a 'wild goose-chase' with an FFI detachment to Le Thoronet. There they were captured by a force of 250 Germans who then 'surrendered' themselves to the three-man patrol when they in turn became surrounded by the FFI a day later. The prisoners were turned over to the FFI anyway. The overpowering fear which the Germans had for the FFI was of scant concern to the Americans at times like this.

With the Germans so thin on the ground, only the unluckiest of paratroopers found themselves surrounded or under fire as they hit the ground. Private First Class Philip Kennamer – the 28-year-old son of Judge Franklin E. Kennamer – had previously had a lucky break in that he had been recently been paroled from prison where he was serving a twenty-five-year sentence for killing a prominent local man in Tulsa, Oklahoma, one Thanksgiving. Now, as he landed near Trans-en-Provence as part of the 560th Parachute Field Artillery Battalion (560th PFAB), his group got pinned down by a machine gun. Phil Kennamer and Lieutenant Harry Moore tried to rush it but both were mowed down. Back in Oklahoma, the *Tulsa World* reported that the Kennamer's death closed the book on one of the country's most publicized slayings. It seems he had a strong premonition that he would not be coming home and hoped that those who had condemned him would hold him differently in their memories.

In the long twilight of summer, troops continued to arrive until 7 p.m. The 551st Parachute Infantry Battalion made what looked like a training jump at about 6 p.m. The British 2nd Independent Parachute Brigade consisted of the 4th Battalion, 5th (Scottish) Parachute Battalion and the 6th (Royal Welch) Battalion. Lieutenant (later Colonel) Oswald Baker was one of the twenty-six South Africans in the brigade, most of whom were commissioned officers with combat experience in the Western Desert, but this was their first combat jump. Baker describes what it felt like to jump into the unknown:

> The sea looked sinister as we flew over it, a dark, still pewter grey. When we crossed the coast of France, the land below looked very inhospitable, a deep smudge of green just before dawn. I was number one in the stick. As I dropped, I shouted to my batman who was just behind me: 'Eaton, where are you?' But he didn't hear me because the wind was wafting men all over the place. We jumped from three hundred feet and it took us only twenty-five seconds to get down. You drop fifty feet before the parachute opens – that prevents the spreading out of the troops. As I fell I thought (while worrying about the tracers coming up towards me): I wish my mother could see me now.[3]

The 5th (Scottish) Parachute Battalion had been allocated the task of capturing Le Muy, but a large contingent had been dropped thirty-five kilometres off course. Baker was one who landed close to the drop zone but was hung up in a tree, unable to reach his knife or his Tommy gun. Fifty-five years afterwards, his memory distorted in the mists of time, Ossie Baker recounted:

> It was a parachutist's nightmare. There was a bit of a battle going on around me. As usual in an airborne landing there is a lot of confusion. When you land among the opposition, they are as scared as you. Everybody was shooting – in

fact, more of us were killed by our own side than by the Germans. You couldn't see who was who. The gliders were coming in now, getting smashed up on the asparagus sticks that the Germans had put up in all the fields. Then to my horror, along came a young German troopie – I learned later he was a Russian, only 14 or 15 years old. He just stared at me, and I just stared at him. Then he said words to the effect that for me the war was over. But over his shoulder, thank God, I could see Eaton creeping along behind him. He came up and put the Tommy gun in the Russian's back and said: 'No, for *you* the war is over!'[4]

Baker now had to organize his platoon. Some were already in action. The platoon sergeant had landed on the roof of a two-storey building full of Germans and had started his war from there. 'It was chaos,' says Baker, blaming it on the 'inexperience of the American sprog pilots'. The brigade was spread out over many kilometres: 'The Germans were as confused as we were. We had troops all over the place, Americans, French, British. We wore identification on our arms, the Union Jack or the stars and stripes, but in the dark it didn't help much.'[5]

Oswald Baker was to become a founding father of the parachute regiment in South Africa, a regular army officer, but it would appear from his personal account, that his memory had become somewhat tainted by the time he was interviewed in later life: 'We had to take two or three villages near the DZ, not only my platoon, but the whole formation, nearly two divisions of parachute troops.' In fact, the airborne formation amounted to less than one division. Baker continues: 'When we went into the village, we were astonished at our reception. To say the villagers were unenthusiastic was an understatement. They were spitting at us, and some of the chaps got browned off at this. It was Vichy France, and those people had not had a difficult war. Certainly no flowers were thrown at our feet. It was the same at Cannes and Nice.'[6] It may be true that a few short-sighted Vichyites were still under the spell of Marshal Pétain, but clearly Baker was uninformed about the dire conditions which existed in Provence. Furthermore, the 2nd Independent Parachute Brigade played only a peripheral role in the liberation of Cannes, although some senior officers visited the city on 25 August. Cannes was liberated on 24 August, and by the time Nice was liberated on 28 August, the whole brigade was back in Italy. In fact, the reception which the Allies received from residents of these two cities was euphoric – as is evident from images and civilian accounts of the liberation. The account given by the leader of Stick 99, accidentally dropped eight kilometres northwest of Cannes, also contradicts Baker: 'I found the French people gave plenty of help & were only too willing to do anything for us.'[7]

It is said that La Motte was the first village to be liberated, but parachutists landed virtually on top of the hamlet of Clastron, and the small garrison surrendered without a fight. Establishing its headquarters at a farm called Le Mitan, one British battalion, reduced in strength, set off to take Le Muy. On reaching the Nartuby River, they found the Germans were ready and waiting in some houses on the opposite bank at a place called La Serre. Trying to cross the bridge, seven British paratroopers were killed, including Lieutenant Arthur Stewart (24) of Wallington, Surrey, the only British officer killed in the whole operation. The Germans had taken worse casualties but they still held onto Le Serre.

After dark, another attempt was made to enter Le Muy by the 6th (Royal Welch) Battalion but at the Nartuby they were caught in the open by illuminating flares, machine-gun and mortar fire and returned to their starting positions. It seems that Brigadier Charles Pritchard, officer commanding the 2nd Independent Parachute Brigade, was reluctant to proceed, and Major General Robert T. Frederick decided to give the job to the recently arrived 550th Airborne Infantry Battalion. American unit histories have suggested that the British 2nd Independent Parachute Brigade was detached from Frederick's command, at his request, because of their lack of aggressiveness.[8]

According to a German source, the Allied paratroopers faced no more than three companies of German combat troops.[9] Others say that Le Muy alone was defended by a battalion-sized force. The strongest defences were sited on the eastern entrance to the town, on the Fréjus road, and on the southern side of town, at Rue Louis Hebreard, with heavy guns covering the road to Sainte-Maxime. With all communications cut by bombing or by the Maquis, German officers trying to organize a defence were forced to dispatch motorcycle couriers, which practically amounted to a suicide mission. Being completely outnumbered and overwhelmed, the Germans became more nervous as the day progressed. Because their own parachute troops were a highly respected elite, they were not keen to tangle with the Allied paratroopers, who, owing to the design of their uniforms, and the knives that many of them had strapped onto their person, had acquired the moniker, 'Butchers with big pockets'.

Most civilians were at first not sure who these soldiers were. Their uniforms, which were covered with blotches of green yellow and black paint, were like nothing they had seen before. When she realized that they were Americans, the 16-year-old Bruna Aldani rushed up and kissed the paratrooper in front of her. She had no idea why she did that but she was aware that this was a day she was never going to forget. Her father volunteered to guide the Americans to their assembly point at Château Sainte-Roseline while her mother took care of injured paratroopers in the living room. Jeeps with white stars on the bonnet came in from the fields, laden with soldiers, and seemed to be heading in the direction of Draguignan. One glider finished its course a mere twenty metres away, and from Bruna's observation point a strange vehicle – a Jeep – rolled out.

For the children, who had never tasted chewing gum before, it was like Christmas with all the chewing gum and chocolate being handed out. The paratrooper's K-rations contained Wrigley's or Dentyne gum, and various types of chocolate bars by Nestlé and Hershey. The sight of the 'gigantic aerial carrousel' overhead was fabulous but there were also lifeless forms on the ground, shrouded with parachutes. Corpses accumulated in front of the Jacquement *boulangerie*. Marthe Georges was twenty at the time and worked at the Le Muy city hall. In her book about her wartime experiences, *C'etait Hier au Muy*, she maintains that 'as morning came everyone wanted to resume work as quickly as possible'. Despite her mother's protests, she went with her father to collect his horse. At the entrance to Rue du Nord, they saw an artillery piece and two Germans standing watch. She tried to get them to move it away from their house, but a soldier simply shrugged and said 'You go … *kaput* … you stay … *kaput* … here, everybody *kaput*.' [10]

At 11.30 a.m. on the 16th, the attack on Le Muy was resumed by elements of the 509th PIB – those not 'lost' at Saint-Tropez – and the 550th Glider Infantry Battalion, with artillery support. House by house the Americans advanced, reaching the town square by early afternoon. At 4 p.m., the German garrison, numbering about 500, surrendered. Tanks from the US 45th Infantry Division had broken out from the beachhead and had already linked up with the paratroopers. Arriving on the outskirts of Le Muy, they provided a strong incentive for the Germans to surrender.

A member of the 550th recalls this stage of the 'battle': 'In one place I could look out over a field and see German foxholes. We discovered they were all old men, members of a construction battalion. They weren't firing, and we just sent men along the line to tap them on the helmet and order them out of the holes – '*Raus! Kommen sie aus!*' They just got up, hands in the air and started walking to the rear.'[11]

Although unconfirmed, there were reports of an incident where a Jewish trooper was murdered and mutilated by the Germans near Le Muy. Private Henry Wikins (otherwise spelled Wilkins), of the 596th Engineer Company, attached to the 517th PIR, was badly injured on landing and could not be moved to the assembly point. The DZ was also under mortar fire, so he was made as comfortable as possible and left behind. Later he was apparently found with his genitals stuffed in his mouth. This information was provided by Technician Fifth Grade (T/5) Charles Pugh, also of the 596th Parachute Engineer Company, and there is indeed a Private Henry Wikins from Pennsylvania buried in the Draguignan American Cemetery, date of death 16 August 1944. It seems that he insisted on wearing his Star of David.

*

The saga of the 'lost legions' of parachutists who were accidentally dropped thirty kilometres off course began in a previous chapter with their sudden appearance in the midst of the Maquis and the members of the OSS near Fayence. About 480 American and 100 British paratroopers, all transported in American C-47 Skytrains, landed between Seillans and Callian. When Jones and Allain were driving down from Fayence to the drop zone in the early hours of 15 August, the first Americans they came across belonged to the 463rd Parachute Artillery Battalion, attached to the 517th Parachute Infantry Regiment.

Those in the leading ten planes jumped in the vicinity of Seillans, and the following thirty-four planeloads landed near Callian and Tourettes. Three major groups and various smaller groups were spread out over twelve kilometres. As this terrain is a jumble of mountains, rocks and forests, it is a miracle that only about 100 men were injured in the night jump. The most common injuries were sprained ankles but those who were too badly injured to be moved were left in the care of their own medics and the Maquis. The only prudent thing to do was to sit tight until daylight before moving out. In most cases, the locals were only too happy to help bundle up equipment and provide directions.

While pouring eau de vie (brandy) and wine for their unannounced visitors, farmers and villagers had maps thrust under their noses. 'Where am I?' was the first question. Pointing to a spot far off the map and mouthing the names of never-before-heard-of towns, it became clear just how far off course they were. When one disorientated trooper hammered on the door of a house, a woman appeared on the balcony and asked what was going on. '*Parachutiste Américain,*' came the reply. The woman just said, '*Oh là là*' and went back inside.

A boy from Callian, who was 16 at the time, had woken to the sound of aircraft overhead. The first thing he saw, shining on the ground, was a packet of Chesterfields. Looking up, there was a parachute hanging in a pine tree. There were red and green and camouflage-coloured parachutes in the woods all the way to Fayence. Next, there were four

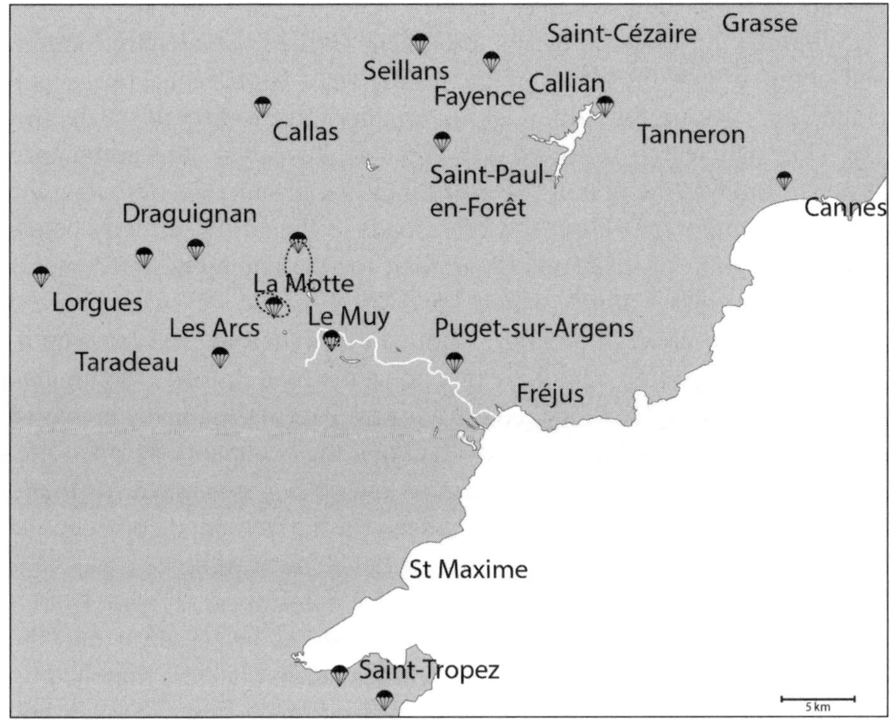

Elements of the FABTF were unintentionally scattered far and wide.

or five Americans lined up by a wall. One of them saw the boy and started speaking in 'American'. All the boy could understand was the word 'La Motte'.[12]

At a farm near Tourrettes, belonging to Lidia Airaud and her husband, an aid post was marked by a white parachute with a red cross in the middle. It was not long before the farmyard was swarming with injured men, *maquisards,* and a few American paratroopers who were thought to be 'negroes' because of their black greasepaint. At about 9 a.m., the assembled paratroopers entered the village and were met with some resistance which lasted late into the afternoon. Captain G. A. Hooper of the 517th had struggled with his parachute harness and jumped later than the rest of his stick, landing somewhere near Saint-Cézaire-sur-Siagne where he immediately became something of a celebrity. After a few days of enjoying the local hospitality, he and one British paratrooper were taken to Montauroux where they met up with fellow countrymen. Numbering about thirty or thirty-five men, this small band carried out a few acts of sabotage and had some brushes with the enemy, but did not attempt to reach their assembly point.

While trying to assemble his men near Callian, Lieutenant Skutnik and about fifteen members of the 517th were approached by several *maquisards* asking for help in taking on thirty-five to fifty of the enemy. The skirmish which followed has come to be called 'the ambulance ambush' and was the first of two ambushes of German convoys along the D 562 on Dragoon D-Day. At a crossroads in the valley, directly below Callian, a group of resistants lay in wait for the enemy reinforcements from Grasse and Cannes which they knew would be rushed to the parachute drop zone. Soon after 7 a.m., a bus with a big red cross on it, accompanied by other vehicles came down the road toward Draguignan. The overzealous fighters opened fire anyway. Part of the convoy managed to turn round but the bus came to a halt and the occupants returned fire. Being only lightly armed with Sten guns and rifles, the *maquisards* found themselves outgunned and had it not been for the immediate presence of the American paratroopers, it would not have ended well.

In the brief firefight which followed, one paratrooper, Private Robert Gruwell, was killed by his own hand grenade as he tossed it into the bus. Six to ten Germans were killed and the survivors were marched up the hill into Callian and locked up in the church. A young French boy remembers that the captives were barely able to walk any more, and they were crying. All had rosaries. They were exhausted and sweating when they got to the town square where there is a fountain. Some of them badly needed to drink but the FFI wanted to prevent them from doing so. An old veteran of the First World War came along and said: 'No, no no, you let them drink. They are prisoners, you let them drink.'[13]

Once the Americans had left the area for their assembly point at Sainte-Roseline, the bodies of the Germans were recovered by their comrades and taken to Saint-Vallier-de-Thiey north of Grasse for burial. From letters of condolence to one of the relatives, it would appear that the bus was in fact a real ambulance evacuating sick and wounded German soldiers further to the rear so as to make room at the hospital in Saint-Vallier for the casualties expected during the coming invasion. This would explain the exhaustion of the prisoners while walking up to Callian.

A second ambush occurred later in the day near the Château de la Colle Noire which at one time was owned by the famous designer Christian Dior. Opposite the château was a stone well – the Well of the Cursed – where a monument stands today. Behind the well was a railway line. From this point, toward Draguignan, the road runs straight along the valley with fields on each side. The German column consisted of about fifteen vehicles from the 327th Reserve Grenadier Battalion of the 148th Reserve Division from Cannes. Having heard of the fate of the ambulance convoy, they were ready to spring into action at the first salvo. One group entered the château and dragged the family out into the road, threatening to shoot them. An old man sitting in the sun, watching the show, was shot for just being there.

There are many versions of what happened next at Colle Noire but it is clear that two Allied fighter aircraft promptly arrived on the scene and began strafing the column on the straight section of road. They made about three passes, annihilating the vehicles and sending both soldiers and civilian hostages scattering. Accounts of this action and the numbers involved vary depending on the source, but up to ten Germans were killed, about five surrendered and the rest escaped into the countryside. It seems that at least three of the German tucks were still in working order and were put to good use.

It is unclear how many paratroopers were involved in the initial contact, but a large contingent joined in to finish the job. A recently assembled group of about sixty men of the 517th under Captain Joe McGeever, together with eighty men of the 5th (Scottish) Parachute Battalion under Major J. A. Blackwood, followed the sounds of battle.

The War Diary of the 2nd Independent Parachute Brigade gives the military version of the ambush, without mentioning the air support:

> Maj Blackwood ordered the group off the road and an ambush was laid. However just before the convoy was due to pass the group, fire was opened up further down the road and the vehicles stopped. Maj Blackwood sent a patrol forward to investigate the source of the firing. During this time an officer from 517 RCT [Regimental Combat Team] reached the group stating that he had a force of 60 men with him as well as an 81mm and a 60mm mortar. A few minutes later the patrol returned with the information that about 15 enemy vehicles were being held up by a mixed British and American force of about 25 men, but they were now being attacked by a force of 60 to 70 Germans. The group then moved down towards the vehicles, took up position and fired on them with LMG [light machine gun] and mortar fire, inflicting heavy casualties on the enemy and damaging several of the vehicles.[14]

Major Blackwood with two escorts forged ahead to report to his HQ that five officers and 110 other ranks of the 2nd Independent Parachute Brigade were on their way. The rest of the column, which was now 400 strong, halted for the night below Bagnols-en-Forêt. On the 16th, one group of British paratroopers under Lieutenant Holden was involved in another fierce skirmish, leaving seven dead Germans and seven prisoners who were handed over to the 'partisans' at Bagnols. Confusion was the order of the day with paratroopers of all nationalities moving in all directions in an assortment of captured vehicles and Jeeps.

At Seillans, as the 517th PIR regimental history relates, it was Colonel Melvin Zais, officer commanding the 3rd Battalion, who rounded up his men. In reality, it was more a question of individuals finding their friends. The column formed up at 8 a.m. only to be bombed by some 'friendly' P-38s. This large group proceeded via Claviers to Callas, where they stopped for the night, and the rest of their journey was relatively uneventful. Many years later, in 1969, General Melvin Zais would be in command of the 101st Airborne Division at the time of their attack on the famous Hamburger Hill in Vietnam.

One group of approximately thirty Americans and British were making their way down to the Argens Valley when they met with a sizeable enemy force. After a short engagement, they withdrew and took a circular route to Sainte-Roseline, only arriving on D+4. Others decided to stay where they were in what would become no man's land for a few days, including the medics manning aid posts which had been set up at Fayence, Montauroux and Callian. They continued treating the wounded from both sides.

The fighting around Fayence went on intermittently for days in what was termed 'individual actions'. Some of the paratroopers joined with the local Maquis and Jedburgh team SCEPTRE in the no man's land which now existed around Fayence and the D562 where some inexperienced *maquisards* walked up to a German convoy thinking they were Americans. In an instant, the *maquisard*s were surrounded and taken to a bridge to be executed. One fell off the bridge into a big oak tree and saved himself. One was wounded and walked three kilometres in the riverbed clutching his stomach. There was a drop of blood every metre of his way and he died that night. In the words of one survivor: 'The Germans were good at war; they had been to Russia, unlike us, who were just jokers.'[15] Of the eight *maquisards* on the bridge, two were killed, four were wounded and two escaped unharmed.

Soon after this, another incident occurred at the same place where the ambulance ambush had occurred on Dragoon D-Day. A gazogène-powered truck on which ten *maquisards* were riding bumped into two German trucks coming from the other direction. In a hail of bullets, the *maquisards* ran off into the woods. 'At that age you can run fast, even when you are wounded,' said one. The Germans did not follow as 'they were afraid, all they wanted to do was surrender'.[16] Almost everyone was wounded. One man, shot through the femoral artery, ran ten metres to a small wall where he bled to death.

Up above Fayence is a rock known as La Roque which had been turned into a strongpoint and was occupied by about 200 or so Luftwaffe aircraft spotters. It was not a fortress or a radar station as many believed. Emboldened by what was happening around them, some inexperienced *maquisards* attacked La Roque but called it off after some were wounded. The garrison refused to surrender and it was only after Operation Dragoon had ended and the entire 517th PIR had started their push eastward that they were prepared to discuss surrender, but only to Americans (more about this in a later chapter).

*

One of sixteen French paratroopers accompanying the FABTF as interpreters and guides was Corporal Claude Jacquement. He had grown up in Le Muy and was thrilled to be able to parachute into his hometown where his father owned a *boulangerie*. His parents had no idea whether he was dead or alive and he could not wait to see the surprise on their faces when he knocked on the door of his family home. Unfortunately, however, when he landed he found himself not in Le Muy, but in the grounds of a château on the outskirts of Fayence. Claude Jacquement had known the area since he was a boy but he was still miles from home and did not make it into Le Muy until the next afternoon.

The Jacquement *boulangerie* had been at the centre of the battle for Le Muy and it was not a pretty sight when Claude arrived home, but a friend who was present at the reunion confessed that the joy and emotion was something that he would never forget. Unfortunately, the culmination to this story is not a happy one. Claude Jacquement went on to fight in Indochina and was captured after the siege of Dien Bien Phu in May 1954. His parents heard nothing more from him and eventually accepted his death.[17]

It was the job of Rugby Force to establish roadblocks on all the main routes and there was none more important than Route Nationale 7 which connected the cities of Nice and Aix-en-Provence, with Toulon in between, and which cut right through the drop zones. A prominent landmark overlooking the RN 7 is a big red rock or bluff called Roque Rousse. From here, the Americans could see all the comings and goings around Les Arcs although some small groups of Germans used the natural cover to slip through to Draguignan where their headquarters was located.

On the RN 7, between Le Muy and Les Arcs, just after midday on Dragoon D-Day, Lieutenant Reardon and his stick of sixteen men stopped a black Mercedes staff car together with another car and a motorcycle. Thinking that this was a German roadblock, the officer stopped and gave a 'Heil Hitler' salute. An anti-tank grenade was fired which failed to explode but it sliced off the top of the driver's head 'as one would slice open a soft-boiled egg. Blood and brains were all over the back floor'. Realizing their blunder, the others made a run for it but six were shot down and one captured. The car was driven back to headquarters and offered to the American colonel for his own use. On seeing the mess on the floor of the car, he turned a little pale but a practically minded paratrooper fired a few shots through the floor, draining out some of the blood.[18] Today there is a pizza restaurant at the scene of the ambush.

Of all the Operation Rugby objectives, the most problematic turned out to be the town of Les Arcs which is situated on the railway line where the RN 7 intersects with smaller roads leading to Trans-en-Provence, Lorgues and Vidauban. The railway runs parallel to the RN 7 just south of the town. It was on and around the railway bridge that the fiercest fighting took place and most of the casualties were incurred. Driving from the RN 7 toward the Les Arcs station today, one will cross over the Pont de la Gare on which there is a monument commemorating the men of the 'Five Seventeenth'.

Approximately 800 metres south of the railway bridge, near where the road branches off to Lorgues, there is another monument to commemorate the bloodiest of all the ambushes, which took place on 15 August. This time it was a group of hot-headed young *maquisards* who, filled with exuberance, and accompanied by two paratroopers rushed over from Lorgues to join in the battle for Les Arcs. According to a local source, there were about twenty fighters in two trucks who had first gone to the district of Les Nouradons, north of Les Arcs, to pick up weapons. On their way back to Lorgues, they decided to pass through Les Arcs, and on the southeastern side of town, on what is now called Avenue des 13 Lorguais, (previously 4 Chemins des Arcs) they were fired on by a German anti-tank gun and a machine gun. Thirteen were killed. Forever known as the *Treize Patriotes Lorguguais*, a small ceremony is held every year to remember them.

A similar incident occurred two days later on the outskirts of Le Thoronet where two trucks of the Lorgues Maquis group known as *Carrara* ran into a strong German column in the process of pulling back. The lives of seven young men were discarded in this little-known incident. Their names are engraved on a large rock. Ceremonies are held here by the local inhabitants, but no details of this incident have been found.

On the evening of 15 August, Major William 'Wild Bill' Boyle and about fifty men of the 517th entered Les Arcs from the southeast, on what is now the Avenue des 13 Lorguais. The small force was cut off and a defensive perimeter was formed close to the railway station. An aid station was set up in a hotel where the American surgeon was assisted by a French doctor. Reinforcements arrived in the form of the 3rd Battalion, the very same 'lost battalion' which had landed thirty kilometres off course near Fayence. Although exhausted from their long hike, they were the only troops available and were given no chance to rest. With artillery and close air support, the Germans were driven back toward the vineyards and the overpass in the east. Some street fighting continued in the town during which a reconnaissance party of fourteen men from the 45th Infantry Division were rescued from their German captors.

After their ordeal, Major Boyle's men withdrew to Château Sainte-Roseline where there was an aid station in a large courtyard. Most of the casualties being treated were those injured in the glider and parachute landings, although some men had been seriously wounded in action. Now that the main invasion force had made its way inland, the paratroopers were temporarily unemployed. While they camped in the shade of multi-coloured supply parachutes, comrades whom they had given up for dead continued to re-emerge.

At the same time as Le Muy and Les Arcs were under siege on D+1, the 551st Parachute Infantry Battalion was tasked with taking the departmental capital of Draguignan. In command was the much-liked Colonel Wood Joerg who would be killed in action at the battle of the Bulge alongside many of his men.

The Americans had artillery support at their disposal but the local resistants sent emissaries to try and dissuade them from shelling the town. One these was Mademoiselle *Hélène* Vidal, daughter of the préfet of the Var. As she had knowledge of English, she was elected to cycle from Draguignan to La Motte, on a dark and winding road, passing through squads of German troops en route. Today Hélène Vidal is recognized for her efforts with streets and schools named in her honour, including a primary school in Les Arcs, near the station.

After dark, the commanding officer of the 551st PIB ordered his men into the city. Their road into Draguignan was the same one that any visitor might use coming from Trans-en-Provence. Today, a monument marks the exact spot at Square Denis Fontès on Avenue Lazare-Carnot where the paratroopers first met up with the FFI at about 10.30 p.m. on 16 August. With the FFI acting as guides, their leather-soled shoes clattering on the cobbles, and white shirts presenting a fine target, small patrols were led through the streets. By daylight the town was cleared and the Americans established their HQ in the Hôtel Madeline.

Huge Nazi flags identified the German HQ, located in the Hôtel Bertin next to the préfecture in the main square. Inside, General Ludwig Bieringer and some sixty-six of his men awaited the opportunity to surrender to the Americans, terrified of being caught by the FFI. The Gestapo, who from their HQ in the Villa Forezienne had terrorized the citizens of the surrounding villages, were long gone. Bieringer was the first German general to be captured by the Allies in the Second World War. When the paratroopers stormed the building, he rose from his desk clutching his monocle. The townspeople threw objects at him as he was taken in a Jeep to Le Mitan where he surrendered all 750 men under his command to General Frederick. The next day, Frederick himself accompanied Bieringer to General Patch's command post at Saint-Tropez.

In the after-action report of the 2nd Independent Parachute Brigade, there is mention of a series of small actions resulting in twenty enemy killed for the loss of one British trooper. Since D-Day, Jeep patrols from the brigade HQ at Le Mitan had been probing in all directions. At an intersection called Quatre Chemins near the Gorges de Pennafort, where the route de Fayence is intersected by the road from Le Muy to Callas, a bridge had been destroyed to prevent a column of German trucks from breaking through to Draguignan. On 17 August, with the bridge repaired, the Germans began to cross. At the same time, a Jeep loaded with Scottish paratroopers bounced through the farm gate and jerked to a halt in the courtyard. A 'young-looking colonel' jumped out: 'Seen any Germans around here?' he enquired. His answer came from the growling of German trucks in the distance.[19]

The farmer grew anxious as he watched the paratroopers preparing an ambush. The German trucks were rolling along slowly with two lines of troops marching on either side. The shooting was all over in three or four minutes and the lifeless forms of six German soldiers lay in the road. The Jeep then disappeared the way it came, through the Garidelle forest toward Le Muy ten kilometres away. Another German patrol arrived presently, and methodically the Boche then set about burning the barns together with the harvested crops, staving in wine barrels, slaughtering livestock, including the farm horse which they shot in the stable. It was all futile considering that the patrol would have run into more paratroopers and FFI further down the road.[20]

*

A motorized reconnaissance patrol of the US 45th Infantry Division coming up from the beaches of Sainte-Maxime first linked up with the paratroopers on the RN 7. Private Arthur Isler of Warren, Ohio, wrote to his parents in great detail about his experience with the 517th from the time he boarded the C-47 in Italy. The letter, quoted in the *Warren Tribune*, his hometown newspaper, reveals how all the intense emotions of the past few days paled into insignificance compared to the relief he felt when he met up with the ground forces coming in from the landing beaches: 'That was the most significant and never-to-be-forgotten sight that I've ever seen, for that meant that our fighting as paratroopers was over. Our joy could not be contained. I thought that we would rip those poor tanks apart. Our mission was successful.'[21]

The balance sheet for Operation Rugby varies according to the date of the tally, but by 20 August 1944, 434 Americans were listed as killed, wounded or missing. The British 2nd Independent Parachute Brigade Group suffered fifty-two killed in action. Despite major navigation errors, the airborne operation – Operation Rugby – would be considered by military historians and senior commanders alike to be the most successful of the war. When paratroopers land in places where they should not have landed, the error is mitigated by the confusion which is created among the enemy.

Nothing could mitigate the tragic loss of seventeen paratroopers of B Company, 509th Parachute Infantry Battalion who dropped into the sea off Saint-Tropez and disappeared forever. It is suspected that the transport plane was flying in a southwesterly direction over the peninsular, which is a maximum of three kilometres wide. Due to the heavy fog, the pilot could not see that he was over water, and the paratroopers jumped either too early or too late. They were wearing Mae West life jackets but either they did not have time to inflate them, or the weight of their equipment pulled them under.

Another five planeloads of troops – Company A of the 509th PIB, and elements of the 463rd Parachute Artillery Battalion – were dropped a few minutes too soon and landed south of Saint-Tropez, narrowly escaping the same fate. Nevertheless, they soon orientated themselves after making contact with the Maquis and decided to start their war from there. Their story will be continued in the next chapter, considering that these airborne troops effectively became part of the amphibious operation.

One of the ninety or so French ships scuttled in the Toulon harbour on 27 November 1942, to prevent them from falling into German hands. (Dale Rooks / US Coast Guard)

Nancy Wake (married name Fiocca) started off in the Marseille underground and became a fully fledged SOE agent.

Eleven young resistants executed
at Saint-Julien-du-Verdon on
11 June 1944.

Krystyna Skarbek, aka Christine
Granville, described by one of
her SOE assessors as 'a very
smart-looking girl, simply dressed
and aristocratic'. A fellow agent
once said that she looked like
'an athletic art student'.

American B-17s drop weapons and supplies to the Maquis of the Vercors on Bastille Day, 14 July 1944. (USAF)

Victims of the massacres which took place on the Vercors Plateau being reinterred at what is now the National Nécropole near Vassieux-en-Vercors.

OSS Major Peter Ortiz, wearing a USMC uniform, inspecting members of the Resistance on 7 August 1944, at Col de la Forclaz, north of Les Saisies, during Mission UNION II. The second man on his right is Capitaine Jean Bulle. (Raymond Bertrand)

American B-24 Liberators directly over Saint-Jean-Cap-Ferrat with Nice to the back and Villefranche-sur-Mer on the right. (USAF)

Bombing mission over Fréjus Plage on Dragoon D-Day. Saint-Raphaël is on the right and the Base *aéronautique navale* runway is the diagonal strip on the left. (USAF)

Paratroopers of the 1st Airborne Task Force jump from C-47 'Dakota' aircraft near Le Muy during Operation Rugby, 15 August 1944.

Paratroopers walk through the vineyards to their assembly point. (US Signals Corps)

A paratrooper at the intersection of the Draguignan road and the RN 7. The villages of La Motte and Le Muy were at the epicentre of the drop zones. (US Signals Corps)

Infantrymen move inland from the beachhead through a pine forest. (US Signals Corps)

Glider pilots injured during the airborne operation receive medical attention at Le Mitan, a farm near the village of La Motte. (US Signals Corps)

Corporal Burl J. Knapp of the 509th Parachute Infantry Batallion pictured with Nicole Célébonovitch, a resistant from Saint-Tropez, soon after the liberation. Burl Knapp was killed in action less than a week later. (US Signals Corps)

German prisoners, mostly *Osttruppen*, hot and thirsty under the August sun, but relieved that for them, the war is over. (Dale Rooks / US Coast Guard)

German PoWs being processed in Saint-Tropez. (US Signals Corps)

Wounded being evacuated by landing craft in the calm waters of the Gulf of Saint-Tropez. (Dale Rooks / US Coast Guard)

Support vehicles and supplies come ashore at Saint-Tropez. By the end of Dragoon, more than 130,000 men, 18,000 vehicles and 7,000 tons of supplies were landed. (Dale Rooks / US Coast Guard)

Audie Murphy, the most
highly decorated American
soldier in history, was awarded
the Distinguished Service
Cross (DSC) for his actions
at Pampelonne Beach on
15 August 1944.

Relieved to be safely ashore,
NCOs drive along the
coastal road in their Jeep.
(Dale Rooks / US Coast Guard)

American GMC 6x6 trucks move inland from the beachhead through wine country. (Dale Rooks / US Coast Guard)

An M7 (Priest) self-propelled gun passing through Brignoles, 20 August 1944. (US Signals Corps)

Vehicles of the US 3rd Infantry Division enter Aix-en-Provence on 21 August 1944. (US Signals Corps)

Shutters, lined with fabric for the blackout, are flung open as American troops pass along the street below. This image was snapped by South African photographer Constance Stuart as she looked up from a truck. (Constance Stuart / American University Museum)

As the Allies raced through the rustic beauty of the countryside, waving people appeared as a kaleidoscopic blur. (Dale Rooks / US Coast Guard)

An incident along the road: *toi et moi, un abri pour deux* – you and me, a shelter for both. (Dale Rooks / US Coast Guard)

Gleb Sivirine (*Vallier*) and some of his *maquisards* at Hyères, 23 August 1944. *Vallier* has his head turned and his hand on the shoulder of one of his men. (Musée de la Résistance Azuréenne)

Commandant Lécuyer (*Sapin*) making a public declaration in Lantosque, 19 August 1944. SOE Major Harvard Gunn has his back to the camera. (Musée de la Résistance Azuréenne)

FFI fighters, some with armbands, posing with items of German uniform and captured weaponry, in Nice, 29 August 1944, the day after the uprising. (Musée de la Résistance Azuréenne)

The start of the *épuration* in Aix-en-Provence. A firing squad is the likely fate for this collaborator being paraded by resistance fighters. (US Holocaust Museum)

In Saint-Tropez, a collaborator holds her shorn locks. An 'ugly carnival' recorded by South African Constance Stuart, soon after coming ashore with the US Seventh Army. (Constance Stuart / National Gallery of Art, Washington DC)

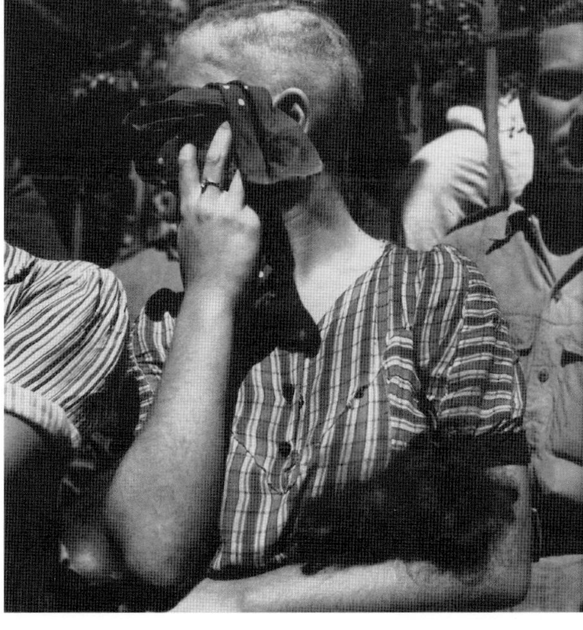

This fighting priest and athletic *maquisard*, wearing the FFI badge, presented a photo opportunity for Constance Stuart who had an eye for anything incongruous. (Constance Stuart / American University Museum)

A German half-track and artillery piece knocked out by an American anti-tank gun. Believed to be at Le Colombier, east of Montélimar, 1 September 1944. In the ditch on the left is a charred German corpse. (US Signals Corps)

American paratroopers with an FFI guide head off on patrol, probably at Col-de-Braus in the Alpes-Maritimes, 4 September 1944. (Musée de la Résistance Azuréenne)

A flyer advertising sightseeing tours for soldiers staying in the United States Riviera Recreational Area (USRRA).

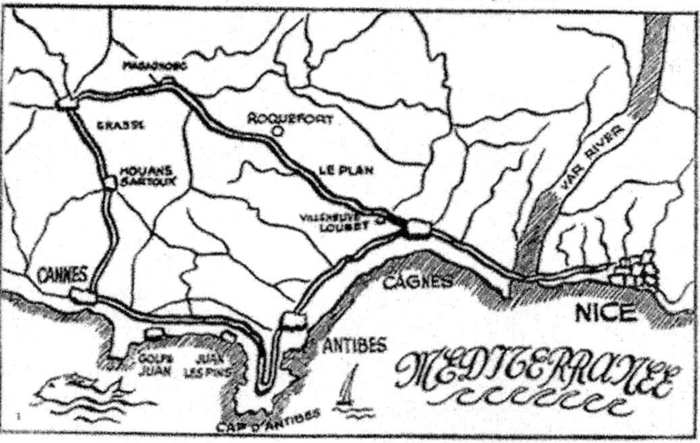

Aerial view showing a small part of Camp Calas which was one and a half kilometres wide and fourteen kilometres long. With military precision, it was divided into battalion, regimental and divisional sections.

Soldiers awaiting repatriation at Delta Base Section transit camps underwent interminable kit inspections. (NARA)

An open-air theatre built into the landscape at Camp Calas at Delta Base Section. (NARA)

Chapter 13

Force

In the early dawn of D-Day, three leading lights of the Brigade des Maures were on the Route de la Belle Isnarde just outside Saint-Tropez, heading toward what they expected to be the main invasion beach. It was just past 4 a.m. when Marc Rainaut, René Girard and Jean Conte heard aircraft low overhead, and, despite the fog, saw vague forms dropping from the sky. Due to a navigation error, worsened by the dense fog, the green light was given prematurely in twenty-nine of the Dakota transports. As a result, 115 men of the 509th Parachute Infantry Battalion plus some of the 463rd Parachute Artillery Battalion landed on the Saint-Tropez peninsula, approximately thirty kilometres south of their intended drop zone at Le Muy. As has been mentioned, Captain Ralph 'Bing' Miller of Youngstown, Ohio, and sixteen of his men were dropped over the Mediterranean, and with their equipment, they vanished without trace.

Had he not hesitated a few seconds after the green light came on, Sergeant Richard Fisco might have become another name on a plaque. In his autobiography, *Your Lives Will Be Beautiful*, he described how he could see nothing through the solid cloud but prepared to extract himself from his harness and jettison the heavy equipment:

> I screamed out to God to please bring me to land. Immediately, a gust of strong, warm wind hit my back and blew me towards land. It was probably the *Sirocco* from North Africa, but as far as I was concerned, it was a breeze from Heaven. I pulled down on my two front risers and slipped landward. I landed on the steps of a villa and sprained my ankle slightly. Since I had prepared for a water landing, there were no leg harness straps to support me, and my legs buckled under me. Sergeant Harvey Sutherland of my company landed in water chest high.[1]

Fisco's first encounter was with a tall, skinny French boy who presented him with a bottle of wine. A soft sea breeze wafted up from the shore, while pine-covered slopes stood before him. After the tough mountain fighting in Italy, Fisco truly thought he had landed in heaven. Somebody over there under the trees was whistling softly, and a man named Murphy recognized the tune. It was 'La Marseillaise'. A Frenchman appeared wearing a reassuring *tricolore* armband. He was a member of the Brigade des Maures, one of the section chiefs who had been alerted by René Girard immediately after the BBC broadcast the previous evening.

Although Marc Rainaut spoke English fluently, the first exchange went something like this:

'Le Muy?'

'*Oh, non, non*, Saint-Tropez!'

It did not take long for all concerned to work out that they were far off course. Referring to his maps, Captain Jess W. Walls, commander of C Company, 509th PIB, realized that he was thirty kilometres away from his objective and had landed in a sector of the invasion zone where the US 3rd Infantry Division would soon be coming ashore. Within an hour, Allied ships and planes would begin pounding the beaches and they would be caught in the middle of it. Hastily, everyone set about gathering their equipment, and guided by the FFI they assembled in a pine forest on the hill called La Belle Isnard.

Having gathered about 250 men of the 509th PIB, and 463rd Parachute Artillery Battalion, Walls and Rainaut decided to join forces to liberate Saint-Tropez. In three columns, they entered the town. The 18-year-old Nicole Célébonovitch, who at this time was still unaware of the fate of François Pelletier, helped guide the paratroopers into the town. As a parting shot, the Germans had detonated mines to render the port unusable, and a huge pall of black smoke polluted the air.

Those Germans who had not already made a timeous departure were occupying the sixteenth-century citadel on the hill. A few others were in a blockhouse overlooking the bay in the Bouillabaisse area, at the opposite end of town. One small group decided to make a stand in the Hôtel Latitude 43 and only decided to give up when a tank from the 45th Infantry Division arrived on the scene from the direction of Sainte-Maxime.[2]

The occupants of a strongpoint at Cap Saint-Pierre, at the point of the southern peninsular, were also holding out. A group of *maquisards* went to demand their surrender, and a young woman who was the mistress of the German battery commander eventually convinced them to come out without a fight. Apparently, the girl was given the assurance that she would be considered a hero of the liberation rather than a collaborator in return for this service. A large amount of weapons were found and distributed among the *maquisards*.

At 10 a.m., the Saint-Tropez section of Brigade des Maures started up the steep hill to attack the citadel. Two attempts were repulsed, and the Germans even managed to muster a counter-attack. An overenthusiastic young *maquisard* by the name of Guy Ringrave was killed. Soon after 3 p.m., the paratroopers brought up a bazooka and the white flag was raised. The prisoners were marched down to the Place des Lices, the main square, with their hands in the air, happy to be out of the war.

The occupants of the Bouillabaisse blockhouse, overlooking the gulf at the entrance to Saint-Tropez, also surrendered, but not before taking the life of 23-year-old Paul Roussel with one last burst of machine-gun fire. By 4 p.m. it was all over. During the day's fighting, seventy-five Germans had been killed and 450 taken prisoner. Two members of the 509th PIB were killed by sniper fire, probably coming from the citadel. The Brigade des Maures and FFI lost four killed and seven wounded.[3] When a column of the 3rd Infantry Division arrived in Saint-Tropez from Pampelonne beach in the mid-afternoon, they found the town to be already under the control of the small contingent of paratroopers together with the Maquis des Maures.

Saint-Tropez, with its harbour and hotels, was an ideal command post for General Patch and his Seventh Army staff officers, and over the following days they moved into the Hôtel Latitude 43, a masterpiece of design with panoramic views over Saint-Tropez – now converted into luxury apartments. Learning of how the Brigade des Maures had assisted his forces, Patch took time out to review these *maquisards* and to award the Silver Star to Marc Rainaut, with letters of commendation to seven others, two posthumously. Nicole Célébonovitch was also given recognition. The moving and stills images of this occasion have made her recognizable all over the world.

*

Just out of Saint-Tropez, on Pampelonne beach, where the 3rd Infantry Division was coming ashore under the cover of smoke, the landing went relatively smoothly. Mines were the biggest hazard, both in the water and on land. Pampelonne beach is longer and wider than most other beaches on the French Riviera. It is a five-kilometre-long stretch of sand between the rocky points of Cape Pinet and Bonne Terrasse, overlooked by the village of Ramatuelle.

Today, in summertime, one can see yachts and pleasure craft of every description gently floating just off the crowded beach. Even at the time, it occurred to some that this was one of the most unlikely sites for a battle.

In their pockets, the 'Yanks' carried packs of Lucky Strike cigarettes and a *Pocket Guide to France* containing useful phrases such as 'I am American', 'Take me to a doctor', 'I am hungry', 'Draw me a map', and 'Take cover!' as well as the everyday expressions like 'Where is the restaurant?'[4]

A few random shells did fall on the beach, and isolated machine-gun emplacements on the hillsides put up a token resistance, but enemy fire had practically ceased by the time the infantrymen and tanks left the beach along narrow roads and across rough scrubland toward Ramatuelle on the hill. A soldier recalls how amazed he was to stumble across a few perfectly harmless little cabanas still standing peacefully intact amid the clutter of barbed wire and booby traps.

Few men had to take excessive risks at Ramatuelle that day but it seems that 20-year-old Audie Leon Murphy managed to find trouble wherever he went. Murphy's story has been told in his 1948 autobiography, *To Hell and Back*, and he played himself in a film of the same name in 1955, but there can be no earlier version than the one which appeared in a small Texan newspaper shortly after his homecoming:

> The perfect landing, military officials call the invasion of Southern France. Maybe it was strategically, but there was nothing perfect about it where I was.
>
> After we broke through from Anzio beachhead and chased the krauts to Rome, the Third Division was moved back to Naples for more amphibious training for the Southern France invasion.
>
> Company B, my outfit, landed near Ramatuelle, on the Rivera at 8 a.m., August 15, 1944, with the first wave of the assault. Since I have been home I've heard a lot of people say the landings in Southern France were soft. That is not true. We had plenty of trouble and the fighting was tough, at least until we had established a hold.

As my rifle platoon and I moved inland from the beach, we were halted by machine gun fire from a rocky ridge around of us. We dropped to the ground and crawled quickly to cover. There was only one thing to do and I could not ask any of my men to do it. I made another dash, this one for 40 yards with bullets whizzing all around me – to a ditch, and returned to the beach. There I found a machine gun squad and borrowed one of their weapons. Another trip through the ditch and another 40 yard dash, the longest 40 yards I have ever run. I told my men I was going to crawl ahead of the platoon and see what I could do about the kraut installation.

'I am going too.' PFC Lattie Tipton 33, of Erwin Tennessee, said. Lattie and I had shared foxholes ever since the invasion of Sicily. He had turned down a sergeant's rating so he could stay with me as a runner. That day he had been shot through the left ear, and was bleeding a lot. But when I ordered him back to the beach for medical treatment, he refused. I knew he would not pay any attention if I told him to stay with the platoon now. I should have made him stay.

We crawled out of the ditch and inched our way 75 yards up the side of the hill. There we found another ditch, and set up the machine gun. As we prepared to fire, the krauts let up in their shooting, and we saw a white flag waving at the top of the ridge.

'This looks funny,' Lattie said, 'but I am going up and [will] get them. Keep me covered.'

He crawled out of the ditch and stood up. There was a burst of machine gun fire, and Lattie fell back in the ditch on top of me. He was dead. I must have gone crazy then. I don't remember much of what happened after that.[5]

In a fit of rage, Murphy wiped out the Germans and continued up the hill, shooting Germans with his carbine and taking prisoners. When the hill was taken Murphy slipped a pack under Tipton's head as a pillow, then sat down and wept, thinking about Lattie's 12-year-old daughter, whose every letter had been shared with him. Lattie Tipton is buried in the Rhône American Cemetery at Draguignan. When Murphy visited the grave in 1948 he was given the freedom of Ramatuelle.

Although he admitted that he was not without fear, and sometimes he could feel his 'insides twist into knots', Murphy put himself in harm's way whenever possible. He ended the war as a second lieutenant and the most decorated soldier in US history. Included in his medal haul are the Congressional Medal of Honor, Distinguished Service Cross, two Silver Stars, Legion of Merit (US), two Bronze Stars, three Purple Hearts, four Bronze Service Stars, Légion d'Honneur, three Croix de Guerre and assorted campaign medals, good conduct medals and efficiency badges.

Leon, as Audie was known before he went into the army, was one of twelve children born into a poverty-stricken sharecropper family in Kingston, Texas. From the age of five, he was hoeing and picking cotton alongside his parents and siblings. In 1939, at the age of 15, Murphy dropped out of school to support his family. A year later, his father abandoned them, which seems to have been too much for Mrs Murphy, who died in 1941. It was the war which rescued Murphy from his circumstances, but afterwards he never fully adjusted to civilian life.

When he returned as a hero to the United States he marched in victory parades, appeared before cheering crowds and featured on the covers of news magazines. In late 1945, he headed to Hollywood and over the next twenty years appeared in a number of low-budget Westerns. His best performance was in 1951 when he played a young Civil War soldier in *The Red Badge of Courage*. Possibly suffering from 'survivor's guilt', he became addicted to prescription drugs. Gambling and bad business deals bankrupted him. On 28 May 1971, Murphy died along with five others in a plane crash while on a business trip. He was buried at Arlington National Cemetery with full military honours, but his passing went almost unnoticed by the media and the public.

For his actions at Pampelonne beach on 15 August, Audie Murphy was awarded the Distinguished Service Cross (DSC), the second-highest US Army medal for valour. The Medal of Honor would come later. However, another man in the 3rd Infantry Division did win the Congressional Medal of Honor at Cavalière on that day. As he hit the beach, Sergeant James Philip Connor from Wilmington, Delaware, was wounded by a shell that also killed his lieutenant. Then the platoon sergeant was killed, and command fell to Connor. Crossing a wide stretch of beach under fire, Connor led his men forward, personally shooting two German snipers in a cluster of buildings. Wounded and unable to move, Connor continued to direct his men from a prone position. His platoon, though reduced to less than a third of its original thirty-six men, outflanked and rushed the enemy with such ferocity that they killed seven and captured forty.

Clearly, there was some determined opposition in this sector because yet another soldier, PFC William W. McNamara of Brooklyn New York, personally killed fifteen men with his BAR and captured thirteen more. Like Audie Murphy, he did it alone. He was also involved in a white-flag incident, having to kill someone who was pretending to surrender, and was awarded the DSC (Distinguished Service Cross).

Perhaps the 3rd Infantry Division was particularly generous with awards: close to a dozen 'Rock of the Marne' infantrymen, including Audie Murphy, would win the Congressional Medal of Honor on the road

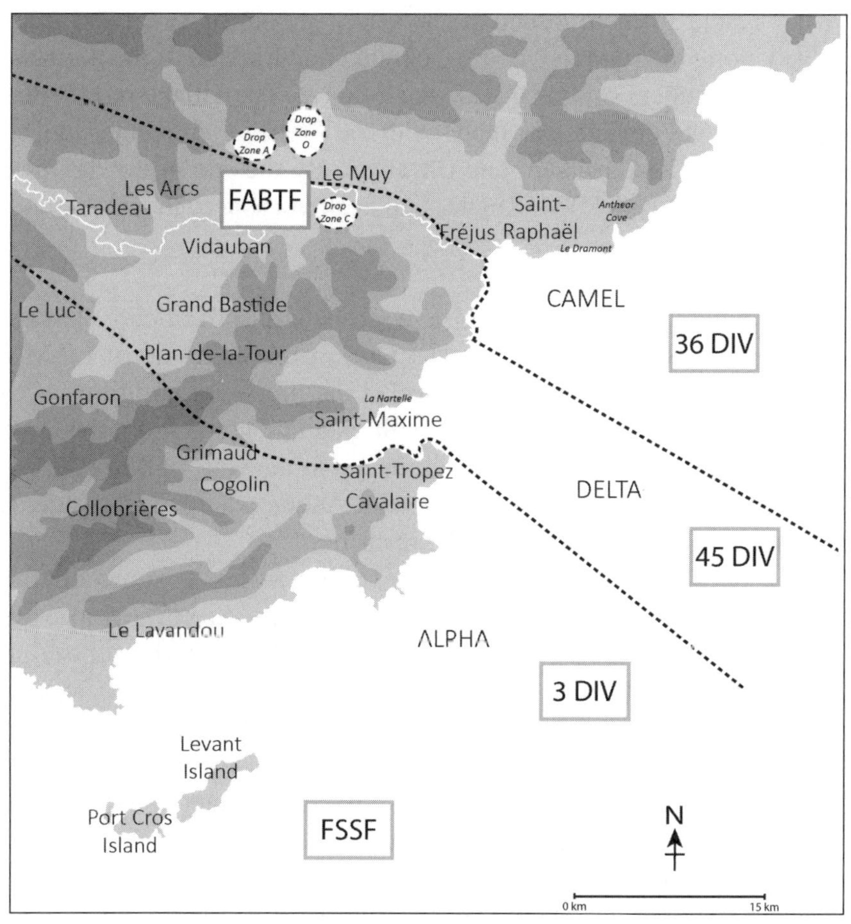

Operation Dragoon airborne and amphibious landings.

to the Rhine. Sergeant Stanley Bender, originally from West Virginia, won his Medal of Honor on D+2 as the 3rd Infantry Division came to La Londe-les-Maures. His heroic actions brought about the destruction of two machine-gun nests, Bender having located their position by standing on top of a tank while bullets ricocheted off the turret at his feet.[6]

In command of the 3rd Infantry Division was Lieutenant General John W. 'Iron Mike' O'Daniel, whose only son, J. W. O'Daniel Jr, was a paratrooper with the 505th Parachute Infantry Regiment and was killed during Operation Market Garden in September 1944. Immediately after landing, at 10.40 a.m., O'Daniel set up his command post in the barnyard of a farm near the village of La Croix-Valmer. While his Jeep radio crackled, the local farmers brought out barrels of rosé wine to toast the victory. Moving inland in three directions, a steady stream of tanks and trucks rumbled along the road to Gassin, Cogolin and Grimaud to the northeast, guided by members of the Brigade des Maures. The village of Cavalière was cleared, and contact was made with the French commandos at Cape Negre between Le Lavandou and Cavalière. By the end of the day, more than 15,000 men and 2,000 vehicles had been put ashore in this sector.

*

The Domaine de Trémouriès is a wine estate conveniently situated one kilometre out of Cogolin on the D98 in the direction of La Môle and Toulon. The Germans had converted the old stone buildings of the château into a strongpoint bristling with machine guns. From the tower, they had a view over a wide area, almost up to the Gulf of Saint-Tropez. Two kilometres down the road is the Val d'Astier, where the Brigade des Maures assembled on the eve of the invasion.

Early on Dragoon D-Day, a group of *maquisards*, some of them unarmed, approached the château from all sides. Alix Macario called out to the occupants to surrender. After a long silence, a Mauser bayonet with a white cloth attached poked through the door. The château, together with a large store of arms and ammunition, was captured without a fight. Now, everyone was well armed. The twenty-eight prisoners turned out to be mainly Azerbaijanis, Georgians and Armenians who invariably refused to fight, and at times turned on their German masters.

Leaving some of their number to man a roadblock outside Cogolin, Macario's men proceeded to take the surrender of enemy garrisons at the nearby Château Saint-Maur and Château des Garcinières. In Cogolin itself, Vichy officials were rounded up and quickly replaced by a Local Liberation Committee (Comité Local de Libération). A few *maquisards* were given the job of guarding the water reservoirs above the village of Cogolin. Had the Germans destroyed them, there would have been problems supplying the great multitude of troops with water.

*

As we saw in a previous chapter, the *Maquis Vallier* had marched from their base on the Canjuers Plateau to the village of Collobrières so as to be ready to play their part in the coming battles. Having camped at Collobrières, which is situated on the backroads from Saint-Tropez to Pierrefeu-du-Var and Toulon, in the forested hills above the landing beaches at Cavalière-sur-Mer *Vallier's* men mounted roadblocks at both entrances to the village on the morning of the 15th. A truck loaded with about thirty German soldiers and all their equipment and supplies was brought to a stop, and three Germans and one *maquisard* were wounded in the ensuing firefight. Expecting no mercy from men such as these, the Germans fled into the forest. Emboldened by this success, about twenty local resistants came forward to join forces with the Maquis *Vallier*.

At about 5 p.m., a column of American tanks and infantrymen of the 3rd Infantry Division, who had landed near Cavalière, came up the road to Collobrières. At first, they were thought to be Germans, and *Vallier's* men opened fire, wounding one American soldier. Spontaneously, *Vallier* cursed in the Provençal dialect and was surprised to hear a GI utter a response in the same vernacular. It turned out that he was a native of the south of France recently settled in the United States.

There was no time for recriminations, however, because a column of enemy vehicles appeared from Pierrefeu to retake Collobrières. They were quickly repulsed by the Americans who then set off in pursuit. Most of the German installations in the area had been vacated – and looted by the locals – but there remained a radar station on the Lambert Plateau to be taken. *Vallier's* Maquis, consisting of forty men, was reinforced with twenty more from Collobrières under the direction of 'Chef Étienne'. An American colonel offered 120 of his men to accompany the Maquis to the radar station. Once at the top, the Americans received radio orders not to attack but the Germans had already 'fled in disarray and disorder', leaving behind a truck, fully laden with weapons and food.

*

The seaside resort of Sainte-Maxime was slap in the middle of the invasion zone. Apart from the anti-tank barriers and bunkers, the centre of Sainte-Maxime looked very much like it does today. Urban sprawl has now engulfed La Nartelle but it is still a separate entity with low-rise buildings and a wide, sandy beach. At La Nartelle today, between the restaurants and beach clubs, is the chassis and tracks of a Sherman tank that lay buried under the sand for decades.

Landing craft lined up along the Nartelle beach, disgorging men and vehicles of the 45th Infantry Division, whose infantrymen had been recruited from the American West: New Mexico, Arizona, Oregon, Nevada and Oklahoma. Within their ranks were a number of Apaches, Choctaws and Cherokees who made excellent radio operators since no one could understand them. The Resistance had already paved the way and apart from random shooting, the landings here were unopposed.

In *The Second D-Day*, Robichon tells of an old man named de la Fargue who opened the front door of his house at La Nartelle to welcome some officers of the US Seventh Army, and had fetched his last few bottles of wine from their hiding place in his cellar. Since 1940, de la Fargue had had no news of his son, François, a naval officer serving with the Free French. As de la Fargue was lifting his hand to clink glasses with the officers, he felt a light tap on his shoulder. He turned to see a tanned young officer in an American naval summer uniform who smiled: 'Don't you recognize me, father?'[7] If the story is true, Ensign François de la Fargue would have been one of a group of about twenty French naval men who were thoroughly acquainted with the various landing sites, and had been assigned to guide the American units to their initial objectives.

Shortly before 8 a.m., the Sainte-Maxime garrison, numbering around 500 German troops, got the order to pull out, leaving only a rearguard to be sacrificed. Those who fled inland were, however, sure to run into the airborne forces. Among those considered to be dispensable was a squad of about twenty grey-haired men, former customs officers. Under the occupation, the church had been used as an arsenal, encircled with barbed wire and it was now turning out to be the 'Alamo' for Germany's 'expendables'.

The Maquis de Maures, now about 400 strong, set about expediting the departure of their tormentors. Every bunker, strongpoint and casemate in the vicinity was attacked. Preferring to wait and surrender to US troops, the occupants held out as long as possible. On the Route du Plan-de-la-Tour there is a monument to the memory of a *maquisard* named Fernand Bessy. It would appear that Bessy was running along the crest of a dam wall on a farm just outside town, where today there is an aqua-park, and he was mistaken for one of the enemy. A trigger-happy American 'commando' pumped him full of .45 calibre bullets from a Thompson sub-machine gun. Fernand's father, Louis, had been shot by the Germans nine months previously – also by accident.[8]

At the Hôtel les Palmiers near the port, the unwelcome Teutonic guests had already checked out by the morning of 15 August. The civilians had been terrified during the bombing but night was followed by a day of ecstasy. Once the mist had cleared, they could see the ships in the gulf. Americans, French and even 'Arabs' came riding in on strange vehicles. Reminiscent of the traffic jams which one experiences there in the holiday season, the military hardware was backed up in all directions. Later, the 'Sammies' occupied the hotel and stayed for six months. Before the former 'guests' departed they wrecked the interior, but the hotel still has pride of place between the church, the old town and the port.

The local townspeople had emerged from their basements and shelters and mingled with the 'Sammies' who looked as though they were on holiday, casually sitting on the low walls on the sidewalk, waiting. Every now and then, a GI would aim at the bell tower and take a pot shot. Inside, the diehard defenders in the cramped space were coughing and gasping with the dust and heat, many near collapse. No more shots were being fired from inside the church, however. Perhaps half of them were willing to call it a day but others threatened to blow up the building and themselves with it.

By now it was past 10 a.m. and a white-haired old lady berated the defenders in fluent German, and ordered them to 'Come down right now!' It was to no avail, and a GI led the grandmother away gently by the arm. It took the arrival of two tank destroyers to get the Germans to change their minds. One ground to a halt in front of the jetty and the other approached ponderously to aim its muzzle straight at the church tower. Presently, a small band of bedraggled old fellows came out with their hands up, amid the taunts and jeers of the onlookers. Looking sheepish, some of them were wearing big, square-cornered caps. One carried an old broom with a white rag tied to it, and another waved a handkerchief.

Only a hundred metres away, at the port, there was still plenty of excitement. At the end of the jetty was a gun turret sunk into a concrete bunker, a fortification known as a 'Tobruk', which could still lob shells into the Gulf of Saint-Tropez. Inside, with barely enough space to stand up, there were six men steadfastly refusing to surrender. The ammunition for their single gun was running low, and yet they kept on firing at the multitude of craft entering the gulf.

The Allied bombardment had hardly made a dent on the Tobruk, so a portly German NCO was sent with a white flag across the jetty to plead with them. He disappeared inside and the door closed behind him, and that was the last anyone ever saw of him. The large crowd of bystanders expected to see a white flag but it was not forthcoming. The tank let loose two 75mm rounds, sending dismembered bodies, together with twisted metal and pieces of concrete into the Bay of Saint-Tropez. Thus ended the 'Battle for Sainte-Maxime'.

Late in the afternoon, a reconnaissance platoon from the 45th Infantry Division set off on the main road to Le Muy. At about 8.30 p.m., the patrol met up with some happy paratroopers of the 509th PIB just south of the town. Morale was high, and General William W. Eagles, a West Point graduate, felt relief at having reached the objectives set for his division, enhanced with the knowledge that their casualty rate for the day had been one per cent – not the expected twenty per cent.[9]

As it turned out, the medical facilities were more than adequate. In addition to the clearing stations and field hospitals, each of the three assault divisions was accompanied by a 400-bed evacuation hospital. The French Army B had two comparable facilities of its own. Before moving inland, the hospitalization units of the 10th and 11th Field Hospitals were agreeably located at Sainte-Maxime, Le Muy, Saint-Raphaël, Cogolin, Cavalière and Plan-de-la-Tour.

By nightfall, the 45th Infantry Division had linked up with the 3rd Infantry Division coming from Saint-Tropez and entered the petite village of Plan-de-la-Tour, finding that the Wehrmacht had already been kicked out by the local resistance, with the loss of only one *maquisard* – Charles Ollivier. As the 'Thunderbirds' of the 45th passed through the village, on foot and clinging onto tanks, they were hailed as liberators, kissed by women of all ages and plied with the best vintages, stored away in anticipation of this day.

*

On the far right flank of the invasion force, the 36th Infantry Division had to fight comparatively hard to take Fréjus and Saint-Raphaël. It seemed that German engineers and their Todt Organization labourers had concentrated their efforts in this sector, building a massive anti-tank wall with a deep moat, masses of barbed wire, concrete blocks and mines. The water was littered with mines and underwater obstructions loaded with explosives. Harmless-looking beach huts and refreshment stands were actually a camouflage for fearsome gun batteries, complete with a warren of communication trenches connecting them with observation posts, underground ammunition stores and concrete dugouts.

From the air, Saint-Raphaël still appeared as it was when F. Scott Fitzgerald lived there: 'A red little town built close to the sea, with gay red-roofed houses and an air of repressed carnival about it.'[10] The blue water is backed by red rocks, white walls, bell towers, domes and Belle Epoch hotels along palm-lined boulevards. Toward the marshes of the Argens River delta, near the airfield now known as Base Nature is Fréjus Plage, designated as Camel Red on the invasion maps. This was expected to be the most critical zone in the sector, and was the responsibility of General John E. Dahlquist's 36th Infantry Division.

The navy called for air support, and a flight of B-24 Liberators of the Fifteenth Air Force took off to make a final attack on Fréjus beach, just ahead of the assault craft. One of the B-24 groundcrew went along for the ride and recorded his impressions. On their way from Italy to the French coast, they passed over Ajaccio in Corsica and saw a great many surface vessels including battleships and three carriers which seemed to be milling aimlessly about the quiet sea waiting for a job to do. It seemed to the untrained eye that the whole of southern France was blowing up. When the aircraft was out of danger, everyone relaxed and began taking off their flak suits. The radioman got a 'hot jive band' on the liaison set. It seemed hardly sporting to fly against so worn an enemy.[11]

On Green Beach at Dramont, east of Saint-Raphaël, the enemy offered virtually no resistance, and the first wave of the 36th (Texas) Infantry Division had no problems. General Dahlquist was in fact the first divisional commander to set foot in Provence. Tank crews were relieved to find that this sector had been subdued by the time they clanked ashore. The only person killed during the assault on Camel Green was Thomas Robert Evans of the Royal Naval Volunteer Reserve when a 75mm shell struck the bridge of his landing craft. He is buried in the Mazargues War Cemetery in Marseille.

At Anthéor Cove, on the divisional right, it was the 141st Infantry Regiment that started landing on Blue Beach at 8.30 a.m. Pillboxes and machine guns had to be neutralized with hand grenades and flamethrowers. Seven of these veterans of Anzio and Cassino lost their lives. At Fréjus-Saint-Raphaël, the main body of the 36th Infantry Division, which was scheduled to land at H+6 – six hours after the first wave – still had a long day ahead. At 1 p.m., as the troops waited in their landing craft, the mine-sweepers attempted to clear a path but were forced to retreat out of range of the German guns. In one final salvo, the big guns of the *Arkansas*, *Tuscaloosa*, *Brooklyn*, *Argonaut*, *Marblehead* and the *Emile Berlin*, six hundred guns in all, swept the shore of the Gulf of Fréjus. Still the enemy batteries were not silenced.

In the blazing heat, at 2 p.m., the first wave set off for Saint-Raphaël but three of the landing craft were hit by shells.[12] One wave of these craft heading for Fréjus was forced to make a U-turn. It was not going to be possible to take Saint-Raphaël by way of a frontal attack. Thus the order was given to abandon their objective, and for all assault groups to proceed to Dramont.

On seeing the Allied flotilla do an about-turn, delirious with joy, the German defenders were convinced that they had repulsed the entire Mediterranean invasion all by themselves.[13] But their celebrations were short-lived as the boats simply went off at a tangent and landed on the Dramont beach, about three kilometres to the east, for the invaders to advance to Saint-Raphaël along the coastal road.

Throughout the morning, the landings proceeded unimpeded. Probably the most serious incident of the day occurred at last light when a bomb was launched from the belly of a Luftwaffe plane and streaked straight toward LST *282*, which was anchored just off Dramont beach. The vessel, about the size of a cross-Channel ferry, was packed with sailors and soldiers, many of whom could not swim, and forty were killed or wounded. Rescuers were at work until the early hours of the morning. Inevitably, the GIs joked that the LST in Landing Ship Tank stood for 'large slow target'.

At 8.43 pm a wave of Do 217 and Ju 88 bombers suddenly soared into sight over the mountains, circled over the landing fleet anchored out at sea as a stream of anti-aircraft fire was sent up into the twilight sky. A few bombs did fall among the vehicles, fuel and ammunition supplies piled up on the beach at Dramont but little damage was done.

Camel Green Beach was the only beach to be bombed by the Luftwaffe on Dragoon D-Day but on D+3 a swarm of five Ju 88s attacked the command ship *Catoctin*, killing six sailors.

While the sharp point pushed forward, the logistic operation swung into action. From the shore to the horizon, the Mediterranean was teeming with every type of vessel, and anti-aircraft balloons blossomed overhead. An endless parade of tanks, DUKWs, Jeeps, trucks, ambulances and bulldozers came off the landing craft and turned left on the coastal road in the direction of Saint-Raphaël. Columns of prisoners shuffled in the other direction and congregated on the beaches before boarding vessels en route to Corsica. A vestige of the landings of the 36th Infantry Division can be seen today in the form of a well-preserved landing craft in the parking lot at the beach.

By evening, all the beachheads were secure, but the centre of Saint-Raphaël was still in enemy hands. Being unable to proceed further than the suburb of Boulouris, it was decided to bypass the obstacle and move on to Fréjus by way of Valescure on the northern periphery of town, meeting up with the airborne assault troops at Le Muy the following day. Already a fighter squadron of the Twelfth Air Force had deployed from Italy to Saint-Tropez, and a reconnaissance squadron had set up shop near Port Grimaud.

Except for the occasional whine of a stray shell and the distant mutter of machine guns, a sudden calm settled over the beachhead. Even in the twilight hour, the heat was merciless, with scarcely a hint of a sea breeze for relief. The natural rhythms of Provence were returning, accentuated by the heavy scents of the eucalyptus trees, the lavender and thyme, as well as the persistent chirping of the cicadas. From the wireless set of a Sherman tank, the melancholy tune of 'Carry Me Back to Old Virginia' floated out of the open hatch. Bing Crosby's radio show *Command Performance* was broadcast to the troops everywhere. This week's episode featured a good dose of comedy with Jimmy Durante and Ginger Rogers as special guests.

In his diary, a battlefield surgeon attached to the 36th Infantry Division recorded smugly that he spent his first night in a villa on the French Riviera and slept well. The following day he explored the battle-scarred countryside around Saint-Raphaël:

> I can see it was a beautiful place in peacetime – villas
> overlooking the sea – small coves that seem to be separate

little lakes, hidden from everything, war included. Saw
Jerry pillboxes dotting the hill that naval shells blasted out
of existence. The LST is still burning. Many prisoners in the
36 Division PoW enclosures. Not looking too happy.[14]

It was another scorching hot day when the infantrymen moved inland.
Their route took them through the parched hills of the Massif des Maures
on narrow, winding roads, cluttered with abandoned old vehicles, carts
and bicycles requisitioned by the fleeing Wehrmacht. Insinuated among
the columns of American troops were coughing Renault vans overflowing
with FFI fighters. Foot soldiers took turns to rest by riding on tanks, with
up to a dozen men clinging on. Patrols were sent out on the flanks to
prevent ambushes and sniping from the overlooking hillsides.

After landing on the far right, the 141st Infantry Regiment proceeded
down the road to La Napoule. Lieutenant William Everett came upon the
site where the Groupe Naval d'Assaut de Corse had been torn to pieces
in the minefield at Anthéor. Everett yelled for the medics to come up
and start helping the wounded who had been lying there for more than
twenty-four hours. There was no time to talk: 'All we kept hearing was
everyone screaming over the radio "keep going, keep going, keep going!"
They were not with you but they were telling you to keep going.'[15]

*

On D+1, the men of the 3ème Division d'Infanterie Algérienne, the 3rd
Algerian Infantry Division, came ashore in the Gulf of Saint-Tropez, their
landing craft weaving through the multitude of ships already anchored
in the bay. Men and vehicles continued disembarking until late in the
evening. In the half-darkness, long columns of leathery North Africans,
rifles slung, packs on their backs, reached the village of Cogolin, four or
five kilometres inland. Shutters were flung open, and people appeared in
doorways in their nightclothes, carrying lighted candles. A voice at the
head of the column yelled out in French: 'Is this Cogolin?'

The next day, General Jean de Lattre set up his first HQ in Cogolin,
where he made his plans for a lightning conquest of Toulon and
Marseille. Alix Macario was called in to see the general who was happy
to receive information and guides from the FFI. Some young men
volunteered their help in bringing supplies ashore and others signed on
with the Free French for the duration. De Lattre was made an honorary

citizen of the town, while the commanding officer of the 3rd Algerian Infantry Division, General De Goislard de Monsabert, established his first command post opposite the town hall.

For the next week or more, colonial or *Indigène* troops continued to arrive in the Bay of Cavalière, on what is today the Plage du Débarquement. On foot, some leading pack mules, they hurried westward on the coastal road through La Croix-Valmer. Although fascinated by their colourful and exotic attire, some onlookers were wondering: 'Do they really expect to defeat the mighty German Army with this motley assortment of *Pieds-Noirs*, Muslim colonials and Black Africans?' Their reputation for rape and pillaging had also preceded them.

The US 3rd Infantry Division went from Pampelonne beach up through Grimaud and La Garde Freinet, to Vidauban and Le Luc on the RN 7, then southwest to Gonfaron and La Londe where Sergeant Stanley Bender won his Medal of Honor. One by one, towns and villages were liberated, setting off a sequence of joyous celebrations which would become par for the course. No soldiers asked for food: on the contrary, locals plied them with bread, wine and fruit despite their children suffering from malnutrition. The high command tried to discourage soldiers from accepting food and wine but it was hopeless.

People were pleasantly surprised by the fresh-faced American soldiers in contrast to the dour, middle-aged German men. One of the most noticeable differences was that these friendly 'Sammies' wore boots with soft soles, not hobnails. They whistled and joked and handed out chocolate and chewing gum to the children, even teaching them to play baseball when time permitted. One company commander scored a hit by teaching his men to sing 'La Marseillaise' – phonetically.

Overall Allied losses for the first twenty-four hours amounted to about 1,000 killed and wounded, including sailors and airmen. Casualties among the landing troops were highest in the 3rd Infantry Division, which suffered 264 losses, 203 of them at Cavalière-sur-Mer, and many were caused by mines. Twenty-five assault ships were sunk between Cavalière-sur-Mer and Anthéor.

Allied warships had fired nearly 50,000 shells and aircraft had carried out 3,733 sorties, including nearly a thousand transporting airborne troops. After twenty-four hours, some 95,000 Americans, Frenchmen, Canadians, Britons and North Africans, as well as a few Pacific Islanders had been disembarked. By the end of Dragoon, more than 130,000 men, 18,000 vehicles and 7,000 tons of supplies were landed. Within days, the Twelfth Air Force fighter squadrons moved closer to the invasion front, first to Saint-Raphaël, and then on to Le Luc.

A French admiral watching the landings from the command ship *Catoctin* waxed lyrical: 'What happiness to recover this coast of France, the most fair, the most amiable, and the most smiling of our country.' The remarks of a naval officer aboard Landing Craft Infantry LCI *233* were more succinct, 'Frankly, this has been the quietest beachhead I have ever seen.'[16] Bill Maudlin, cartoonist and correspondent for *Stars and Stripes* was on usual form: 'This is the best invasion I ever attended.' Adolf Hitler is reputed to have later said, 'The 15th of August was the worst day of my life,' but this was partly due to what was happening on the Normandy front.

Chapter 14

Fraternity

Operation Dragoon ended with the breakout from the beachhead and accomplishment of all the primary objectives by 18 August 1944. Just the previous day, the intelligence services had deciphered a message in which the German high command ordered all forces in southern France to begin a fighting withdrawal. Only those defending Marseille and Toulon were expected to fight to the last man. Already ahead of schedule, the US Seventh Army now fanned out in three main directions to pursue the enemy and prevent him from escaping into Germany.

While the term 'Champagne Campaign' is most commonly associated with the 1st Airborne Task Force and the advance to Nice, some might say that it applies to all aspects of the invasion of southern France where each liberated area brought forth champagne and flowers for minimal casualties. To the north, the first real resistance was encountered about 150 kilometres north of Marseille, in the Department of the Drôme, but the taking of Toulon and Marseille would be anything but 'a walk in the park'.

While the American forces moved north up the Rhône Valley and also east to Nice and the Italian border, the French forces, l'Armée B (Afrique), or Army Group B, headed west in the direction of Toulon and Marseille. The liberation of these cities by French forces would be important for the nation's psyche. In the vanguard of the Allied forces disembarking in Provence were the volunteers of the Commandos d'Afrique. It was they who seized the German batteries at Cape Nègre on the night of 14/15 August 1944. The other elite formation was the 1er Bataillon de Choc attached to the 3ème Division d'Infanterie Algérienne.

The French Army B, under the command of General de Lattre de Tassigny, consisted of the 1ère Division Française Libre (1 DFL, the 1st Free French Doivision) 3ème Division d'Infanterie Algérienne (3 DIA, the 3rd Algerian Infantry Division) and 1ère Division Blindée

(1 DB, the 1st Armored Division). The latter was an armoured division comprising 73 per cent Europeans and 27 per cent *indigènes* (indigenous to Africa). Somalis, New Caledonians, Tahitians, Indochines, Syrians, and Lebanese were also part of this multinational force. 'General de Lattre is a terrible man to serve under,' said one, 'but I wouldn't care to serve under anyone else.' Some considered him to be the greatest soldier to serve France since Napoleon. 'His sharp gaze, like Napoleon's, subjugated, pierced and ruthlessly stripped naked everyone on whom his eyes rested.' Another described him as 'very pleasant, very volatile' and 'very soldierly'. In 1914 he killed two of the enemy with a sword his father had carried in the Napoleonic Wars, but was impaled by a German lance. One of his men had to pull it out with a foot on his chest. His personal motto was *Ne pas subir* (don't give up). In peacetime, as a staunch Catholic, he used to carry the sick at Lourds, and in wartime he ensured that there was always a priest around to give the last rights.[1]

Initially, de Lattre had been loyal to the Vichy regime but the German occupation of the *zone libre* was too much for him to bear, and, like many other once-faithful servants, he was locked up. With the help of his 15-year-old son, Bernard, and the Resistance, he escaped from prison and fled the country. In the early dawn of 18 October 1943, he parachuted from an RAF plane on to the field at Tangmere. Clearly, Jean de Lattre, at 55, was not your average general. Known as *Roi Jean* (King John) for his love of pomp and ceremony, he had a West African soldier sound a trumpet whenever he made an appearance. Visitors might wait all day to have an audience with the general who, as an aide explained, was 'nocturnal'. It had been de Lattre's hope and ambition that he, rather than General Alexander Patch, would be in overall command of the invasion. In de Gaulle's estimation, he was 'ardent to the point of effervescence'. His faults derived from 'the excesses of his virtues'.[2]

The 1ère Division Française Libre and the 3ème Division d'Infanterie Algérienne were the first two French divisions to land at Cavalière and Saint-Tropez respectively. The 1ère DFL was under the command of General Diégo Brosset, a barrel-chested, rugby-playing man with a passion for literature. After the First World War, he joined the colonial army and spent fifteen years patrolling the North African desert with a camel-mounted cavalry unit. When France capitulated, he refused to carry out the orders of the Vichy government, and pledged allegiance to de Gaulle. Considering that Brosset could not be part of the first wave on Dragoon D-Day, he remained aboard the troopship *Sobieski* until 16 August, seething with impatience. Like many on board, his eyes filled with tears when surveying the coastline of France. During the coming weeks, he would be instrumental in the taking of Mont Redon, Hyères, Le Touar and La Garde before entering Toulon. Three months later, when crossing a bridge in the Haute-Saône on 20 November 1944, the general's vehicle overturned into a river and he was killed.[3]

In the sleepy fishing village of Le Lavandou, the days leading up to the liberation were darkened by the violent spasms of a desperate and cornered enemy. Situated on the fringe of the invasion zone, on the coastal road leading to Toulon, the population had been terrorized by the mostly Armenian conscripts serving in the Wehrmacht. The nearby Cap Nègre had fallen to the Commandos d'Afrique, and Le Lavandou was in their sights. Some civilians had slipped through the German lines to report on the progress of the Allies, and the townspeople were eagerly awaiting their arrival. Waves of aircraft surged overhead. Not knowing which way to turn, the Germans panicked and imposed a curfew, and shot at anything that moved. On this night, resistance fighters came out of the shadows and fired back. A reckless policeman took a shot at the captain of the Saint-Clair battery as he rode by on a motorcycle with fatal consequences – to himself.

Having lived through the intensive bombing of the coastal areas, which reached a crescendo on 14 August, the day of the invasion dawned with naval bombardment. Le Lavandou was in the target area – a gun position had been hit and an ammunition dump was on fire. Many inhabitants had already taken refuge in the surrounding hills but some refused to budge from their homes. Two old spinsters, the *demoiselles* Ruef, had never before left their little seaside villa, and a few days previously, they had apparently asked God to allow them to be taken together by the same bomb. Jeanne Calvet, a friend and neighbour who documented her experiences of 15, 16 and 17 August 1944, last saw them when she returned an empty basket which the two kindly old ladies had filled with carrots as a gift. The bodies of the Ruef sisters were later found together in the rubble of their house.

On the waterfront at Le Lavandou were two jetties which provided a mooring for fishing boats, but for the Germans they represented a potential harbour for warships. At about 1 o'clock on the afternoon of the 16th, the Germans blew up the bigger jetty using tons of mines, bombs and other explosives. The smaller jetty had already been blown up a few days previously, and the townspeople knew what to expect. Windows were shattered and huge rocks came crashing through roofs. Some looked for shelter under a railway bridge which was already filled with wounded Germans lying on their jackets. Having been given fifteen minutes' warning, Jeanne Calvert took refuge in the old cemetery among the tombs of her ancestors.

Acting like men possessed, the Germans began rounding up civilians from wherever they were hiding. An officer with pistol in hand was shouting, 'Hostages, hostages!' A bedraggled group of about 300 men women and children were formed into a column. Beaten with rifle butts and barrels, they were hurried along the steep and winding road to the village of Bormes-les-Mimosas about three kilometres up the hill behind Le Lavandou. As the cortège made its way up the steep, winding road, one man carried his grandmother on his back, and two young boys helped shove an overweight woman up the hill using their shoulders like the second row of a rugby scrum. Aircraft circled overhead but did not attack.

Night was beginning to fall when they reached the Place Saint-François in Bormes. In front of the Café de La Terrasse, an officer, notebook in hand, demanded names and identity papers. It appears that the Germans were looking for resistance fighters believed to be among the hostages. A cordon of soldiers with machine guns was set up around the square and the hostages were told to seek accommodation wherever they could. The hospitality of the residents of Bormes would never be forgotten. The message from the Germans was that 300 people would be shot the next day, regardless of whom they were or where they came from.

That same evening, two platoons from the Commandos d'Afrique had just reached the outskirts of Le Lavandou, and on approaching the first houses at the edge of town they were told about the abduction of the hostages. Colonel Bouvet decided to attack the village at daybreak and it was a race against time. All 300 hostages tell a slightly different story, but for Jeanne Calvert the night seemed strangely short. She felt as though she and the other hostages had been abandoned to their fate and had all but given up hope. As the dawn glowed pink over the landing beaches in the east, sounds of firing could be heard in every direction. It was Bouvet and his commandos, desperately hoping that they would not be too late.

At about 6.40 a.m. on 17 August, rifle barrels and helmets could be seen glinting in the first rays of the sun, but it soon became clear that these were not Germans. Hugging and sobbing, the hostages realized that there was nothing more to fear. Although there were shouts of 'The French are here', it seems that the first troops to arrive in Bormes were Americans of the 3rd Infantry Division. En route from Cavalière-sur-Mer, via the Forêt Domaniale du Dom, they came upon the hostages purely by chance. Meanwhile the French commandos who had come up from Cap Nègre and Cap Benat, had overrun the town of Le Lavandou.

Giving thanks for the liberation of Le Lavandou and the rescue of the hostages, the parish priest said mass on the waterfront, and then, flanked by a platoon of Commandos d'Afrique, the liberation parade made its way through the streets. Almost immediately, the reprisals began. A mob of young men calling themselves FFI, but derogatorily known as *résistants de la dernière heure* (last-minute resistants), set to work in front of the *mairie* shaving the heads of women suspected of consorting with the Germans before parading them throughout the town. One of those accused of being a *libertine* had secretly been a staunch supporter of the local Maquis.

Nazis who had strutted arrogantly about town, and committed atrocities, now shed their uniforms and tried to blend into the crowd, but were quickly identified and put to death. Neither was any mercy shown to the five German soldiers who were responsible for blowing up the jetty. They were taken behind the Hôtel Beau Rivage and shot out of hand. One Armenian soldier who was found to have his pockets full of rings, some with the fingers still attached, was dealt swift justice.

The young Claude Gritti and his friends were tasked with combing the German blockhouses to retrieve any food the Germans had left behind. Large quantities of black bread, bottled soup and jam were taken to the community hall, from where it all disappeared overnight. A hospital was set up in the Hôtel de Provence, and when sheets ran short, the children were sent to collect more from other hotels. The boys were then sent on a mission to collect firearms which had been left behind in the blockhouses. It is a miracle that nobody was hurt because the weapons were usually loaded.

On what is now the Avenue de la 1ère Division Français Libre, motor vehicles of every description clogged the roads, generating much interest among the locals. The North Africans, for the most part, marched on their feet under the scorching sun. The rank and file loped alongside their mules and sheep. The mules, which they had used in the Italian campaign from the Volturno River to Sienna, carried their equipment and were sometimes used to clear minefields. Sheep served as rations on the hoof. A lieutenant of the French colonials documented his first few days on campaign:

> In our backpack, among other things, four days of food, received on board the troop transport before disembarkation, because we did not know at all when the next resupply would take place. All this is rather heavy, of course, especially under the August sun on the Côte d'Azur of the Var. On the beautiful coastal road, are scents of resin and aromatic plants. We successively pass through Cavalière, La Croix Valmer, Rayol, Canadel, Pramousquier, then we cross the big town of Lavandou, where the population gives an enthusiastic reception to the black Tirailleurs [colonial infantrymen]. The wine of Provence flows freely in the districts, but we must tell Lavandourains that Africans fear alcohol, and that they need their legs and brains for the fight that awaits them.[4]

From Bormes-les-Mimosas, the next town on the road to Toulon is La Londe-les-Maures, which was reached by the US 3rd Infantry Division on the evening of 17 August. Most of the residents had taken to the hills, but inside the village, a young *boulanger*, a baker, by the name of Louis Busonne, decided that he would try and prevent the Germans from blowing up a bridge, the pont de Pansard, having just witnessed the destruction of the pont du Maravenne. Unfortunately, he was spotted while trying to defuse the explosives and was captured. While being marched off to the feldgendarmerie – the German military police – with his hands above his head, he managed to exchange a few words with his friends. On the property of a well-known family in La Londe, the brave Louis Bussonne was shot multiple times in the back of the head. As was their custom, the Germans waited for the opportunity to surrender to the Americans but the chief of the feldgendarmerie was picked out of a column of prisoners and lynched. His body was thrown down a well.[5] There is a side street, a few blocks from the River Pansard in La Londe, named Rue Louis Bussone.

Down the road from La Londe, on the site of an old French fort, the Mauvannes battery consisted of four naval guns which covered the entrance to Hyères from the east. It had been bombed by Allied aircraft and bombarded from the sea with no result, but on 18 August, sixty African commandos infiltrated through the minefields and captured the casemates.[6] The next minor obstacle on the approach to Hyères was the Gapeau River where pleasure boats are now moored cheek by jowl. It was not all plain sailing for one company advancing in Indian file, on the sides of the road, a few inches from the ditches which provided cover in an emergency – although they were often mined:

> Captain Parison falls shouting 'Jesus, Mary and Joseph!' Lying among the vine stocks, I feel a violent pain in my left shoulder, and the blood begins to flow abundantly on my khaki shirt. Parison, very near, gives no sign of life. A Tirailleur died to my right, another gently moans, and the German shells continue to rain very hard … As usual, the blacks have stuck to the ground, nose on the ground, their fingers relaxed on their weapons and they await the continuation of fatal events … The morning is warm, the August sun darts its rays on the men of the 2nd Company, pinned down by the batteries of 88mm guns firing from the hills overlooking the city of Hyères.[7]

While the Free French were advancing on Hyères, another hostage drama was playing out. It appears that four German officers had been killed and mutilated, probably by Armenian deserters. Maddened with rage, the Germans arrested over a hundred men, young and old, in their homes on the night of 18 August. In their nightclothes and barefooted, they were marched through the streets, then onward in the direction of Toulon. Nervous of an ambush, the thirty or so guards fired left and right.

While passing a hospital, a young nurse, Mademoiselle Jaume, had come out into the garden to see the column going past. She was shot dead with a burst of machine-gun fire. Although the hostages were held in a schoolyard and told they would be executed, the guards eventually came to their senses. The culprit who killed Mademoiselle Jaume was identified among the thousands of prisoners, and after being judged by a tribunal, was executed at what is today the Hyères-Toulon airport, also known as Palyvestre.[8]

The toughest nut to crack on the way into Hyères, just to the right of the coastal road, at Hyères les Palmiers was the Golf Hôtel, an impossibly strong, seven-storey, concrete structure which had been fortified by German engineers and that featured a network of underground cellars. The approaches were protected by barbed wire and mines, as well as the thirty-metre-wide Gapeau River. No amount of shelling could dislodge the occupants. General Brosset had not planned to spend forty-eight hours overcoming each obstacle in his way. The newly captured guns of Mauvannes were turned on the hotel but only succeeded in chipping the concrete.

To make things harder, the hotel was dominated by a hill, about 1,000 metres to the northwest, which would have to be taken first. Volunteers were called for from the 1er Bataillon d'Infanterie de Marine du Pacifique (BIMP/Pacific Naval Infantry Battalion), a unit consisting of New Caledonians and Tahitians. The volunteers were divided into six teams of about ten men, each one being given a specific task. Fortunately, for the attackers, they had on their side a young man who knew the building intimately, having worked on the site as part of his compulsory STO labour.

In the early afternoon, Sergeant Marcel Nallier and a man named Salviani were ordered to clear the mines in the saltpans on the approach to the fortress. Hardly had they moved a dozen metres when there was the crack of a Mauser. Salviani dropped the mine detector and fell into the salty water, muttering in his rough Corsican accent, 'I'm hit.' The bullet had entered his belly, passing through the first-aid dressing on his belt and exiting near the spine. The sniper could have killed both men but he stopped shooting. The machine guns now took over and bullets whistled overhead as the men sank lower into the salt marsh:

> In front of me, my Thomson seems ridiculous. It is hot, very hot. The mosquitoes devour us. Each time Salviani raises an arm, the bursts begin again. He begs me to finish it. I make him wait as long as I can. Nobody can come to fetch us. The afternoon is long, very long under this sun. The sun begins to drop, a deluge of fire and smoke falls on the Golf Hotel. Around 7 p.m., it's all over. They come to get us. 160 Germans are made prisoners of which about forty are wounded. Salviani died at the age of 64 years, but was paralyzed in the lower limbs.[9]

It was decided to first take the high ground at the back of the hotel, and the BIMP were able to attack from the rear, under cover of smoke fired from ships at sea. By 7 p.m. on 21 August, the 'hotel' had been captured, room by room. General Brosset came flying up in his Jeep and, bizarrely, performed a splendid athletic vault. He first congratulated the Germans on their 'beautiful defence' and only then praised his own men. The prisoners were then lined up against a wall. Thinking the worst, they began to vehemently denounce Hitler and the Reich. General Brosset yelled: 'Don't kill the prisoners, do not kill the prisoners!' According to one of the French soldiers, their intention had been only to search them, not shoot them. Around midnight, the liberation of Hyères was accomplished by the 1er Bataillon de Légion Etrangère – the 1st Battalion Foreign Legion – and the way to Toulon was open. In the district of Gapeau, the Golf Hôtel no longer exists, the pock-marked hulk being demolished over time. A gendermarie barracks building now stands there – next door is a school, the Lycée Golf-Hôtel – but various plaques remind the visitor of the events of 1944. '*Passant, souviens-toi*' (passerby, remember) is the message to visitors who fly in and out of the nearby Toulon-Hyères airport.

When things had quietened down, *Vallier* caught up with his diary, outlining the events leading up to the capture of La Garde. Leaving the sick and wounded at Collobrières, he had followed the American armour to Pierrefeu where elements of the Free French were still congregating after only coming ashore on 19 August. *Vallier* had little to say about this stage of his campaign except that he and his men, sixty-five in total, were heavily shelled for an hour and a half on the slopes of Mont Redon in a pine forest which caught alight. Situated just three kilometres outside of La Crau, Mont Redon is today the site of a holiday campsite. In their first taste of conventional war, several of *Vallier's* men were wounded. Mont Redon held out until the 20th; three days later, the Maquis *Vallier* played a role in the battle for Hyères by capturing a gun position on the Giens Peninsular. In due course, *Vallier* and a few of his men would sign on with the Free French for the duration.

Situated on a peninsular at the entrance to the Gulf of Toulon, the Saint-Mandrier Peninsular guns had a range of thirty-six kilometres. By now only one of the turrets was still in working order. The battery, set on a rocky hillside covered in pines, was difficult to spot from the air; nevertheless, three of its four guns had been put out of commission by persistent bombing. An underground network included ammunition stores and bunkers deep in the earth some distance away from the guns. These defences were intended to counter a direct attack from the sea. One turret with two huge barrels salvaged from the French battleship *Provence* was called 'Big Willie'.

The presence of these guns was one reason why the Allied landings took place farther to the east. From all other directions, Toulon is protected by white rocky hills extending from Bandol to the Grand Cap Massif. Only the coastal plain to the east, the area from La Valette to La Crau and Le Pradet favoured the French forces. The three highpoints to the north of the city are Mont Caumes, Mont Coudon and, of course, Mont Faron, the summit of which can today be reached by cable car. From this vantage point, one has a panoramic view of Toulon. In addition to Musée Mémorial du Débarquement, one can find old fortifications and various monuments commemorating the events which took place there.

On 22 August the way to La Garde was found to be wide open and flat. The hour of liberation had arrived for Marcelle Zunino, the young mother and resistant from La Garde. With the sound of the approaching battle, she tried to persuade her husband to take refuge in a tunnel in the mountain. 'You must leave the house, it is too close to Mauvannes to be safe,' she said to her husband, Roger. 'No, I'm always fleeing, this time I'm staying!' he responded. Marcelle left by herself, defying the curfew, and was immediately spotted by a small plane which bore down on her: 'I plunge into the ditch. When the alert is over, I go to the tunnel. It is crowded with fugitives like me. I do not stay there long, worried about leaving my husband in the turmoil.'[10]

At the first light of day, the people of La Garde welcomed their first liberators with laughter, joy and drinking. A reminder of that night is the François Accusano stadium, named in memory of a local young FFI fighter. On returning to their house, the Zuninos found it looted but there was a happy surprise. Marcelle's brother, Milou, was there as an officer with the Free French. As a reward for her services to the Resistance, Marcelle Zunino was immediately appointed to the Comité Français de la Libération Nationale – the only woman out of six members – and with pride took her place in the town hall. Toulon was now only a few kilometres down the road.

It was in the mountainous Maquis stronghold of Siou Blanc near Signes that the Algerians first made contact with the FFI group known as the Maquis *Camolli* on the night of 19/20 August 1944. When approaching the Algerian lines, the Maquis were challenged, '*Halte-là, qui vive?*' Not expecting to hear French coming from that quarter, the shouted reply was to the effect of: '*Hey! Qui êtes-vous là-bas, français ou quoi?*' ('Hey! Who are you over there, French or what?') Congratulations and warm embraces followed. A monument now marks this remote spot.

On 20 August, the 3rd Algerian Infantry Division reached Mont Faron and the encirclement of Toulon began. By the following day, they had reached the village of Le Camp at a crossroads halfway between Toulon and Marseille, preventing the Germans from escaping in that direction. An enemy roadblock was swept away, and, aided by enthusiastic members of the FFI, the 1er Bataillon de Choc infiltrated the centre of Toulon in small groups and engaged in some chaotic street fighting around what is now the Avenue du 1er Bataillon Choc.

The Groupe de Contre-Sabotage de la Marine Français, codenamed GÉDÉON, which had infiltrated at LZ *Fantôme,* near Brue-Auriac, thirty kilometres northwest of Brignoles on 12 August, now arrived in the Signes area. The long-suffering population could wait no longer for their day of liberation. On 19 August, four days after the landings, the French marines joined forces with the Maquis and two rescued American airmen to take control of the village of Signes. Contact was then made with the Allied *avant-garde* during their advance on Toulon.

Whereas some Allied commanders wanted nothing to do with these unconventional commando-type brigands, and ordered a halt to their operations at the first opportunity, it seems that General de Lattre de Tassigny was happy to have the support of a team of French commandos during the fight for Toulon. A member of the SAMPAN team, Enseigne de Vaisseau Sanguinetti, made his way through enemy lines to report to General de Lattre de Tassigny, who described the ensign as 'something thin and feverish looking like a Corsican bandit'. Sanguinetti then guided Captain Allain (*Lougre*) into Toulon, but he did not reach there until 23 August, five days before the city was liberated.

In charge of GÉDÉON was Enseigne de Vaisseau Première Classe Jean Ayral, a highly decorated officer who had served with distinction in the Royal Navy and, as part of the special operations forces, had already completed several missions in France. Said to be the first Allied soldier to enter Toulon on 21 August, Ayral was mistaken for a *milicien* and shot by advancing members of the French Bataillon de Choc. His last words were 'France! France! France!'[11] His eternal reward is in the naming of the street where he fell.

Meanwhile, Senegalese riflemen of the 9th Colonial Infantry Division liberated communities on the northern side of the city and seized Mont Coudon. Defending the fort on the top of Mont Coudon was a garrison of 120 German naval troops who seemed determined to fight to the last man and last round as their Führer had decreed. Led by their company commander, the attacking Senegalese gained access to the fort by taking off their boots and scaling the ten-metre-high outer wall. During hand to hand combat the German commander called down artillery fire which fell on attackers and defenders alike. Few escaped without injury but the colonials won the day.

On the northern side of Mont Faron was La Poudrière de Saint-Pierre, an underground quarry used by the Germans for storing ammunition in tunnels in the side of the mountain. Using French-made tanks which were rushed out of the tunnels at opportune moments, and artillery bombardments which were called down on tunnel entrances, the Germans kept the French at bay. French tank destroyers pounded the approaches to the powder magazines. Some of the defenders took refuge in the tunnels, refusing to surrender. During the night, tanks closed in and fired directly through the tunnel openings. At 9 p.m. on 21 August, a shell hit an ammunition dump and the mountainside exploded. Rocks and debris rained down over the entire neighbourhood. Hundreds of corpses were pulled out of the rubble and it is believed that some still remain there. Today the German government would like to see La Poudrière declared a place of collective memory although there are developers wanting to reclaim the land.[12]

The 5ème Régiment de Chasseurs d'Afrique (5 RCA) was part of the 1ère Division Blindée and equipped with light Stuart tanks as well as Shermans. After disembarking at La Nartelle beach on 19 August 1944, two squadrons sped through Grimaud, La Garde Freinet, Gonfaron, Flassans, Brignoles, Tourvès, Rougiers and Saint-Zacharie to Auriol on the outskirts of Aubagne. Two other squadrons approached Toulon from Cuers and arrived at the village of Solliès-Pont on 21 August 1944. On the old road, alongside what is now the A57, Sherman tanks broke through Solliès-Pont and made a dash for the hamlet of La Farlède – about ten kilometres north of Toulon. Here the lead tank blew up on a mine and the Germans cut down two huge plane trees to block the retreat of the rest of the column. They were then able to pick off eight more Shermans at will until the Senegalese infantry arrived to save the day.

Again, without waiting for the infantry, the 2nd Squadron 5 RCA rushed ahead with Stuart light tanks and the surviving Shermans. That night, the small force was cut off at a crossroads called La Pierre Ronde. This area is today a vast commercial district at the northern entrance to Toulon where there is a giant Ikea store and a Carrefour supermarket, just off the highway. During the battle, it was a ghost town, with shutters closed and no sign of life. The tanks were low on fuel and ammunition, but with the help of local *maquisards*, they managed to form a perimeter and hold out until help came.

During the night of 22 August, a *peleton* – a platoon – of light tanks was sent up to La Valette to try and rescue the isolated group. The lead tank *Bretagne* was blown onto its side by a well-concealed 8.8cm anti-tank gun. The driver and one other man managed to get out of the burning wreck but the others were trapped and dazed by ammunition falling from the twisted racks. The gunner had his fingers caught in the turret hatch and was blocking the exit. After calmly considering their options, the man said to his commander: 'Take your knife, *chef*, and cut off my fingers.' The tank commander refused, leaving the gunner no alternative but to take out his knife with his spare hand, open it with his teeth and cut off his own fingers. At the German dressing station he said to the doctor: 'I wish I had a better knife, because I struggled to saw through the bone.'[13]

In what is now Avenue du char Verdun, in La Valette, one can see a pristine M4 Sherman tank, with 'Verdun' stencilled on the side. The attendant plaques pay homage members of the 5 RCA who were killed in the liberation of La Valette. Passersby are asked to remember them. On 22 August, Roger Saulas, the radio operator of the unlucky *Verdun* had his skull crushed by the recoil from the gun. Next day, the same tank was blasted point-blank by a panzerfaust, killing three more crewmembers. Two light tanks, *Artois* and *Aquitaine*, were also knocked out, with three fatalities, and two more Shermans, *Rouen* and *Rochefort* were damaged. The Senegalese infantry had spent the night at a place called Le Logis Neuf in Solliès-Ville. At eight o'clock on the morning of the 23rd, they renewed their attack on La Valette and the tankers were rescued after their forty-eight-hour ordeal.

Mont Faron was captured by the 1er Bataillon de Choc after climbing up the vertical southern face. They found the summit to be deserted, but the Germans called in an artillery bombardment from guns sited on Mont Touar. A plaque which can be found on top of Mont Faron proclaims that Capitaine Lamy, at the head of the 3rd Company of the 1er Bataillon de Choc, was the first to get to the top on 22 August and was killed on the field of honour. Another monument marks the spot where Lieutenant J. M. Chipier of the 3rd Algerian Division was killed on 23 August in carrying out a support mission for the Bataillon de Choc. Shells also rained down on a company approaching the port. Residents had barred their doors and it was particularly disheartening not being able to take shelter in friendly houses.

A section of the 1er Bataillon de Choc, under l'Aspirant, or Officer Cadet, Bonnard made its way into the centre of Toulon and holed up in a building off Place Martin Bidouré. A strong detachment of German infantry, supported by two 20mm guns, launched an assault on the morning of the 23rd. Bonnard and seven of his men fought until they were out of ammunition and then laid down their arms. The Germans lined them up in the street and executed them with their heavy weapons. Bonnard was shot in the legs and left for dead. Another man ran between the two guns and got away. A plaque with the names of the seven commandos 'assassinated by the Germans' proclaims that the Toulonnaise never forget.

In the Place de la Liberté in the heart of Toulon is a plaque stating that on 23 August 1944 elements of the colonial forces caused the French flag to fly again in Toulon. In fact, the symbolic hoisting of the *Tricolore* on the sous-préfecture building was carried out by a diverse group so that all units might share equally in the glory. The city was still far from secure when a sailor, assisted by a pretty young woman raised the flag while the small representative group presented arms. Standing quietly to one side were the *collabos* who had backed the wrong horse and were nervously contemplating their future.

Characteristically, General Diégo Brosset was one of the first into Toulon. He would give his driver the cold sweats, always insisting on being at the front. On the return journey, Brosset met up with his leading troops encouraging them saying, 'Go ahead, I have just kissed at least two hundred girls!' In his diary, Brosset confirmed that his reconnaissance by Jeep resulted in him being accosted and kissed (*baisé*) by a crowd of crazy women.[14]

It seems that the garrison troops took seriously Hitler's order to fight to the last man considering that they held out for more than a week against overwhelming odds. In some isolated areas the Germans fought to the death rather than surrender, but a thousand or more prisoners were taken at Fort Sainte-Catherine near Bandol after their commanders were assured that they would be surrendering to the French army and not the Resistance. There was still no official surrender, and, becoming exasperated, the French sent a message on the 25th to the effect that if the last defenders did not immediately capitulate, the Senegalese would be ordered to massacre them all. All resistance ended in the city and the official surrender came into effect on 26 August, but still the naval gunners on the Saint-Mandrier Peninsular held out.

For three days the occupants, shaken from the bombing and shelling, had been holed up in the Saint-Mandrier bunker, surrounded by a scarred and scorched landscape, scattered with wreckage. Deciding to get serious, Allied ships pounded the fortress from a distance of about eight kilometres until the defenders finally agreed to give up at 6 a.m. on 28 August 1944. In total, 17,000 Germans were taken prisoner in Toulon, and untold numbers killed. Once the shooting stopped, both sides saw each other as human, and out came the family photographs and cigarettes. Thirteen days had passed since the Allied divisions had landed in Provence. At the liberation parade three weeks later, American, British and French sailors marched together.

De Lattre's intention had been to liberate Marseille after first taking Toulon. However, when his forces secured the village of Le Camp early on during the encirclement of Toulon, he decided to allow them to move on Aubagne, even farther to the west. Le Camp is at a crossroads up in the hills above La Ciotat and Bandol. The doomed prisoners en route from Gestapo headquarters in Marseille to Signes would have passed through here on what is today called the Route du Maquis. It was partly because resistance leaders such as Robert Rossi had been recently executed here that the FFI in Marseille, although numerous, was divided and disorganized. As a result of the premature uprising by the population of Marseille, de Lattre was forced to immediately lend support to the FFI.

The task of taking Aubagne, the gateway to Marseille, and home of the Foreign Legion, was assigned to the 6,000-strong Groupements de Tabors Marocains (GTM) who had only recently arrived on foot from the landing beaches. 'Tabors' is the generic word for these Moroccan irregulars although individually they are called Goums. They wore sandals and striped cloaks, many had beards and carried vicious-looking knives. The Germans put up a stiff resistance, inflicting a number of casualties, especially among the French officers but Aubagne was in French hands by the morning of 23 August, and all communication was cut off from the defenders of Marseille. Other Moroccan units captured the coastal town of Cassis; their legacy is an Avenue des Goums in Aubagne and an Avenue des Goumiers in Marseille.

The hot, dusty sirocco wind had been blowing for three days over Marseille, and many of the oil refineries in the area had caught fire during the latest air raids. Now, with the strong wind blowing, they were belching out clouds of thick, oily smoke that spread over the city in a heavy blanket of suffocating air. Although not as well defended as Toulon, there were nearly 200 artillery pieces and 20,000 German troops in Marseille. Many were Kriegsmarine troops who may have been slightly older than the ideal, but they were seasoned veterans from the Eastern Front and all ethnic Germans.

Putting on their FFI armbands, the large underground movement in Marseille went on the offensive on 18 August, starting with the looting and distribution of food. General insurrection was announced over loudspeakers mounted on trucks. A proclamation declared that the Vichy government was no longer in control, and the préfet of the Bouches-du-Rhône prudently handed over power. Immediately, the various political factions began arguing about how the new dispensation would be run. The *épuration* – the purge – began early with the execution of a Gestapo agent and a *milicien*. Roadblocks sprang up and black marketeers and other collaborators were arrested. Even at this stage, it was uncertain whether or not de Lattre would be bypassing Marseille.

On 22 August, de Lattre called a meeting of his commanders at a classy hotel on the outskirts of the city where there is now a street named in his honour. On the *terrasse* he was annoyed to see elegant young men and women sipping cool drinks, seemingly oblivious to the fact that there was a war raging a few kilometres away. On the orders of the *chef* (de Lattre), the French Army was to remain on the outskirts, but when the FFI came pleading for immediate help, General Joseph de Monsabert decided to establish his headquarters in the city centre, next to the préfecture which had been seized by the FFI. A couple of half-tracks and machine guns were set up outside on the pavement as protection.

A thin line of French troops now extended from Aubagne, through the suburbs, to the Vieux-Port. In the city of Marseille itself, many Germans refused to surrender or retreat and took the only remaining option. Monsabert, met with General Hans Schaefer, the German commander, and tried to persuade him to surrender but only got an angry response regarding the behaviour of the FFI, which according to him, was not a military force, and he vowed to continue shelling the city. Meanwhile, more troops were filing into Marseille, guided by FFI scouts who had knowledge of every pillbox and landmine.

Two strongpoints which remained were sited at the Vieux-Port and the hill on which stands the Cathedral of Notre-Dame de la Garde. This hill has a commanding view of the city and had to be taken post-haste. On 25 August, a large force of Algerians, supported by tanks, was assembled to make the attack. The steep, narrow streets did not make an ideal tank battlefield, but from Boulevard de la Corderie a troop of Shermans proceeded up the Montée de la Bonne Mère. Local residents poked their heads out of their windows and cheered them on.[15] Several unarmed Germans asked for and received protection from the bishop inside the cathedral, fearing what the Resistance and the North Africans might do to them.

The lead tank, *Jeanne d'Arc*, rode into a storm of panzerfausts, grenades and flamethrowers. Three of the crew were killed and the tank was incinerated like its namesake. The second tank, *Jourdan*, hit a landmine and was stopped in its tracks. The commander, named Loiliot, told his men to escape one at a time and acting on impulse he grabbed the *Tricolore* off its mounting and carried it up the hill. He, and a resistance fighter who came to his side, dashed through a hail of bullets to tie the flag onto a railing in front of the Basilica – on which physical signs of the fighting can still be seen today. A resurrected Sherman, also named *Jeanne d'Arc*, is the centrepiece of a monument in the street leading to the Basilica, the Montée de la Bonne Mère.

In his memoirs, General Schaefer made much of the fact that he refused to damage the Cathedral of Notre-Dame de la Garde even though his positions were being fired on from there – probably by resistants. On the evening of 27 August, he requested a ceasefire, and the next day, in scorching heat, the final surrender was signed on the bonnet of a Jeep. In a final twist of irony, the German officer carrying the documents stepped on a mine, shredding the papers and him.

It so happened that Marseille and Toulon were liberated on the same day, and this feat had been accomplished by the French themselves. The victory parade which was held at the Vieux-Port in Marseille on 29 August 1944 was charged with emotion. The FFI took pride of place, together with the men of the multicultural French Army, as the crowd went wild with joy. The surviving Germans fled north up the Rhône Valley in gazogène-powered and animal-drawn vehicles, and anything else they could commandeer from the French. Ernst Dunker and the rest of his Gestapo colleagues had already run, but they would have nowhere to hide.

As a German field hospital packed up and prepared to leave a village betweenTarascon and Saint Rémy de Provence, the chief medical officer told the owner of the villa, 'We're obliged to leave now, but we'll be back. We're putting the finishing touches on some terrible secret weapons that will win the war for us. We'll be seeing you soon, Madame.' In whatever vehicles they could find, they drove out of the courtyard and north toward Avignon and Orange.

With the sound of guns continuing in the distance, urban residents half expected the Germans to return. Anxiety was fuelled by the ambulances rushing through on their way to hospitals in the rear. During an unforgettable evening at the end of August, a continuous rumbling was heard in the main street of Saint-Étienne du Grès, then a cry, 'The Americans, the Americans are here!' Large green vehicles, loaded with soldiers, were passing through. The village crowded round, shouting, 'Long live the Americans!' But the helmeted figures called out, 'We're not Americans! We're French!'

In the days that followed, the real Americans arrived in Saint-Étienne and set up camp across from the post office. Skinny, undernourished kids hung around their trucks and tents, scrounging chewing gum and especially those 'magical little tin cans full of candy and cookies'.[16] From that point on, life seemed to calm down, and it might even have become a bit boring if there hadn't been so many living things for a child to discover in the garden, at the foot of the olive trees.[17]

Some of de Lattre's forces continued to Arles and Nîmes and one detachment got as far as Montpellier, while the main forces turned north up the Rhône Valley. The 11th Panzer Division made several feint attacks toward Aix-en-Provence to try and hinder the Allied pursuit. While the French were celebrating their victory at the Vieux-Port of Marseille, the three American infantry divisions were locked in battle at Montélimar, north of Avignon. The French Army B – redesignated the First French Army on 25 September – would be given the honour of being the first to enter Lyon, France's third-largest city, before continuing its advance toward Germany.

Chapter 15

Persistence

It was another sweltering hot Provençal day when the 36th (Texas) Infantry Division tramped through Draguignan, and the men stopped at the fountains to take advantage of the cool water. Wine flowed freely, and the Americans reciprocated with chocolates, cigarettes and K-rations. Food was now particularly scarce in the Var since the links with the rest of the country had been completely broken, but one shopkeeper broke open crates of tomatoes and tossed them to the soldiers who crunched them like apples.

The early success of the landings brought about logistical problems. Vehicles and fuel were in short supply although captured fuel stores at Draguignan and elsewhere did help. German and civilian vehicles were pressed into service, and handfuls of troops could cling onto the back of armoured vehicles. Mostly, the infantrymen had to rely on their traditional mode of transport – their feet.

In an article dated 21 August (delayed), a *Stars and Stripes* correspondent with the US Seventh Army in southern France, Sergeant Stan Swinton, wrote of an encounter with an aristocratic former American, whom he called 'The Countess from Plainfield N.J'. It is not known where the countess in question was encountered, or indeed whether or not she had a claim to the title. She simply said to a GI: 'Have you got a Lucky Strike? I'm dying for one.' Her name was Countess Frances Gruiociardini, and for four years she had sought safety on a small farm buried in the vineyards. Sixteen years previously, she had come to Paris where she was introduced to a certain Count Horace Gruicciardini. A few months later the American girl was a countess. In 1940 she and her two children, François (14) and Mary, (11) fled to southern France. Her family urged her to return to America. 'But I was no child when I married – I had my eyes open and knew what I was doing. It was only right to stay with my husband,' the attractive, blue-eyed countess said:

> 'My husband stayed until our money was gone and then he returned to Paris. I weigh only 95 pounds but my son and I broke the earth in the backyard to make a garden and grow potatoes. I spread manure and tilled the earth. All day I did nothing but scramble for food for my children. In the morning I would get on the bicycle and ride everywhere until I found food. Now you soldiers have given me food. But it was very hard.
>
> 'The Germans? They were very correct. And they were lonely – always they wanted to show pictures of their children and family. When they began to trample through my living room to use the telephone they paid half of the telephone bill. They were very correct but they were the enemy. Ten days ago many of them left for the north. We knew that if you invaded you would have little trouble here. But we thought you would not come to this little, forgotten village.'
>
> The countess is slender, with grey hair and clear features. She dresses like an American – white-slacks and a lacy white blouse. And now that she can, she still will not leave France. She will stay in the little house with its century-old painting of the Gruicciardinis. She has waited for Paris to be freed so that she can be with her husband once again.[1]

In the days following the liberation the residents of Draguignan saw only Americans, not individual units; consequently both the 36th Infantry Division and the 517th PIR have been given credit for the liberation of their town whereas it was the less glamorous 551st PIB who should have been credited. In Draguignan, the mistake has since been rectified with a monument honouring the 'GOYAs'.

The capture of the German hospital in Draguignan was achieved early on the 17th when a couple of soldiers bluffed that they had it surrounded. A field hospital was then established behind the church of Notre-Dame-du-Peuple. The resident cleric, Raymond Boyer, was stopped in the street by the American chaplain driving in a Jeep named *Ave Maria* and asked if a service could be given in the church for some of the soldiers. A good twenty arrived, armed to the teeth, faces smeared with camouflage. 'We prayed,' said Boyer who spoke good English. 'It was moving.' Later he would get to know the medical staff when they installed themselves for the long haul. Most surprising for Father Boyer was the fact that each American doctor had brought with him a substantial library of medical books.

Liberation came to Lorgues on 17 August but the lives of fifteen of its townsfolk were lost in the process, mistakenly killed by American artillery fire. The unpleasant details of this incident seem to have been conveniently forgotten, but in 2015 an impressive monument was erected at the site opposite the tourist office in Boulevard Mistral. The names of the twenty FFI fighters who lost their lives at Les Arcs and Le Thoronet between 15 and 17 August 1944 are also remembered there.

Of course, the most significant memorial in Draguignan today is the Rhône American Cemetery. Although the mayor of Draguignan offered to have the American dead buried in the town cemetery, it was decided that a bigger piece of land would be needed. A beautiful twelve-acre tract situated at the foot of a hill, covered with cypresses, olives and oleanders was chosen. Some trees would be left in place; the soil was good for digging. Although the United States government was prepared to pay for the land, the townspeople wanted to contribute something. The first to be buried here on 19 August were from the FABTF and the 36th Infantry Division. The 3rd Infantry Division had buried their initial casualties at Cogolin just inland from Saint-Tropez but like most battlefield burials, they were ultimately exhumed and reinterred.

The Rhône American Cemetery in Draguignan is the final resting place for 861 Americans killed during the landings and in the subsequent campaign. On the wall of the missing there are 294 names. The dead represent every state in the Union, except for North Dakota. Some are from the District of Colombia and Puerto Rico. There are sixty-two graves of unknown soldiers, and two sets of brothers buried side by side. Lieutenant Aleda Lutz, a flight nurse, is the only woman buried here. She was killed on 1 November 1944 when her C-47 crashed in severe weather south of Lyon. Families of the fallen were given the option of repatriating the remains, and 40 per cent chose to do so. The other 60 per cent preferred to have their loved ones buried among their comrades.

Draguignan soon found itself in the rear echelon and firmly under the control of the liberation committee. Even staunch Vichyites changed their tune and welcomed the Americans now pouring through. A clandestine newspaper, *La lutte patriotique*, published an article giving some credit to the Americans for assisting in their liberation. Under the heading, '*Salut a nos frères d'armes des USA*', (Salute to our brothers in arms, the USA), it stated:

> It is with immense joy that the population of the Var welcomes the first 'Sammies' landing on our soil and coming from far to help with the liberation of France. From the bottom of all our hearts, a gigantic *merci* is addressed to our valiant Allies whose military valour, combined with an unbelievable degree of production, has allowed us to live for this long-awaited day.[2]

On passing through Draguignan, a diarist recorded that 'There was no war damage worth mentioning – people all very cordial and seem honestly pleased that we are here. One fellow who could talk English said that the Germans were correct but not nice – the Americans are nice.'[3] Broadcasting from the beachhead on the afternoon of the first day, Eric Sevareid, a stalwart of the CBS broadcasting company, spoke of the reception which they received from the locals:

> Apparently many French Fascists and Vichyites were living here and are here also. One is the Director of one of the worst pro-Nazi, anti-Semitic French newspapers, which was a great help to the Germans in confusing the French before the war began. The village and countryside people have welcomed us most sincerely, but not with a tremendous amount of enthusiasm ... there are a few strained tears. And they are people who suffered a long, long time ... They are a little more shrewd than the Italians, and are not counting upon the unending flow of manna from the American armies. And we are only the beginning.[4]

The *Pocket Guide to France*, which GIs may or may not have studied before landing on French soil, reminded the conquering troops: 'You are a member of the best-dressed, best-fed, best-equipped liberating Army now on earth. You are going among the people of a former ally of your country. They are still your kind of people who happen to speak democracy in a different language. Americans among Frenchmen, let us remember our likenesses, not our differences.'[5]

It had to be drummed into the men that despite what Nazi propaganda had tried to portray, the French were allies – not collaborators – and had fought valiantly but in vain during the battle for France in 1940. Mention was made of the Frenchmen who had rallied to the *Tricolore* in the Tunisian campaign and in Italy, as well as the ordinary men and women who had risked a firing squad by joining the Underground. It was thanks to them that 'our fliers have come back to base after falling into the very jaws of the Nazis'. Many French lives had also been lost as a direct result of Allied bombing. Some bitter feelings existed, and Americans were told to avoid sensitive subjects: 'Don't you help anybody to dig up past history in arguments. This is a war to fight Nazis, not a debating society.'[6]

*

While the main American and French forces chased from behind, an independent force of 3,000 men and about 1,000 vehicles under General Frederick Butler had been assembled with the goal of racing north to outflank the Germans. Known as Task Force Butler, this flying column of Sherman tanks, M10 tank destroyers, artillery and motorized infantry was put together with elements from all three American divisions which had come ashore on 15 August. The force had no specific mission except for carrying out a reconnaissance-in-force. Departing from the coast on 18 August, the task force spent their first night in Le Muy then passed through Draguignan, Salernes and Barjols before turning north toward the confluence of the Verdon and Durance rivers.

Worried about being strafed by their own planes, a reconnaissance squadron of the 117th Cavalry carried yellow smoke canisters as they scouted ahead on the road to Salernes. Three kilometres outside of Draguignan the senior German officer in the region, General Ferdinand Neuling, had had his command post built into the hillside. Having first declined to surrender, one or two rounds from a tank encouraged him and his staff to come out with their hands up – all covered in dust.

On the evening of 19 August, Task Force Butler arrived on the outskirts of the spa town of Digne-les-Bains which sits astride both the River Durance and the Route de Napoléon. The Germans had prepared a defence, and there was a skirmish, but when confronted by tanks and fighter-bombers, all resistance crumbled. The Gestapo HQ in Digne, where Francis Cammaerts had been held, was now deserted, but some of their loyal acolytes faced a popular tribunal and then a firing squad. It was at this point when Francis Cammaerts offered his services to General Butler and was snubbed. From Digne, the flying column moved to Aspres-sur-Buëch in the direction of the Rhône Valley, hoping to cut off the retreating German 19th Army.

*

As the 36th Infantry Division moved inland from the coast, the paratroopers stood down and assembled at a school in Puget-sur-Argens, on the Fréjus road.[7] It was from here that the FABTF began its three-pronged advance to the River Var. The 517th PIR was allocated the left of the line in the hill country to the north. The first pocket of resistance which they met in this sector was in the mountains at Fayence, where some of the so-called 'Lost Legions' of the 1st Airborne Task Force had accidentally ended up on D-Day. Two hundred German troops were still ensconced at La Roche in Fayence and had fought off all attacks by the stranded paratroopers working with the Maquis. Now the 517th PIR prepared to occupy Fayence for a second time.

After some shelling from artillery positioned at Saint-Paul-en-Forêt, the German commander sent word that he was prepared to negotiate. It was Captain Walter Hanna of Jedburgh team SCEPTER who met the German delegation at a neutral house in the village and warned that the paratroopers were preparing for an all-out assault. With the assurance that they would not be handed over to the Maquis, the relieved men came down from the rock on the morning of 21 August and laid down their arms.

In the neighbouring villages of Callian, Fayence and Montauroux, American medics who had been left behind on D-Day to look after the wounded and injured paratroopers, were found to be carrying on with their work, treating all nationalities equally. A little house-to-house skirmishing was required to take the village of Callian. Again it was a Jedburgh who is credited with taking the town. T/5 James Bryant of SCEPTER induced the surrender of twenty-eight Germans by waving a pistol and using a captured German as a shield.

Having breached the first line of resistance on 21 August, the 517th moved off in the direction of Saint-Cézaire-sur-Siagne, fifteen kilometres southwest of Grasse, thirty kilometres from Cannes and fifty-two kilometres from Nice. The town is built on high cliffs on the eastern side of the Siagne River – a natural fortress. Probably because of the accidental parachute landings in the area, the town had since been invested by several hundred Germans. Apart from Captain Grand Hooper, who had parachuted in by chance on 15 August, the first American to reach the town was an OSS intelligence officer attached to the 36th (Texas) Infantry Division. Wearing full military uniform, Lieutenant Walter Willard Taylor was behind enemy lines to try and find out what the German intentions were in the vicinity of Grasse. Were they planning to counter-attack or retreat?

A local FFI leader, León Roux, exhausted after a week of non-stop action, zigzagged up the road to the town of Saint-Cézaire in an open Citroën, with Taylor in the passenger seat. The plan was to drop Roux off, and wait for him while he went into Grasse. Near the entrance to the town, a row of mines had been strung across the road and Roux climbed out to investigate. He got no further than three metres from the car and was shot in the head. At first, thinking that they were being attacked by the Maquis, Taylor tried to reverse out of trouble and was knocked out by the blast of a grenade which also shredded his thumb.

With an infected hand, he was taken successively to Grasse, Ventmiglia, Genoa and Alexandria, then to Verona, Mantua and through the Brenner Pass. Along the way Taylor experienced what life was like for his enemies – being strafed whenever they ventured out on the roads. Nobody knew what to do with this 31-year-old archaeologist. Having been in the Marine Corps before joining the intelligence services, he ended up in a naval prisoner of war camp. While in captivity, Taylor met up with the fellow marine and OSS officer, Major Peter Ortiz, and together they plotted their escape; however, events overtook them. In 1954, Professor Taylor would publish a groundbreaking and controversial work on the study of archaeology which earned him the reputation of prophet, pariah and pioneer in his field.[8]

On 22 August, when the 517th began their assault on Saint-Cézaire they had no idea of the drama which had played out there the previous day. In fact, the trauma did not end there. Roux's body was left lying in the road and some German soldiers went down to have a look. One of them then stood on a mine and was blown to pieces. Later in the day, after the August heat had already had an effect, the swelling bodies were brought up to the village in a wheelbarrow.

Captain Grand Hooper was detailed to lead the attack on Saint-Cézaire, whose citizens had afforded him hospitality when he parachuted in a week previously. Following an artillery barrage, which killed one civilian, G Company went up the steep, terraced slope under mortar fire and became bogged down while I Company waded across the River Siagne and in darkness climbed a steep cliff to get behind the defenders. Five members of G Company lost their lives, one of whom, Private Richard Sailor, was a full-blooded Indian, predictably called 'Chief'.

When the commanding officer of the 517th Parachute Infantry Regiment, Colonel Rupert Graves, went over the battlefield, he found nine dead Germans from a reconnaissance battalion that had been sent to hold the town. Most of them looked to be about 18 or 19 years old. However, these were the best of the German Army, rabid Nazis, and as ordered had held their positions until killed.

It appears that one man, Sergeant Frank Dallas, a skinny country boy from Pennsylvania, had single-handedly accounted for most of the enemy dead. The citation for his Silver Star states that he climbed up a thirty-five-foot cliff and found himself behind the enemy positions. With deadly efficiency, he picked off about seven Germans among the rocks at the top of the cliff and silenced the machine-gun and mortar positions. Because his officer was later killed, Dallas had to wait until 1997 before being awarded his medal, by which time he was a retired colonel with a chest full of other medals, having served in Korea and Vietnam.

In the morning, people came out of their basements and found the street full of Americans, 'big, tall, unshaven guys with beards, covered in gear'. They were hungry, they asked for bread but the villagers had none. Instead, they were offered tomatoes, which were devoured with a speed which left the French aghast. Having subsisted on tinned food, anything fresh was particularly relished. More and more soldiers arrived in the village throughout the day, and were showered with kisses, hugs and fresh fruit. At the end of the day, Captain Hooper was reunited with his former hosts.

As usual, when the Germans retreated booby traps were left in the narrow alleys, and some days later, on 28 August, three young *maquisards* were killed trying to defuse an anti-tank Teller mine that was booby-trapped. Antoine Colmars (20) was disembowelled. When the local doctor said that he could do nothing Colmars was put in a car to be taken to the military hospital at Draguignan, but by the time they got down to the valley, he was dead. The ten Germans who had been killed in the battle of 22 August were buried in a single pit without ceremony. Boys from the village would visit from time to time, but only to spit and urinate on the grave of the 'filthy Boche'.

*

Just as the Normandy landings had given rise to a *faux depart* in June, so the landings in Provence, or Dragoon D-Day, was a second false dawn for the Resistance in the Alpes-Maritimes. Convinced that the Germans would have their hands full in dealing with the entire US Seventh Army, *maquisards* came down from their mountain hideouts and occupied some villages lower down in the foothills. Consequently, the villages of Levens, Aspremont, La-Roquette-sur-Var, Saint-Martin-du-Var and Plan-du-Var, situated at the confluence of the River Var and its tributary, the Vésubie, would be at the centre of unwanted attention during the last two weeks of August.

Filled with newfound enthusiasm, the 47-year-old resistance leader, Commandant Marcel Gérôme, went into Aspremont with the intention of demanding the surrender of the German garrison. A group of about eight soldiers was sitting around a table on the *terrasse* of the Trastour restaurant, as Gérôme approached them. One hot-headed *maquisard*, Charly Michenon, unfortunately drew his weapon and shooting erupted. Pionier Ernest Richter (27) was killed, and another German wounded. Gérôme was struck by a bullet in the vital organs, yet he helped carry the Germans into the church so that revenge would not be exacted on the village.

Through clenched teeth, muttering '*marche ou crève*' (march or perish), the unofficial motto of the French Foreign Legion, Gérôme stayed on his feet for twenty minutes before being laid out on a stretcher. There was no doctor in Aspremont, and the one from Colmars had to be summoned by force, but surgery was done too late. It transpired that the Germans had not fired a shot in the encounter and that it was a French bullet that killed him. Marcel Gérôme had been a pilot in the First World War and had suffered serious injuries when shot down. Originally from Nancy, for health reasons he moved to Nice where there is now a square named Place Commandant Marcel Gérome.

Farther to the north, two companies of FTP *maquisards* occupied Plan-du-Var and Levens on 16 August. One detachment went as far down as Saint-Martin-du-Var where the young communists called a meeting of the liberation committee then sang *La Marseillaise* with gusto and looted shops before leaving the village with their fists in the air. The citizens were less than impressed with these armband-wearing warriors of the last minute, at least a few of whom were turncoats known to have denounced real resistants and later used their newfound powers to settle personal scores.

Overlooking the valley of the Vésubie a few kilometres from its confluence with the Var is the village of Levens, where the FTP showed up on 16 August. Isolated and unmotivated, the small German garrison was more than willing to capitulate. Only the NCO in charge remained obstinate, irritating the *maquisards* with the usual prophecies of Germany's ultimate victory. But when he realized that they had murder on their minds, the NCO pulled out photographs of his family. Regardless, he was taken into the forest and shot in the head by a young resistant, going by the name of *Cobra*, angry over the recent loss of his father. Some say that the German was made to dig his own grave but according to another version, he was buried in a hole made by an uprooted olive tree.

Although Levens is located only about twenty kilometres due north of Nice, the presence of the FFI had been ignored by the Germans until 24 August. Now that the Var River had become the front line, a unit which had been fighting in the Cannes area – 164th Reserve Grenadier Battalion of the 148th Reserve Division – was ordered to take back control. As a column came grinding up the road, it ran into an ambush at a secluded place called Sainte-Claire, between Levens and Tourette-Levens.

Pandemonium ensued as a large force of experienced troops immediately returned fire and gave chase. The 23-year-old Max Mauvignant (*Médel*) was wounded in the stomach and was carried down to the road where he was heard telling the Germans that the Americans were not far away and would give the 'dirty Boche' a beating. Then a gunshot, and *Médel* collapsed, slowly rolling into the ditch, his head on his knees, his fists on his face. The manhunt continued throughout the day, and at least four were taken prisoner – but quarter was neither given nor expected.

An aggravated 164th Battalion resumed their attack on Levens on 25 August, and although the resistants had had some successes since the disastrous affair at Saint-Claire, they decided to abandon the town. As they withdrew, some were seen to remove their armbands and hide them in the cracks of stone walls along the roadside. As expected, the arrival of the Germans in Levens was marked by round-ups, interrogations and threats of death, but thanks to interventions by the priest and the doctor, who had treated German wounded, the village was spared.

Meanwhile on Route 202, which runs in the valley alongside the River Var, near the Pont Charles Albert, a group of Germans on bicycles met with a fusillade of shots, killing an 18-year-old recruit, Grenadier Johann Schmidt who was buried on the roadside. The letter of condolence to his family mentions all the right things about being one of the best soldiers in the company because of his friendliness and helpful manner – 'brave and bold at all times'. The company commander ended with a 'Heil Hitler!' and words to the effect that Schmidt had given his young life for the existence of the glorious Reich.

After taking back Levens, the164th Battalion moved straight on to the village of La-Roquette-sur-Var which is perched above the Var River valley and has a commanding view. When they arrived in the village, the Germans went berserk with rage, determined to find 'terrorists'. Banging on doors, and shouting *'Raus!'* a house was set alight, and the animals in the attached barn were burned to death. Two young men who looked to be of fighting age were taken out into the street and shot. The parents of Prosper Bovis, one of the dead boys, came upon the bodies while making their way to the church in the square. As the distraught mother wept over Prosper's blood-covered corpse, one of the murderers told her, 'This is war and German mothers are also crying.'

Some genuine *maquisards* were in fact hiding in the community clubhouse. Those who were able, made their escape, but one wounded man remained hidden under the pool table. A hand grenade was thrown through a window, the effect of which traumatized some children there for the rest of their lives. Two *maquisards* and two civilians were dead, and the rest of the villagers were herded into the square by ferocious-looking soldiers with leaves and branches camouflaging their coalscuttle helmets. Expecting the worst and shaking with fear, the men and boys were locked up in the church and told that they would be shot if the 'terrorists' carried out further attacks, but for now the resistants had retreated into the mountains north of the Vésubie River. The war was not over for La-Roquette however, as the Americans would arrive on the west bank of the Var on 26 August and launch an attack on the town the following night.

The appearance of the 517th Parachute Infantry Regiment at Le Broc on the west bank of the Var, opposite La-Roquette, spurred the Resistance back into action. All the various factions joined forces to carry out a *grande attaque* on Levens on 26 August. Armed with both American and German machine guns, the *maquisards* opened fire on the village from positions low down on the slopes of Mont Férion, trying not to hit any civilians. Deadly accurate mortar and artillery counter-fire quickly drove them back up the mountain. Some didn't get the message to pull back, and were cut off. Only one *maquisard* was killed but the testimonies of those involved in this *grande attaque* are characterized by stories of bravado and miraculous escapes.

One small group had to lie low while the Germans scoured the slopes. Their hopes rose and fell in unison with the sound of guttural voices and jackboots on rocks. One joker whispered that he would light a candle 'this big' to the Holy Mother if they managed to survive. After dark, they crept up the slope and crossed the road into a vineyard, biting into sour green grapes to quench their thirst. A farmer agreed to feed them provided that they did not come near the house. His daughter carried the basket of food into the forest, making the hungry boys think of *le petit Chaperon Rouge* (Little Red Riding Hood).

The crossing of the River Var at La-Roquette would be accomplished without loss to the Americans, thanks to the assistance of the Maquis. Ten days earlier, the head of the FFI in the Alpes-Maritimes, Jacques Lécuyer (*Sapin*), had driven all the way to Saint-Raphaël to try and convince General Frederick to make a dash for Plan-du-Var via a northerly route. Frederick preferred to play it safe, but did send a small patrol through enemy lines that arrived safely at the Var on 17 August.

As a professional military officer, *Sapin* dressed impeccably with shoulder boards on his starched khaki shirt. On his belt he now wore a fine-looking Colt given to him by General Frederick. *Sapin's* right-hand-man was a Scottish SOE agent, Major Harvard Gunn, an Oxford man who spoke five languages, although he was not a man of many words. Himself an accomplished artist, Gunn was an admirer of Cézanne and Van Gogh, emulating them in painting the Provençal countryside. When the war broke out he was living in Saint-Tropez where he owned a cottage. Originally serving in the Seaforth

Highlanders, he had transferred to the SOE in 1944. Perhaps because of his height, his codename was *Bambus* (Bamboo), but he was not exactly thin. Gunn was part of the Inter-Allied Mission commanded by Christian Sorensen, which operated mainly in the Alpes-Maritimes and the Var once the invasion was underway. He trained in Algeria with Christine Granville and worked with Francis Cammaerts. Gunn's orders were to wear uniform in the field and 'maintain the proper status of an Allied officer'. His usual 'uniform' was his Seaforth Highlanders kilt which bemused the French wherever he went.

A day ahead of the main forces, Harvard Gunn entered Saint-Martin-du-Var and found the FFI (mainly FTP) to be 'very disordered and very political'. Conventional wisdom holds that while the pro-communist FTP dominated in Nice, the hinterland was under the control of the FFI, led by Lécuyer and his deputy, Pierre Gautier (*Malherbe*). In a smuggled message dated 22 August and signed by Lieutenant-Colonel William Blythe and Captain Geoffrey Jones at their headquarters in Fréjus, the FFI were instructed to try and prevent the enemy from retreating into Italy.

Higher up on the River Var, is Puget-Théniers where the Route de Grenoble (R202) heads west through Digne. The town and surrounding area had been in the hands of the Resistance for some time. History relates that it was *Sapin* who persuaded the entire German garrison to surrender on 19 August; however, a photograph exists of *Sapin* and his entourage in the village of Lantosque on 19 August, fifty kilometres away, on dangerous roads. A few days later, six of the original thirteen members of Operational Group RUTH, under lieutenants Brandes and Strand, joined the *maquisards* who were protecting the bridge at Puget-Théniers. By 28 August, a patrol of the 517th PIR had passed through, and RUTH was withdrawn to Grenoble where all the OSS operators in southeastern France gathered prior to being disbanded.

On 23 August, while the 3rd Battalion 517th Parachute Infantry Regiment was enjoying the fruits of victory in Saint-Cézair, the 1st Battalion moved north and occupied the remote village of Saint-Vallier-du-Thiey. Passing through Grasse, the day after it had been liberated by the 1st Special Service Force, the 517th PIR took a left fork and headed through Bar-sur-Loup, high up in the hills to Bouyon, not encountering any opposition, apart from the tortuous roads, until they came to the River Var.

Being under observation from high ground at La-Roquette, any attempt made by the Americans to cross the Charles Albert Bridge was met with a hail of shot and shell. Clearly it would be necessary to cross the river elsewhere and take the high ground before the bridge could be used. It fell to E Company of the 517th PIR to cross the river at a ford and attack La-Roquette from the rear, departing from Le Broc at 1.30 a.m. on 28 August. The men of E Company were convinced that this would be a suicide mission, and ate all their chocolates beforehand. A new supply of candy rations had just arrived, and each man received a box of peanut-covered chocolate Clark Bars. Nobody wanted to die with such treats in their pockets for someone else to find. (The army Hershey Bar on the other hand, was bitter and hard; it tasted no better than a boiled potato and was rated as one of 'Hitler's secret weapons'.)

Although it was the dry season, the Var was still flowing quite strongly and it appears that the FFI guides were not sure of their directions. At about 2 a.m. they started down the cliff toward the river. The paratroopers had not gone far before they were in over their heads, but made it across without losing too much equipment. Although expecting to receive a welcome from the German guns at any moment, they were ignored because 'the Kraut knew anyone with any brains at all would never try and cross that river at night. They were not aware of the fact that we were paratroopers, thus not very bright'.[9]

After gathering themselves, and dismissing their incompetent guide, the company made their way round the back of La-Roquette and by mid-afternoon, were on the outskirts of town. While the FFI had not performed as well as hoped, they had already paid a price for their enthusiasm. Two messengers sent out from Le Broc to inform *Malherbe* of the imminent crossing were captured and taken to Levens where they were held in the Place de la République. A village official heard the commotion in the middle of the night and went to see what was happening. The two men were trussed up, lying on the ground, with one screaming for his mother. The other *maquisard* was calmer and gave their names as Jean Garente (31) and Richier Joseph (37). In the morning, they were taken into a field and shot and buried one on top of the other in a shallow pit.

On reaching the outskirts of La-Roquette, a squad of paratroopers set up an ambush on the Levens road. Two Germans on a motorcycle trying to get out of Levens came around the bend: the driver was shot first and the passenger ran toward a barn in vain. A search of their bodies revealed that they were carrying top secret despatches. From the cover of grapevines and trees, the paratroopers watched reinforcements march into town with their hobnailed boots, and assemble in a courtyard. Some were lying on the grass when the shooting started. The Germans were in panic. Some put up a fight, some ran inside the buildings, and some jumped over the cliff.

By this time the main body of 164th Battalion had pulled back to Levens, eight kilometres away, leaving mostly Polish troops who were only too willing to surrender. However, Hitler Youth fanatics, almost all under the age of 18, fought to the death. When the dust settled, eleven bodies were found in the village and one down on the Charles Albert Bridge. Far from being a suicide mission, the battle for La-Roquette was a walkover for the 517th PIR who sustained no fatalities.

It seems that the booby traps devised by the Boche were particularly vicious of late. Two *maquisards* had hit a landmine on the road between Vence and Tourettes-sur-Loup, on 28 August. A crater had been made in the road. When a company of American engineers arrived they found the two bodies lying in the bottom of the crater. The grief-stricken father of one of the *maquisards* begged the engineers to retrieve the bodies. Although the mine-detector did locate some mines, the German engineers had been too cunning. As the second corpse was being dragged out, there was a chain explosion that killed two of the engineers as well as a Frenchman on the spot. A third engineer, Private Olaf Kaastad, died the next day in hospital at Draguignan. This characterful 35-year-old had left Norway as a teenager and then lived in Minnesota for many years. His body was repatriated by his family in Norway after the war.

*

While the Americans did not cross the Var until 29 August, the northward advance up the Route de Napoleon and into the Hautes-Alpes had been lightning-fast. Gap was liberated on 20 August and Briançon was reached on 23 August. These early successes can be attributed partly to Task Force Butler, and partly to the FFI supported by teams of special operators. On the Italian border in the Hautes-Alpes during the second half of August were OG NANCY, plus two Jedburgh teams, NOVOCAINE and CHLOROFORM, as well as the IAM CONFESSIONAL consisting of captains Robert Purvis and John Roper under Commandant Jacques Pelletier (no relation to François).

CHLOROFORM had ended up in the Hautes-Alpes, although they were supposed to stay in the Drôme after landing east of Montélimar on 30 June 1944 – long before most other Jedburghs arrived. They narrowly missed being caught up in the Vercors but were on hand to give assistance to the survivors. They moved up into the mountains on 7 July 1944 with Colonel Jean Drouot (*l'Hermine*), a 37-year-old former air force officer, who was now appointed *chef* of the Central Alps area. It seems the newcomers were not well received by the existing Maquis command.

Henry McIntosh, the commander of CHLOROFORM, was long remembered in the area since he had the strongest southern (American) accent anyone had ever heard, and he spoke French as he spoke English. The junior team member, and radio operator, was a Frenchman, Lieutenant Jean Sassi, who raised the ire of the ordinary *maquisards* because he ordered them around   even at gunpoint – and had an 'attitude' because he was a Jedburgh. According to the local heroes, he did nothing out of the ordinary to earn his Légion d'Honneur.

Be that as it may, Sassi rose to the rank of colonel and covered himself in glory at Dien Bien Phu in Indochina in 1954. Shortly before the base was overrun, planeloads of legionnaires volunteered to parachute onto the battlefield to try and rescue their comrades, despite it being a lost cause. Sassi led an operation called 'Desperado' which was unable to prevent the fall of Dien Bien Phu, but he was able to use his skills in unconventional warfare to exfiltrate about 200 men through the jungle.

Francis Cammaerts was being held by the Gestapo at Digne between 13 and 17 August, and was thus incommunicado immediately before, during and after the Allied landings. On his return to his headquarters at Seyne, he found that even more special operations missions had arrived and needed instructions. These included IAM UNION III that consisted of Englishman Major D. E. F. Green and Canadian Major C. B. Hunter, together with a BCRA team of four French officers, both teams landing at Chabanon in the Alpes-de-Haute-Provence on 13 August.

Jedburgh team EPHEDRINE was also waiting in Seyne at this time. The American team member was Lieutenant Lawrence 'Larry' Swank of Washington DC. Late in the afternoon of 13 August, having learned that Cammaerts had been arrested, the entire group – Green and Hunter, the three Jeds, and the four Frenchmen – decided to move toward Barcelonnette and the Larche Pass, but then happened to meet up with

Christine Granville who advised them to join those groups already in Vallouise in a hidden valley, twelve kilometres southwest of Briançon.

While Granville embarked on her efforts to get Cammaerts released, the ten men in a charcoal-burning truck turned north from Barcelonnette and started up the road toward Guillestre. Near Saint-Paul, a careless accident occurred. One of the French instructors had left his loaded weapon stacked in the back; a sharp turn caused it to fall over and discharge. The bullet struck Swank who died several hours later. He was buried in the local cemetery on 15 August, just as his fellow countrymen were landing in the south.[10]

Gap, the capital of the Department of the Hautes-Alpes, is situated on the Route de Napoleon, and General de Gaulle dearly wanted to be able to claim that the FFI had liberated the town by themselves. Despite the threat of a large-scale uprising in the town, the German garrison refused to surrender to the Maquis. Under pressure from his superiors, Jean Drouot (*l'Hermine*) had to rely on guile to get the Germans to lay down their arms before the Americans got there. While Task Force Butler was still fifty kilometres away, between Sisteron and Digne, *l'Hermine* persuaded just one tank commander to advance to the outskirts of Gap and fire a few shots, resulting in the immediate surrender of the 1,200 Germans.

Thus, on 20 August, the important crossroads of Gap was technically liberated by the FFI. Perhaps the man of the hour was the priest, Père Robin (*Ludovic*), already a legend for hiding weapons and Jews in his parish at Champoléon. Dressed in his cassock, he fought like a madman for the liberation of Gap, and almost murdered a German who was found with objects from the church in his pack.[11] In the memory of the locals, it is actually Commandant Paul Héraud (*Dumont*) who must be credited with the liberation of Gap, although he had been killed five few days before. The interlocutors, Jean Drouot and his Jedburghs, had evidently done no more than execute the plan and accept the surrender.

Paul Héraud, aka Commandant *Dumont*, was a charismatic FFI leader who had helped to bring unity to the squabbling resistance factions in the Hautes-Alpes. Francis Cammaerts himself wrote that Héraud was Christine Granville's one 'special friend' in whom she found 'purity and perfection'.[12] Not yet 30, Paul Héraud was a keen mountaineer and professional Alpine skier, with a remarkable knowledge of geology, history, poetry and music. Gap was his hometown, and gloomily he now said: 'The end is coming, but not everyone will see it,'

Only a week before Cammaerts was arrested, on 9 August 1944, Héraud and a friend were travelling by motorcycle on the road near Tallard, south of Gap, when they ran into a German column. Héraud tried to run for it so as to dispose of the papers he was carrying. While his friend was shot on the spot, Héraud managed to get far enough to tear up the documents but was eventually brought down.[13] A menhir stone marks the spot where he fell and on it is inscribed 'Hard as a rock'.

When the first American forces coming up from the landing beaches arrived in Briançon on 23 August, the reception was even more rapturous than usual since the Germans had left only two hours before. During the chaos, the leader of IAM CONFESSIONAL, Jacques Pelletier, was accidentally shot in shoulder by a boy with a revolver who had been in FFI for about an hour, thus ending his part in the proceedings. Briançon has the distinction of being liberated twice. On seeing the large American force approaching from the direction of Gap, the German troops abandoned the city and retreated into the surrounding forests. Thinking that it was all over, the Americans moved back toward their main axis of advance, leaving only a small force behind.

On 28 August a temporary task force of about 1,000 American troops under Lieutenant Colonel Harold S. Bibo, took over the defence of the area so as to protect the right flank of the 45th Infantry Division on their drive north. During the night, a counter-attack was carried out by hardened German troops from across the Italian border. Bibo withdrew his headquarters twenty kilometres down the Grenoble road. American outposts were overrun; C Company of the 83rd Chemical Battalion, a mortar support battalion, was cut off and suffered heavy losses. The fit young *maquisards* who had so impressed Jedburgh Team NOVOCAINE were surrounded. Many were killed, and ten others captured and executed on 29 August 1944.

Now abandoned by the Allies, Briançon was subjected to a reign of terror. From the mountaintops the Germans had witnessed the outpouring of joy in the village, as well as the disrespectful treatment of the dead they had left behind, and they were incensed. A number of citizens were taken hostage and a member of the local liberation committee was shot. The second liberation came at the cost of eighteen North African infantrymen, and today the town and the ancient fortresses are covered in monuments and plaques of remembrance.

Assisted by NOVOCAINE and the FFI, the last remaining enemy troops were driven out of Briançon on 6 September by the 4ème Régiment de Tirailleurs Marocains (4 RTM), which had arrived in France on D+10 from Italy and had come up straight up from the coast. This forgotten corner of the Southern Alps along the Italian border, and the pass itself, remained in German hands until the following spring.

Chapter 16

Desolation

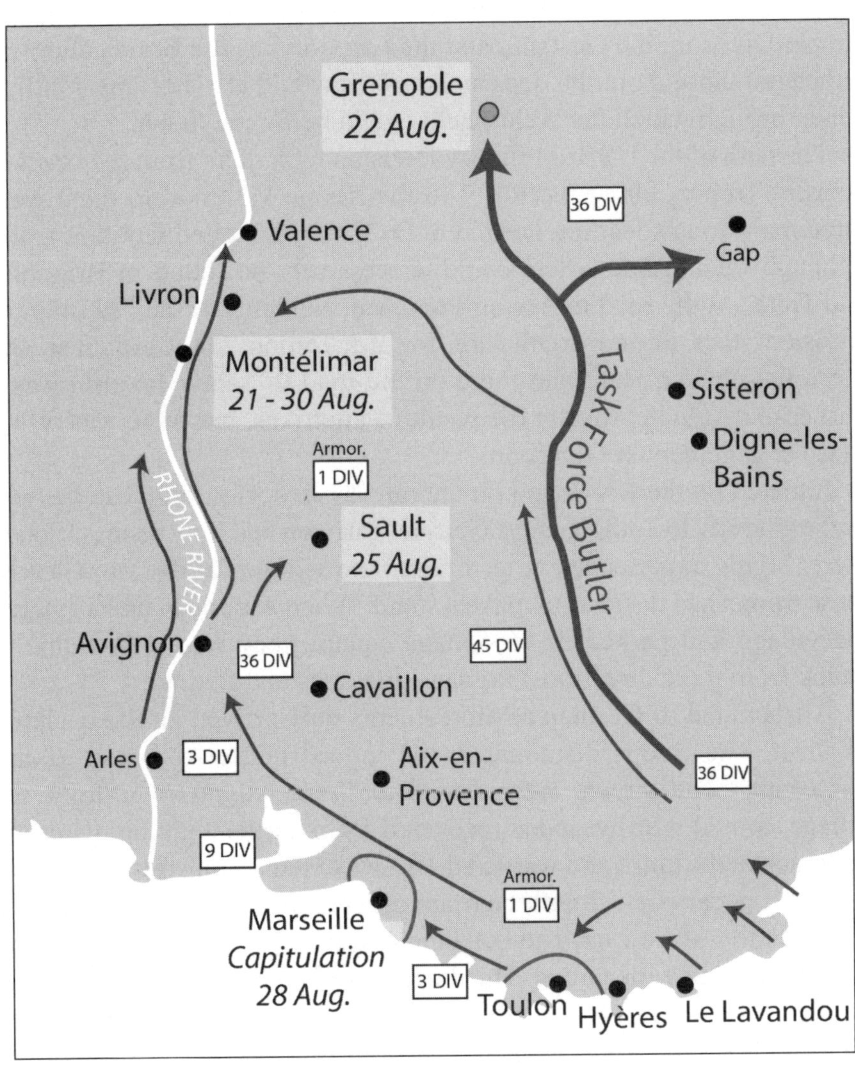

Pursuit up the Rhône Valley and the taking of Toulon and Marseille.

If there is such a thing as quintessential Provence, it is perhaps the rolling hills of the Luberon in the Vaucluse Department, where vineyards give way to lavender fields as the land rises toward Mont Ventoux. Whereas the upper Rhône Valley with its smokestacks, industry and major highways would always call for a heavy German presence, it was the proliferation of Maquis groups and drop zones which drew the unwanted attentions of the occupiers up into the hills. Situated between the Massif Central and the Alps, the Vaucluse has been called *carrefour de la Résistance*, the crossroads of the Resistance. In the summer of 1944, the 11th (Ghost) Panzer Division, the Gestapo, and their auxiliaries, the Brandenburgers rampaged throughout the department. This would also become a killing zone, through which the Wehrmacht would be forced to flee.

The path of the US 3rd Infantry Division took them from the beaches at Saint-Tropez, along the RN 7 to the Rhône Valley were there were three main routes leading north. On D+1, they liberated Gonfaron, and although their headquarters could successively be found in Brignoles and Trets, on the road to Aix-en-Provence, elements of the 3rd Infantry Division also turned southward toward Toulon via Carnoules and Pierrefeu-du-Var. Here and there on the road to Saint-Maximin was a burned-out vehicle, mostly the result of airstrikes, but there was also a sharp engagement at Gonfaron.

Situated on the RN 7, and on the railway line, Gonfaron can be seen as the gateway to Toulon, and a German garrison had long been stationed there, highly experienced at terrorizing the villages of the Var. Clearly, these troops had decided to make a stand. When American tanks entered the village and parked in the village square, they were vulnerable to attack from three directions: Pignans, Flassans and Le Luc.

A truckload of German reinforcements duly arrived on the outskirts of town. The troops dismounted and moved house by house toward the centre. The streets were deserted. Some young men from the village, armed with weapons recovered from earlier fighting, carefully approached the tanks and warned the crews of panzerfausts lying in wait. Just then, a car packed with German officers in full flight arrived from the direction of Le Luc. The machine gun mounted on a Sherman tank wiped them out with a burst. The demoralized enemy fought desperately before surrendering. Now acting as guides, the young *maquisards* led the Americans to the German command post located in a château on the road to Pignans where the occupants surrendered without a fight.[1]

After bivouacking at Rians on the night of 19 August, a battalion of 600 Americans from the 45th Infantry Division, hitherto untested in this campaign, probed westward parallel with the Durance River. Being unable to get across the river, the formidable 11th Panzer Division made a stand at a crossroads on the RN 561 between Peyrolles and Meyrargues, obliterating eight American vehicles and scattering the infantry following behind. Fighting went on throughout the day and well into the night before the Germans withdrew. As the bridge at Mirabeau was no longer usable, the Americans called on the help of local people to clear a path through the river. Tank destroyers and amphibious vehicles were able to cross, but the rest of the column had to wait for the engineers to build a bridge.

Although the Germans had virtually abandoned Pertuis on Dragoon D-Day, and the *Tricolore* flew in place of the swastikas on all the buildings, a nervous atmosphere prevailed until the day of their actual liberation – 20 August 1944. The bells rang incessantly as the 45th (Thunderbird) Infantry Division came into town and settled around the fountain in the square to wash for the first time in five days. As they reorganized their kit, inquisitive young boys hovered about to see what they could scrounge.

On 21 August 1944, the day that de Lattre's advance guard entered Toulon, the headquarters of the three US infantry divisions could be found in the following locations: 36th Infantry Division at Sisteron, east of the Rhône and north of Digne; 45th Infantry Division at Mirabeau, east of the Rhône and south of Digne; and the 3rd Infantry Division at Aix-en-Provence. At all points north, French men and women studied their maps to pinpoint the location of the Allies, and to estimate how long it would be before their own day of liberation arrived.

Having crossed the Durance, the Americans were now in the territory of the Maquis Ventoux. First contact was made with a reconnaissance patrol on 18 August in the village of Banon; nothing but a Jeep could have got up the steep and narrow access road. From here on, the FFI would be fighting side by side with the regular army and over the next few days, they carried out a series of attacks on German convoys in order to hinder their withdrawal. The escalation of this threat rattled the German command and it was the ordinary civilians who paid the price with their own blood. In groups or individually, scores were taken hostage, beaten, robbed and shot. Their homes and even historical edifices, like the 800-year-old Château du Barroux northeast of Carpentras, were destroyed out of spite.

Apart from a few *kampfgruppen* – battlegroups – the only proper fighting force which the Germans had available was the 11th Panzer Division. Their role was as the rearguard, protecting the northward retreat of the 19th Army, which also meant keeping the Maquis under control. Based around Carpentras and Auzon as from mid-August, the 11th Panzer Division, veterans of Operation Barbarossa and the battle of Kursk, marauded through towns and villages of the Vaucluse. Violence was visited on Saint-Hubert, Méthamis, Sault, Apt, l'Isle-sur-la-Sorgue, Le Barroux, Mormoiron and Mazan – all east of the Rhône.

At a place called Coustellet, a key crossroads between Cavaillon and Gordes, an FTP Maquis group set up a roadblock on 19 August 1944. During the night, a column of tanks of the 11th Panzer Division arrived from the west. Reinforcements from another Maquis group rushed in to help, but crossed paths with a German armoured vehicle, and twelve eager young fighters were killed. At the poignant memorial ceremony less than six weeks later, children sang 'Chant du Départ' as the monument immortalizing the twelve names was unveiled.

Fighters from various groups including the Maquis Ventoux and the Maquis Vasio set up an ambush on the road between Le Barroux and Malaucène, near border of the Drôme. On 20 August, more than a dozen men, hidden behind rocks, opened fire on a small convoy. Two Germans were killed; the remaining seven abandoned their vehicles and took cover inside a tunnel. During the firefight, the 23-year-old Fernand Blanc was hit in the forehead. There are many versions of how Fernand Blanc was killed; he was from Avignon and not well known by the others. Some say that he tried to seize a sidecar to be able to take a wounded comrade to safety, but as another *maquisard* soberly put it: 'No, we were all there. We shot, and they shot. And Fernand was dead. That's all.' If there was any hero, it was the 17-year-old Simon Sochacsenski who went into the tunnel with a grenade in each hand, and in fluent German demanded the surrender of those inside.

In the tranquil riverside town of l'Isle-sur-la-Sorgue, which was a popular leave destination for German soldiers, a massacre took place on 22 August 1944. Perhaps in retaliation for the recent ambush at Le Barroux, nine hostages were taken but after the pleadings of the local mayor and the handing-over of money, jewels and other goods, five were released. The other four were taken to the school courtyard and shot at 6.30 p.m. Their bodies were thrown into the garbage pit. Vicarious revenge came the way of the people when one morning a large aircraft was seen flying at low altitude, south of Cavaillon toward the north, with two fighters in pursuit. An eyewitness described how the faster planes rushed at it, spitting flame. Then a column of smoke appeared in the sky over Velorgues. It turned out to be a German plane that ended up against a row of poplars facing the Jonquiers wine cellar in l'Isle-sur-la-Sorgue. The pilot was buried next to the road.

*

Despite having once had a narrow escape from the Gestapo, SOE agent John Goldsmith returned to France for a third mission on 19 July 1944 to work with FFI leader *Archiduc* who ran a busy airstrip and parachute drop zone in the Vaucluse. From the moment that his feet touched the ground, Goldsmith noticed a change in the professionalism and strength of the Resistance in comparison to his previous visits. A series of ambushes was carried out during the month of August, with the Maquis Ventoux successfully punching above their weight.

On a lonely stretch of road between Apt and Sault, near the hamlet of Saint-Jean-de-Sault, is the Château de Javon, a formidable castle, over a thousand years old. It was near here that five Germans, four of them officers, were killed on 4 or 5 August. A few days later, on 8 August, a larger party of Germans coming from Apt was ambushed in the narrow gorge on the road from Sault to Montbrun-les-Bains; one witness counted 120 Germans lying on the ground. Despite the inevitable reprisals against resistants and innocent civilians alike, the Maquis carried out even more daring attacks in the coming days.

The most ambitious action took place two or three kilometres north of the hamlet of Saint-Jean-de-Sault, on the RN 143. A sizeable convoy of vehicles of the 11th Panzer Division was spotted travelling from Avignon to Digne on 22 August 1944. Because of the large number of 'terrorists' around Apt, the convoy took a detour through Sault. The alert was given via a telephone call to Saint-Jean-de-Sault, and the Maquis forces set the trap overnight. To have taken on the 11th Panzer Division and won was a feat of arms seldom seen in the shadow war; however, in this type of terrain, the odds were stacked in favour of the Maquis.

It appears that Goldsmith has either confused or combined the action of 8 August with that of 22 August. The steep, narrow gorge which he so vividly describes is closer to Montbrun-les-Bains, whereas the country around the hamlet of Saint-Jean-de-Sault and Château de Javon is more undulating and far from the actual slopes of Mont Ventoux. Although Goldsmith was under the impression that the battle was a personal one between the Maquis of the Ventoux and the Gestapo of Avignon, there were much bigger players involved in the plan to disrupt enemy movements after the landings. Although he mentions no dates, it is most likely the ambush of 22 August 1944 that Goldsmith describes in his memoir, *Accidental Agent*. Wearing the uniform of a major in the Royal Armoured Corps, he fought alongside the Maquis Ventoux, and many of his fellow SOE operatives would have envied his participation in this battle. During all the years of stealth and hiding, they dreamed of facing their enemy in the open.[2]

Crouching under the shade of a withered olive tree on the barren slopes of Mont Ventoux, Goldsmith watched mesmerized as a German column clanked its way slowly up the 'steep incline'. Two thousand or so well-armed *maquisards* covered a wide area on both sides of the road. The leading tanks were allowed to get well up onto a plateau before they were fired on by anti-tank guns, and when they limped back down the hill they found themselves cut off and unable to turn around or reverse out of trouble. As they retreated down the sunken road, hugging the sides to escape the fusillade, Goldsmith bowled grenades down on them in cricketing style. Peculiarly, the sky of Provence was not its usual bright blue. The mountain was 'shrouded in a dirty brown haze that smelled of charred twigs, cordite, melting rubber and dust'. In Goldsmith's imagination the air seemed to reek of Germans too: 'a sour odour of sweaty tunics and stale cigars'. The part-time partisans had held their discipline and passed up many inviting targets before the order was given to open fire. 'The pent-up frustrations of years of suffering, injustice, hunger and humiliation, exploded in a relentless fury' on the men of the 11th Panzer Division, and no mercy was shown to the wounded after the shooting died down.[3]

To Goldsmith's knowledge, only one *maquisard* was injured; in his excitement, he shot his own finger off. Although Goldsmith mentioned that 250 enemy dead were counted, more cautious accounts speak of 110 dead and perhaps 250 'put out of action'. Commandant Rayon's orders were to take no prisoners, and only to pursue fleeing Germans up to a point. Cleverly, the Maquis had not corked the bottle into which the enemy had been lured so that they would not turn mad with the desperation of men for whom there is no hope.[4] A few vehicles which had not yet entered the kill-zone did manage to make a U-turn on the narrow road, and drove twenty kilometres to pitch camp in a forest on the Plateau d'Albion (near Saint-Christol) after dark. Next day, they went on their way, leaving their wounded behind at the mercy of the French. Goldsmith attributed the 'ruthless efficiency' of the Maquis to the 'masterful leadership' of Commandant Pierre-Michel Rayon.

Three members of Rayon's SAP had fallen into the hands of the 11th Panzer Division and were being held in the principal town of Apt, situated in the basin below Sault. All the Maquis from Pertuis, Céreste, and Manosque, as well as Jedburgh teams GRAHAM and CITROËN converged on Apt, but arrived too late for any action. Sensing that trouble was coming, most civilians had left town, and the German garrison decided it was time to head back to Cavallion. On the afternoon of 22 August 1944, at 2.50 p.m., after a hurried meal in town square, the column mounted up and cautiously drove off in the direction of Beaumettes, twenty kilometres to the west, with the Maquis nipping at their heels. The three *maquisards* were used as human shields and tied onto the bonnets of vehicles at the head of the convoy. On reaching the entrance to Beaumettes, they were no longer needed so they were taken off and shot.

On the roads throughout the Luberon at this time it was not safe for either side as German stragglers tried slipping through the net, and American patrols scouted far and wide into enemy territory. Everyone was in a state of insecurity, not knowing who was where. On 20 August 1944, a German column from Carpentras entered the village of Bédoin, at the foot of Mont Ventoux, causing panic among the inhabitants, some of whom fled. Lieutenant Marius Bastidon, of the Maquis Ventoux, unwittingly rode into the town on a motorcycle and was mortally wounded by a burst of machine-gun fire. Then, on 23 August, American scouts coming from Sault arrived at Auzon and found the village still in hostile hands. An American officer was wounded, his Jeep was seized and a half-track was destroyed in the skirmish.

The liberation of Cavaillon on 24 August was bittersweet because it came too late for so many. The town had been a base for the barbarities of the 8th Company, 3rd Regiment of the Brandenburg Division which installed its command post at the Hôtel le Splendid. The population was traumatized, and most of them eventually left the town. Although not the first or the last to be executed here, five men were arrested on 1 July 1944, kept in a farmhouse, tortured for four days and then finished off. In order to conceal their deeds, the German auxiliaries dynamited the house. Two months later the mutilated bodies were discovered in the rubble. Among them were some of Cavaillon's favorite sons like Jean-Louis Bastide, a leading light in the sporting and cultural affairs of the town.

Even after the Germans departed, blowing up the suspension bridge over the River Durance behind them, many residents were too afraid to come out of hiding. Then, word came that the Americans were at the entrance to town. The manager of the Cheval Blanc – the White Horse – took a keg of beer out into the street to offer the liberators a drink. French flags appeared on the facades of buildings. First to appear was a Jeep with two young soldiers, happy to accept refreshments. It was, as usual, very hot.

People, who had been used to living under brutal repression now began to express their true feelings, and congratulated each other in loud voices as if they wanted to take credit for the liberation. Someone then came rushing up the Avignon road shouting, 'The Germans are coming back.' The flags disappeared as quickly as they had appeared, but it was a false alarm. The next morning, locals were thrilled to find a Sherman tank parked on the pavement of the Grand Café Moderne, with men of the 3rd Infantry Division sleeping on the ground in Place Gambetta. Throughout the day, vehicles loaded with troops and equipment passed through the town and went on down the Avignon road.

*

The sights and sounds of the *gris-verts* retreating inundated the villages of the Vaucluse. Hanomag half-tracks and BMW motorcycles with their sidecars were caught in traffic jams at the Rhône, having to wait at the three ferry-crossing stations at Arles, Avignon and Tarascon. The grey Wehrmacht personnel carriers, heavily camouflaged, resembled a forest in motion. The troops inside sat quietly, no longer singing their patriotic songs as they had done for four years, parading and strutting through France. Sweat-stained and weary, these men had barely had a moment's respite since D-Day. Those who had escaped the cauldron would now end up in the fire of Montélimar.

After dark, the roar of the German motorized columns, instead of abating, seemed to get louder. In the streets below them, villagers heard distant guns, muffled voices, jackboots tramping, squeaks of overloaded wagons, the neighing of horses and the clip-clop of their hooves on the asphalt. Troop movements took place in the middle of the night so as to avoid the Allied aircraft that were masters of the sky. Bolting their shutters, residents worried that an army on the run might turn to looting.

Drunken soldiers did on occasion enter the homes closest to the road to steal a horse or a bicycle.

While Task Force Butler forged ahead to the Rhône Valley by the fastest possible routes, the 36th (Texas) Infantry Division followed behind using all available roads. One contingent turned right at Draguignan toward Grasse, and then moved up the Route de Napoleon. Stephen Weiss, a 19-year-old from Brooklyn, was part of a twelve-man rifle squad which advanced 144 kilometres along this route in fourteen hours. As they raced through the rustic beauty of the lower Alps, waving villagers appeared as a kaleidoscopic blur:

> If we paused for a moment's respite, our shirts bathed in sweat and covered with dust, our mouths parched with thirst, they would run to greet us, arms outstretched, with tears of joy streaming down their cheeks. Four years of emotional deprivation expressed itself in a volcanic surge of feeling, which engulfed us all. I was hugged and kissed by people of all ages until my face and ribs ached. When I shared my rations with them or made small talk with pretty girls my own age, the melancholy of war seemed very far away. Amidst their wine and our cigarettes, against a backdrop of olive-green tanks and trucks, we struggled for the appropriate words in either language that somehow never expressed or matched the moment. It was ineffable. When all the towns along the highway – Castellane, Digne, Sisteron, and Gap – were set free in four days, the spirit of liberation was sublime.[5]

Montélimar is situated on the east bank of the Rhône in the Department of the Drôme. Farther north, beyond La Coucourde, the bridge over the Drôme had been destroyed by the Resistance. The bottleneck which resulted on the RN 7 turned the upper Rhône Valley into a killing field. Apart from isolated groups of stragglers, the bulk of the German 19th Army had reached Montélimar by 21 August, and was moving through the gorge at La Coucourde. Butler's task force arrived at the same time, and from the hills overlooking the Rhône valley blasted the convoys with everything at their disposal.

Infantry was however needed to cut off the escape route, and the fifty or so *maquisards* accompanying the task force were clearly inadequate. Suffering from a shortage of ammunition, fuel and everything else, Butler called on the US 36th Infantry Division for help: 'French infantry support absolutely unsatisfactory repeat absolutely unsatisfactory. Request one infantry battalion by motor without delay.'[6] In his turn, the FFI leader in the Drôme, Commandant de Lassus, was critical of General Butler, saying that he lacked mobility and daring.[7] Most military types, however, hold up Task Force Butler as an American version of blitzkrieg.

All three American infantry divisions were spread over a wide area from Grenoble to Gap, Digne and Guillestre – on the road to Briançon. By 24 August, the whole of the 36th Infantry Division had reached the battle zone and occupied defensive positions along a forty-kilometre-long strip. From 25 to 30 August, they were subjected to daily attacks in an attempt to cut their supply lines and encircle them. The fighting was confused with no single front line, and the enemy on all sides. Reinforcements from the US 45th Infantry Division were deployed forty kilometres north of Montélimar near Crest, which in turn is twenty kilometres upstream from Livron-sur-Drôme. The aim was to obstruct the German withdrawal up the Rhône Valley, as well as to counter any German reinforcements that might be pushing south.

From their elevated gun positions, US artillery turned the valley floor into a valley of death. During eight days of fighting, the various artillery regiments fired more than 75,000 rounds. From the air, P-47 fighter-bombers strafed vehicles and pounded bridges, forcing the enemy to remain on the east bank of the river. A news sheet originally printed at Anzio, *The Beachhead News*, gave the following optimistic statistics:

> For 18km north and south of the town [Montélimar] the highway was a smoking double-column of knocked-out vehicles, dead horses and men. There was no stretch of road that did not contain some degree of destruction. In total,

Blaskowitz and Wiese's troops suffered 11,000 casualties and lost 1,500 horses. The Americans took some 5,000 prisoners at Montélimar and destroyed more than 4,000 vehicles, as well as the 189th and 338th Divisions.[8]

Within the Rhône Valley, between Montélimar and Valence, the battle was fluid over a distance of fifty kilometres. Such was the level of confusion, that elements of the American and French armies had already reached Romans-sur-Isère on 22 August, nine days before its final liberation. Two short-sighted *miliciens*, still faithful to the Nazis, fired on the French troops as they arrived in town. A number of *maquisards* and Senegalese were killed and wounded on 22 August as is evidenced by the plaques of remembrance dotted around the town.

A contingent of FFI, mostly veterans of the Vercors under the command of Narcisse Geyer (*Thivollet*), was fighting alongside the regular French troops in Romans. When it was all over, the two *miliciens* tried to blend in among the liberating soldiers and *maquisards,* but *Thivollet* had them arrested and shot the following day. One of the snipers was an agent of the Gestapo, and the other had participated in the massacres on the Vercors plateau. They were shot an hour apart on the morning of 23 August by a firing squad made up of Senegalese soldiers. Images show them with their hands tied behind their backs, kneeling down in front of iron railings on the northern side of the Jacquemart Tower.

Roadblocks were set up, but when a strong column of the 11th Panzer Division broke through to Romans-sur-Isère from Valence on 27 August, the FFI was no match for them. Many of the citizens fled, shops were looted and hostages were herded together at the Café Glacier. Having been so closely involved with the happenings on the Vercors, everyone expected the worst. When the officer in command of the German column, the reputable Major Karl Thieme, visited the hospital to see his men who had been wounded on the 22nd, he discovered that they had been captured by regular troops, some of whom were also in the hospital. Thus retaliation was avoided, and there would be no more dark threats.

Although they were guilty of a number of outrages throughout the Vaucluse during the last two weeks of August, the 11th Panzer Division fought a magnificent rearguard action. When confronted by hit-and-run tactics employed by the Maquis, they had been shattered and frustrated, but against the conventional American forces, their tactics were superior.

General Wend von Wietersheim's 'Ghost Division', so-called because it would appear out of nowhere, got out with 75 per cent of its armour intact, and remained effective until the last days of the war. Thanks to them, the 19th Army lived to fight for the Fatherland another day.

*

As we have seen, the US 36th Infantry Division had begun arriving in the battle zone on 22 August. Charlie Company of the 1st Battalion, 143rd Regimental Combat Team, approached Valence from the direction of Chabeuil and was ordered into the attack immediately. It was 24 August 1944, and this was the first real resistance the combat team had encountered since landing at Saint-Raphaël. Stephen Weiss was riding into battle on the back of an M-10 tank destroyer (TD), which with its thin armour was better suited to defence than attack. Even with two TD battalions and a contingent of FFI in support, the attack was repelled by German 8.8cm guns which knocked out three TDs in quick succession.

During what became known as the battle at Les Martins, Weiss and seven other members of his squad became separated from their company and spent the night in an irrigation ditch, within twenty metres of the enemy. Hyper-vigilant, and attuned to the slightest noise or movement, Weiss felt like a sacrificial lamb:

> Charlie, a ghost company, disappears as if it never existed. Simmons [the company commander] has vanished. I'm outraged. By bugging out, by taking off [retreating], he has thrown us to the wolves and lost the battle. I'm overcome by a sense of desolation, and feel betrayed.[9]

During the morning of 25 August, the eight men managed to slip away and took refuge at a nearby farm. The farmer, Gaston Reynaud, contacted a gendarme who was also a member of the Resistance: 'I have a bit of a problem,' he declared. 'There are eight Americans hiding in my hayloft.' In a daring operation the eight were dressed in blue gendarme uniforms and transported in stages through German roadblocks into Valence. To reach momentary safety, they had entered a world of signs, counter-signs, of cover-stories, agents and cover names. Back home in Brooklyn, Stephen's parents received a 'missing in action' telegram, which so often meant that the person was dead and the body not yet found. In some cases, the family waited forever, and the name remained eternally on the list of the missing.

After crossing the Rhône in a rowing boat, the men were taken on foot to Alboussière in the Ardèche Department, about sixty kilometres north of Montélimar where the three American infantry divisions were still engaged a struggle to prevent the 19th Army from escaping across the Drôme. Valence was still in German hands. In Alboussière the eight Americans were accommodated at the Hôtel Serre, which served as the headquarters of the FFI leader, former French army captain, François Binoche (*Auger*). When asked to provide instruction in the handling of American weapons obtained in a recent arms drop, they proved to be less competent than their supposed 'trainees'.

Most of their time with the Maquis was spent flirting with the girls as they did their laundry at the stone *lavoir* in the village, but there was violence as well. Weiss was invited to join a firing squad being assembled for the execution of a *milicien*. He declined, but stayed to watch with the rest of the crowd. The execution was scheduled for 2 p.m. on a plot of open ground between the café and the church. While waiting for the arrival of the condemned man, members of firing squad mingled in the crowd, glass of wine in one hand and rifle in the other:

> The accused stood erect (without the benefit of a wooden post) and waved off the blindfold [Gendarme Lieutenant] Mathey offered, with a flick of his wrist. Given the opportunity to say a few parting words, he refused with a Gallic shrug of his shoulders and a toss of his head … Matthey shouted one order after another, the firing squad tried pulling itself together; little sounds persisted, the buzzing of an insect, the rustling of leaves, as I sucked in my breath like the others, watching, waiting, We stood behind the line of armed men, pointing their Lee Enfields at the accused, taking aim, Matthey shouted, 'Fire!'; the crack of musketry ricocheted off the wall. At a distance of not much more than an arm's reach, most bullets found their mark.[10]

The man toppled sideways, and lay twitching and writhing on the ground. Mathy rushed forward waving his pistol. He pulled the trigger, but there was only a click; he pulled a second time – another click. Taking aim, for the third time, Mathy's hand was shaking. The crowd stared in disbelief. Mercifully, an 'old curmudgeon' came forward, placed the muzzle of his rifle against the man's head, and fired. The twitching stopped and the townspeople walked away muttering in disgust.

Despite the ineptitude of some of the *maquisards,* Stephen Weiss was content to serve under François Binoche, and considered him to be a better leader than his own incompetent company commander, Captain Simmonds.

It was with regret, therefore, that he got news of an American OSS officer who had come looking for them, requesting that they join his OG about sixty kilometres to the west, in the remote hamlet of Devesset. One or two members of the team had been wounded, and they could use the extra manpower. Operational group LOUISE consisted of the usual fourteen or so other ranks under the joint command of lieutenants W. H. McKenzie and Roy K. Rickerson, known to everyone as 'Rick'. The OG had been in the area for some time and had achieved great success, together with their FFI allies. Apart from blowing a vital bridge, they had harassed German columns travelling through the Ardèche. On 25 August, the force occupied a position overlooking the town of Vallon, where there were reportedly some 10,000 German troops. OG LOUISE had the rare distinction of receiving an airdrop of four 37mm anti-tank guns, one of which was damaged. Incidentally, John Goldsmith remembers 6-pounders being dropped – each weighing a ton – and on one occasion a single outsize artillery piece being flown in by a Hudson aircraft, together with a gunnery officer. The obsolete 37mm guns were used to shell Vallon 'to good effect', but the resulting counter-attack necessitated that they be abandoned.

The eight men of Charlie Company were not the only strays to throw in their lot with OG LOUISE. Three shot-down American pilots also became honorary members of the team. In an ultimate coup, on 31 August, LOUISE joined forces with the newly arrived OG LAFAYETTE to bring about the surrender of 3,000 to 4,000 German troops. Rickerson had bluffed the Germans that he had a much larger force, and if forced to attack, he would not be taking any prisoners. A number of high-ranking officers were among the haul, and fearing the vengeance of the FFI, insisted that they were surrendering to the Americans and the Americans only. It is said to be one of the biggest success stories of the OSS in France.

OG LAFAYETTE had been transported from Algiers in three B-24 bombers on the night of 29 August. It was a still clear night, and below them they saw the Allied forces stretched out along all the roads north as far as Montélimar, where the destroyed vehicles of the German 19th Army were still smouldering. While Stephen Weiss and his comrades had been missing in action, they had missed out on one of the biggest battles of the campaign where the 143rd Infantry Regiment of the 36th Infantry Division had distinguished themselves by taking more than 1,000 prisoners in the final mop-up around Loriol on 29 August.

By this time, the eight missing men of Charlie Company had teamed up with OG LOUISE.

They were impressed by Rick Rickerson's leadership, and especially his ability to command airdrops, bringing whatever he desired, whereas the infantrymen knew that they would be lucky to scrounge a stale D-ration chocolate bar from the company supply sergeant. This was the type of war that Stephen Weiss wanted to fight. Rickerson had planned one last attack on the 11th Panzer Division before they withdrew into Lyon. Having witnessed their fearsome capability firsthand, Weiss was not too keen on the idea but in the end the mission did not materialize. From Lyon OG LOUISE was withdrawn to Grenoble, 120 kilometres farther south, where all the special operators in this sector were to be disbanded.

The liberation of Valence, the seat of the préfecture in the Drôme, was achieved in the early hours of 31 August and was credited to the FFI under Commandant de Lassus (*Legrand*). Francis Cammaerts and Jedburgh team MONOCLE were also there, but this would be the swansong of the SOE in the south. A young girl from Valence, named Christiane, wrote a sixteen-page letter to her friend, a week later chronicling – and sometimes exaggerating – the events of the past two weeks:

> Between Montélimar and Livron, the road was strewn with corpses. In a field near Livron, the Boche corpses were piled one metre high. At one place, there were 78 pieces firing at once. You imagine the hell it must be. The Boche, seeing themselves lost, began to flee, and the Valentinois, with the joy you can imagine, saw the army routed for days and nights.[11]

These broken men had so recently been overjoyed to be assigned to the comforts of southern France instead of facing the infernos of Normandy or the Eastern Front; it is estimated that 600 Germans were killed, 1,500 wounded and about 5,800 taken prisoner. American casualties at the battle of Montélimar amounted to a total of 1,575 and a substantial cemetery sprung up there. It was all over by 29 August, and this date marks the end of the pursuit. Task Force Butler was disbanded, and by 2 September, the 3rd and 36th US infantry divisions had stopped outside Lyon. The 45th Infantry Division took a slightly easterly route, moving through Grenoble and then north along the Swiss border.

The privilege of being the first to enter Lyon on 3 September was given to General Diégo Brosset's 1ère Division Française Libre. It was a symbolic gesture because the Resistance had already cleared the city, and the 36th US Infantry Division had been the first to reach the outskirts. But it was only fitting that they should hold back, because of the importance of Lyon to the French psyche. Lyon had been an important centre of resistance, and it was here, at the Montluc prison, where so many had suffered and died at the hands of Klaus Barbie, the Butcher of Lyon.

In their final spasms, the Gestapo of Lyon had killed 109 prisoners, and used their corpses to fill bomb craters on Bron Airfield. Now Werner Knab and Klaus Barbie were bent on exterminating all the political prisoners remaining in the Fort of Montluc. On 20 August, about 120 souls were transported to the Fort de Côte-Lorette in the town of Saint-Genis-Laval, southeast of Lyon. In groups of six, with hands tied behind their backs, they were led up to the first floor where they were shot by the Gestapo and their *miliciens*. When the upper level was full, the killing continued on the ground floor with blood trickling through the floorboards. Then the building was set alight. Further massacres at Montluc were prevented when an FFI leader disguised himself as a Gestapo officer and convinced the commandant that he had orders from Barbie to free the prisoners.

Atrocities were also uncovered at Grenoble which had liberated itself – with some outside help – on 22 August. At a fort called the 'Polygone', two mass graves were discovered containing forty-eight victims of the Gestapo who had been executed on 13 July and 11 August. Only 29 of the terribly mutilated bodies were identified, one of whom was Father Yves de Montcheuil, the Jesuit priest from Lyon who was seized at the Grotte de la Luire during the Vercors episode. It is hardly surprising that the citizens of Grenoble showed no mercy to those believed to be collaborators. A war correspondent, John Osborne, confessed that he wanted to cry at the sight of ten young, wretched, unshaven Gestapo 'underlings' in the courtroom dock. Six of the ten were taken to the training base where the Gestapo had previously carried out their executions. Although tied to stakes, their bodies seemed to fall 'slowly, slowly, slowly in dreadful unison'.

Even before the uprising in Lyon, the FFI had been told to disband. Fighters could choose to demobilize or join the regular forces for the duration. Of those under *Sapin's* command, 500 signed on at Nice. An NCO academy was established at Puget-Théniers for training in the use of American weapons and equipment. Although many were graduates of Saint-Cyr, and veterans of 1939–40, the Maquis found it difficult to fit into de Lattre's First Army, whose regulars looked down on the self-promoted *maquisards* and their lack of proper training. Whereas de Lattre was inclined to recognize the FFI as equal to his conventional soldiers, others, de Gaulle in particular, were scathing of their lack of discipline and training as well as their propensity to award themselves high rank.

According to a leading historian of the French Resistance, Julian Jackson, the clearing of the road to Grenoble was one of the major strategic achievements of the Resistance. Although they were unable to completely cut off the retreat of the German 19th Army, the destruction of the bridge at Livron on 16 August allowed the Allies to inflict terrible damage on the enemy. All the while, the FFI were 'yapping at their heels like angry terriers closing in on a fox'.[12]

The essence of the pursuit phase was captured by William Henry 'Bill' Maudlin, a sergeant attached to the 45th Infantry Division. Of course, he was also a talented cartoonist who in 1945, at the age of 23, won a Pulitzer Prize for his wartime body of work. Willie and Joe, with their scruffy and sarcastic demeanour were the much-loved characters featured in his cartoons. By March 1944, Maudlin was working for *Stars and Stripes,* roaming the front in his own Jeep, and publishing six cartoons a week throughout the European Theater of Operations (ETO). In his memoirs, Maudlin nicely summarizes this phase of the campaign:

> Even though the campaign was a very fast one for the first few weeks, it was not an easy war. No war is easy for those who fight it. The guys were tired from constant

marching and they were running into stubborn resistance in spots, but it was such a tremendous change from Italy that their morale was a little better. They had expected a rough beachhead, and even tougher mountain fighting. They were much relieved to find that they could push ahead. The Maquis and FFI helped a lot, particularly in the mountains. By actually pitching in and helping to chase the Krauts out, the French saved many of their own towns from destruction. The French were honestly and sincerely glad to see the Americans come, and the farther north we worked the more hospitable the people became. I had a feeling that we were regarded truly as liberators, not as walking breadbaskets. It was a far cry from Italy.[13]

The countryside was in chaos. Stray Germans, groups of French and American soldiers, refugees and civilians roamed about not knowing who was in control. An air of anti-climax prevailed, especially for those whose usefulness had now ended. John Goldsmith had orders to rally with other members of the SOE in Paris. He took his leave of Pierre-Michel Rayon at the beginning of September, and in Avignon he briefly met Francis Cammaerts, who was down with a heavy cold, probably brought on by the stress of his stay in a Gestpao prison. It was a surreal and melancholy journey to Paris on roads littered with burned-out vehicles and useless tanks lying in ditches.

*

Stephen Weiss stayed as long as he could with OG LOUISE, and even applied for a transfer to the OSS, but because of the dire shortage of combat infantrymen, it was refused, and he now had to catch up with the 36th Infantry Division headquartered at Vittel, a spa on the western slope of the Vosges Mountains. Working his way north from Lyon, he saw how the rear echelon types fought the war as civilians in uniform. They worked nine-to-five while girls their own age waited for them at sidewalk cafés and quays along the river. It was a far cry from the precarious existence of an infatryman.

The infantry accounted for 14 per cent of the US Army's overseas strength but sustained 70 per cent of the casualties. It was quite rational for an infantryman to wonder not whether he would be hit but when and how bad. All who wore uniforms are called veterans, but the vast majority of them were as uninformed about the killing zones as those on the home front.

Coming from a culture that values life and the individual, the realization that he was expendable was difficult for Weiss to accept, especially when so many had comfortable jobs in the rear. Although he was promoted to sergeant on his return, he was close to breaking point. Most of his rifle squad had become casualties of some sort or another. In a rifle company, almost 30 per cent of all casualties were psychological casualties, but the twin taboos of desertion and battle fatigue were hushed up. There were many levels of desertion, ranging from not being in the right place at the right time to being 'on the trot' for months.

On two occasions, Weiss deserted his post, or went absent without leave – 'over the hill' in GI jargon. The second time was under fire and in the face of the enemy. At 4 a.m. one cold, wet October day in the Vosages, while his position was being heavily shelled, he simply walked down the hill and kept going until he reached Lyon. The court martial resulted in a dishonourable discharge, loss of all pay and benefits, and six winter months of confinement in a Disciplinary Training Center (DTC).

After serving his time, Weiss was given a second chance and remained in France as an army photographer. Fortuitously, while in Paris, he ran into François Binoche, the resistance leader from the Ardèche, who was now a colonel with the French Ministry of Defence. In a short space of time, he decorated Weiss with both the Croix de Guerre and the Médaille de la Résistance Française.The latter was awarded for 'remarkable acts of courage which contributed to the resistance of the French people against the enemy'. Over the years, Stephen Weiss earned a master's degree in clinical psychology, and a master's degree and a doctorate in war studies from King's College London. In 1999, France bestowed on him her highest honour, the Légion d'Honneur, but tellingly, he has not been shown the same appreciation by Uncle Sam.

Chapter 17

Momentum

Following the breakout from the beaches, the US Seventh Army simultaneously struck out in all directions. While the three American infantry divisions and the Free French Army concentrated their efforts in the Rhône Valley, it fell to the 1st Airborne Task Force, which equated to less than a single division, to advance eastward along a wide front in the direction of Nice and the Italian border. The hilly section on the far left of the line was allocated to the 517th Parachute Infantry Regiment, as we have seen, while the 509th Parachute Infantry Battalion and 551st Parachute Infantry Battalion moved up the coastal road. The centre axis was assigned to the 1st Special Service Force.

On the night of 19/20 August, the British 2nd Independent Parachute Brigade moved to a concentration area at Gallieni on the northern periphery of Fréjus and would play no further role in the liberation of France. With unseemly haste, brigade HQ flew back to Italy on 23 August and the rest followed by sea two days later. While other British paratroopers were making history at Arnhem, the 2nd Independent Parachute Brigade spent the remainder of the war in the backwaters of Greece, and thereafter went to Palestine. Some believe it was because their commanding officer invoked General Frederick's ire for failing to take Le Muy, their main objective.

After a flurry of 'conferences' and contradicting orders, during which time, in the language of their own war diary, 'slight chaos reigned', at the HQ of the 2nd Independent Parachute Brigade. Word came on 21 August that they would be replaced by the American-Canadian 1st Special Service Force, which had previously served under Frederick's command in Italy and was now under Colonel Edwin A. Walker. Known as the 'Black Devils' or 'Forcemen', this was the same unit which had captured the islands off Hyères at the outset of the invasion.

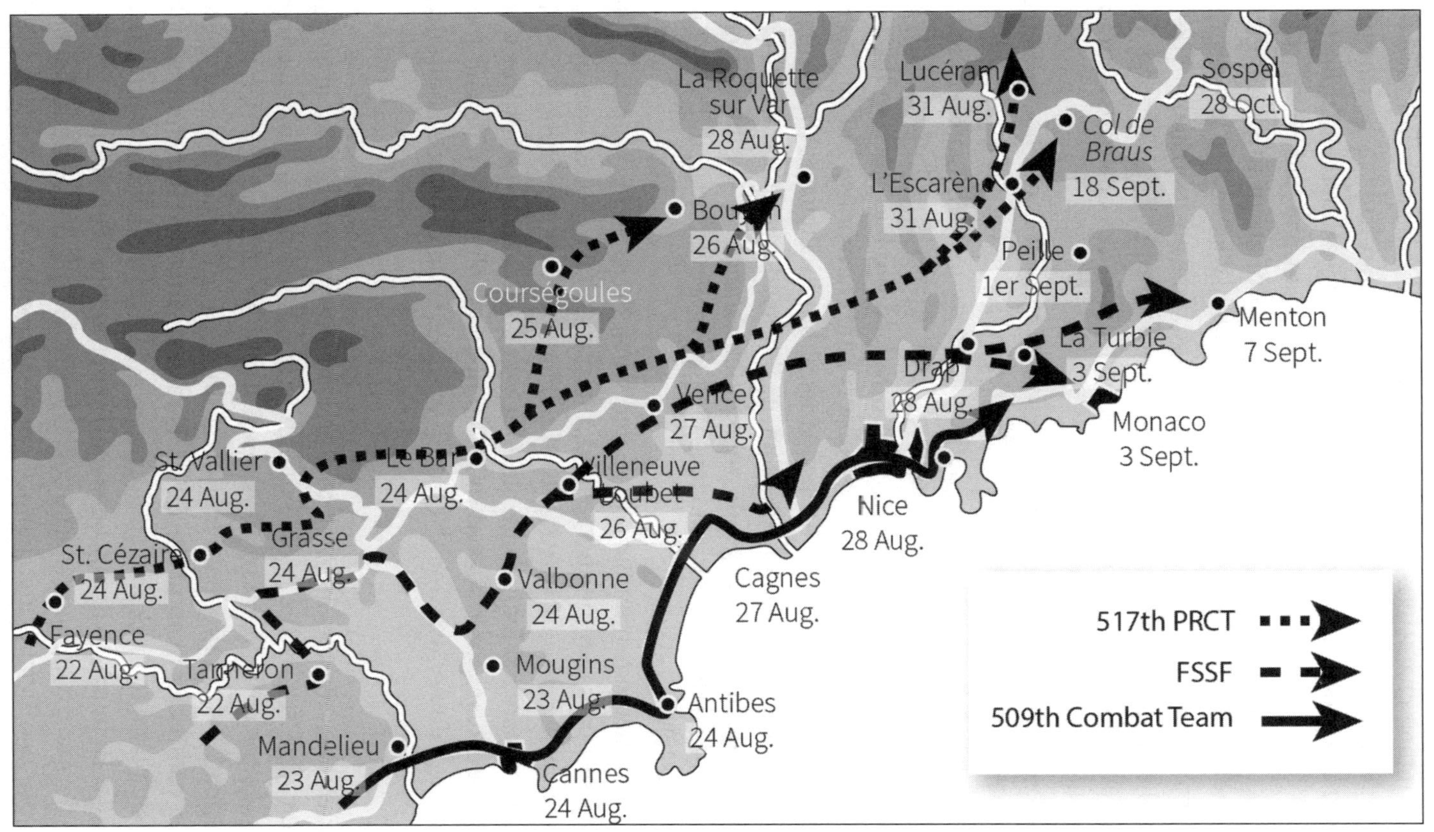

FABTF advance to Nice and the Italian border.

With their characteristic sense of urgency, the Forcemen followed the RN 7 east through Les Adrets, and by 22 August they had reached the tiny village of Tanneron, stretched along a narrow ridge, about ten kilometres inland from Mandelieu-la-Napoule. The Germans had had no intention of making a stand in Tanneron, but one group of about fifty stragglers was sheltered in a comfortable farmhouse called Château de la Verrerie, one and a half kilometres south of the village. This position had not been well chosen because it was in a valley overlooked by high ground; but the occupants did not expect to see Americans – or Canadians – so far from the invasion beaches.

The Hôtel des Voyageurs is now a restaurant, but it still occupies the same vantage point in the heart of Tanneron. From here it is possible to see almost all the way to Nice, and while studying their maps around a table on the *terrasse*, the Canadian officers were warned of the enemy presence nearby. Local people offered to lead the Forcemen to the top of a hill from where they could observe the farmhouse below. There are many versions of what happened next, but Lieutenant Allan 'Spud' Wright went forward and was shot in the head by a German officer who was determined to go down fighting, and who, within seconds, accomplished that goal. Lieutenant Wright, however, lived to the age of seventy-eight.

Fire rained down on the house, and when the shooting stopped, four scorched bodies lay on the ground, the others gave themselves up. As was often the case, it was left to the locals to bury the bodies, which were first searched for documents. One was an older man, an officer who held in his blackened, clawed fingers a photograph of his wife and four children. Another was found to be 17-year-old Gunner Josef Knödlseder.

*

Incidentally, these were not the first reverberations of the invasion which were felt by the people of Tanneron. Returning to the parachute drops in the early hours of 15 August, it will be remembered that many planeloads of paratroopers had been dropped off target. One of these was a pathfinder team of the 509th Parachute Infantry Battalion, which was supposed to mark the landing zone at Le Muy, but was dropped in a forest at Belluny – halfway between Tanneron and Montauroux.

After a terrifying approach through intense flak, the fourteen pathfinders, plus two unofficial extras, jumped into the darkness. Many spent the rest of the night suspended in pine trees while the scattered team tried to regroup. At daylight, with the eager help of *maquisards* and ordinary folk, the parachutists were cut down from the branches. Nobody had been hurt except the leader, Lieutenant Dan DeLeo, who had a gash on his head from a flak fragment. It seems that the pathfinders were in no hurry to move off their mountaintop since they only walked into Tanneron after two days. From Belluny, the paratroopers would undoubtedly have been able to hear and see the convoy being ambushed and strafed at La Colle Noire near Fayence on D-Day. Yet they decided to go in the opposite direction toward the coast.

Tanneron is situated higher up from Belluny, on a sharp ridge no more than a hundred metres wide in places, and there are panoramic views toward Grasse on the one side and toward Fayence on the other. A short walk south of the centre of the village gives one a balcony view of La Napoule and the Lérins Islands. While the pathfinders were relaxing in the village, one of their French guides came running: '*Les Boches sont là*' (the Germans are here); and three or four of them went out to challenge the column of Germans marching up the road. As the Germans lifted their weapons, the Americans opened fire, killing two. The Americans retreated into village where a brief firefight ensued, ending with the surrender of the remaining Germans. One of the dead turned out to be 17-year-old Georg Vogel whose twin brother, Max, had been killed in Normandy the previous month.[1]

Leaving some of his men in the village, at least one of whom was wounded, Lieutenant DeLeo, together with a small party, was guided through enemy territory on 20 August to organize their extraction. En route, his pathfnders were mistaken for Germans and shelled by American artillery. The men had just stopped by a house to take a rest as some children came out to sit with them. Charles Petty gave one of the little girls a chocolate bar and in return she gave him a small medallion which he attached to his dog tags. Suddenly, shells began exploding all around. Petty got the girl down in a ditch, and stayed there until it was over. Later he found out that on the medallion was written '*Toi et moi, un abri pour deux*' which means 'You and me, a shelter for both'.[2]

An article which appeared in *The New York Times* on 7 September 1944 reveals that it was none other than the New York heiress, Isabel Townsend Pell, who guided the cut-off paratroopers through the German lines. Known as *la femme à la mèche blonde* (the woman with the blond streak), Isabel Pell was living less than ten kilometres away at Auribeau-sur-Siagne near Grasse with her partner, Claire, la Marquise de Forbin. It may be remembered that it was at Auribeau where the French commandos captured at Anthéor Cove were freed from their captors, and that the group had then been conducted to Tanneron. Isabel Pell had been interned, together with her maid, at Puget-Théniers during the Italian occupation, and had simply walked out when the Italians capitulated. Since then she had been with the Resistance, avoiding the Gestapo. Now, on D+5 she led her fellow-countrymen down to the landing beaches where a war reporter was on hand to get the story:

> In the tiny town of Tanaron [sic], shortly after dawn on Aug. 15, Southern France's D-Day, a parachute sergeant was in a bad fix. He and 15 men had been dropped 10 miles from their assigned landing zone, had fought a quick battle and captured a dozen Germans, but were finally cut off and surrendered. Three wounded needed quick attention. Suddenly the townspeople started shouting. Striding toward a street barricade, came a slim, athletic woman, her face deeply tanned, a flashing lock of pure white standing out in her brown, bobbed hair. 'The girl with the blonde meche [lock of hair], Frederika!' 'It's Miss Pell'. She wore the *tricolore brassard* of the FFI, but she spoke to the sergeant in pure American. 'Okay Kid', she said, 'It's all right now'. She stood a moment, the tears rolled down her smiling face, then Isabel Townsend Pell, 43-year-old New Yorker, who looks ten years younger, ended four years in the French underground by showing 16 fellow-Americans how to get to safety through the German lines.[3]

The breakout from the beaches in an easterly direction, toward Cannes and Nice, had been led by the 141st Infantry Regiment of the 36th US Infantry Division. Its mission was to protect the right flank of the invasion. Immediately upon landing at Anthéor Cove, this detachment turned right toward La Napoule and advanced swiftly though the Massif de l'Esterel, a range of red rock mountains stretching from Saint-Raphaël to Cannes. Any resistance was easily overcome thanks to naval artillery support which was on permanent call. German accounts tell of being 'shot to pieces' by the huge guns of a multitude of 'battleships'. Spotter planes overhead would direct fire onto even a single person who showed himself.

Some shells inevitably fell short, and among the victims of friendly fire on 20 August was the 29-year-old Lieutenant Henry (actually Heindrich) Apperman, an affable and debonair German Jew who had escaped from Germany and became an officer in the US Army. Despite his gruesome injuries, he remained undaunted during the long, bumpy ambulance ride over cratered roads but was dead on arrival at Saint-Raphaël. American wounded were mostly evacuated to Naples from Saint-Raphaël, which had become a logistical hub.

An invading army is like a tunnelling machine with a sharp point of fighting troops, followed by a long shaft of logistical support. Air bases also followed on behind the front. Fighter-bombers of the Twelfth Air Force deployed from Italy to begin operating from Saint-Tropez, Sainte-Maxime, Grimaud and Saint-Raphaël. General Frederick moved his headquarters into the Hôtel Courier in Saint-Raphaël while captains Geoffrey Jones and Alan Stuyvesant, another OSS (SI) officer, who had parachuted in on Dragoon D-Day, found accommodation nearby at Valescure.

*

Along the coast, on the advance to Nice, the first line of resistance was at La Napoule which was reached by the 141st Infantry Regiment on D+1. Strung out between the coastline and Le Tremblant on the RN 7, about three kilometres inland, they faced a strongly defended position on Hill 84 – also known as Castle Hill. Here, the advance would be held up until 21 August by deadly artillery and sniper fire which was responsible for the deaths of fifteen men of the 141st Infantry Regiment on 16 and 17 August.

As of 20 August the La Napoule sector, along the coastal road, was taken over by the 509th PIB and 551 PIB, thereby relieving the 141st Infantry Regiment which was withdrawn to the communes of Bagnols-en-Forêt and Callian. From their staging area at Puget-sur-Argens, the entire FABTF began their eastward advance in the heat and dust, unshaven and unwashed for five days and still wearing the same clothes they had jumped in. Due to the shortage of vehicles at this early stage, the mode of transport for the airborne troops was foot-slogging. From now on, they would look no different to ordinary infantry, except for the jump boots and big pockets on their battledress.

It is only thirty kilometres from Puget-sur-Argens to Le Tremblant, and the paratroopers carried out the relief during daylight. Enemy artillery made the most of this opportunity, sending the paratroopers scrambling for foxholes dug by their predecessors in the rocky ground. For what felt like an eternity, men prayed and the wounded cried out for their mothers as the shellfire traversed up and down, bursting in the pine trees. Within a few hours of their arrival, on 20 August, three men of the 551st had been mortally wounded and another nine were killed in the battle for Hill 105 the next day. When the dust settled, the Germans watched passively from a short distance away as the 'Amis' collected their dead and wounded.

When the probability of fighting in their neighbourhood became apparent, the inhabitants of Le Tremblant had left their homes to stay with relatives or in caves in the mountains. On their return, they found their houses had been ransacked, not by the Germans but by fellow Frenchmen. Among the detritus of war which surrounded a home at the foot of Hill 105, was the bloated body of a German soldier. It appeared that he had been wounded and someone had tried to make him comfortable with a rolled-up blanket under his head; but such corpses were often booby-trapped. Only after a week did a team from the *mairie* arrive to bury the body. They simply dug a hole and rolled him into it.

At the same time as members of the 551st PIB were in action near Le Tremblant, on 21 August, the 509th launched an attack on Hill 84. The 'castle' on top was occupied mainly by Polish *Osttruppen* who were very ready to surrender but their more fanatical leaders managed to inflict thirteen fatalities among the 509th. The ravine between them and the enemy was rocky and there was nowhere to hide. One of those killed by a sniper was the rugged-looking Corporal Burl J. Knapp, who only a week before had been photographed in the company of Nicole Célébonovitch and other resistance fighters in Saint-Tropez.

Plan Sarrain is situated between La Napoule and Mougins, and on 22 August, while the American lines were only a few kilometres away, some *maquisards* had moved into the village. One of their number, wanting to be remembered as a hero of the liberation, went up to a harmless German in the square and shot him without warning. More soldiers came running and a skirmish ensued. Afterward, the entire village was taken hostage, including women and children. Two *maquisards* had been captured in the fight and were immediately taken aside and shot. The remaining villagers were saved through the intervention of the priest, who offered his own life in their stead.

Up to ten kilometres inland, there was nowhere to hide from the naval guns. Pibonson is a country estate near Mougins in the hills overlooking Cannes where German soldiers, mainly officers, were sent to relax for a few days away from the front. On 23 August a spotter plane flew overhead and directed fire onto the villa where the young men were sunbathing around the swimming pool. Heavy shells crashed into the property, killing three and leaving pieces of flesh hanging from the chandelier. The mangled bodies were buried under some olive trees at a nearby crossroads. When they were exhumed in 1952 the boys were found to be aged 18 and younger.

The bridge on the RN 7 over the Siagne River north of La Napoule attracted regular attention from the big guns. The road was littered with debris, glass, wires and burned-out vehicles when Carl Cryon ran the gauntlet and was lightly wounded in the hand by shell fragments. After having the hand bandaged by his unteroffizier, his NCO, he walked back to Cannes where he found a dressing station set up in the living room of a house. Next morning, the wounded were loaded onto a truck and transported to Nice. As they crossed the River Var, a fighter aircraft appeared but on seeing the red crosses on the side of the truck, the American plane turned away. Stopping for only a few hours in Cimiez, where the main German military hospital was overflowing and the dead were piling up, the ambulance truck continued on through Monaco and Ventimiglia to San Remo in Italy.

Everywhere along the coast, from Cannes to Antibes, German troops were pulling back, destroying stores and equipment. Reduced to eating grapes and whatever else they could forage, the first German line of resistance was crumbling. Some veterans of the Eastern Front chose to fight to the death, but the aggression and élan of the Allied paratroopers, with the support of the naval guns, was too much for the occupation troops.

In desperation, the Kriegsmarine tried to hit back at the Allied ships. Three small torpedo boats were dispatched from Monaco on the night of 20/21 August and attacked American ships off Cannes near the Lérins Islands. Although they approached slowly and stealthily, they were caught in the searchlights of an American cruiser. Unable to make smoke or fire torpedoes, one torpedo boat tried ramming the cruiser but was blown out of the water before it could get close. The survivors managed to swim to Île Sainte-Marguerite. From there they were transported to

Nice the next day. The other two torpedo boats headed back to Nice at top speed, but chased by destroyers and with daylight approaching, they decided to beach in the Gulf of Juan and get help for their wounded.

Francis Tonner, one might recall, was the MUR *maquisard* who on D-Day organized the escape of the French naval commandos, the survivors of the minefield ordeal at Anthéor, while they were being taken on foot to Grasse. Now at La Napoule, his hometown, Francis and a small band of fighters offered to lead the Americans across the River Siagne. In the vicinity of the Cannes-Mandelieu airport, where the rocky ridges descend to a well-watered plain, the Germans decided to put up a last big fight before withdrawing through Cannes to the River Loup.

On the evening of the 22nd, Francis Tonner had arrived at his parent's humble home in the company of an advance party of American paratroopers, much to the surprise and consternation of his family. His brother, Fernand, also a resistance fighter, wanted to accompany them back to the American lines, but was persuaded to stay home for the sake of their mother. The next day, eight men of the 509th PIB and three *maquisards* were wiped out by heavy artillery. Henri Bergia, the son of a *boulanger* in Cannes, and Francis Tonner were apparently vaporized by the first shell. The Americans came and picked up the bits of torn flesh and human debris, including Henri Bergia's left hand, but there was no trace of Francis. Convinced that he was only wounded, the Tonner family spent weeks searching military hospitals as far afield as Draguignan. The distraught mother was finally made to accept the terrible truth. A man had gone to the Saint-Cassien Bridge and had found the back pocket of Francis's pants hanging in a tree. The pocket was still buttoned shut with his wallet in it.

For seventy-four years, the Tonner and Bergia families lived with the belief that their heroes had no proper graves, but new information has come to light as a result of the work of Jean-Loup Gassend, a forensic scientist turned battlefield archaeologist. Burial records show that the body of a 'GI' exhumed from a civilian cemetery in Cannes and reinterred at Draguignan had no dog tags, no boots, no equipment – and most tellingly – no left arm. The odds are that this is Henri Bergia but the final resting place of Francis Tonner is less certain. Today, there is an Avenue Francis Tonner in Cannes, and the square in which Henri Bergia's home once stood is now named in his memory.[4]

The Germans responsible for causing such carnage on the bridge over the Siagne were no more than a rearguard left behind for the withdrawal from Cannes. The main forces had made a timely withdrawal, harassed by FFI, and the city was now wide open. When the Americans did not enter Cannes right away, resistance fighters and civilians went up to the American lines and asked, 'When are you coming to liberate us?' As a parting gift the Germans had mined the roads by making holes in the asphalt. Tragically, one of these mines blew up a medical Jeep, indiscriminately killing a talented young surgeon, Captain Roy Baize, who had recently distinguished himself in combat.

The liberation of the celebrated city of Cannes, on 24 August 1944, was a memorable milestone in the campaign. While camped at the Cannes Golf Club, the paratroopers got themselves spruced up for the parade and because they had few vehicles of their own, they piled onto the back of tank destroyers belonging to the 645th Tank Destroyer Battalion. The sidewalks were swarming and the police were having difficulty keeping back the crowd. After a long wait, the first American armoured vehicles arrived, packed with rather tired-looking soldiers. Flags which had been hidden in attics were dusted off and people were shouting, '*Vive la France, vive l'Amérique.*'

The road to Antibes, and the town itself, was wide open. Most of the defenders had slipped away in the night, by road and even in small boats. Throughout the morning of 24 August, members of the resistance had been taking over public offices and making arrests. The Americans arrived in the evening, cementing the myth that Antibes had liberated itself. The only action took place at the bridge over the River Brague, east of the city. As would be the case with Nice a few days later, the uprising only happened once the powerful Allied armies were gathered on the outskirts of the city and the Germans had already decided to vacate it.

In the afternoon, the FFI got word that a column of *miliciens* and regular Wehrmacht was returning to make a stand at Biot, a community just inland from Cannes on the Brague. A group of lightly armed gendarmes and *maquisards* rushed to the bridge and erected a roadblock. On seeing the barricades, a van full of *miliciens* made a quick U-turn and headed back to Villeneuve-Loubert. A strong contingent of German troops succeeded in breaking through briefly before being pushed back to the River Loup. Two *maquisards* were killed in this action; the Resistance could be proud of their role in the liberation of Cannes. The Americans now took up positions on the banks of the Brague for two days of relative peace.

On 23 August, while the 509th PIB was crossing the River Sigane to enter La Napoule, the 1st Special Service Force was in the centre of the line, moving up the Route de Draguignan (D562) in the direction of Grasse. A German 8.8cm gun sited at Peymeinade had been particularly troublesome, killing two Forcemen on the road between Les Veyans and Peymeinade, but a direct hit on their ammunition wagon brought about the gunners' own destruction. The following day, while looters were removing boots and other items, a teenage boy noted details which stuck in his memory:

> One still had his helmet on, so they were in combat position. One was lying against a wall, it seemed like he had dragged himself to the wall. One had his mouth open and his two front teeth were missing ... Another had flies that were eating his eyes. One of them must have been shaving, because he was half shaved and there was a piece of mirror in the branch of a tree. And there was one who had eaten tomatoes; a shell fragment had slit his belly open and there was a tomato in his stomach.[5]

At Grasse itself, the Germans left only a small rearguard; these were the same troops who had been mauled at Saint-Cézair twenty-four hours earlier and now sensibly gave themselves up after firing a few shots. The town, which is of course famous for being the capital of the perfume industry, was taken during the night of 23/24 August and in the morning the locals woke up to the sight of the Forcemen in their streets. Children watched in awe as an armoured bulldozer brushed aside the anti-tank pyramids. Four Canadians in a Jeep stopped to give a boy a ride. They laughed constantly – something the child had not experienced for years.

No liberating or conquering army could have been better received. All along the road between Grasse and Valbonne the Americans were met with near hysterical joy. Farmers working in the fields dropped their tools and ran to the road. Children picked bunches of flowers to give to their liberators. No longer did they have to worry about the Gestapo or treacherous *miliciens* in their midst. General Frederick moved the FABTF HQ to Grasse the next day, 25 August. The town became a collecting point for bodies of soldiers who had been killed in the fighting at the coast.

Guided by a handful of local men, the FSSF crossed the river and filtered silently into Villeneuve-Loubet, capturing the garrison of the

Villeneuve Castle while they were fast asleep. Elisabeth de Vanssay spent the night in the cellar listening to the guns with a mixture of excitement and fear. In the morning, she was woken from her restless slumber with the shout of '*Les Anglais sont là!*' (the English are here). It turned out they were Canadians. While some of the surprise guests rested, others invaded the kitchen making a terrible mess but they sure knew how to cook.

The imposing château had been captured without loss to the Allies, but the Germans counter-attacked with determination, ensuring that the Forcemen paid a price for the town. A sniper's bullet hit Lieutenant Ross Samuel in the thigh on 26 August. The femoral artery was severed and the wound proved fatal. Lieutenant Samuel was a fine-looking 22-year-old and had a brother serving in the air force. On returning from the memorial service at his home in Ottawa, the Samuel family got word that their other son was missing in action over the North Sea.

That afternoon, the 24-year-old Sergeant Floyd Schmidt was also hit in the thigh, by a bullet from a Schmeisser machine pistol. He was laid out on the grass near a garage workshop where the medics and a local doctor tried in vain to stop the bleeding. His body was covered with a poncho and there it remained until the next day. Popular among his comrades, and at home in Elmira, Ontario, Floyd was an only child. To help raise the spirits of folks at home, a Canadian war correspondent who was accompanying the FSSF wrote:

> I have seen them start marching with full packs under a broiling sun, trudge all afternoon along a dirty, dusty road, or throughout the forests of southern France, in order to reach the starting line by nightfall, so they could fight. I have seen them fight for 60 hours straight to capture a town, then still have enough energy left to celebrate their liberation in an all-day party before they moved forward again at night.[6]

As had become their practice, the Germans left their dead behind – at Villeneuve-Loubet – and it was two or three days before they were collected for burial. Bayonets, boots and other leather items had typically been taken but helmets were not touched. The Italian immigrants of the town, so recently full of arrogance, were made to dig the masss grave and transport the dead in a cart. No proper records were kept of the names or even the number of the German dead. It was not until 2007, through the initiative of Jean-Loup Gassend, that the grave was discovered and fourteen bodies exhumed. Twelve of the soldiers were identified and of these, eight came from Poland and other territories no longer part of Germany.

A few kilometres north of Villeneuve-Loubet, at La Colle-sur-Loup, the bridge over the Loup had been blown, and four *maquisards* offered to inspect the damage and find a way through. In the words of one of the men, who remains anonymous: 'We were young and had no military training, and we set out like four imbeciles.' Areas such as this were always infested with mines but one of the local men led the way confidently. As they went under the bridge, they heard a loud bang. The man in the lead was wounded and the others were hit with shrapnel. They all got the fright of their lives and afterward exaggerated their wounds so as to get some pampering from the young girls who called themselves nurses.[7] At Cagnes-sur-Mer it was madness as usual: all and sundry were brandishing *brassards* while Sten-toting warriors were suddenly infused with courage after the Germans had gone.

Meanwhile, the 1st Special Service Force reached Saint-Paul-de-Vence, ten kilometres inland. Fortunately, this old walled city was spared as the occupants had departed in the night. Using valueless slips of paper or at gunpoint, the Germans requisitioned cars, bicycles, donkeys, mules and carts to make their escape. As the first Canadian and American Jeeps began arriving in the town square on 27 August, the bells rang and people surged onto the streets. At the Hôtel Colombe d'Or, Colonel Walker of the FSSF signed the register immediately below the names of German General Otto Fretter-Pico and his staff who had checked out on 27 August. Out of nowhere about thirty young men appeared in the town square, all wearing armbands of the FFI or FTP. With relish, the head-shaving began, while political hopefuls scrambled for power.

By 27 August, the first two defensive lines – Siagne Valley and Loup Valley – had been overcome, and now it remained only to cross the River Var before Nice. The valleys and ridges that lie at right angles to the coastline, stretching from Nice to Monte Carlo, were also formidable barriers. A document which fell into Allied hands made it clear that the German 148th Reserve Division under Major General Fretter-Pico would pull back toward the Italian border, and make a last stand on a line linking Col-de-Braus with La Turbie and Cap d'Ail just west of Monte Carlo. The order warned that the terrorist-infested city of Nice should be given a wide berth.

*

It had taken two weeks exactly for the Allies to advance from the invasion beaches to the west bank of the Var at the portal of Nice. Higher upstream, at La-Roquette-sur-Var, the first crossing was made on 28 August, but between the coast and Saint-Jeannet, the remainder of the 1st Airborne Task Force and 1st Special Service Force were still assembling their troops. Inside the city of Nice the Resistance could wait no longer and began their insurrection at 6 a.m. on 28 August. Key points had been preselected, which included the préfecture, police stations, hospitals, SNCF railway station and water supply, but attacks took place all over the city, wherever German soldiers dared to move. Once the chaos started, men of all ages clamoured for weapons to join in on their own liberation although a few *miliciens* with suicidal tendencies remained faithful to their masters.

At the préfecture, which was to be the nerve centre, not all the staff were enthusiastic when a group of heavily armed men under René Canta burst in and declared that the patriots were now in control. These Vichy puppets were terrified by the sight of the *maquisards* taking up defensive positions on all the floors. The telephone exchange was siezed early in the morning and was kept working throughout the day, permitting insults and threats to be transmitted both ways.

At a location referred to as 'the level crossing' on the Boulevard de Cessole, north of the railway station and Place Gambetta (now Place de la Libération), a fortified roadblock was set up by about thirty resistants. With hand grenades, a machine gun and some old rifles and handguns, they destroyed two trucks and captured additional weapons. Fighting went on all day at the level crossing, bringing about a death toll of twelve resistance fighters. Traffic from all directions was being barred. German troops retreating from the upper or middle reaches of the River Var found themselves unable to enter Nice, and headed back up into the hills to bypass the city.

It was at the level-crossing roadblock that a staff car was shot up, the driver killed and a knapsack full of documents was found in the hands of a high-ranking officer. Some quick-thinking fighters immediately took their find to the Allied commanders on the far bank of the Var. Although they demanded to be paid, the goods were ultimately handed over to Captain Geoffrey Jones, the OSS man who was now acting as General Frederick's intelligence officer. The bag was caked in the blood of the driver and the papers had got wet in the river. One intelligence officer, who spoke fluent German, was flabbergasted to find that it was a field order – written that very afternoon. Throughout the night, by candlelight, Jones and his team worked on translating General Otto Fretter-Pico's order which contained the latest plans for the withdrawal of German forces to fortified positions on the Italian frontier, complete with maps. In the early hours of the morning, Jones was ready to wake Frederick and show him what he had. Far from being annoyed at having his sleep disturbed, he told Jones to fly down to Saint-Tropez in his personal aircraft and show it to General Alexander 'Sandy' Patch.

Despite repeated attacks, the Germans were unable to regain control of the préfecture. When armoured vehicles failed to get through the gates, the Germans resorted to ultimatums and threats of mass executions and wholesale destruction of the city. With shells crashing through the roof, the gentlemen of the préfecture turned white with fright, begging the resistance fighters to surrender, but they remained steadfast. In any case, those who fell into enemy hands were invariably executed. In the Fabron district, one captive survived the executioner's bullet and played dead while his two companions had their throats slit.

Isolated groups of fighters, with no way of communicating with each other, had no idea of how the overall battle was going. Were they all alone? Were they surrounded? The narrow alleys of the old town were killing zones. Saint-Roche and Pasteur hospitals were filling up. When shells began bursting in Place Garibaldi some began to wonder if the revolt was rash and useless. As one FTP fighter put it, there was 'enthusiasm in the morning, hesitation at noon and euphoria in the evening'. A food depot was set up in Rue Fodéré near the port to keep fighters from all the neighbourhoods going.

Under the state of martial law which now existed, the citizens of Nice were to stay indoors and anyone found on the streets was liable to be executed. Retreating troops, in convoys or on foot, were fired at from windows and rooftops with shotguns and hunting rifles. Hand grenades were dropped into vehicles passing below. General Fretter-Pico ordered that retreating troops take hostages and keep them on the back of trucks when passing through suspect neighbourhoods. At least twenty-five dead Germans were found in the streets but it is unknown how many were carried off in vehicles. French casualties included twenty-nine resistants killed in action, and six who died accidentally or after being taken prisoner by the retreating Germans. All the casualties, including the thirty-two civilians killed in the crossfire, have been recognized as *mort pour la France.*

As the battered Wehrmacht streamed eastward on the famous Corniche or cliff roads, the sniping continued. From out at sea, ships targeted the luxury villas of the rich and famous at Saint-Jean-Cap-Ferrat. William Somerset Maugham later returned to find his roof damaged and art collection looted. Having been all-conquering rulers until only a few days before, the Germans, together with a battalion of Italian 'Blackshirts' vented their frustration on the inhabitants of Menton. Ostensibly looking for terrorists, German troops ransacked houses and in a 'sadistic frenzy' shot five civilians and an unarmed gendarme accused of being snipers.

As at 29 August, the American forces were still assembling on the western side of the Var. Small patrols made their way into the city, and celebrated with the locals. One advance party was met by a delegation of city officials in a black car. A universal experience, it seems, is that the members of these patrols came back blind drunk. It was not until late on the 30th that the men and vehicles of the FSSF, 551st PIB and 509th PIB forded the river in a corridor marked by white tape. Proceeding up Avenue de la Californie and Rue de France to Place Masséna, this was not technically a parade, but the reception was the same as always.

*

General Frederick moved his headquarters from Grasse to Nice on 5 September, taking over the Villa Alhambra on the Cimiez Heights. Although he tried to stay out of local politics and personal disputes, his office was besieged by people accusing their neighbours of being Nazi sympathizers or communists. To help deal with civil affairs, he employed Isabel Pell, who had earlier helped out a group of 509th PIB pathfinders stranded in the village of Tanneron after Dragoon D-Day. Coincidentally, her *nom de guerre* in the Resistance was *Frederika*. Although there are those who say that she was more of a collaborator than a resistant, the town square of Puget-Théniers was promptly renamed after her.

By the middle of September, General Patch's Seventh Army had cleared south and central France, taken some 100,000 prisoners at a cost of some 13,000 casualties. Even before the shooting stopped, the battle for political power had begun. Posters proliferated on the grubby walls of even the poorest villages. The communists were at the peak of their power, and the Communist Party of Draguignan was quick to claim credit for defeating the Fascists. In Paris, the battle was still ongoing but de Gaulle would soon be perpetuating the myth that the French had liberated themselves:

> The 16th of August will remain a great date for our town of Draguignan. In a series of battles resulting from many years of armed struggle, a group of our valiant Francs-Tireurs, together with the armed civilians from Draguignan, seized the town. During the course of the night, American troops entered the town and finally delivered us from a long nightmare. The Francs-Tireurs' brilliant feat of arms is a marvellous example for all of us. Having left everything behind, and risked their lives for four years, the FTPF formed a large force, disciplined and valorous, among whom were an uncountable number of heroes. The French Communist Party pays a warm tribute to the regular troops of the FTPF integrated into the FFI.

Between 14 and 18 September 1944, General de Gaulle made a flying visit to the southern cities of Bordeaux, Toulouse, Marseille, Toulon and Lyon. It seems that the main purpose of the tour was to ensure that the 'Army of the Shadows' re-entered the ranks. The message which he carried was: 'Tomorrow, the FFI will finish its task because there will be only one French army.'

Speeding in from the Marignane airport outside Marseille, de Gaulle and his entourage made their way to the préfecture where the future president of France spoke to a huge crowd chanting *'Vive de Gaulle, vive la République.'* A contingent of the FFI calling themselves descendants of the original Regiment La Marseillaise – after which the national anthem is named – was lined up for inspection.

From Marseille, the general drove to Toulon where, in the late afternoon, he saw the sunken ships in the harbour. 'The fleet is destroyed.' he said 'We will rebuild the fleet. We will rebuild France.' The city of Nice was not on the agenda for this trip but on 9 April 1945, one month before the victory in Europe, he told an adoring crowd: 'Nice, on 28 August 1944, by the heroic sacrifice of her children, liberated herself from the occupier. Nice liberated. Nice Proud. Nice glorious.'[8]

Chapter 18

Stagnation

Leaving the Comité Local de Libération – the local liberation committee – and the citizens of Nice to sort out their political strife, and deal with collaborators, the 1st Airborne Task Force converged on the road to Monte Carlo and then spread out into the mountains. During the first week of September, the 1st Special Service Force carried out 'aggressive patrolling', passing through the Col-de-Braus, and occupying Tête de la Lavina – names which would become all too familiar. Unfortunately, the enemy was allowed to re-occupy these strategic heights while the American forces reorganized themselves. It would take weeks of hard fighting to get there again.

In the coastal zone, the 509th and 551st were approaching La Turbie, northwest of Monte Carlo. A seven-man patrol of the 551st PIB went out in the direction of Tête de Chien, a rock outcrop on which there was a solidly built fort. At a farmhouse above La Turbie, the paratroopers were greeted by a young Frenchman named Charles Calori who fed them with information and alcohol. It turned out that there was a machine-gun emplacement 350 metres up the hill, which had been interdicting the road between La Turbie and Nice.

Half drunk, and keen for action, the squad decided to attack the machine-gun post rather than return to base as instructed. Guided by Charles Calori, they achieved complete surprise and rolled two hand grenades through the door. Calori remembers that they then 'ran around the shack like Indians, firing into it …' When the shooting stopped, the group sat down in front of the shack puffing like steam engines from the effort and excitement. One of the troopers danced up and down like a little boy and grinning from ear to ear saying, 'I got two of 'em!'[1] Within minutes, the Germans were mortaring their own outpost, but the patrol got down the hill by leaping down the terraces, two metres high, with no injuries more serious than a sprained ankle. Two of the three Germans killed at La Turbie on 31 August were aged seventeen. Their comrades never returned to this outpost to retrieve the bodies, and for the families, their deaths remained unconfirmed for fifteen years.

Allied ships shelled the cliff roads and even fired at the magnificent Hôtel Vistaero on the Grande Corniche at Roquebrune-Cap-Martin, sending the German 'guests' hurrying for the door. Residents of Beausoleil will not easily forget an incident where a carload of *maquisards* was blown up by a mine on the Moyenne Corniche, killing eight. It was 3 September, and the 509th PIB was at the gates of Monaco but only a few Jeeps went into the city because of the principality's neutrality. Unlike their predecessors, the Allies fully respected Monaco's sovereignty, and posters were put up at the entrances declaring the territory to be off-limits to all Allied military personnel. Monaco did not escape the war altogether. It was bombed on 27 August and the heights above the city were shelled the next day. Ministers of this state, which pretended to be neutral, were justifiably nervous about their futures.

The village of Peille, inland of Monaco, had been the scene of yet another uprising by the Resistance, prompted by the sound of the guns approaching from the invasion zone. To the surprise of the residents and holidaymakers, a group of about 130 resistance fighters took over the town on the afternoon of 15 August. By prearrangement, the garrison of the fortress on Mont-Agel gave themselves up. Groups of *maquisards* from the surrounding area, and gendarmes from Sospel responded to an appeal for reinforcements. Even some of the holidaymakers joined in. For five days they held out against ever more serious attacks, and threats of annihilation, but in the end it was just another battle of the 'clay pot' against the 'iron pot'.

While the Americans were massing and reorganizing, the Maquis took it upon themselves to capture the fortifications on the top of Mont-Agel, from where one can survey the entire coastline of Monte Carlo. Today, the ancient fortress is used by the French Air Force as an air defence station, and the Monte Carlo Golf Club is located on the lower slopes. The attackers included two groups of inexperienced *maquisards* and a group of fit, young Marseille firemen under the FFI leader, *Capitaine Tilley*. When the shooting started, and people got hurt, they retreated in disorder. From the sea, Allied cruisers shelled the fortress, and while providing fire support on 5 September, *Le Malin* and *Ludlow*, were attacked by five German midget submarines, three of which were sunk and one captured. The garrison sheltered in the deepest recesses but the 8-inch guns had the desired effect.

A patrol of the 1st Special Service Force, approaching stealthily, found the place deserted apart from two Polish deserters and a multitude of booby traps. In fact the Germans had already pulled out of Menton. The front line was now drawn through the mountain villages of Castellar, Sospel and Turini along the Italian frontier. This would become the 'forgotten front' and would remain essentially unchanged until April 1945.

Although Menton was now devoid of enemy troops, the preceding two weeks had been chaotic and devastating for the town. Austrians, Prussians, Bavarians, Poles and Czechs had brawled at the Hôtel du Globe. Blackshirted bullies were the first to flee to Ventimiglia and San Remo on the other side of the border, placing mines as they left. Even after the liberation, the town was always in range of the German batteries, and the Allies seemed powerless to silence them. Shops were boarded up, hotels catered only for lonely soldiers. The scatterlings of Menton started to return in April 1945 and by June there was a population of 5,000, but it did not reach prewar levels until 1965.

While the 1st Special Service Force was advancing along the coast toward Menton, a motorized patrol was scouting up toward Col-de-Braus, a mountain pass at an altitude of 1,002 metres, reached by a road with tight switchbacks. At Col-la-Madone a Jeep carrying four artillerymen hit a landmine, scattering their remains among the bushes and rocks on the sides of the road. Moving at a speed of about one mile an hour, a platoon with a half-track, guided by partisans, reached Touët-de-l'Escarène on 31 August. The railway tunnel which runs from Touët-de-l'Escarène to Sospel under the pass had been converted into a convenient fortification with a blockhouse at either end.

From the 75mm gun mounted on their half-track, the Forcemen fired about 90 rounds into the tunnel. Terrible screaming was heard from the depths, and the platoon moved closer to the entrance. However, the Germans were not yet done, and opened up with a machine gun, wounding one. The attack was called off, and the Germans pulled back to Sospel of their own volition, blowing the tunnel behind them. For a short time Col-de-Braus, the pass overlooking Sospel, was left unoccupied.

Situated on the River Bévéra, twenty kilometres inland from Menton, the historic town of Sospel is considered to be the gateway to the Roya Valley and Italy. Once they realized the significance of this, the

Wehrmacht entrusted its defence to the 28th Reserve Jäger Battalion, a light infantry unit and the most reliable troops they could muster.

The citizens of Sospel had borne the brunt of the occupation since 1940. First it was the French Chasseurs Alpins, then the Italian Alpini, and now the Boche. From the outset Salel Barracks had been used as an internment camp for 600 prisoners. The previous month, on 9 August 1944, the Gestapo and their henchmen brought fifteen partisans, mostly Italian, to the prison where they were tortured for two days and two nights, traumatizing the villagers with their cries. Looking like the living dead, on 12 August, the condemned men were transported in a cart through the village to the place of execution in the courtyard of the agricultural cooperative, behind the railway station where they were shot three by three. A plaque is now affixed to one of the pillars used to tie up the martyrs, and a joint French-Italian ceremony is held there on 12 August every year.[2]

When the booming of American guns was heard on 2 September, some inhabitants of Sospel took refuge in caves in the banks of the Bévéra. Sandbags half sealed the entrances and after dark, blocks of wood were added because of the fear of rape. Before each bombardment, a spotter plane was seen dropping smoke bombs to mark the target. As the artillery duel continued over the next few days, some civilians risked their lives, crossing the lines to provide information to the Allies.

The 1st Airborne Task Force was manning an eighty-kilometre-wide front from the sea to the mountains along the Italian border. Farthest south, on the coast, was the 1st Special Service Force. On their left was the 517th PIR, then the 509th PIB, then the 551st PIB, and finally the 550th Glider Infantry Battalion in the north around Col-de-Larche. A battery of the 460th Parachute Field Artillery Battalion (PFAB) had just sited their guns and dug their foxholes near the railway station at l'Escarène below Col-de-Braus when they were heavily shelled on 5 September, signalling the start of a bitter struggle for the strategic town of Sospel.

Overlooking the pass of Col-de-Braus from the north was an even higher hill called Caire-de-Braus which had to be seized. On the night of 5/6 September a small attacking force of the 517th PIR climbed up a steep cliff to surprise the platoon-sized German force on the crest, killing six or seven and taking a number of prisoners. However, the Americans were forced into a defensive semi-circle on the edge of the cliff as repeated counter-attacks were made. Private Felix Povinelli earned the

Silver Star, and the gratitude of his comrades, for running back five or six kilometres in record time to fetch reinforcements.

Altogether, the 2nd Battalion of the 517th had seven of their number killed during the fighting of 5/6 September on 'Purple Heart Hill', one of whom was PFC Travis McDonald, hit by a Pak 36 (panzerabwehrkanone) on 6 September. Private S. D. Moxon wrote to McDonald's widow, saying 'He was just like a brother to me. It hurt me just as much as my own brother's death did.' The whole truth about what a 37mm anti-tank round does to the human body was skillfully avoided: 'The kid lived awhile after being hit, but the shock and loss of blood was too much. He was smiling all during those hours he was dying. He smiled until the morphine put him to sleep.'[3]

On 7 September, the 3rd Battalion of the 517th relieved the 2nd Battalion, and sent out a three-man patrol to reconnoitre enemy positions on Tête de la Lavina, the high point on the right of the road to Sospel. When the two sergeants and a trooper were about half way up the hill, they were fired at from a pillbox. Bluntly put, Sergeant Robert Miller 'had his head blown off' and the other sergeant, although badly wounded in the stomach, made it back down the hill. Two separate accounts relate how the third soldier, although unwounded, was terribly shaken and nearly tore out his nails trying to dig a hole in the ground with his hands. He had to be evacuated, and was never seen again by his friends. Although extremely common and well documented in other campaigns, one does not associate the 'Champagne Campaign' with mental breakdowns. There were few, if any, desertions among airborne troops; nevertheless, accounts of soldiers losing their sanity do exist.

A platoon-strength fighting patrol led by lieutenants Arthur Ridler and Dick Spence at Col-de-Braus on 9 September resulted in a number of unnecessary casualties for G Company of the 517th PIR. Lieutenant Arthur Ridler, described by one of his men as a 'soldier's soldier' seems to have been determined to get a medal. As it transpired, he was posthumously awarded the Silver Star. Many others were badly mangled on this ridge known as 'Bloody Stump'. At 1 p.m. they moved into the attack supported by a strong artillery concentration. As they passed the first bunker, the enemy fired at point-blank range. Outnumbered and outgunned, the platoon fell back leaving four dead, including Lieutenant Ridler. One man, who had been given up for dead, crawled back after dark.

A carefully planned but disastrous attack took place on 11 September. When the commander of I Company, 517th PIR, was found to be 'in a state of nervous collapse' the battalion leader, Captain Joe McGeever, decided to lead the attack. Once again, the German positions were in well-camouflaged bunkers with an open field of fire over the gently sloping ground. With McGeever in front, they walked until the silence was shattered by gunfire. A medic named Wilbur 'Bill' Terrell went to the aid of three men cut down in the fusillade. First, he went first to Captain McGeever who was lying on his back: 'He was already gone. I suspect he died instantly, for he had been stripped of all personal belongings.'[4]

Clearly, it was going to need the utmost determination to take Tête de la Lavina, and after a few days of softening up by the artillery, a company of the 517th PIR launched at least four attacks – on the 13th, 14th, and 15th – but were beaten back every time. Defending this strongpoint were battle-hardened veterans of the Eastern Front belonging to the 34th Infantry Division, but by 19 September, Hill 1098 was permanently in American hands.

North of Sospel, just out of Peïra Cava, is a hill covered in spruce trees, named Tête du Pin. On 2 October, a patrol had been ambushed and the 517th PIR had two men killed plus one taken prisoner. In search of payback, a platoon led by Lieutenant Howard Hensleigh immediately went back up the hill and took the Germans by surprise while they were eating and facing the other way. The firefight lasted about an hour, and ended in the surrender of all the Germans but one who kept firing his machine gun from behind a bush. Hensleigh saw the leaves vibrating, and emptied the whole clip of his M-1 in reply.

Twenty-seven-year-old Feldwebel Georg Rieck had been shot in the head, and going through the sergeant's pockets, Lieutenant Howard Hensleigh found a set of wedding photographs originating from a photographic studio near Nuremberg. In 2012, Hensleigh made contact with the grandson of the man he had killed, filling in the gaps. The German soldier who had been manning the machine gun during the first ambush in which two Americans were killed, Gefreiter (Private) Gerhart Höfig, had written to Georg Rieck's widow, who was five months pregnant, expressing his profound gratitude to the heroic Herr Feldwebel for taking over the MG after he was wounded, thereby saving his life.[5]

Conditions in Sospel had become so dire that the Red Cross in Menton went in to negotiate for the evacuation of the remaining civilians, but the

Germans needed them as hostages and workers. Allied bombardment, mostly from the sea, had killed 687 people and damaged or destroyed 700 homes in the area. By 26 October, patrols into the city reported that the Germans were evacuating. Numerous large explosions were heard, one of which signaled the demolition of an eleventh-century bridge over the River Bévéra.

When the Americans eventually entered Sospel on 27 October, there were no flowers, flags or wine. The people had little to celebrate. There had been more than the usual quota of torture and executions. Most of the people had been evacuated to escape the shelling, and those who stayed behind were starving. Sospel was the last sizeable town in France to be liberated, and the citizens could not understand why it had taken so long. Few of the buildings were fit for habitation but on 4 November, a company of paratroopers moved into an abandoned house. During the night, a massive device exploded, killing five men as they slept.

*

In almost every town, the residents lined the streets and celebrated their day of liberation. However, there were always those who hid behind closed shutters knowing that this was their day of reckoning. Even before the Americans arrived, there began a 'wild purge' or *épuration sauvage*. Some have classified it as the 'neighbourhood purge' because of its local character. Those unfortunate citizens subjected to popular justice included not only collaborators who had actively aided and abetted the Germans, but also black-marketeers who profited from the misfortunes of their countrymen.

Once a commune was liberated, the FFI set up their own 'courts' almost immediately. These tribunals were particularly harsh where the Milice had imposed a reign of terror. In the most extreme cases, the condemned men would be paraded through town and made to dig their own graves. On the evening of 28 August, before the last German was run out of Nice, a collaborator was pursued on the tracks of the Saint-Roche station and mutilated by having an arm placed under the wheel of a locomotive. At another suburban station in Nice, Gare de Riquier, a couple of collaborators and their dog were hanged on a lamppost. This type of rough justice was carried out daily with the approval of the new authorities as a necessary part of the transition to a new order.

The *épuration* was not altogether spontaneous. Advance notice was given by the Resistance in various ways. A calling card by the MUR gave this ominous warning: 'The French Résistance is communicating with you: The time for settling of accounts is approaching. Your Germanophile sympathies are known. The IVth Republic will not forget if you persist in your attitude.'[6] Some communities did not even wait for liberation before carrying out summary executions or extra-judicial killings. Possibly thousands of collaborators were summarily executed by local – mostly communist – resistants in so-called 'wild purges'.

Typically, these punishments took place publicly, either in the village square or in front of the town hall. It is estimated that less than half were related to 'horizontal collaboration'. Other offenders were those who had economically collaborated or denounced people to the occupiers. Women who consorted with Germans had their heads shaved as a public symbol of their shame, which remained for as long as it took their hair to grow out. Head shaving can be seen as a ritualized punishment of women for the independence which many of them had enjoyed, and even flaunted, during the occupation. If shaving was not enough humiliation, the women had swastikas painted on their foreheads or were stripped naked.

As has been intimated, the large majority of women who found themselves in compromising positions with occupying soldiers were those who worked in cafés or hotels frequented by Germans. Some said it was only the 'tarty' girls who gathered around soldiers in the cafés. Clandestine relationships were most prevalent in the cities where the populations of German soldiers were highest and the anonymity of urban life provided opportunity. Now they were being named and shamed in notices pinned up in the town square.

For the little boy who lived with his grandmother in a village in the Bouches-du-Rhône, the liberation brought a new batch of incomprehensible adult words and unforgettable events. The south was still a violent place. First of all, there was a new sort of soldier, local types, proud to display their armbands and sub-machine guns and 'the young housemaid, who has just given birth to a fatherless little girl, has become very discreet, and one can hardly imagine a person capable of shearing those abundant curls that make her so attractive'.[7]

Although they may have varied in intensity, purges were carried out in most, but not all, towns and villages in Provence. In Peyrane, a small village near Apt in the Vaucluse, the head of the local Maquis received a notice from the Comité d'épuration – literally the purge committee – ordering him to arrest those accused of collaboration, including the Vichy mayor, the town clerk, the town notary and the principal grocer. After reading the telegram, the resistance leader tore it into pieces, proclaiming that in this village they sorted out their own affairs: '*Nous réglons nos affaires en famille!*'[8]

Denise Layet was the manager of a bistro in Avignon, a regular meeting place for collaborators and *miliciens*. Following the liberation in August 1944, she and her husband, an active member of the Milice, were arrested. Denise survived the *épuration sauvage* but her husband was shot out of hand before the court of justice started its work. During her interrogation, she admitted to wearing a Milice armband at a rally, but claimed that her husband made her wear it. Charges were eventually dropped after she named various people who could attest to her innocence.

When a collaborator was a well-known member of a tight-knit community, it was harder to mete out justice. Léon Michel grew up in Gap, and had been known for his lack of judgement from an early age. Now aged 23, it seems the Gestapo made him an offer he could not refuse. Having been a member of the Maquis before he was turned, he was in a position to denounce former comrades – but he seldom did. Instead, he used his new position as an agent of the Gestapo to blackmail and extort ransoms from Jews and other vulnerable people. Some of his former friends could not believe that he had done anything more than work as driver for the Gestapo. Following legal process, the tribunal found him guilty of having taken part in the arrests, looting, arson and torture, and on 3 May 1945 he was sentenced to death. He was shot on the edge of River Luye, previously a favourite Gestapo execution spot. When asked whether or not he wanted a blindfold, he replied, 'As you please, I don't care anymore.'

Because of the large number of Italians in southeastern France, this region had the highest number of extra-judicial killings – around 120 in the Alpes-Maritimes. More than a thousand suspected collaborators were arrested, half of them of Italian origin. Women of a lower social standing and Italian women bore the brunt of the 'justice of the people'. In his book, *La Tour de Siagne: Des enfants terribles en Provence* Max Stèque mentions that it was the *réfractaires* – those who hid from the STO but were too afraid to join the Maquis – who carried out the *épuration* at Saint-Cézaire-sur-Siagne. All the poor women of Italian descent who had supposedly slept with the enemy were shaved. Although the *réfractaires* and the imbeciles in the street laughed, it truly was an ugly carnival. American soldiers were sickened by these scenes, but were advised to stay out of local matters. It was not always easy for an outsider to understand the character of the French people, or the dynamics which existed in occupied France. A day or so after the liberation of Nice, Peter Cottingham and other representatives of the 1st Special Service Force were tasked with finding suitable premises for their battalion headquarters. In a fashionable suburb, they drove up to an imposing villa on a hill, overlooking an orchard. They parked their Jeep in the courtyard and were welcomed into the house by a middle-aged lady who spoke perfect English. It turned out she was a widow who had lived in California until her late husband moved to Nice just prior to the war. She willingly put her home at the disposal of the Forcemen, and that evening they enjoyed a meal around her dining room table.

The next morning, Peter Cottingham went out to get his shaving gear from the Jeep and was met in the courtyard by an unkept looking bunch of 'freedom fighters'. The leader stepped up, pounding his chest, demanding that the woman who owned the villa be handed over. He claimed that she had collaborated with the officers of the German occupation by entertaining them in her home.

There were about ten or twelve heavily armed men in the group but Cottingham sent them packing with sarcastic comments about there being plenty of Germans left to fight, which would be a better test of their bravery than terrorizing a single woman. The freedom fighters departed and were not seen again, but Cottingham spotted the woman about a month later, sitting at a pavement café and, on sitting down to join her for a drink, complimented her on her hair, which thanks to him, she still possessed. Perversely, Frenchwomen who were bald or wearing wigs or scarves were believed to be particularly 'easy' by GIs intent on a bit of their own 'collaboration'.

Survivors of the internment camps did not always know who had betrayed them, and often they were too weak to take revenge. Members of the underground, some of them just thugs or 'resistants of the 25th hour' took vengeance on their behalf. This unbridled blood-letting was carried out by small groups and involved a bullet in the nape of the neck, or a burst from a machine gun, without even a sham trial. The bodies would later be found in the street or floating down a river. Through their mouthpiece *Combat*, the FFI exhorted their members not to use their *tricolore brassards* as an excuse to 'steal, pillage and extort'.

The *épuration* was widely reported on, and openly encouraged, in many of the newspapers which sprung up in the wake of the liberation, such as the leftist *L'Espoir de Nice*. Within these pages, defendants were referred to as monsters, harmful beasts and aggressive little shrews.[9] The entire front page of *Le Chant du Départ*, which called itself an organ of liaison between the Francs-Tireurs and Partisans of the Basses-Alpes, was devoted to instigating acts of revenge and retribution. The huge headline screamed: '*Épurons! Épurons!*'

Although isolated cases of rough justice spilled over into 1946, the *épuration sauvage* theoretically lasted until a special accelerated legal system was established on 20 September 1944. One of the first candidates for the tribunal in Nice was César Fiorucci, a taxi driver working for the Gestapo. He was convicted of being involved with the arrests and subsequent hanging of Torrin and Grassi in Place Massena. Fiorucci was shot by a twelve-man firing squad at the Quai des Etats-Unis, near the flower market in the old town. It seems that taxi drivers were particularly cooperative with the Nazis as at least thirty taxi operators in Nice were fined or had their licences revoked for collaboration.

It was not easy to halt the momentum of popular justice. On 14 March 1946, a baker named Joseph Innocenti, known for his fascist opinions, was found dead in his *boulangerie* in Nice, riddled with bullets. The last extra-judicial killing in the Alpes-Maritimes took place on 8 October 1946. Jacques Meyzenc, a medical doctor and well-known collaborator, was executed at Pasteur Hospital. He had initially been sentenced to forced labour for life, but some resistants refused to accept the court's decision, and on their second attempt carried out the death sentence of their own accord.[10]

Collaborators could change allegiances with impressive speed. While staying at the Hôtel Westminster in Nice, shortly after the liberation, a resistance leader was called to intervene in a situation where a woman had 'jumped on the sentry like a lunatic'. He went downstairs, sub-machine gun in hand, and asked, 'Madame, what is going on?' 'This guy got all my family deported!' she screamed. 'He killed my entire family!' For people like him 'there was no tomorrow'.[11]

Some escaped the execution squads by paying a ransom. Fake resistants found it particularly profitable to arrest rich residents of

Monaco. The actress Mireille Ballin, considered to be one of the most beautiful actresses of French cinema in the 1930s, lost a fortune in this way, but it did not save her from utter devastation. Her downfall was that she had had a love affair with a young Austrian officer. The two were arrested in September 1944 by the FFI in Beausoleil while trying to escape into Italy. The actress was beaten and raped by drunken FFIs, then incarcerated in Nice while her paramour seems to have been summarily shot. Her career and health in tatters, Mireille Balin lived out her life in poverty and oblivion on the Côte d'Azur. She died aged 59, in 1968.

After the liberation, Jean Moulin's former comrade, Raymond Aubrac, was appointed as the Regional Commissioner of the Republic in Marseille and was in charge of prosecuting collaborators throughout the southeast. Once a student of engineering at MIT and Harvard, the 30-year-old Aubrac was now an important public figure. He also had a personal interest as his Jewish parents had perished at Auschwitz. Assisting him was Maxime Fischer, a former lawyer who had been second-in-command of the Maquis Ventoux.

It was part of Aubrac's job to decide on appeals for clemency, and he once said: 'I signed at the right, the fellow was shot the next day at 6.00. At the left, he was sent to prison. It was terrifying.' The first two collaborators to be put to death in the Vaucluse were small fry. It was a judgement meant to satisfy public wrath. Aubrac had once decreed that a defendant had no right of appeal, but this was later rescinded. He was eventually relieved of his post, ostensibly because a private security force that he had founded engaged in rape, torture and murder. De Gaulle instructed his successor to 're-establish a Republican order, and reattach a region to France which is completely out of control'.[12]

Prime candidates for prosecution were those who had served foreign governments especially in the Department of Jewish Affairs or those who had been part of collaborationist organizations such as the Milice and Parti Populaire Français (PPF). If one had published articles, brochures or books or given speeches in favour of the enemy, one was deemed to be a collaborator. Of course, many who genuinely deserved to be prosecuted went scot-free. Gendarmes who had hunted down STO dodgers with a vengeance in the early days were forgiven if they later became sympathetic to the Resistance. Writers and intellectuals were targeted, but construction workers who had helped build the Mediterranean Wall were likely to be left alone – although certain construction companies were placed in provisional sequestration.

Italians, naturalized citizens or not, were targets of both the *épuration légale* and the *épuration sauvage*, and the line drawn between the two was often blurred. On 23 September 1944, at Fort Carré, which overlooks the yacht harbour in Antibes, ten Italians with questionable sympathies were executed before the law could fully take its course. The imposing fort had been used as an internment camp at the beginning of the war, and was now holding approximately 500 people suspected of collaboration. Ostensibly in revenge for the killing of one of their own, a group of FTP members demanded that the commander of Fort Carré hand over ten prisoners so that retribution could be carried out. In command of this FTP rabble was Louis Piétri whose story of being interned at Sospel has been touched on in a an earlier chapter. He claims to have been given the approval of the mayor of Antibes for what he was about to do.

A firing squad of twelve volunteers was assembled under 'Capitaine' Piétri's command. The victims, also selected by him, were then taken out into the moat facing the sea. Each of the executioners supposedly fired two shots. According to Piétri, it was a military act, but other prisoners, who were detailed to pick up the bodies, say that the victims had been randomly selected, then beaten until their faces were unrecognizable, before being machine-gunned.

This affair is known today as the Fort Carré tragedy, and the families of the ten victims are campaigning to have their names cleared and their honour restored. It has been claimed that many detainees had been denounced for reasons of jealousy and revenge, and their only crime was that they were Italian. One man was a victim of mistaken identity, and one of the females, 16-year-old Carmen Raveu, had done no more than help her father to sell a political newspaper sympathetic to the occupier. Piétri was tried twice for his deeds, but in the end his 'punishment' was being sent to a combat unit on the front line in the Alps. When the descendants of the condemned recently requested that a plaque be erected at the entrance to the fort, providing visitors with the facts, Piétri made the statement that exoneration would constitute 'an insult to the Resistance'.[13]

It was in fact the fake *maquisards*, those who enthusiastically participated in the *épuration*, who did the most damage to the reputation of the Resistance. These were the *résistants de la dernière heure* who would march through town enjoying the adulation and the kisses. When they got to the other end, they would let the real soldiers continue the fight. As one eyewitness observed: 'You know, there weren't many FFIs. Do you know when they did come out? When all the Germans were gone, then they came out of the houses. When the storm had passed, they all came out. There were armbands here and armbands there; that was the Resistance for you …'[14]

But not everyone could be tarred with the same brush, and the official attitude of the US Seventh Army was more considerate. All ranks were reminded that the Maquis were the recognized armed forces of an Allied nation:

> These people have been in constant combat against the invaders of their country; in so doing they have taken far greater hazards than the usual military forces of a country are expected to do; for more than four years, many of them have carried their lives in their hands; their participation in resistance has exposed their families to hostage and revenge by an unscrupulous foe; tens of thousands have been tortured and killed; hundreds of thousands have been robbed, imprisoned and expatriated; the self-sacrifice and patriotic devotion of those who survive and continue to fight should readily ensure them the respect and confidence of the Allied forces of liberation from whom they expect so much and for whose advance they are in a position to so ably pave the way.[15]

*

Only the bravest or most fanatical *miliciens* were foolish enough to stand up and be counted after the Normandy landings of 6 June 1944. There was only one way out for them and that was to flee to Germany. Many went into exile and became members of the SS whether they wanted to or not. As one of them remarked, 'It was either the SS or striped pyjamas.' Those who chose to remain in France had nowhere to hide and some chose to go down fighting.

One *milicien*, Maurice Giannardi, must have been an eternal optimist. He had gone to Paris from Provence with the idea that he would be needed to keep law and order there in the event that the striking gendarmes were disarmed. In a letter dated 15 August 1944, he wrote to his wife in Digne, telling her that he still believed in the National Revolution and Germany's ultimate victory. Had he written one day later, he might have mentioned the landings in Provence and the breakthrough in Normandy. Maurice Giannardi escaped into Germany but was caught in March 1945 in Italy and brought back to Aix-en-Provence to face justice.[16]

As of February 1944, approximately 300 *miliciens* had enlisted in the Waffen-SS. This was largely due to an impassioned speech given by Joseph Darnand the previous year in Nice, where he declared that he would fight alongside Germany and asked that others join him. But this was a relatively small proportion of the 10,000 or so active members of the Milice. Perhaps it was an indication that relatively few of them were young and fit enough to qualify physically.[17] Joseph Darnand had become the strong man of the Vichy state since it began imploding at the beginning of 1944.

Although a number of Frenchmen were already serving with other SS units, the Germans authorized the recruitment of a special French unit of the Waffen-SS, the Charlemagne Division. The original French unit in the German Army was the Légion des Volontaires Français contre le Bolchévisme (Legion of French Volunteers against Bolshevism), or LVF. Whoever thought of calling this new unit the Charlemagne Division knew their history because King Charlemagne represents a link between France and Germany who both claim him as their own. Both Napoleon and Hitler invoked the name of Charlemagne for their own purposes. Those who joined the Charlemagne Division as a last resort, after the liberation of France, numbered approximately five thousand.[18] The few surviving members of the Sturmbataillon Charlemagne, having burned their bridges in their homeland, were the last defenders of Hitler's bunker complex in the rubble of the Reich Chancellery. On 8 May 1945, while at Bad Reichenhall in Bavaria, General Phillipe Leclerc was presented with twelve captured Charlemagne Division soldiers. He asked one of them: 'Why are you wearing a German uniform?' The defiant Frenchman then asked in return: 'Why are you wearing an American one?' Leclerc told his men to 'get rid of them' and without further ado, they taken out and shot. A few survivors found a home with the Foreign Legion, and one Charlemagne veteran lived to tell his story in the 1969 documentary *Le Chagrin et la Pitié* (*The Sorrow and the Pity*).

Reasons for joining the Wehrmacht varied from adventurism to fascism. One of the 20,000 Frenchmen who volunteered for the Waffen-SS was André Bayle who defined himself as 'Provençal, French, Catholic and European'. Although only 16, his main motivation was to save Europe from the 'Reds' but he also regarded the British as the enemies of Europe. In addition, he admired German society and their smart military. Until his death in Marseille in 2010, he was ostracized and discriminated against for his Nazi past.

While the Allies were closing in on Marseille, the resident Gestapo agents and their auxiliaries, scrambled to get out of town, and, where necessary, paid for their space in a car heading for Germany, but justice eventually caught up with most of them. The Jew hunter, Charles Palmieri (*Merle*) left Marseille with his Gestapo bosses on the day of the Allied landings and made his way to Berlin. With little choice in the matter, he was given training in explosives, and as part of a small team, including his brother, Alfred, parachuted back into France at the end of 1944. Alfred dislocated his knee on landing and opted to swallow his cyanide pill rather than be captured by the French police.

During his long trial in Marseille, Palmieri angrily divulged the names of people holding 'resistance credentials' in spite of being collaborators. The list included police officials and other notables, who he said were just as guilty as he was in arresting Jews and collaborating with the occupier. He was executed on 22 August 1946 at La Malmousque just outside Marseille. Palmieri mentioned at his trial that a second sabotage team, consisting of three SS members, had been inserted earlier, their mission to attack a pipeline in the Rhône Valley. Interestingly, in the Vaucluse, there was a case of possible sabotage by fifth columnists.

The Château de la Simone outside Pertuis, on the road to Villelaure, was occupied by a company of former resistance fighters of the Ventoux-Luberon Maquis, waiting to join the regular forces on their march into Germany. Three months after the liberation of Provence, on 25 November 1944, a mysterious explosion occurred, completely destroying the château and killing thirty-one *maquisards*. To this day, it is unclear whether this was an accident or sabotage. Newspapers at the time blamed a 'fifth column' for an act of revenge.

As a rule, restraint was exercised by the tribunals, and genuine Resistance members were frequently dismayed to see so many suspects pardoned or let off with light sentences. The overriding consideration was whether or not the defendant had been merely following orders. It is estimated that less than 10,000 executions of collaborators occurred in France overall, but numbers are vague because summary justice did not leave much in the way of documented evidence. Approximately a quarter followed due process. The other three-quarters were summary executions, and over half of these took place during the occupation, before the Allied landing.

The death sentence was thus a rare form of punishment in the context of the *épuration légale*: sometimes it would be commuted to hard labour. Functionaries of the many préfectures which had implemented the Nazi policies were thrown out of office, and many thousands of civil servants and police suffered some sort of sanction. The purge was particularly severe for writers who, by the nature of their work, were in no position to deny their past affiliations. Robert Brasillach, a fascist French author, journalist and cinema critic, had once called for the summary execution of all captured resistance members. Immediately before his own execution, Brasillach called out, '*Vive la France quand même!*' – 'Long live France all the same!'

In September 1944, Pétain, Laval and other bitter-enders relocated to Sigmaringen in Germany, and the Vichy regime was over. Fast-forwarding to April 1945, as General George Patton's army closed in, the Vichy ministers were forced to find another sanctuary. Pierre Laval was flown to Barcelona in a Luftwaffe plane but was expelled and imprisoned at Fresnes Prison where so many of his adversaries had been subjected to a living hell.

Being a lawyer, Laval hoped to convince his fellow countrymen that he had been acting in their best interests all along, but it was futile, and even members of the jury jeered him. In an attempt to cheat his executioners, he took cyanide but was kept alive by having his stomach pumped and was dragged in front of the firing squad. Joseph Darnand, leader of the Milice and fully fledged SS officer, was captured by the British in northern Italy in June 1945. At his trial, he predictably claimed to have been a soldier carrying out orders but he too was executed by firing squad a few months later. The venerable old Philippe Pétain would escape the executioner, probably because of his senility, but spent the rest of his life in prison where died in 1952 at the age of ninety-five.

Chapter 19

Deliverance

There was snow on the high mountains in mid-November 1944 when the 1st Airborne Task Force was withdrawn from the Italian border for three weeks of reorganizing, near Nice. With winter coming on, it had been decided that if elite troops were to maintain their aggressive spirit, they should be spared the static mountain warfare in miserable conditions. Replacing them was an element of the 14th Armored Division, nicknamed 'The Liberators' who had landed at Marseille only two weeks previously. They in turn would be replaced by the Free French Army.

The 1st Airborne Task Force was deactivated at the end of November; General Frederick was given command of the 45th Infantry Division. Having been a composite force formed for a special purpose, the 1st Special Service Force was completely disbanded on 5 December in a field near Menton. On this occasion the *Montreal Standard* wrote: 'The significance of this force is that is that it was the first joint force of its kind, drawn from two neighbour democracies, and that it was a brilliant success throughout.'[1] After the breakup, the Canadians mostly went to the 1st Canadian Parachute Division, and the Americans transferred to either the Rangers or other airborne divisions.

For some reason, either because there was no transport, or in order to teach discipline, the 517th PIR was made to march back from Sospel, through Nice to La Colle-sur-Loup – a total distance of sixty-two kilometres. They spent the first night on the road at La Pointe de Contes, huddled under their frost-covered ponchos. It was a bedraggled group of paratroopers which passed through Nice the next day, walking along the Promenade des Anglais to bivouac at the racetrack at Cagnes-sur-Mer. A short uphill hike on the third day brought them to La Colle-sur-Loup, ten kilometres northwest of the Nice airport in the direction of Saint-Paul-de-Vence. Members of the 509th PIB were billeted higher up in the hills at La Gaude overlooking the River Var.

While the quartermaster issued new clothing and equipment, company clerks brought their personnel records up to date. A third of their number had been killed or wounded, and new replacements were brought in. The troopers spent the next two to three weeks renewing their acquaintances with the girls in Nice. More than one GI managed to tie the knot with their French sweethearts before moving out during the second week of December. To accomplish this, there were many obstacles and attitudes to overcome. The pocket guide for GIs made that clear:

> Should you find some girl whose charms induce thoughts of marriage, here are a few points to think over: In your present status as a soldier, marriage to a foreign girl has many complications. The same reason that caused so many of your comrades, as possibly yourself, to forego marriage at home – the uncertainty of future movements, the hazards a soldier faces – apply here even more so. From time to time, regulations may vary with regard to marriage abroad, but here are some ideas as to what you may run into: During the war, and for six months thereafter, the government will not pay for the transportation of dependents of military personnel from the theater of operations to the US nor from theater to theater. After the war, when you are shipped home for discharge, there will be no transport available for a wife. Nor is there likely to be any for a long, long time. In any case, you can't marry without the permission of your commanding officer.[2]

Sergeant Richard Fisco, the B Company, 509th PIB paratrooper who believed that a divine wind had prevented him from landing in the sea on Dragoon D-Day, had thoughts of marriage from the minute he saw Louise Cecchetti walking down a street in Nice. During a weekend away from the front at Sospel he had won her over with a gift of camouflage parachute silk, which she promptly turned into an item of haute couture – she was a dressmaker. Although Louise was only 17, her father consented to the marriage. A French girl was normally given a free rein at this age, but it helped that Richard was a staunch Catholic. A pearl and diamond engagement ring was paid for with four cartons of cigarettes. The wedding took place on 8 December in the Basilique Notre-Dame de l'Assomption, situated on Avenue Jean-Médecin in the centre of Nice. The couple spent their wedding night in the original Palais de la Méditerranée on the Promenade des Anglais, and the next day Fisco entrained at Antibes and moved north into the battle of the Bulge.

During the last two weeks of December of 1944, at the battle of the Bulge, the paratroopers, formerly of the 1st Airborne Task Force, faced their toughest test yet in the icy forests of the Ardennes. All available resources had been sent to reinforce that sector, a breakthrough was narrowly prevented, and on 27 December, General Patton relieved the town of Bastogne. Then, on 31 December, the Germans launched Operation Nordwind against the depleted US Seventh Army and French First Army in the mountains of the Upper Vosges, south of Strasbourg. This was Germany's final offensive, and for a while the fighting was desperate.

In the Alpes-Maritimes, the advance had ground to a halt. The advance to Germany took precedence over what was simply a holding operation. It was not a priority to drive the Germans out of southeastern France as they were expected to withdraw of their own accord when the Allies progressed up the boot of Italy. A limited offensive had been launched in the Apennines in Italy to coincide with the Wacht am Rhein offensive in the Ardennes, but effectively, both campaigns on the Italian side were static until the following spring. It is not without reason that this was called the 'forgotten front'.

At first it wasn't so bad holding this part of the line. 'It's like camping in the Adirondacks,' remarked one GI before the winter set in. The two sides watched each other from their respective heights, not inclined to take unnecessary risks. Shelling and patrolling continued throughout the winter, with the main danger coming from mines and booby traps, but the odd firefight did erupt. Various formations came and went; among them was the 442nd (Nisei) Infantry Regiment, comprised of second-generation Japanese troops, mainly from Hawaii and the West Coast. Having just come from heavy fighting in the Vosges, their task of holding a twenty-kilometre front was considered to be almost as good as a rest.

Another ethnic unit which overwintered here was the 65th Infantry Regiment consisting of Puerto Rican troops, and when they went into the line at Piera Carva, on 12 December 1944, it was their first experience of combat. Their commanding officer was the 42-year-old Colonel George A. Ford, a Virginian and a West Pointer. In his letters to his wife and three children he described his surroundings as 'the most gorgeously magnificent scenery I have ever encountered. It is futile to attempt to describe it, a tumbled sea of mountains all around, rugged gray masses dusted with snow and snow-covered ranges interspersed … The morning and evening light on the mountains is lovely beyond description, and each turn of the road reveals a new and fascinating vista'.[3]

The regiment had previously been guarding fuel depots and railheads, and this was the first time in six months that George Ford had felt happy. Such enjoyment could only be a waste of taxpayer's money, he concluded. To be in the combat zone and to have a command of his own unit was crowned by the fact that his was a 'quiet little war' and his family need have no concern for his safety. 'My only risk,' he wrote, 'is of bumping my head on a cloud' before ending off with wishing 'a merry, merry Christmas to the best and sweetest wife and family ever'.

Two weeks later, Colonel Ford's enthusiasm had waned. He was bumping heads with his second-in-command, and his Puerto Ricans were suffering in their freezing foxholes. In order to boost morale, on 5 January 1945, Ford took the unusual decision to personally lead a twelve-man patrol to scout positions being held by battle-hardened men of the German 34th Division. On approaching the enemy position, which was in a 'cable house', Colonel Ford told his men to wait while he and Captain Daniel Logan went forward to within twenty metres of the house. The colonel stepped out from behind the tree to the left and took about four steps, slightly crouching, when a single shot rang out. Logan later reported:

> I asked the colonel: 'Where are you hit, Colonel. He replied: 'Logan, I'm hit in the back.' Right after he said that, he drew his knees up, and stretched out and quivered. I could see blood was flowing from his mouth. After that, I called the Colonel: 'Colonel come to me,' and there was no answer. I remained in my position about a minute, and before I left, I took another look at him, and he looked to me like he was dead.[4]

As it looked like the Germans were trying to outflank him, Logan withdrew to where some of his men were waiting. One had been mortally wounded. Staff Sergeant Jose Robles was ordered to go and bring in the colonel's body but when he realized that an enemy patrol was enveloping his flank, he retreated, leaving behind the colonel's body and the wounded man, who now no longer had a pulse. Since his death could not be confirmed immediately, Colonel George A. Ford was first listed as missing in action, and his remains were recovered only once the war was over. No tags were found, and he had to be identified by dental records.

When a man was killed on a deep patrol in these mountains, far from his own lines, his body had to be left behind and might not be recovered for months. In no man's land, there was no time for even a hasty battlefield burial. After being exposed to the elements and wild animals, identification was very difficult if not impossible. Nevertheless, the Graves Registration Unit at Draguignan went to great lengths to get a positive identification using dog tags, personal effects, fingerprints and dental records. A member of the same unit would usually be asked to describe the circumstances of the death.

The last battle fought on French soil before the fall of Berlin was at Authion, among the high peaks and hidden pastures, about thirty kilometres north of Sospel. Overlooking the valleys of the Vésubie, the Bévéra and the Roya, Mont Authion has been described as 'a natural fortress in a bucolic setting'. The 'forgotten front' was now being held by the 1ère Division Française Libre and on the northern end was the French 27th Alpine Division which included ex-FFI fighters, legionnaires and colonials. The 1ère DFL had recently been involved in the pursuit to Germany, and moved to the Alpine front on 28 February 1945. In the middle of March, the order came for them to seize Mont Authion and push toward Turin. General de Gaulle was keen to conquer and keep some Italian soil in retaliation for the recent occupation of the Alpes-Maritimes, and Menton in particular. When he visited Nice in April 1945 he made his feelings known: 'Gentlemen, I am aware of the sacrifices that I ask of you. The campaign which opens will be hard, I know it. It will open the doors of the Piedmont and you will drive to the Tyrol … We want to take back the natural frontier of our country.'

It was to be an all-French affair, with supporting fire from French ships at sea, and close air support from French pilots stationed at the Californie airfield, the site of the present-day Nice Côte d'Azur International Airport. The French troops lacked warm clothing and wore a mishmash of American and French uniforms, with some British battledress and civilian clothing thrown in. The former FFI fighters were still equipped with antiquated weapons.

On the opposing side, the German 148th Reserve Division had been replaced by the 34th Infantry Division. Although it had an impressive war record, it now consisted largely of older replacements, unfit for combat duty; nevertheless, they were Nazi fanatics. Some of their most reliable auxiliaries were 3,500 Italian Blackshirts, commanded by German officers. French *miliciens*, who had fled from France, were now also deployed on the border of their former homeland.

On Mont Authion, the defenders occupied five forts from a bygone era, strengthened by new casemates, forming part of the Ligne Alpine, the Little Maginot Line. Not only were they formidable defences, they were also quite comfortable in comparison to how the attacking troops lived – exposed to the elements. Having spent the winter there, they knew the lie of the land, and had all their weapons ranged in. Nevertheless, the morale of these troops was not good, and sickness was prevalent as a result. Recent snowfalls had made it difficult to transport supplies. There was, of course, bad news from home, and the defeat of the Wehrmacht in the Ardennes had been a huge blow.

Even when the end was in sight, a last-ditch attempt was made by the Kriegsmarine to hurt the Allies. On 17 April, a suicide canoe was used to strike at a French destroyer. Twenty were killed, and the ship was sent limping back to Toulon. Encouraged by this success, further attempts were made on 23 April, but the Allied ships were now on the alert and three canoes were sunk at Cap Martin and a fourth at Antibes.

After an ineffective preliminary bombardment from French artillery on 10 April 1945, the 1er Bataillon d'Infanterie de Marine et du Pacifique (BIMP) launched the first attack on Mont Authion from the south but were repulsed with heavy losses. The next day, the same battalion continued the attack on the forts using flamethrowers and bazookas. At the end of the day, the French could assemble on the plateau, and only one fortress was still standing. At the end of the third day, 12 April, the final assault was made by four or five infantrymen supported by a single Stuart light tank which had struggled up the steep hill in the thin air at 2,000 metres above sea level. Corporal Césaire le Mercier, a Breton belonging to the BIMP, entered the fort alone and came out with 38 prisoners. The entire German front collapsed on 24 April 1945, opening the way into Italy.

Simultaneously, in the Apennine Mountains north of Florence, the American Fifth Army broke through the Winter Line to Bologna and the plains of the River Po. The French forces found themselves only seventy kilometres from Turin but de Gaulle didn't get his wish. American and South African troops were ordered to occupy Turin, the Italian Riviera and the Aosta Valley – to which the French were laying claim. The 1ère DFL was ordered to return to base at Menton on the French side of the border. The war in Europe officially ended on 8 May 1945, although in Italy, General Kesselring had capitulated a few days earlier.

*

Unlike most other military campaigns, the final phase of the 'Champagne Campaign' was fought in close proximity to one of the world's favourite tourist destinations. From Monte Carlo, one could look up and see the bleak battlefields around Col-de-Braus. Every two weeks, the men were granted 48-hour passes to Nice or Beausoleil, where bar fights resulted in what the GIs referred to as 'non-Purple Heart casualties'. From his beachfront hotel room a soldier on R&R in Nice could see the cold mountains where death and discomfort was the daily reality.

Up and down the coast, hotels and villas were requisitioned to provide accommodation to troops of all nationalities. Although the leftist Liberation Committee claimed to have no great affection for the Americans, the men and women in the street were more than welcoming. Most were happy to share their space, and may even have considered it an honour. The Americans always asked property owners if they could take over a house, even if the previous tenants had been German.

Marseille was geared more for military business than for pleasure although the 'oldest profession' thrived in its side streets. Like others before and after him, T/5 Harold Coons of the Black Panther Division wrote disparagingly of France's filthiest city: 'Here I am in Marseille, for the last time, I hope,' he confided to his wife. 'Though the second largest city in France, I think it is the dirtiest and smelliest.'[5] The same sentiments were expressed by T/5 Alfred 'Al' McCarthy of the 9th Armored Division:

> Prostitution is the business in Marseille, and one sees women are waiting everywhere. They are in bars, cafés all along the streets, under every street light, waiting to be

316

asked to go somewhere. I become sick in my heart and in my mind, because so many men have lost their pride, and will go along, dragging themselves and the American uniform into the quagmire and filth of vice and prostitution in the lowest form.[6]

A rash of prostitutes from Paris, Bordeaux and Toulouse invaded the length of the Riviera, bringing venereal diseases (VD) with them. When the military police raided a nightclub in Nice on 3 July 1945, sixteen prostitutes were arrested, and fifteen of them tested positive for VD. Police estimated that there were 508 'professional' and 1,136 'clandestine' prostitutes operating in Nice alone in 1945, eight times more than the previous year. Most disturbing was the prevalence of child prostitutes who could earn up to 10,000 francs per day, at a time when the average monthly salary on the Côte d'Azur was 3,000 francs.

The *Pocket Guide to France* warned GIs that if a girl did not carry a prostitute's card, then she was an 'irregular', but 'regular' or 'irregular', either kind could present one with a nasty souvenir to take back home. Despite *préservatifs* – condoms – being freely available, there was an explosion of VD. Colonel Aldo Bagnulo, commanding an African-American engineer regiment, noted that the infections picked up in Marseille were resistant to all treatments – including penicillin. One source states that the rate of infection among coloured troops was three times that of the whites.[7]

Allied soldiers returning from leave were subjected to FFI (free from infection) inspections also known as 'short-arm' inspections and in high-risk areas such as Marseille, weekly inspections were required. A pamphlet entitled 'do's and don'ts – while on leave' strongly advised men not to risk venereal disease, but if they had done so, they were urged to visit the clinic at once. In the US Army, prostitution was accepted. Morality became a disciplinary matter only when it resulted in venereal disease or incapacitation through substance abuse.

Nice had been a playground for the men of the 1st Airborne Task Force from the time they entered the city on 29 August 1944 until the first week of December when they departed for the Ardennes. While engaged in the fighting around Col-de-Braus, it was possible to return to Nice and Beausoleil for short periods of rest, and after they were withdrawn from the line, the FABTF spent three weeks around La Colle-sur-Loup, in what is known as the 'back country'. This neighbourhood is today congested with commuters working in Nice, Grasse and Cannes. After the cessation of hostilities, the only vehicles on this road were army trucks crammed with soldiers making day trips to these same cities, but accidents still happened. Reckless driving on narrow roads resulted in about twenty accidents between June and August 1945, leaving nine dead and twenty-four injured in the Nice area alone.

Monte Carlo was closer than Nice to the battlefields, but it was off-limits, and Menton was a ghost town. The feelings of goodwill which came with the liberation, soon dissipated when the locals realized that the paratroopers, in particular, might have been good soldiers but made bad tourists. Bar fights, theft, and breaking windowpanes was all part of a paratrooper's fun. On one occasion in Beausoleil they locked the gendarmes up in their own cells.

Although the *Niçois* may have heaved a sigh of relief when the paratroopers departed for the Ardennes, the Yankee occupation was only just beginning. Designated the United States Riviera Recreational Area (USRRA), an official rest area was established in January 1945 encompassing the cities of Nice, Cannes, Antibes, Juan-les-Pins and Grasse. Men arrived by the trainload several times a week, representing every division of every Allied army in Western Europe.

Battle-fatigued and feeling like fugitives from the law of averages, soldiers could not believe their luck. The fun started at Dijon where they stopped over for a meal at an establishment called the 'Merry Messing Center'. Nearing the Côte d'Azur, travelling through countryside which reminded them of California and the Sierra Nevada, they felt the warmth of the sun through the carriage windows.

On arrival in Nice, tired and dirty, but excited, each soldier clutched an envelope which included his hotel reservation and a small booklet informing him about the facilities and scheduled events. The instruction book and guide listed the twenty-six or so hotels allocated to military guests, and indicated their location on a map. Directions on where to find American beer and Coca-Cola led to the 'Shopping Center' housed in a former exposition centre, the Palais des Fêtes, centrally situated at 34 Boulevard Victor Hugo where the army ran a cafeteria, perfume shop, numerous barber shops and a hairdresser for the Women's Army Corps, the WACs. In charge of this whole operation, which employed 2,400 civilians, was Colonel Thomas F. Gunn, a past president of the Rotary

Club in Pasadena, California. The Rotary Club of Nice got going soon after liberation and directed its energies to looking after orphans and hosting young soldiers.

For a whole seven days and seven nights, before returning to the front, soldiers had comfortable beds and could sleep for forty-eight hours, or even stay drunk if they so pleased. Few did because there was just so much to do. In addition to strolling or cycling along the Promenade des Anglais, shopping in Avenue de la Victoire, and people-watching in Place Massina, there was everything from pedal boats in the Baie des Anges to underwater spearfishing, from yachting to golf, from surfing to roller-skating, from pinball to bicycles, from girlie shows to opera, from tennis to swimming in a heated pool at 9 Rue de le Buffa.

The favorite amusement of young French people was simply taking a *promenade* which can vaguely be defined as 'an occasion where people go somewhere for recreational purposes only'. It may be a short walk down the street, or a picnic in the woods or an outing on a boat; it may be made by a family on a Sunday afternoon or by a couple in love; even a single person, walking in what seems to be an aimless manner, may be said to be taking a *promenade*.

Film footage taken on a spotless Promenade des Anglais during the American occupation shows that some things never change. Multitudes of walkers risked being run over by wobbly cyclists and roller-skaters, while groups of young people lounged on the pebble-beach below. There was no sign of the barbed wire and sandbags with which the Germans had defaced the beachfront, but a concrete blockhouse provided a nice flat surface for sunbathing and picnicking.

Drinking is part of the culture of the military and part of the masculine mystique.[8] In a theatre of war, heavy drinking was quite acceptable provided that a man did not incapacitate himself or become unruly. Alcohol was, however, to blame for many acts of disorderliness, with a clear link between alcohol and sexually transmitted disease. Alcohol served the function of blunting the sex drive, acting as a type of sexual anaesthetic. It made prostituted sex more acceptable. Without doubt, alcohol was also to blame for many of the road accidents which occurred, especially during the postwar period.[9]

To maintain harmonious relations with the natives, the military made a point of educating soldiers about the café culture in French towns and villages. Provençals are generally a sober people, and, according to the *Pocket Guide to France*, 'the café is much more and much less than a bar. It's the social center':

> The neighborhood French café is the most French thing in all France. If you want to be welcome when you come back a second time, use the café the way the French do. As you'll see by looking around you, the Frenchman comes there with his family. It is NOT a place where the French go to get drunk. Like all wine-drinking people, the French don't drink to get drunk. Drunkenness is rare in France. Conversely, the only thing the French have never been able to say against the Nazi Army of occupation is that it was a drunken army. Don't let them say it about the American Army. And don't forget that the Nazi propaganda agents have already given the French a pretty picture of the way Americans act on a Saturday night.[10]

On every programme, for every rest area, 'tea-dances' featured prominently. This common pastime was nothing more than dancing at teatime, whether it was ballroom or big-band. The preferred source of female company was nurses and WACs. Incidentally, a survey found that 40 per cent of unmarried WACs were celibate, 55 per cent were sexually active on occasion and 5 per cent were promiscuous.[11] Many of the facilities in the recreational areas and staging areas were run by Red Cross women. Soldiers found them to be always kind and helpful, but alas, not always the most beautiful.

Sergeant Harold Levy, a tank commander in the 2nd Armored Division, and his friend, John Pellicci, a platoon sergeant in the same 67th Regiment, had been together ever since they first joined the army. Aside from time spent recovering from wounds in hospital, this was the first time that either of them has been away from their unit. After watching a floor show and drinking cognac in one of the GI bars, they walked back to their hotel, arm in arm with two girls. Wafting through the doors of the Red Cross Casino Club, across the Promenade des Anglais, was the sound of Glen Miller's 'Moonlight Serenade', causing them to wonder if perhaps they had been killed in action, and this was heaven. Coming to the end of their stay, the two sergeants shared their experiences with *Yank* magazine staff correspondent Sergeant Ralph G. Martin:

> So the first night Levy and Pellicci went on a binge, got drunk enough to get all the war tension out of their systems. Levy carried Pellicci up seven flights and put him to bed that night. After that they didn't drink any more, except for some beer. They went everywhere, saw everything, didn't miss a trick. They took the excursion to Grasse to see the perfume factories, went along on a boat ride to Monte Carlo. They swam, rode bicycles, did some shopping and went fishing (Pellicci used to like to go trout fishing near Pelham, NY). 'We did lots of things that I never thought I'd be doing again,' said Levy who was once wounded three times in a single afternoon. 'I wish all the guys up front would get a chance to come here.'[12]

At a push, the USRRA could accommodate 18,000 soldiers, and there was once talk of expanding it to three times that size. The hosting of the 100,000th restee was celebrated on 20 July 1945 with the presentation of a golden key at the Negresco Hotel. On a typical day in September 1945, there were 9,916 restees in Nice, 974 in Cannes, and 700 in Juan-les-Pins.[13] A big sign in the lobby of the USRRA headquarters in Nice said, 'GI paradise, off limits to officers.' Elsewhere in Nice there were signs declaring, 'No saluting required.' Cannes was reserved for officers only; NCOs and enlisted men had the freedom of Nice while nurses and WACs stayed in Juan-les-Pins and Antibes. An advertisement in *Stars and Stripes* announced that American dancing partners would be provided for officers at a dance to be held on the Starlite Terrace of the Hôtel Provençal in Juan-les-Pins.

Soldiers would talk for hours about the *Niçois* women: how they wore their clothes, the way they wore their hair, the way they rode bicycles, the way they looked in bathing suits. At a time when only the most daring American girls sported skirtless swimsuits on the beach, two-piece *maillots de bain* were very much the mode on the Riviera. The consensus was that the women were terrific and the best thing was that there were so many of them. 'That's the number one important thing about Nice – the women,' wrote Sergeant Ralph Martin in *Yank, The Army Weekly*. 'They're absolutely positively the most sensational, the most terrific, the most beautiful, wonderful, glamorous women I've ever seen in all my life,' said another soldier 'or maybe I've just been in the line too long.'[14]

To help soldiers get the girl, their phrasebooks contained such expressions as 'You have charming eyes', 'I am not married' and 'Are your parents at home?' A one-liner in *Stars and Stripes* pokes fun at the phrasebook at the back of the *Pocket Guide to France*: in a letter to the publication, one supposedly wrote to the editor: 'I said "vooley-voo-promenade-aw-vec-mwa" and she said "wee wee." Now what do I do?' Evidently, when it came to impressing the ladies, nothing worked as well as paratrooper boots, although rear-echelon types in their crisp khaki, lightweight uniforms had the long-term advantage.

Rumour held that France was inhabited by 40 million hedonists who spent all their time eating, drinking and making love. Recruiting pamphlets had sold the war to young men, not so much as a struggle for freedom as a sexual adventure. Italy was equated with sun-browned bodies and sexual promiscuity. France was portrayed as one big brothel by the 'enlistment entrapment' experts although the *Pocket Guide* did concede that 'France is full of decent women and strict women'.

For the lucky and the few, the promised land was everything they hoped it would be: 'When I was in combat, I used to daydream, like everybody else, about all the things I'd like to do if I ever got out alive,' said Private LaVern Sellard of the 377th Parachute Field Artillery Battalion, which fought at Arnhem and the battle of the Bulge. 'But now I can say that during my seven days and nights here, I've done absolutely everything I ever dreamt about. And then some.' This was one of the comments on the USRRA questionnaire which soldiers were asked to fill out on departure. The only gripe they got was from a soldier who said, 'I don't like this place because the girl at the information desk won't go out with me.'

French girls who did not see a future for themselves in war-torn Europe were keen to marry a GI just to get to the United States. After an outbreak of such marriages, a Nice newspaper felt compelled to publish an article entitled: 'Not all the "Sammies" are millionaires.' During the war, the number of weddings had grown every year and a report in *Stars and Stripes* of 29 December 1945 correctly predicted a baby boom in 1950, followed by a demand for children's clothing and an increase in school enrolments in 1955, and then a second marriage boom … and so on.

What the reporter did not foresee was that hasty embarkation marriages often ended up on the rocks, although due to the morality of the time, some chose to live with their mistakes.[15] A long-term study of Californian university students and recent graduates who joined the American armed forces showed that marriages were at greater risk during the war years. In 1946, there was indeed a spike in divorces, but marriages established during the war were no more likely to dissolve than marriages begun at other times. It appears, therefore, that it was the long separation rather than the lack of courtship which caused the problems.[16] A one-liner in *Stars and Stripes* quipped that a newly married bride was waving goodbye to a corporal on an outgoing train. Suddenly she shrieked, 'Darling, I forgot to ask you; what's our last name?'

In the last days of the war in Europe, on 27 April 1945, an article entitled 'They want to go' appeared in *Yank, The Army Weekly*, concerning the large number of applications by women wanting postings to Europe. The Office of Strategic Services had advertised 200 jobs for women aged 23 to 42 and was overwhelmed at the response. 'If the mountain will not come to Mahomet,' the article begins, 'Mahomet will go to the mountain.' OSS officials reckoned that the money was as great a lure as husbands and boyfriends overseas. The weekly pay, including living allowance, of about $70 per week was double the usual salary of a clerical worker.

Gwen Mallach, a petite brunette from Farmington, Long Island, who was at the time a clerical worker at Grumman Aircraft, was quoted: 'Why do I want to go overseas? Why, I want to see all those places I've been reading about in the papers since the war started. The reason I would like to go to Paris particularly is because my boyfriend is in the army, and he is in England. No of course, that's not in France, but its closer to him than I am now, isn't it?' 'Yes it is dear,' added the condescending correspondent.

A veteran of the 14th Tank Battalion, 9th Armored Division, who saw action at the Bulge, T/5 A. V. McCarthy, wrote 268 love letters to his future wife, the ravishing Oneta Blashke, in Cleveland, Ohio. Mailed from training camps all over the United States, then from England, then France, then Belgium, the letters all began with 'My Oneta' and contained snippets of news mixed in with a feverish torrent of passionate prose. The final and most urgent ones were written from Camp Calas in the Delta Staging Area near Aix-en-Provence. The couple had been apart for three years, and Al was getting worried that Oneta wouldn't wait for him. Fidelity was a common theme, and his pleading was unrelenting: 'You are the only good, pure, clean, and virgin young woman I know' and 'Be mine alone, be mine always, because I want to come out of this bad dream and live again.'[17]

Not everyone preferred the 'squeaky clean' girls at home. Sometimes, late at night, one could hear a merry bunch of soldiers walking the streets of Nice, raucously singing:

> *The girls are fairer*
> *Down on the Riviera*
> *So give a vive la, vive la France.*
> *The wine is stronger;*
> *The kisses, linger longer.*
> *So give a vive la, vive la France.*

According to *Yank* magazine, the feeling was mutual as far as the *Niçois* women were concerned. A girl named Simone Randon, who was studying to be a pharmacist liked the informality of the 'Sammies', and the way they could 'jitterbug'. All the boys called her 'Shorty' and straight from the phrasebook, absolutely everybody told her, 'You have a pair of very beautiful eyes, baby.' The language barrier was there, but not insurmountable. A 'cute brunette' called Josette who worked in the information booth at the Hôtel Negresco, said that the soldiers seemed a little stiff and awkward: 'From the way they talk and joke with us, it seems as if they are trying to get into practice again on how to act with women ... But they are always very clean and very lively, like children.'[18]

Occasionally, especially on their first night in Nice, some of the 'children' got a little too lively. When that happened, the MPs stepped in, but these were no ordinary MPs. Almost all of them either wore Purple Hearts or Combat Infantryman badges. They understood the need to blow off steam and instead of locking up an inebriated soldier, they took him home to his hotel and put him to bed. A key feature of USRRA policy was a gentleman's agreement on behaviour: an absolute minimum of regulations, providing the soldiers did their part.

Authorities claimed that there were surprisingly few drunks, but it goes without saying that where there are 10,000 soldiers out on the town there would be problems ranging from street fights to traffic accidents. French civilians were frequent victims of assaults, some of them deadly. Soldiers were blamed for attacking the newly elected mayor, Jacques Cotta, one night after leaving a function, but having just defeated the communist candidate, he would have had many enemies.

Generally, the first port of call for members of the armed forces was the American Red Cross Casino Club situated in Palais de la Méditerranée on the Promenade des Anglais. It had been, and is again today, a luxurious gambling casino identifiable by its high arches. One could relax in deep, soft chairs on the *terrasse* and watch the world go by, or make use of the myriad facilities and activities they offered. One could select from any of the following: sitting lounge, reading and writing room, games room, ping-pong tables, jitterbug lessons, ballroom dancing lessons, bike tours to Cagnes, a USO play (*Ten Little Indians*), checkers tournament, photography, home hospitality service, shopping service and package wrapping. Tea was served in the lounge every afternoon, and the snack bar was always open. On a particular day in September 1945 the 88th Infantry Division band was playing in the ballroom, a string quartet played gypsy music in the lounge and bingo was taking place in the Bamboo Room.

At the Red Cross Club, the ice-cream and Coca-Cola was free, but for adult entertainment one would almost always end up at one of the nightclubs where there were soft lights, smooth orchestras, fast-moving floor shows, 'boucoup' good-looking women, and good service. Reynaud's, located on the Quai des Etats-Unis, fronting the sea, was one of the most glamorous rendezvous on the whole Riviera. Most popular though, was the spacious Crown Club at the Ruhl Hotel where hostesses were provided. Enlisted men frequented the Copacabana, Queens, Maxim's, and Christie's, while the Plantation Club catered for the few officers staying in Nice.

After a night of debauchery, there was the possibility of repenting one's sins in any number of churches, from Russian Orthodox to Christian Science. Confessions were heard in French or Italian at the Catholic Cathedral, and a squadron of army chaplains provided counselling. Most GIs just wanted to relax after a night on the town – stretch out in the sun, snooze a little, stare at the women in their scanty bathing suits and forget about the war for a while. At the Hôtel Beau Rivage, just opposite the beach of the same name, a GI could make three-minute recordings which were sent to his home radio station. Corporal Joe Jackson of the 95th Infantry Division told the folks at home: 'I think this is the nicest place in the world, with the exception of Brooklyn.'

The most highly decorated American soldier of all time, Audie Murphy of the 3rd Infantry Division, was one of the visitors to the French Riviera during May 1945. It will be remembered that he won the Distinguished Service Cross at Ramatuelle on 15 August 1944 and for his actions of 25 January 1945 he would be awarded the Medal of Honor. Now a lieutenant, he was in Cannes while the rest of his division put on a victory parade in Salzburg. Already showing signs of post-traumatic stress disorder (PTSD) and survivor's guilt, the 20-year-old Murphy took it easy, walking on the beach, contemplating what the future held for a poorly educated son of a Texas sharecropper.

After VE Day, visitors to the USRRA came mostly from occupation duties in Germany or from the transit area around Marseille. Now that the borders were almost back to normal, soldier-tourists from Italy started venturing into Monaco, France and Switzerland. Although many GIs were unaware of the fact, a coalition of many nations had helped to drive the Germans out of Italy. They were a little surprised therefore, when they met South African soldiers in Nice. With their unfamiliar uniforms and accents, some were unsure whether these fair-skinned Africans had been allies or enemies. The colonials in turn, observed the Yanks with amusement as they mangled the French language along the lines of 'Hey, garcon, how about some ice cream, toot sweet.'

The 6th South African Armoured Division had ended their campaign in Milan and after a short stint of border duty in the Aosta Valley near Turin, they were comfortably installed in resorts along the Italian Riviera, from San Remo to Rapallo. During his six-month wait for transport home, Corporal John Hodgson and a small group of friends made the trip from San Remo to Nice on a number of occasions. After the squalor of Egypt, and deprivations in Italy, he enthused about his visit to France:

> We got there at about midday after a pleasant trip; on the way we passed through Monte Carlo, and saw the famous casino; also the 'Hotel de Paris' which is renowned to be the finest in the world. As you can well imagine these two

places need more than words to describe them. In Nice itself we had excellent food at American controlled restaurants, visited 'the' hotels of the French Riviera, which are far beyond my sphere of explanation. These were also taken over by Americans for rest hotels so all of the prices were very cheap. The shopping centre was very nice to look at, but the outstanding prices soon took the idea out of our heads of doing anything. We also spent a fair amount of time on the promenade surveying the sights on the beach. I can assure you that it was an eye-opener to French dress and certain of their ways. It was really a wonderful experience to be able to have a look round such a renowned city. There was plenty of beer to be had, and any amount of ice-cream and cakes at the American Red Cross Club. It is hard to describe at all in such a short space all that we saw and did, so I think it had better wait until I get back which I hope will not be long now, and then I will be able to give you all the details. We got back here to our hotel at four o'clock on Saturday morning.[19]

The pebbly beach below the Promenade des Anglais, however, did not impress Hodgson, who described it as a strip of stones about fifteen yards wide which in South Africa, would not even be called a beach: 'As far as the styles of costumes [bathing suits], I have seldom seen anything like it; the majority were only costumes in name, there was so little of them; also such a thing as a bathing-booth is not employed, everyone dresses and undresses on the beach.' At the Rhul Hotel one could hire bicycles during the day, and in the evening, there was dancing. Hodgson found the French girls to be 'streets ahead of these decadent Italians'.

A few weeks later, Hodgson again visited 'GI Paradise'. At the Forum Theatre, which reminded him of his local cinema in Johannesburg, he watched one of the latest films with Bette Davis in *The Corn is Green*. At the Red Cross Club he indulged in coffee and doughnuts 'at the expense of the Yanks'. After a fairly late supper, the rest of the evening was spent at the Ruhl Hotel where the floor show was the main attraction. Two 'very pretty blondes in long white dresses' came out and did the 'Blue Danube' in ballet style – 'and could they dance!'

A programme of forthcoming attractions in Nice and Cannes was provided in *Stars and Stripes*: at the Olympia Theatre at 67 Rue d'Antibes in Cannes, Ginger Rogers was starring in *Weekend at the Waldorf* and at the Forum Theatre, at 45 Promenade des Anglais, Lee Tracy was starring in *I'll Tell the World* – admission free for armed forces only. Americans who happened to be in Nice on their Independence Day – 4 July – could wallow in nostalgia watching the fireworks display in front of the Negresco Hotel. It so happened that VJ Day – Victory over Japan – and the first anniversary of the invasion of Provence fell on the same day: 15 August 1945. It was an occasion for both wild celebration and quiet contemplation.

Comedy with an American flavour was sadly lacking in France, but in the summer of 1945, Bob Hope did a show on a lit-up platform on a soccer field in Nice. The much-loved Maurice Chevalier was in the audience, and Bob Hope called him up on stage to do a song – against the advice of his staff. Chevalier was under a cloud since it was reported that he had toured Germany in 1941. He claimed to have only given one concert at a PoW camp – as did Edith Piaf in 1943. Chevalier was eternally grateful to Bob Hope for bringing him back into the limelight. That night he sang his 1929 English hit song, 'Louise'.[20]

By September 1945, there were thirty-nine orchestras in the USRRA ranging from three- to ten-piece outfits as well as an all-girl orchestra. By Broadway standards they were judged to be fourth and fifth rate. One jaded customer described these tea-dances as 'two hours of tea, lousy doughnuts, and dancing to an army band' but some of the open-air venues were spectacular. During the glorious summer of 1945, pavement cafés sprung up everywhere. Moving images show a swing band playing aboard a sunset cruise to Villefranche-sur-Mer where, for a while, there was even a floating dance hall. Jazz connoisseurs were critical of the local French musicians who played American music in a 'weird half-jump tempo to which it is all but impossible to dance' but also noticed that GIs 'don't mind it a bit'. [21]

Looking back on a momentous year in the European Theater of Operations (ETO), *Stars and Stripes* pronounced 1944 as 'possibly the greatest twelve months in history'. Highlights were said to be the liberation of Paris, as well as Dinah Shore and Marlene Dietrich visiting the continent. It was also in *Stars and Stripes* of 27 December 1944 where it was reported that Glenn Miller's plane had been missing since

15 December. It had mysteriously disappeared over the English Channel on a flight from London to Paris. No other members of his forty-five-piece Army Air Force Band was on board. On 25 April 1945, the musicians flew from Orly airport to Nice aboard three C-47s. Accommodation was provided for them at the world-renowned Martinez and Carlton hotels in Cannes. On the *terrasse* of the nearby Hôtel Miramar, some lucky officers and their partners had the rare privilage of dancing to the sounds of the world's greatest swing band. Before returning to Paris on 6 May, the Glenn Miller Orchestra held two concerts a day for other ranks at the Red Cross Casino Club in Nice.[22]

The 9 July 1945 cover of *Life* sported a picture of a curvy model wearing a zebra-striped two-piece suim suit. Inside was a history of bathing suit fashions from 1905 to 1945. Following the same theme was a photo spread under the sub-title 'American boy meets French girl at famed prewar resort now a US recreation area'. A good-looking infantryman, Sergeant Jimmy Stewart – no relation to the film star – was photographed with a local beauty named Josette Chanzal in a romantic pose on the Colline du Château overlooking Nice, tanning on the beach at Juan-les-Pins, strolling on the Promenade des Anglais, and sipping a drink at the Hacienda nightclub. When the magazine appeared on the newsstands in his hometown there was much speculation among Jimmy's family and friends. Two years later, when *Life* learned that Josette had been crowned the 1947 Nice Carnival Queen, the photojournalist decided to do a follow-up. In a piece entitled 'What became of Jimmy?' it was revealed that he had gone back to his decidedly plain prewar sweetheart in Morrilton, Arkansas, where he was running his own insurance company.[23]

Chapter 20

Monotony

Because of political infighting and the dire shortage of food, it took a long time for law and order to return to the cities of the south. Food riots loomed and the black market was rampant. While the war persisted, fishing was still restricted, especially night fishing, due to the danger of enemy attack. Only in mid-1945 did the supply of fruit, vegetables and meat improve. Children in particular, were undernourished and lacking milk. Citizens of Nice felt particularly hard done by, accusing Marseille of keeping the lion's share. The Var was slightly better off for a change. German stores were found at Sainte-Maxime and Draguignan and boatloads of flour, sugar and other staples started arriving in Saint-Tropez just two weeks after D-Day. Despite German efforts to destroy them, the three major ports of Toulon, Marseille and Nice were open for business within three weeks of their liberation.

Distribution would prove to be a problem however, because of the lack of road and rail transport. Some stockpiles in Toulon were impregnated with diesel oil, and in Saint-Raphaël, broken bags spilled flour over the dirty, wet floors but it was salvaged anyway. Private companies were contracted to move supplies, and once again it was a challenge to keep these supplies from getting into the hands of the black market. American soldiers hawked army rations, clothing and equipment out of the back of trucks and were involved in cross-border smuggling of olive oil.

As was the case in Italy and elsewhere, the theft of army supplies and equipment was rife. Motor pools had to be closely guarded to prevent batteries, tyres and even whole vehicles from being stolen. The culprits could be anything from naughty French children to criminal syndicates of servicemen. A report revealed that as of 25 November 1945, a total of 2,345 people were arrested for pilfering army property in the Marseille area. It was usually the small-time thieves who were sentenced while connected operators openly sold shiploads of looted goods. A sign in a shop window read 'If you don't see the overseas article you're looking for, just ask us and we'll get it.' Another advertised, 'You can march to kingdom come in these beautiful imported boots.'

For the purposes of supplying the armies to the north, a depot called the Continental Advance Section was established in Marseille. This den of iniquity now became an important headquarters, and a hive of activity, especially around the port and the Saint-Charles railway station where daredevils drove their Jeeps down the monumental steps. Some of the less-salubrious areas were off-limits to American troops. Compared to Marseille, Nice was a GI paradise, which is what it came to be named.

The food shortage was a bone of contention for everyone during the weeks and months following the liberation. When a French baker refused to sell a loaf of bread to a soldier because he could not produce a ration card, the American was irate: 'Some gratitude,' he wrote, 'we should have left the Germans there,' Nonetheless, he could not help feeling sorry for the poor housewives who stood in line hoping to get a loaf before it was all gone.

Officers who went to the Hôtel Negresco in the early post-liberation days handed over their army rations to be prepared and served to them on silver platters. As long as it tasted good, one did not ask a restaurateur what it was that you had just eaten. Between the fish soup or rabbit hors d'oeuvres and the dessert of cognac-soaked cherries, there might well have been some horsemeat camouflaged within the plat du jour.

In some ways, Marseille is quintessential Provence. Here, the *bouillabaisse* and southern accents are the thickest, and pastis is the beverage of choice. In a letter to Anaïs Nin on 22 June 1933, Henry Miller suggested that they did not meet up in Marseille, describing it as 'a dirty thieves' den, full of bums, full of misery, full of wind. It has a semi-Provincial air, too. There is only the port, and that's for men – a place to knock around in'.[1]

Described in a serviceman's news sheet, *The Delta Stage*, as the 'crossroads of the world with over one million people', Marseille both attracts and repels. An amateur correspondent tried to capture the essence of the city: 'It takes all kinds of people to make the world, and a cosmopolitan city like Marseille is a little world in itself. Here live representatives of virtually every race, colour, creed and nationality, ranging from the scum to the apex. The choice of association rests largely with the individual – and it is a known fact that water tends to seek its own level.' These were the same stinking alleys which had assaulted the nostrils of the German occupier and allowed the Resistance to flourish:

> Marseille is a unique city, only a few hours in it will take a big place in the scrap book of memories. Unforgettable for GI noses is the town's conglomerate smell, that of garlic, salt air, sidewalk stall latrines, fish, sewerage running in gutters, and perfumes, all combined with traditional city odors … Le Vieux Port with its narrow twisting streets and dingy houses shelters honest fishermen, prostitutes, white slave traders, pimps, gunmen, dope peddlers, and internationally-hunted criminals. [2]

Through the ages, visitors to Marseille have strolled along the Corniche Longchamp and climbed up to Notre-Dame-de-la-Garde. An extra attraction in 1945 was the wreckage of the German harbour defences. 'Off-limits' signs proliferated around the port, and MPs patrolled the side streets to save the GIs from being lured by streetwalkers. For the more cultured there was the opera, but the most popular venues were the Times Square Club, where Coca-Cola was free, and the two bars, the Pink Elephant and the Green Elephant, where a bottle of American 3.2 per cent-alcohol beer cost three to five francs.

For those small purchases at the PX – Post Exchange – stores at Camp Calas, one could use coupons known as Calas francs, and the exchange rate was favourable. A man who spent two long months at Camp Victoret, adjoining present-day Marignane International Airport, complained that he was bored because he was always broke. It was pointless going into Marseille if one had no money to spend on one's vices.

Although the public relations people liked to say that there was almost nothing for a man to spend his money on in the USRRA, since almost everything was free, soldiers habitually wrote home despairing of their lack of funds, and the high cost of everything. The locals had many ways and means to separate the soldier-tourist from his hard-earned pay. When Al McCarthy went from Delta Base into Nice for a spot of R&R, he planned to have two rolls of film developed. From the negatives he would have some snapshots printed and maybe some enlargements made. The problem, he said, was that 'the damn French want beaucoup many francs for each print, because they overcharge us for everything.'[3]

MONOTONY

Whenever the opportunity arose, soldiers endeavoured to send photographs to their loved ones. In Marseille, outside the Red Cross Club on La Canebière, street photographers would 'snap your picture as you walked by'. They would give you a ticket and then you could go back the next week and pick up a copy of the photograph. Cameras, films and exposed prints were not allowed to be carried into a battle zone, and films could only be processed by commercial photo-finishers who had been investigated and approved by the US Army. It was forbidden to send undeveloped film out of France, and prints being sent in the mail were subject to censorship.

Without money, one could not even participate in the games of dice that went on at all hours of the day and night in the transit camps, but anyone could play pinochle, a popular non-betting card game at the time – especially in France. Frenchmen were fascinated by the game of Horseshoes which they construed as a 'sort of pétanque played without boules'. The other favourite pastime was listening to the 'local talent', usually some southerner from Texas or Georgia who played the guitar and sang Hillbilly or Western tunes. These distractions did break the monotony of life and the long days of inactivity, but one got tired of 'I'm Walking the Floor Over You' and 'Down Yonder' after hearing them a thousand times.

In the sweltering summer of 1945, while waiting for shipping to become available, life was a dull routine of sweating the discharge announcements, counting points, rumours of being sent to fight the Japanese, preparing for kit inspection, listening to music, odd trips to Marseille, looking forward to PX rations of peanuts and beer. Feeling like caged animals, men got lazy, both mentally and physically, joking that they would have to build their own boats.

Homesickness was a condition so all-encompassing that it can be considered the one experience which united all soldiers away from home. Whether they were on the front line or in some base camp, homesickness pervaded their entire existence. One might well ask why it is that these men were not happy living it up in postwar Europe, with the spoils of victory so freely available. An anonymous poet ponders the same question in a poem called 'In Exile'. The first of seven verses asks:

> *Oh tell me why I always long for home,*
> *Why not satisfied that I can so freely roam.*
> *What is it that calls me, and will not let me be,*
> *That saddens me – that maddens me – in this land across the sea.*

A points system was used to determine who went home first. Every GI was in possession of a 'credit card' or service record; points were allocated for the number of days in combat, medals and awards, and family commitments. One had to have a total of ninety points to qualify for a discharge. The less fortunate were in line for transfer to the Pacific theatre of war. Much of their time was spent in training or standing in line to receive inoculations against typhoid, dengue and other jungle diseases. Once Japan had surrendered, even seventy-pointers were sent home.

It was tempting to apply for a transfer to join the occupation troops in Austria and Germany where enlisted men were rumoured to live in hotels. Many of these jobs went to those newly arrived in the ETO, who knew nothing of the struggle to stay alive, and were scorned by both veterans and civilians. Even if one's posting meant staying until the end of the Nuremberg War Crimes Trials in late 1946, it was preferable to being in the Dust Bowl of Delta Base for any length of time. Although fraternization with German girls was discouraged, if not forbidden, one was always on the lookout for a 'piece of frat'. Women outnumbered the men and would 'do anything' for cigarettes or silk stockings but American occupation troops remarked that German girls looked fresher and more wholesome than the French girls: they wore less makeup.

The magnitude of the American-built staging area in the Rhône delta beggars description. Soldiers awaiting repatriation or redeployment to the Pacific theatre were housed in sprawling camps within the triangle formed by Marseille and Aix-en-Provence in the east, and Arles which is a hundred kilometres to the west. There were in fact three main staging areas: Calas, Saint-Victoret and Arles – collectively known as Delta Base Section (DBS). This conglomeration of camps encompassed numerous towns and villages, including the communes of Calas, Cabriès, Vitrolles, Miramas and Rognac which is to the north of the present-day Marignane airport. Depending on which town was the nearest, the camps were known as Camp Calas, Camp Victoret and so on. With military exactitude, the camps were divided into sections and blocks designated battalion, regimental and divisional areas. Camp Calas by itself occupied a rectangular tract of land, one and a half kilometres wide and fourteen kilometres long.

Depots and annexes were scattered over a wide area, right up to the Vieux-Port of Marseille. These included a vehicle park at Vitrolles, a sports stadium in the Quartier du Griffon, a military hospital and cemetery near Luynes, and various fuel and ordnance depots. The tentacles of DBS reached as far as Lyon. When a competition was held to find a name for a news sheet in the staging area, someone came up with the name 'Caviar' which was a combination of the first two letters in Calas, Victoret and Arles. Other suggestions included 'Dust Bowler', 'Mess Kit', Carrier Pigeon', and 'Jungle Fever'. Ultimately, the paper came to be called *The Delta Stage*.

Rognac and Miramas are situated on the banks of Lake Berre where one could play volleyball on the sandy beaches. This area was used primarily for storing of equipment and supplies and would be the first to close once everything had been packed for reshipment to the East. The final crating-up was done at the Vieux-Port where the clatter of hammers could be heard day and night as wooden crates were built around the odd-shaped apparatus of war. German prisoners doing the crating work were skilled carpenters and lived in a camp on the site of the Jewish ghetto which had been demolished by the Nazis.

To estimate the total capacity of the staging area is like trying to hit a moving target, but may have reached 200,000 at its peak. This would have included the inmates of the Disciplinary Training Center plus the German PoW camp. The more commonly used figure of 100,000 probably refers only to American troops in transit. Saint-Victoret on its own had a capacity of 40,000, but Camp Calas was even bigger than that with 5,500 tents and 1,300 prefabricated buildings divided into ten compounds. Another 3,000 permanent structures were later erected. The tents had wooden floors and electricity but no beds. Every blade of grass had been removed and when the Mistral blew, no amount of water could dampen the dust, so a mixture of diesel and water was sprayed on the ground.

Bulldozers and excavators levelled the area, and at Camp Calas alone, the Americans constructed twenty-five kilometres of roads. Running down the centre of Camp Calas was a wide boulevard, always busy and requiring a pointsman at the main intersection. Apprehensive GIs en route to the Pacific called it 'The Great Tokyo Road'. The tent city had five theatres or cinemas, sports stadiums, chapels, libraries, numerous PX stores, seventeen clinics and a hospital, and even a dog pound for returning war dogs. Every day the three military post offices consigned a treasure trove of 75,000 items to the United States.

Besides the boredom and the dust, men griped most about the interminable queuing. More than a hundred mess tents and kitchens were strategically positioned throughout Camp Calas but one had to wait in long queues for food, and then eat standing up. Likewise, one had to queue for hours to have a cold shower in one of the sixty ablution blocks, hoping all the time that the water wouldn't run out first. There were twelve bars or beer gardens in Camp Calas but one had to stand in line for hours to get a luke-warm beer.[4]

Not surprisingly, the bars in Calas and other small villages within the staging area attracted GIs like moths to a flame. Whisky was their drink of choice, but it was virtually unheard-of in Provence. While in Normandy, some soldiers had developed an appreciation for cognac and Calvados, which made acceptable substitutes. Too much of this firewater, however, resulted in regular 'incidents' for which the military police had to be called in. According to witnesses, fighting between black and white Americans would erupt at the drop of a hat. Prostitutes, mostly from Marseille, were also attracted to the bars in satellite towns, knowing that there would be no shortage of clients. As with the canteens and the showers, men had to queue for their services.

The few young women who lived in Calas and other villages in the delta found themselves in great demand whenever there was a dance organized. One girl remembers being transported to the venue in the back of an army truck, and being *secoue comme des pruniers* – shaken like a plum tree – but laughing all the way. Sometimes a truckload of GIs would come to town to play football against the locals. Other little things which made a lasting impression on the local girls were discovering nylon products, powdered coffee and eating those 'funny cakes with a hole in the middle' which the boys loved so much. The GIs were said to be mostly well-behaved, but not as well-behaved as the German occupiers had been. One witness remembers that it was not safe for a girl to go out on the streets of Calas at night. Men would follow them, harass them, and undoubtedly there were cases of rape.

The job of maintaining morale was taken seriously by the military, civilians and celebrities alike. In outdoor theatres, soldiers were treated to films, concerts and United Service Organizations (USO) shows. Under the stars they watched such classics as *The Texans* and *Zorro Rides Again*. The biggest open-air theatre at Camp Calas was named in honor of the late Glen Miller, and another was baptized 'Marlene

Dietrich'. One theatre was named after General Leslie McNair who had been killed in Normandy by friendly fire on 25 July 1944. The most intimate venue was wistfully named 'Shangri-La' after a mythical and harmonious valley, isolated from the world.

Using the methods of the ancient Greeks, these amphitheatres were built into semi-circular valleys, making use of the natural contours. The seating capacity of each venue was supposedly five thousand. The camps had their own orchestras and troupes of actors, but when Bing Crosby, Marlene Dietrich or Micky Rooney played here, crowds of up to 17,000 spectators lined the slopes, finding rocks to sit on. Bob Hope and his 'radio pal' Jerry Colanna, played in all the main venues of the 'Dust Bowl'. Enjoying the success of her latest film, *The Miracle of Morgan's Creek*, released in 1944 and hit song of the same year, 'It Had To Be You,' Betty Hutton did a one-woman show at Calas. Edith Piaf, known as 'La Mome' or 'The Little Sparrow', was already the highest-paid entertainer in France and made an unforgettable appearance in one of the venues near Marseille:

> She walks forward to the footlights, so that they make her seem taller than she is. She seems to plant her feet on the stage, and sets her body much in the manner of an athlete who is about to perform a strong and difficult feat … With her voice, with her songs of unrequited love, of prostitutes, of dead soldiers, she may set the listener aflame … Only the nod of her head comes in response to the audience's adulation.[5]

One did not need to understand French to be mesmerized by Edith Piaf's voice. She famously said that she could move an audience to tears while singing the words from a telephone directory. Nevertheless, her most appreciative audience at the Delta Base would have been the 2,000 French troops being trained there. At one time there were more than 16,000 French civilians employed on the base, a number of young women among them. The romances which blossomed were mostly short-lived.

Although the homesick GI might not have considered it entertaining, the most popular film in Provence throughout the 1940s was Marcel Pagnol's 1932 production, *Marius*. The story is about a young man torn between his love for a girl and his longing to go to sea. It is centred around a family-run bar on the Marseille waterfront. The French loved it because it was a true reflection of their own lives. Pagnol was from Aubagne, and in his work he portrays the social rituals, accents and culture of Provençal life, in particular the lower classes.

Delta Base Section included a DTC as well as a special camp with a capacity of 3,000 for displaced persons, including rescued Allied military personnel and ex-prisoners of war. Since the start of the campaign, German prisoners had been held in a PoW cage around a small lake called Lac du Réaltor near Calas. But as the trickle turned into a flood, the Continental Central Prisoners of War Enclosure – CCPWE 404 – grew to become one of the biggest in Europe, with a capacity of 45,000 prisoners, although the actual numbers were lower.

On arrival, MPs stripped the prisoners of their filthy rags, deloused them and gave them American clothing to wear. They were then classified according to their skills, and assigned to appropriate services. When a delegation from the International Red Cross based in Geneva inspected the PoW camp, they found that prisoners were well fed, well clothed, and well cared-for by German doctors. There were separate compounds for

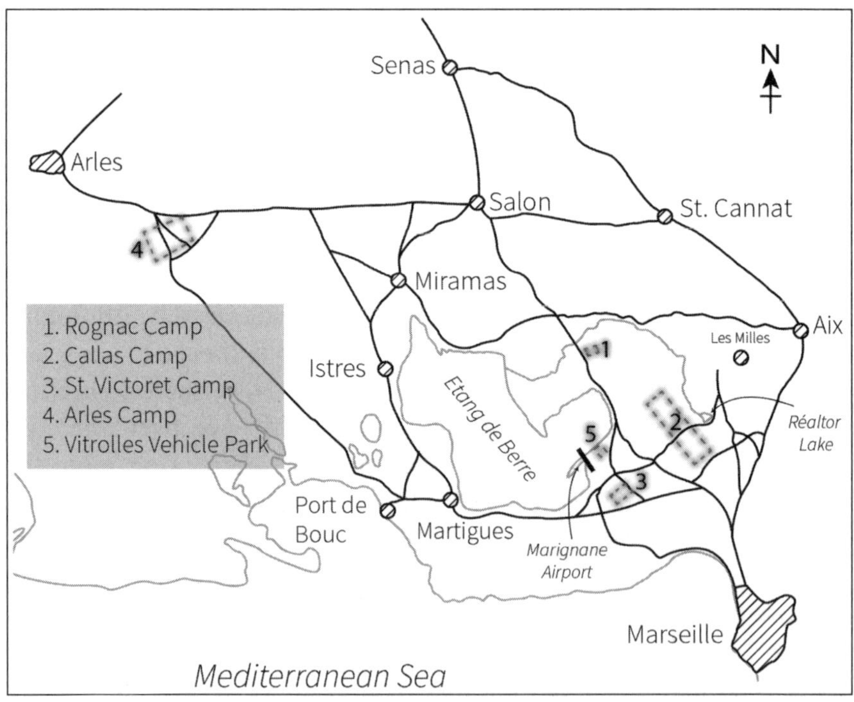

Transit camps of Delta Base Section.

Hungarians, Yugoslavians, Romanians, invalids, amputees and youths under 18, of whom there were more than a thousand. SS troops were under tighter security than the rest while they underwent interrogation to determine whether or not they were war criminals. *Lagerführers* – camp leaders – were elected to take charge of each of the twenty-five compounds and ensured that the running of the camp was exemplary. Even in the American section of Camp Calas, the kitchens were run by German prisoners, and the consensus was that the food was good.

Older men found it hard to sleep on the ground under canvas, especially when a mistral was blowing or when it rained. Nevertheless, they were happy to have survived the war and were well behaved. Life was more comfortable for those who lived and worked in the centre of Marseille. German prisoners worked six days a week and were paid a decent wage. In addition to crating up equipment at the port, they worked in kitchens making ice-cream and doughnuts. Bread was made in a central bakery in Nice and trucked down to DBS. After a truck full of mines, cleared from the Californie airport in Nice, exploded on 18 September 1944, killing five American engineers, German PoWs were used for mine-clearance in the blockhouses, pillboxes, tank traps and on the beaches. Some PoWs remained in France until 1948, working on farms and rebuilding the infrastructure.

German PoWs were treated better than the American inmates of the DTC who received no luxuries apart from eight packets of cigarettes a month and enough toiletries to keep clean. The DTC was a prison facility for US military personnel who had been convicted and sentenced by court martial to serve more than four months' confinement. Opened on 1 May 1945, the Delta Base Disciplinary Training Center was located on the airfield in what is now part of Les Milles industrial area on the outskirts of Aix-en-Provence. Covering almost twenty hectares, the site was surrounded by barbed wire and machine-gun towers.

There was little to distinguish the companies of prisoners from ordinary soldiers, apart from the liberal sprinkling of white-helmeted MPs among them. If a man successfully completed the rigorous retraining programme, he was allowed to return to active duty status. Incorrigible criminals who gave no indication that they were rehabilitation material would be evacuated to the United States to serve their terms in federal prisons. The so-called 'trainees' were drilled from dawn to dusk, with extra drill for any further violations of regulations. Depending on the seriousness of the infraction, trainees could be burdened with extra weight or sent to solitary confinement. Every evening on parade, the 'legions of the damned' lined up behind their white flags with black lettering, as the officers looked on. When the marching band commenced playing, the neighbours in the nearby village of Calas would say: '*Tiens, le bal est commence*' (Hello, the dance has begun).

Deserters and petty thieves were locked up alongside murderers and rapists facing the death penalty. A disproportionately large percentage of inmates were black, rear-echelon soldiers confined for committing civilian-type crimes such as theft and armed robbery. A total of 94 American military prisoners, in all theatres of war, were executed by hanging or firing squad under military authority for crimes committed during or shortly after the war. The overwhelming majority of executed soldiers were black, and the two shot by firing squad at Les Milles on Monday, 15 October 1945 were in fact African-American. Sidney Bennerman, from Wilmington North Carolina, murdered two people in France, and Woodrow Parker, born in Alabama, date of birth unknown, had murdered a Polish man and raped a Polish girl in Germany. The remains of these men were reinterred in Plot E of the Oise-Aisne American Cemetery in northern France. Plot E is a section specifically built to hold the 'dishonoured dead' as all had been dishonourably discharged from the US Army just prior to their execution. The area is separated from the main cemetery, hidden from view and is closed to casual visitors.

Happily, the vast majority of those millions who passed through Delta Base Section, stayed no longer than two or three weeks. Only those involved in the running of the camps were permanent residents. Among the last to return home was T/5 Harold Coons of the 66th 'Black Panther' Infantry Division which arrived in May 1945 to oversee the repatriation process and provide a security force for the Disciplinary Training Center. Coons was based at the Arles transit camp, appropriately called the 'Dust Bowl'. In many of his letters home, Coons mentioned the dust and the wind but it seems that on 20 September 1945, the mistral was blowing in full force:

> The surroundings and the winds are not conducive to writing. The only pleasant place is the sleeping bag, and though it's only 6 p.m., I feel like crawling in, covering my head, and going to sleep. This morning I placed my blankets inside the sleeping bag with the aid of the blanket pins and

should be considerably warmer tonight. I was getting a little ripe not being able to take a shower since leaving our chateau, and since we still have no shower facilities here in the Dust Bowl, I took what is known in army parlance as a 'whore's bath' by using my helmet. Anyway, I don't smell as much like a goat as I did.[6]

It may not be common knowledge that the financial empire which is now American Express had its beginnings as a banking facility for soldiers on R&R. The organization opened offices in Nice and Marseille, and was asked by the army to organize sight-seeing tours under the supervision of the Special and Information Services. Day excursions were made to Saint-Paul-de-Vence and Grasse which are still on the itinerary of almost every American tourist in this region. Clean and tidy Switzerland was a two-day road trip away from the war-ravaged South of France.

History lovers much enjoyed a tour to Nîmes and Pont du Garde with a guide who in his previous life had been a university lecturer in Roman History, and was now a GI. Situated at a crossroads between Italy and Spain, Arles was a 'little Rome', originally called Arelat. It might have occurred to some of the more cerebral soldiers that the Romans had used exactly the same flat terrain as a staging area for their operations in Gaul and northern Europe.

For the sake of keeping up morale, the Information and Education Section of the US Army sent deserving candidates on courses to further their education and develop skills. One could also apply to attend the Biarritz American University where 275 civilian and military instructors and professors taught 241 courses ranging from agronomy to Shakespeare.[7] Al McCarthy was sent to Nice to do a course in hotel management. Harold Coons was an attorney in civilian life and had the opportunity of doing a law course in Edinburgh, but took up a law-enforcement position in Paris instead. His account of the journey on an overnight train from Marseille to Paris will resonate with anyone who has undertaken the journey during a railway strike when services are reduced. The train had come from Nice and Cannes, and in a compartment for four, he found seven interesting travel companions:

On my right, next to the window was a Polish girl, a 2nd lieutenant, first on my left was a 2nd lieutenant, a dentist from Kentucky, and the last man was a PFC from Pittsburg who was oblivious to everything and slept like a log with his feet all over everyone else. Then reading from left to right across from me was an English 1st lieutenant, a French movie starlet by the name of Gerry Garland, a Pfc from Birmingham, and a Polish captain. The two Poles talked far into the night until he and I exchanged seats and she cuddled up against him. The movie gal, who looked like twenty-five last night and like thirty-five this morning, cuddled up with a lieutenant, and I cuddled up with my field jacket.[8]

As from the end of November 1945, the camps began to clear out. A GI's last day on French soil was spent completing the reams of paperwork and stuffing superfluous pieces of kit into bulging duffel bags. Space had to be found for one's war souvenirs among the blankets and sleeping bag plus a half tent complete with tent pole and pegs, first aid packet, army records, overshoes, overcoat, two sets of fatigues, sweater, and steel helmet. Then it was a short trip in the back of a 6x6 truck down to the docks where the 'Victory Ship' was waiting.

In his last letter from Nice, Al McCarthy wrote: 'How are you this morning? I love you and I wish we were able to get our lives on the same track, because I love you with every bit of me, and I will never be happy until I hold you in my arms and feel your tears of happiness running down your cheeks.'[9] Inevitably, those trained in the science of killing had changed as a result of habit, discipline and mass psychosis. The returning soldier was prone to profanity, chronic complaining, scepticism, irritability, brutality, disrespect and envy of civilians, loneliness, fatalism and hatred of monotony[10] The same system was, however, also likely to instil in a man many countervailing virtues like punctuality, neatness and respect for those who earned it.

When DBS emptied out in January 1946, there remained a mother-lode of surplus material and equipment which was auctioned off. Lines of Jeeps and trucks extended from horizon to horizon at the army ordnance depot near Vitrolles. The camps themselves were occupied by the French Army for a short while, before being abandoned and demolished by salvagers. Even now, the terrain yields rich pickings for souvenir hunters with metal detectors. One of the more interesting finds is a Saint Christopher medallion which is engraved on one side with the words, 'To Bill with love, Bob' and on the other side 'I am a catholic, call a priest'.[11]

After the Americans had packed up and left, the French would have to live with themselves. The years of suffering and sacrifice under foreign occupation cast a long shadow. People still struggle to come to terms with the painful past of split allegiances and empty stomachs which epitomize the dark years. Although the families of thoses wrongfully accused still campaign for justice, the subject of collaboration is taboo in polite circles.

Wanting to fit back into French society, the Jews preferred to accept the official narrative that it was the Germans who had persecuted them whereas in fact the Vichy regime had participated just as willingly. Everywhere in Provence, there are graves with markers proclaiming '*fusillies par les hordes Nazis*', '*assassiné par la Gestapo*' or by the '*barbares Nazis*'. The major role of the Milice and the Frenchmen serving with the Brandenburg Division in these atrocities is conveniently forgotten.

Ostensibly, the sins of the fathers have been forgiven, but collective guilt has ramifications for contemporary society. Once the savagery had dissipated, leaving the population of Europe exhausted, a culture of tolerance and pacifism would prevail. The bravest and the most patriotic had either died or had the spirit of nationalism extinguished within them. All and sundry were invited in to enjoy the fruits of peace and help rebuild, thereby sowing the seeds of future discord. Germany is now considered an ally, but the zeitgeist of the dark years still stalks the land.

French communists have been criticized for embellishing their role in the Resistance and exaggerating the extent to which their members were martyred. Because of the need to obscure reality, certain resistance myths have taken hold. Lacking documentary evidence, the Gaullists and communists of the Resistance immediately started writing their own myth-histories – on a blank slate. Small communes and individuals have also cleansed their past and developed their own narratives about their previous commitment to the struggle.

Contributing to the heroic but false narrative of self-liberation is de Gaulle's refusal to acknowledge the role of the SOE and the OSS. After the liberation of Paris, all foreign agents became *persona non grata* in France.[12] Captain Harry Despaigne observed: 'Even today when you visit the museums of the wartime Maquis and what have you, SOE is never mentioned. It is the French that have done it all.' Despaigne goes on to say that there could have been no resistance if they did not get their money, guns and ammunition from London, 'But France has forgotten that.'[13]

For a top-down perspective of the intelligence services and the Resistance, one can turn to Major André Dewavrin, better known as *Colonel Passy*. He was the head of the BCRA, de Gaulle's intelligence services in London. He once described the resistance in France as having 'an abundant desire to do well, brave thoughts and exalted imagination which translated into disorganized actions without real effectiveness'.[14] But the sacrifices cannot be denied; the legions of the dead don't lie. It has been said that in war 'there is only one incontrovertible "truth", that of the man in his final death agony. The stories of all other individuals are necessarily fractured'.[15]

Although the words *ne oublions jamais* – never forget – have been chipped into stone, some of those who suffered the most have had to remain silent for the sake of national reconciliation and cohesion, and did not cry out for revenge. A survivor of the Vercors killing fields expressed a yearning to live, live intensely, dance to the music of an accordion, and take a special interest in the Tour de France. Nature seemed more beautiful, the flowers more colourful, the songs of birds more harmonious. How does someone who was there explain to the *étranger* – meaning both stranger and foreigner – that one's destiny was arbitrary. The past is delicate in a French Provençal village, so perhaps it is best to let sleeping dogs lie.

Glossary of Terms and Abbreviations

Glossary

agent de liaison	liaison agent (usually female)
armés jusqu'aux dents	armed to the teeth
arrive qu'arrive	whatever happens happens
baiser	to kiss, shag
Boche	pejorative term for Germans
bonheur	happiness, joy
boucherie	butchery
boulangerie	bakery
boules	a game similar to bowls
brassard	armband
brouilleé	to be feuding
brouille	a quarrel
carrefour	intersection
chacun sa méthode	each to their own method
chaleur	heat
chansons	songs
charnier	mass grave
cheminots	railwaymen
chérie	darling (f)
chez le juifs	home of the Jews
chez nous	our home
citoyen d'honneur	citizen of honour
clocher	bell tower
cul	ass or arse (impolite)
débarquement	the landings or invasion (disembarkation)
demoiselle	unmarried woman
des jours meilleurs	better days
drôle	funny or strange

eau de vie	brandy
épuration légale	legal purge
épuration sauvage	wild purge
faux depart	false start
Feldgrau (German)	Field grey, the colour of the German uniform.
femmes de mauvaise vie	women of ill repute (prostitutes)
fête	celebration
flics	police (slang)
fréquentations	visitations
fusillé	shot or those who have been shot
gendarmes	police
gendermarie	police station
goutte de mercure	drop of mercury
gris-verts	grey-greens, nickname for German soldiers
interlocuteurs	interlocutors
je suis	I am
la dernière heure	the last hour (literally) or last minute
l'exode	the exodus
le chagrin et la pitié	the sorrow and the pity
Le Petit Chaperon Rouge	Little Red Riding Hood
libertine	a hedonist, a person of loose morals
lycée	high school
maillots de bain	bathing suit
malfaiteurs	criminals
ma petite maman chérie	my dearest mum
Maquis	group of resistance fighters
maquisard	resistance fighter
Marche ou crève	March or perish (motto of the French Foreign Legion)
mon tout petit frère adore	my beloved little brother
mon petit papa aimé	my beloved dad
Monegasque	people from Monaco
mot de passé	password
mort	dead
mort au combat	killed in action
Mentonnais	people from Menton
milice	militia

milicien	militiaman
ne pas subir	don't give up
Niçois	people from Nice
nom de guerre	pseudonym/code name
ouvrages	works
panier à salade	salad basket or Black Maria
partir	to leave
passant souviens-toi	passer-by, remember
passeur	smuggler or conductor (ferryman)
paysan	peasant
personnage important	very important person (VIP)
pied noir	French colonial (literally, black foot)
poche	pocket
poste de contrôle	command post
poupée	doll
préfecture	departmental government or the building which houses it
profonde	deep
pur et dur	through and through
putain	whore or general expletive
quand meme	all the same
rafle	raid or roundup
réfractaire	fugitive from compulsory work
relève	relief work
sanglier	wild boar
se débrouiller	to make do (to get by)
sizaine	group of six
soldat Allemand	German soldier
soldats de l'lombre	soldiers of the shadows
toubib	Doc (familiar for Doctor)
tourisme pédestre	touring on foot, hiking
traître	traitor
trentaine	group of thirty
vallon	valley
Varois	people from the Var
vendange	grape harvest
Viens douce mort	Come Sweet Death (song title)

French Abbreviations

AS	Armée Secrète
BCRA	Bureau Central Rensiegnements et d'Action
BCRAA	Bureau Central de Renseignements and d'Action Alger
CDL	Comité Départemental de Libération
CFLN	Comité Français de Libération Nationale
CLL	Comité local de Libération
CMR	Comité médical de la Résistance
CNR	Conseil Nationale de la Résistance
FFI	Forces Françaises de l'Intérieur
FFI	Forces Françaises de l'Intérieur
FFL	Forces Françaises Libres
FN	Front National
FTPF	Francs-Tireurs et Partisans Français
FTP	Francs-Tireurs et Partisans
LVF	Français Contre le Bolchévisme
MP	Milices Patriotiques
MUR	Mouvements Unis de Résistance
ORA	Organisation de la Résistance armée
PCF	Parti Communist Français
SAP	Section atterrissage et parachutage (Landing and Parachuting Section)
STO	Service du travail obligatoire

Italian Abbreviations

OVRA	Organizzazione per la Vigilanza e la Repressione dell'Antifascismo

German Abbreviations

GFP	Geheime Feldpolizei
SD	Sicherheitsdiens
SiPo	Sicherheitspolizei

SiPo-SD	Sicherheitspolizei-Sicherheitsdiens
SS	Schutzstaffel

English Abbreviations

AFHQ	Allied Forces Headquarters (Mediterranean Theatre)
CP	command post
DBS	Delta Base Section
DTC	Disciplinary Training Center
ETO	European Theater of Operations
FABTF	1st Airborne Task Force
FSSF	1st Special Service Force
GI	slang for American soldier (der. General Issue)
IS	British Intelligence Service
IAM	Inter-Allied Mission
MAAF	Mediterranean Allied Air Force
MI5	Military Intelligence Section 5, UK's domestic intelligence agency (Security Service)
MI6	Military Intelligence Section 6, UK's foreign intelligence agency (Secret Intelligence Service)
MI9	Military Intelligence Section 9, UK's intelligence agency for escape routes and evasions (War Office)
MTO	Mediterranean Theater of Operations
OG	Operational Group
OSS	Office of Strategic Services
OSS/SO	Office of Strategic Services/ Special Operations
PIB	Parachute Infantry Battalion
PIR	Parachute Infantry Regiment
PoW	prisoner of war
PX	Post Exchange (retail store operating on US military bases)
RAF	Royal Air Force
SAS	Special Air Service

SHAEF	Supreme Headquarters Allied Expeditionary Forces
SIS	Secret Intelligence Service (British)
SO	special operations branch of the OSS
SOE	Special Operations Executive
SPOC	Special Projects Operations
USAAF	United States Army Air Forces
USMC	United States Marine Corps
USO	United Service Organizations
WAC	Women's Army Corps

Timeline of Events

1939

3 September   Britain and France declare war on Germany.

1940

10 June   Italy declares war on Britain.
18 June   Charles de Gaulle's call to arms (*L'Appel du 18 juin*).
22 June   France signs armistice with Germany and Italy invades France.
24 June   France signs armistice with Italy.
28 June   Britian recognizes de Gaulle as leader of Free French.
10 July   Vichy regime established.

1941

21 April   Peter Churchill enters Antibes by submarine on first mission.
25 April   Albert Guérisse becomes 'Pat O'Leary' on landing in southern France.
29 August   Varian Fry given 2 hours to pack his belongings and leave France.
20 September   SOE F-Section agent Francis Basin lands in Perpignan.
7 December   Japan attacks Pearl Harbor.
8 December   Allies declare war on Japan.

1942

1 January   Jean Moulin parachutes into the Alpilles Mountains, near Eygalières.

30 July	Harry Despaigne, Henri Frager, Nicholas Bodington land at Antibes.
28 August	Peter Churchill arrives to take charge of URCHIN and establishes SPINDLE.
23 October	Allied victory at the Battle of El Alamein; turning point in the war.
2/3 November	SOE operative Odette Sansom (*Lise*) lands on a beach near Cassis.
8 November	Operation Torch (Anglo-American invasion of French North Africa).
8 November	Germans occupy Marseille.
10 November	Germans invest the *zone libre* and Italians expand their presence.
27 November	Scuttling of the French fleet in Toulon.

1943

22–24 January	Roundup of Jews in Marseille and Nice.
6 February	Fred Brown, the first OSS operative in the Var, lands at La Roche Escudelier on the submarine *Casabianca*.
24 March	Francis Cammaerts (*Roger*) arrives at Compiègne by Lysander.
16 April	Peter Churchill and Odette Sansom arrested at Saint-Jorioz, Haute-Savoie.
23 April	SOE agents Ted Coppin and Yvonne Experton arrested in Marseille.
14/15 May	SOE agent Sidney Jones infiltrates by Lysander on second mission.
27 May	Jean Moulin forms the Conseil National de la Résistance (CNR).
31 May	Berty Albrecht hangs herself in Fresnes Prison, Paris.
8 July	Jean Moulin dies in captivity after interrogation by Klaus Barbie.
8 September	Italy capitulates and Italian occupation of Provence ends.
15 September	Cammaerts courier Cecily Lefort arrested by Gestapo in Montélimar.

1944

2 January	9 *maquisards*, 1 civilian killed in firefight at Limate Farm near Signes.
21 February	Operation against the Maquis begins at Sèderon.
22 February	35 maquisards arrested at Izon-la-Bruisse executed in Eygalayes.
29 February	Henri Frager arrives back in France to head DONKEYMAN circuit.
23 March	SOE Captain Charles Skepper arrested in Marseille.
29 March	Jacques and Charlotte de Prévaux arrested near Le Lavandou.
15 April	Peter Churchill parachutes in at Saint-Jorioz near Lake Annecy.
29 April	Nancy Wake and Major John Farmer parachute into the Auvergne.
27 May	3,012 French civilians killed by Anglo-American bombs.
4 June	American Fifth Army enters Rome.
6 June	D-Day: Normandy landings (Operation Overlord).
7–9 June	Premature risings in Valréas, Vaison, Barcelonette, Aups and elsewhere.
10 June	Massacre by Waffen-SS of 642 people at Oradour-sur-Glane in the Limousin.
10 June	Uprising at Vaison-la-Romain crushed, approximately 20 dead.
12 June	Germans rampage through Valréas and execute approximately 53.
12 June	62 *maquisards* killed on the Plateau of Manivert, Roque-d'Anthéron.
12 June	All Normandy beachheads linked up.
13 June	28 resistants executed on a farm near Lambesc and Roque-d'Anthéron.
13 June	SOE Major Alistair Hay killed in action near Barcelonette.
13/14 June	Muthular d'Errecalde (*Lucas*), joins Mission MICHEL near Cucuron.
13/14 June	Counterscorch team SAMPAN drops near Cucuron, Vaucluse.

16 June	15 *maquisards* massacred at Saint-Martin-de-Bromes.
17 June	8 *maquisards* shot after arrest at Roboeuf farm on the Siou Blanc Plateau.
24 June	Jedburgh Team DODGE led by Cyrius E. Manierre dropped in Isère.
25 June	Weapons drop of 420 containers on the Vercors Plateau.
28 June	IAM EUCALYPTUS led by Major D. Longe parachutes in at Vassieux-en-Vercors.
29 June	OG JUSTINE parachutes in at Vassieux en Vercors.
29 June	Jedburgh Team CHLOROFORM drops into the Drôme.
2 July	Henri Frager arrested by Feldwebel Hugo Bleicher.
6/7 July	Mission PAQUEBOT and Christine Granville parachute onto Vercors Plateau.
7 July	Séraphin Torrin and Ange Grassi hanged at Place Masséna in Nice.
9 July	10 Maquis recruits shot near Saint-Julien-du-Verdon.
12 July	Epic aerial battle over Provence, four B-24 Liberators shot down.
14 July	Second large weapons drop on Vercors Plateau and start of German assault.
15 July	Henri Chanay of Mission MICHEL arrested by Gestapo in Marseille.
16 July	Mass arrest of resistance leaders in Oraison.
17 July	SOE-RF/BCRA Mission CAIQUE at DZ *Armature*, Vaucluse.
18 July	Major John Goldsmith drops at DZ *Armature*, Lagarde d'Apt, Vaucluse.
18 July	Second Signes massacre, 29 captives shot near Mont Sainte-Baume.
19–23 July	Fighting on Vercors Plateau, Haute-Savoie, 640 resistants killed.
22 July	12 *maquisards* and civilians killed at Aups and Canjuers Plains.
24 July	Arrest of François Pelletier and Muthular d'Errecalde in Saint-Tropez.
27 July	8 members of Battaglia detachment killed near Salernes in Moyen-Var.
27 July	10 hostages held at Brignoles prison are arbitrarily shot.

TIMELINE OF EVENTS

31 July	Antoine Saint-Exupéry disappears on reconnaissance flight.
31 July/ 1 August	Two 15-man sticks of 1er Bataillon de Choc parachute into Drôme.
1 August	Major Peter Ortiz arrives at Les Saisies with SO Mission UNION II.
3 August	IAM TOPLINK, drops at Seyne-les-Alpes, DZ *Assurance*, Alpes-de-Haute-Provence.
3/4 August	OG RUTH parachutes in at La Roque Esclapon near Brovès.
4 August	Softening-up operation begins, and continues until Dragoon D-Day.
6 August	Jedburgh Team NOVOCAINE lands at DZ *Assurance*, Seyne-les-Alpes.
8 August	Ambush carried out by the Maquis Ventoux at Montbrun-les-Bains.
9 August	IAM TOPLINK with Xan Fielding and Julian Lezzard arrives at DZ *Assurance*.
10 August	Flight Lieutenant Rostron lands at LZ *Spitfire*, Saint-Christol, Vaucluse.
10/11 August	Counterscorch Mission GÉDÉON (Jean Ayral) at DZ *Fantome*, Brignoles.
10/11 August	Mission LOUGRE with M. T. Jones and Allain arrives at DZ *Prisonnier*.
11 August	19 *maquisards* killed or executed at Sainte-Croix-du-Verdon.
12 August	Pelletier and d'Errecalde among 9 prisoners executed at Signes.
12 August	Jedburgh Team EPHEDRINE (Lawrence Swank) arrives at DZ *Assurance*.
12 August	IAM UNION III (majors Green and Hunter) at DZ *Assurance*.
12/13 August	OG NANCY lands at DZ *Armature*, La Garde d'Apt, Vaucluse.
13 August	Francis Cammaerts and two other SOE agents arrested by Gestapo.
12/13 August	Jedburgh Team CITROËN lands at La Garde d'Apt, DZ *Armature*.

13/14 August	Jedburgh Team CINNAMON to DZ *Fantome*, Brue-Auriac, Brignolles.
13/14 August	Jedburgh Team SCEPTRE to DZ *Prisonnier*, Montagne du Malay.
14/15 August	Airborne invasion of Provence (Operation Rugby) FABTF.
15 August	Amphibious landings of Operation Dragoon.
15 August	Murder of 8 prisoners by Gestapo at Villa Montfluery in Cannes.
15 August	Murder of Hélène Vagliano and 22 others in the Ariane district of Nice.
16 August	Premature Maquis uprisings in Levens, Saint-Martin and Plan-du-Var.
16 August	Allies and FFI meet up in Draguignan at 10.30 p.m.
17 August	Le Lavandou liberated by the US 3rd Infantry Division and Commandos d'Afrique.
17 August	Salernes and Lorgues liberated.
18 August	All Operation Dragoon objectives achieved.
19 August	Jacques and Charlotte de Prévaux plus 20 others murdered near Lyon.
19/20 August	FFI liberates Gap with the help of one American tank crew.
20 August	Pertuis is liberated.
20 August	120 political prisoners murdered by the Gestapo near Lyon.
21 August	Village of Gordes suffers reprisals.
21 August	Fayence captured by the 517th PIR.
21 August	First French troops enter outskirts of Toulon; Jean Ayral of GÉDÉON killed.
22 August	Germans evacuate Grenoble.
22 August	11th Panzer Division ambushed by FFI near Saint-Jean-de-Sault.
22 August	Romans-sur-Isère in the Drôme is liberated for the first time.
23 August	Briançon is liberated for the first time.
24 August	Liberation of Cannes, Antibes and Grasse.
24–26 August	Reprisals and attacks at Levens and La-Roquette-sur-Var.
25 August	Paris is liberated.

28 August	Nice, Toulon and Marseille liberated.
28 August	Montélimar in the Drôme is liberated.
30 August	Second liberation of Romans-sur-Isère in the Drôme Department.
3 September	Lyon is liberated; Americans enter Monte Carlo.
4 September	Battle of Col-de-Braus begins.
6 September	Briançon liberated for the second time.
17 September	Operation Market Garden (battle of Arnhem) begins.
10 September	Liberation of Dijon.
23 September	10 political prisoners executed by the FTP at Fort Carré in Antibes.
5 October	Henri Frager executed in Buchenwald concentration camp.
27 October	Americans enter Sospel.
16 November	1st Airborne Task Force replaced by 442nd (Nisei) Infantry Regiment.
23 November	Liberation of Strasbourg.
25 November	Explosion at Château de la Simone near Pertuis kills 31 *maquisards*.
6/7 December	517th PIR entrains at Antibes for journey north.
15 December	Glen Miller's plane goes missing.
16 December	German Ardennes offensive (battle of the Bulge) begins.
27 December	General Patton relieves Bastogne.
31 December	Germans launch Operation Nordwind in Alsace and Lorraine.

1945

25 January	Audie Murphy wins the Medal of Honor.
6 March	Collapse of Colmar Pocket.
9 April	General de Gaulle visits Nice.
10 April	Battle of Authion begins.
28 April	Mussolini captured and killed by partisans.
29 April	Liberation of Dachau concentration camp.
30 April	Hitler commits suicide in chancellery bunker.
7 May	General Alfred Jodl signs unconditional surrender.
8 May	Churchill and Truman proclaim VE Day.
9 May	German surrender ratified in Berlin.

Sources

Archives

Archives départementales des Alpes-de-Haute-Provence, Lettre du milicien Maurice Giannardi à son épouse, Paris, 15 août 1944 (43 W 207).

Archives départementales des Alpes-de-Haute-Provence, Rapport du gendarme Boyer commandant provisoirement la brigade de gendarmerie d'Oraison, 17 juillet 1944 (42 W 105).

Archives départementales du Var – Draguignan, Cote / n° inventaire, 132 PRS 1 23/8/1944, Journal clandestin, *La lutte patriotique*, Organe officiel de la section de Draguignan du Parti Communiste Français.

Archives départementales du Var, Draguignan, 1 W 79, Tract de la Résistance rédigé par les Mouvements Unis de la Résistance (M.U.R) issu du fonds de la préfecture du Var.

Archives départementales du Var, Draguignan, 1 W 80, Correspondance du directeur de la police de Toulon au préfet du Var reproduisant le texte d'un tract, 2 May 1943.

Archives Municipales de Cavaillon, Cavaillon 1944, de L'ombre a la Liberté, 24 août 2015.

Archives nationales, 72 AJ 104, le Kommandeur de la *SIPO* et du *SD* de Marseille, Rapport final Affaire Catilina, Marseille, 6 juillet 1944, signé Dunker, *SS Scharführer*.

Imperial War Museum, Boiteux-Burdett, Robert René, IWM Oral History, Catalogue number 9851.

Imperial War Museum, Cammaerts, Francis Charles Albert, IWM Oral History, Catalogue number 33036.

L'Établissement de communication et de production audiovisuelle de la Défense (ECPAD).

Liddell Hart Military Archives, Kings College London, O'Regan, Capt Patrick Valentine William Rowan (1920-1961), GB0099 KCLMA O'Regan.

SOURCES

Literature

517th Parachute Regimental Combat Team, Turner Publishing Co., Kentucky, 1998.

Arnaud, C., (Translated by L. Elkin & C. Mandell), *Jean Cocteau: A Life*, Yale University Press, London, 2016.

Atkinson, R., *The Guns at Last Light: The War in Western Europe, 1944–1945*, Henry Holt & Co., New York, 2013.

Aubrac, L., Konrad, B., & Wing, B. (trans.), *Outwitting the Gestapo*, Lincoln: University of Nebraska Press, 1994.

Aubrac, R., & Aubrac, L., *The French Résistance: 1940–1944*, Paris: Hazan Editeur, 1997.

Bailey, R., *Forgotten Voices of the Secret War: An Inside History of Special Operations during the Second World War*, Edbury Publishing, 2008.

Beavan, C., *Operation Jedburgh: D-Day and America's First Shadow War,* Penguin, London, 2006.

Benstock, S., *Women of the Left Bank: Paris, 1900–1940,* University of Texas Press, Austin, 1986.

Bernstein, J., *P-47 Thunderbolt Units of the Twelfth Air Force*, Osprey Publishing, Oxford, 2012.

Binney, M., *The Women who Lived for Danger: The Women Agents of the SOE in the Second World War*, Hodder & Stoughton, London, 2002.

Bishop, C., *SS Hitler's Foreign Divisions: Foreign Volunteers in the Waffen-SS 1940–45*, Amber Books, United Kingdom, 2005.

Blandford, E. *Green Devils – Red Devils: Untold Tales of the Airborne in the Second World War*, Leo Cooper, London, 1993.

Bleicher, H. E., *Colonel Henri's Story: The War Memoirs of Hugo Bleicher, Former German Secret Agent*, William Kimber, 1954.

Bourhill, J. F., *Come Back to Portofino: Through Italy With the 6th South African Armoured Division*, 30° South Publishers, Johannesburg, 2011.

Bourke, J., *An Intimate History of Killing*, Granta Books, London, 2000.

Bourne-Patterson, R., *SOE in France 1941–1945: An Official Account of the Special Operations Executive's 'British' Circuits in France*, Pen & Sword, Barnsley, 2016.

Brome, V., *The Way Back: The Story of Pat O'Leary, GC, DSO, RN, Croix de Guerre (Belgian & French)*, Cassel & Co. Ltd., London, 1957.

Broumley, J. T., *The Boldest Plan is the Best*, Rockey Marsh Publishing, 2011.

Bryant, C. D., *Khaki-collar Crime: Deviant Behaviour in the Military Context*, The Free Press, London, 1979.

Burrin, P., *Living with Defeat: France Under the German Occupation, 1940–1944*, New York, 1977.

Carles, E., *A Wild Herb Soup: The Life of a French Countrywoman*, Orion Books Ltd., London, 1996.

Carré, M-L., *J'ai été la Chatte*, Morgan, 1959.

Caver, J., Ennels, J. A., & Haulman, D. L., *The Tuskegee Airmen: An Illustrated History, 1939–1949*, Newsouth Books, Louisville, 2011.

Chalou, G.C. (Ed.), *The Secrets War: The Office of Strategic Services in World War II*, National Archives and Records Administration, Washington DC, 2002.

Churchill, P., *All About the French Riviera*, Vista Books, London, 1960.

___________., *Duel of Wits*, Hodder & Stoughton, London, 1953.

___________., *The Spirit in the Cage*, Hodder & Stoughton, London, 1954.

Clarke, J. J. & Smith, R. R., *From the Riviera to the Rhine: United States Army in World War II, European Theater of Operations*, Centre of Military History, United States Army, Washington DC, 1993.

Coons, P. M., *Letters Home: From a World War II 'Black Panther' Artilleryman*, iUniverse Books, Bloomington, 2012.

Cooper, A. & Beevor, A., *Paris After the Liberation: 1944–1949*, Penguin Books, 2007.

Costello, J., *Love, Sex and War: Changing Values*, Collins, London, 1985.

Cottingham, P. L., *Once Upon a Wartime: A Canadian Who Survived the Devil's Brigade*, Privately published, 1996.

Crwys-Williams, J., *Mood of a Nation: A Country at War 1939–1945*, Ashanti Publishing, Rivonia, 1992.

Danby, J., *Day of the Panzer: A Story of American Heroism and Sacrifice in Southern France*, Casemate, Drexel Hill PA, 2006.

Danielson, A.G., *A Traveller's History of Côte D'Azur*, United States, 2012.

de Linares, F., *Par les portes du Nord: la libération de Toulon et Marseille en 1944*, Nouvelles Editions Latines, Paris, 2005.

de Linares, François, *Par les portes du Nord: la libération de Toulon et Marseille en 1944*, Nouvelles Editions Latines, Paris, 2005.

Dear, I., Sabotage and Subversion Classic Histories Series: *The SOE and OSS at War*, The History Press, Stroud, 2016.

SOURCES

Dinter, E., *Hero or Coward: Pressures Facing the Soldier in Battle*, Frank Cass & Co. Ltd., London, 1985.

Dodd, L. & Lees, D. (Eds.), *Vichy France and Everyday Life: Confronting the Challenges of Wartime, 1939–1945*, Bloomsbury Academic, London, 2018.

Eldridge, W. J., *Finding my Father's War: A Baby Boomer and the Second Chemical Mortar Battalion in WW II*, Pagefree Publishing, Otsego, MI, 2004.

Faith, W. R., *Bob Hope: A Life in Comedy*, Da Capo Press, Cambridge, MA, 2003.

Falgoux, D., Marnette, J., & Brusson, A., *L'Amérique en Provence, le camp de Calas 1944–1945*, Editions Persée, Aix-en-Provence, 2015.

Fielding, A. W., *Hide and Seek: The Story of a Wartime Agent*, Secker & Warburg, London, 1954, reprint by Paul Dry Books, 2013.

Fisco, R. D., *Your Lives Will be Beautiful*, Arbor Books, New York, 2011.

Fitzgerald, F. S., *The Complete Short Stories, Essays, and a Play*, Volume 1, Scribner, New York, 2004, pp. 881-883.

Flavian, C. L., *Ils furent des homes,* Nouvelles Editions Latines, Paris, 1948.

Foot, M. R. D., *SOE in France: An Account of the Work of the British Special Operations Executive in France, 1940–1944*, London, Pimlico, 1999.

Forbes, R., *For Europe: The French Volunteers of the Waffen-SS*, Stackpole Books, Mechanicsburg, 2010.

Funk, A. L., *Hidden Ally: The French Resistance, Special Operations, and the Landings in Southern France, 1944*, Greenwood Press, Westport, 1992.

Fussell, P., *Wartime: Understanding and Behavior in the Second World War*, Oxford University Press, New York, 1989.

Garrett, M., *Provence: A Cultural History*, Oxford University Press, New York, 2007

Gassend, J-L, *Operation Dragoon: Autopsy of a Battle: The Allied Liberation of the French Riviera August–September 1944*, Schiffer Publishing Ltd., Pennsylvania, 2014.

Gaujac, P., *La guerre en Provence, 1944-1945: une bataille méconnue*, Presses universitaires de Lyon, 1998.

__________., *Special Forces in the invasion of France*, Historie & Collections, Paris, 1999.

Georges, M., *C'etait Hier Au Muy*, Cultures Croisées, France, 2004.

Germain, M., *Le sang de la barbaríe: chronique de la Haute-Savoie au temps de l'Occupation allemande, Seprembre 1943–26 Mars 1944*, La Fontaine de Siloé, Montmélian, 1995.

German, A., *Les chemins de la mémoire, 'le Toubib des Maquis du Var', Soixante cinq ans au service de la résistance*, Broché, Imprimerie Bonneaud, 2007.

Gilda, R., *Fighters in the Shadows: A New History of the French Resistance*, Faber & Faber, London 2015.

Gold, M. J., *Crossroads Marseille 1940*, Random House, New York, 1980.

Goldsmith, J., *Accidental Agent: Behind Enemy Lines with the French Resistance*, Pen & Sword, Barnsley, 2016. (First published by Leo Cooper Ltd., 1971).

Grehan, J. & Mace, M., *Unearthing Churchill's Secret Army: The Official List of SOE Casualties and Their Stories*, Pen & Sword, Barnsley, 2012.

Gritti, C., *Le temps de l'occupation au coeur des Maures*, Claude Gritti, Le Lavandou, 2008.

Guillon, J. M. & Laborie, P. (Eds), *Mémoire et histoire: la Résistance*, Éditions Privat, 1995.

Harris Smith, R., *OSS: The Secret History of America's First Central Intelligence Agency*, The Lyons Press, Guildford Conneticut, 2005.

Helm, S., *A Life in Secrets: Vera Atkins and the Lost Agents of SOE*, Little, Brown, Hachette Digital, London, 2009.

Jackson, J., *France: The Dark Years, 1940–1944*, Oxford University Press, New York, 2003.

Jacobs, P., *Setting France Ablaze: The SOE in France During WWII*, Pen & Sword, Barnsley, 2015.

Jefferson, A. & Carlson, L. H., *Red Tail Captured, Red Tail Free: Memoirs of a Tuskegee Airman and POW*, Revised Edition, Fordham University Press, New York, 2017.

Jenkins, R., *A Pacifist at War: The Silence of Francis Cammaerts*, Random House, London, 2009.

Jones, B.F., *Eisenhower's Guerrillas: The Jedburghs, the Maquis, and the Liberation of France*, Oxford University Press, New York, 2016.

Jones, T., *The French Riviera: A Literary Guide for Travellers*, I. B.Tauris, London, 2007.

SOURCES

Kaplan, P., *The Bomber Aircrew Experience: Dealing out Punishment from the Air*, Skyhorse Publishing, New York, 2016.

Kaufmann, J. E. & Kaufmann, H. W., *The American GI in Europe in World War II: The Battle in France*, Stackpole Books, Mechanicsburg PA, 2010.

Kedward, H. R., *In Search of the Maquis: Rural Résistance in Southern France 1942–1944*, Clarendon Press, Oxford, 1993.

Kennedy, P. A., *Battlefield Surgeon: Life and Death on the Front Lines of World War II*, University Press of Kentucky, Lexington KY, 2016.

Kershaw, A., *The Liberator: One World War II Soldier's 500-Day Odyssey From the Beaches of Sicily to the Gates of Dachau*, Hutchinson, London, 2012.

Klingbiel, P-E., *Le front oublié des Alpes-Maritimes (15 août 1944–2 mai 1945)*, Serre, France, 2005.

Krivopissko, G., *La vie à en mourir: Lettres de fusillés, 1941–1944*, Points Seuil, Paris, 2006.

Kundahl, G. G., *Riviera at War: World War II on the Côte d'Azur*, I. B. Tauris, London, 2017.

Kurowski, F., *The Brandenburger Commandos: Germany's Elite Warrior spies in World War II*, Stackpole Books, Mechanicsburg PA, 2005.

Le Chene, E., *Watch for Me by Moonlight: A British Agent with the French Resistance*, Eyre Methuen, London, 1974.

Lécuyer, J. (Sapin), *Méfiez-vous du toreador: des soldats sans uniforme témoignent de leur combat pour chasser l'occupant Cartonné*, Agpm, France, 1987.

Leslie, P., *The Liberation of the Riviera: The Resistance to the Nazis in the South of France and the Story of its Heroic Leader, Ange-Marie Miniconi*, Wyndham Books, New York, 1980.

Levendel, I. & Weisz, B., *Hunting Down the Jews: Vichy, the Nazis and Mafia Collaborators in Provence, 1942–1944*, Enigma Books, New York, 2011.

Levendel, I., *Not the Germans Alone: A Son's Search for the Truth of Vichy*, Northwestern University Press, Evanston IL, 1999.

Lieb, P., *Vercors 1944: Resistance in the French Alps*, Osprey Publishing, 2012.

Liptak, E., *Office of Strategic Services 1942–45: The World War II Origins of the CIA, 1942-45*, Osprey Publishing, Oxford, 2009.

Lloyd, C., *Collaboration and Resistance in Occupied France: Representing Treason and Sacrifice*, Palgrave Macmillan, New York, 2003.

Ludewig, J., *Ruckzüg: The German Retreat from France, 1944*, University Press of Kentucky, Lexington KY, 2012.

Mahoney, K.A., *Bombing Europe: The Illustrated Exploits of the Fifteenth Air Force*, Zenith Press, USA, 2015.

Maudlin, W. H., *Up Front*, Henry Holt & Co., New York, 1945.

McCarthy, O., *Love and War: A Story of World War II in 268 Love Letters*, Travis Publishing, Canada, 2008.

Monahan, E. & Neidel-Greenlee, R., *And if I perish: Frontline U.S. Army Nurses in World War II,* Knopf Doubleday Publishing Group, New York, 2003.

Moye, J. T., *Freedom Flyers: The Tuskegee Airmen of World War II*, Oxford University Press, New York, 2012.

Mulley, C., *The Spy Who Loved: The Secrets and Lives of One Christine Granville, Britain's First Female Special Agent of the Second World War*, Macmillan, London 2012.

Murphy, A., *To Hell and Back,* Henry Holt & Co., New York, 1949.

Nelson, M., *Americans and the Making of the Riviera*, McFarland & Co., Jefferson NC, 2008.

Nemirovsky, I. *Suite Française*, Alfred A. Knopf, New York, 2006.

Nin, A., *The Diary of Anaïs Nin 1939–1944*, Volume 3, Harcourt Publishing, San Diego, 1971.

Orfalea, G., *Messengers of the Lost Battalion: The Heroic 551st and the Turning of the Tide at the Battle of the Bulge*, The Free Press, New York, 1997.

Ottis, S., *Silent Heroes: Downed Airmen and the French Underground*, University Press of Kentucky, Lexington KY, 2001.

Ousby, I., *Occupation: The Ordeal of France, 1940–44*, Pimlico, Bournemouth, UK, 1999.

Pemler, G., *Route Nationale Nr. 7: Tagebuch einer militarischen tragodie* (German Edition), Druffel-Verlag, 1985.

Pigoreau, O., *Sanglante randonnée, les Français de la division Brandebourg et des formations de chasse SS*, Histoire at Collections, Paris, 2013.

Rabino, T., *Le réseau Carte, Histoire d'un réseau de la Résistance antiallemand, antigaulliste, anticommuniste et anti collaborationniste*, éditions Perrin, Paris, 2008.

Richards, B., *Secret Flotillas: Clandestine Sea Operations in the Mediterranean, North Africa and the Adriatic, 1940–1944*, Volume 2, Frank Cass Publishers, London, 2004.

SOURCES

Ring, J., *Riviera: The Rise and Rise of the Côte d'Azur*, Faber & Faber, London, 2011.

Roberts, M. L., *What Soldiers Do: Sex and the American GI in World War II France*, University of Chicago Press, Chilcago, 2014.

Robichon, J., *The Second D-Day*, Arthur Baker Ltd., London, 1969.

Rosencher, H, *Le sel, la cendre, la flame*, éditions Du Félin, France, 2000.

Ruby, M., *F Section SOE: The Story of the Buckmaster Network*, Leo Cooper Ltd., London, 1988.

Sivirine, G., *Le Cahier rouge du Maquis, journal de résistance*, Editions Parole, Artignosc-Sur-Verdon, 2007.

Souyris-Rolland, A., *Les Chantiers de la Jeunesse dans la Résistance et les combats de la libération, Mémoire des Chantiers*, CERPA, Paris, 2009.

St. John, P. A., *The Liberator Legend: The Plane and the People*, Turner Publishing Co., Paducah KY, 1992.

Stout, M. & Yeide, H., *First to the Rhine, The 6th Army Group in WWII*, Zenith Press, St Paul MN, 2007.

Stuhlmann, G., (ed.), *A Literate Passion: Letters of Anaïs Nin & Henry Miller, 1932-1953*, Harcourt Brace & Co., San Diego, 1987.

Sussna, S., *Defeat and Triumph: The Story of a Controversial Allied Invasion and French Rebirth*, Xlibris Corporation, 2008.

Taggart, D. G., *History of the Third Infantry Division in World War II*, United States Army, 1947.

Thomas, G. & Lewis, G., *Shadow Warriors: Daring Missions of World War II by Women of the OSS and SOE*, Amberley Publishing, Stroud, UK, 2016.

Tickell. J, *Odette, the Story of a British Agent*, Chapman & Hall, London, 1949.

Tucker-Jones, A., *Operation Dragoon: The Liberation of Southern France*, Pen & Sword, Barnsley, UK, 2009.

United States, Office of Strategic Services, Congress, *The Secrets War: The Office of Strategic Services in World War II*, National Archives and Records Administration, 1992.

Vaughan, H., *Sleeping With the Enemy: Coco Chanel, Nazi Agent*, Chatto & Windus, London, 2011.

Vinen, R., *The Unfree French: Life under the Occupation*, Yale University Press, New Haven CT, 2006.

Weiss, S. J., *Second Chance: In Combat with the US 'Texas' Infantry, the OSS, and the French Resistance During the Liberation of France, 1943–1946*, Military History Publishing, 2011.

Weitz, Margaret Collins, *Sisters in the Résistance: How Women Fought to Free France, 1940–1945*, John Wiley & Sons, New York, 1998.

Winter, J. M., *Remembering War: The Great War Between Memory and History in the Twentieth Century*, Yale University Press, New Haven CT, 2006.

Wylie, L. W, *Village in the Vaucluse*, Harvard University Press, Cambridge, 1977.

Yung-de Prevaux, A., *Love in the Tempest of History: A French Resistance Story*, The Free Press, London, UK, 2001.

Zaloga, S. J., *The Atlantic Wall (3) Südwall*, Osprey Publishing, Oxford, 2015.

Periodicals

After the Battle, No. 174, The Battle of the Vercors, Battle of Britain International Ltd., 2015.

Austriaca, No. 19, Ecrivains autrichiens exilés en France, Université de Rouen, Centre d'études et de recherches autrichiennes, November 1984, pp.28-30.

Buchanan, A., "I Felt like a Tourist Instead of a Soldier': The Occupying Gaze: War and Tourism in Italy, 1943–1945', *American Quarterly, Vol. 68, No. 3*, 3 September 2016, pp. 593-615.

Daily Mail, 'Forgotten WWII spy tortured by the Nazis died penniless after her British pension was halted without explanation', 21 September 2010.

Daily Mail, 'Testimony of Harold Osmond Le Druillenec', 31 March 2016.

Daily Telegraph, Obituary of Nancy Wake, 8 August 2011.

De Tarle, A., 'In Occupied Provence: A Childhood Memory', Translated from the French by J. Weintraub, *Michigan Quarterly Review*, Volume XLIII, Issue 2, Spring 2004.

La Gazette Locale, Le 10 juin 1944 vu par le chef du Maquis Vasio, 11 June 2014.

Los Angeles Times, Obituary of Marie-Madeleine Fourcade; French Resistance Leader, 22 July 1989.

Nice Matin (Cannes), 'Les corps de deux héros de la Résistance cannoise finalement retrouvés 74 ans après la libération de la ville?', 23 août 2018.

SOURCES

Nice-Matin, 'Antibes Fusillés du Fort-Carré : 65 ans d'intérrogations', 20 septembre 2009.

Nice-Matin, 'De l'Occupation à la liberation, hors-série édité par le group', août 2010, pp. 4-56.

Paris Match, 'Jacques et Lotka de Prévaux, Les amoureux de la Résistance', 28 August 2014.

Pavalko, E. K., & Elder, G. H., 'World War II and divorce: A life course perspective', *American Journal of Sociology* (95) 5, 1990, pp. 1213-1234.

Pécout, C., 'Les Chantiers de la Jeunesse (1940–1944): Une Expérience De Service Civil Obligatoire', *Presses de Sciences Po (P.F.N.S.P.)*, 2008/1 No. 47, pp. 24-33.

Stars and Stripes, 'Sweat-it-out-U, A unique GI school has sprouted up in old Biarritz', 16 September 1945.

Stars and Stripes, Marseille Edition, 4 December 1944.

Stars and Stripes, Southern France, 16 August 1945.

Stars and Stripes, Southern France, 23 August 1945.

Sugarman, M., 'Captain Isidore Newman, SOE', *Jewish Historical Studies*, Vol. 41, 2007.

Tagliabue, J., 'Clues to the Mystery of a Writer Pilot Who Disappeared', *The New York Times,* 11 April 2008.

The Australian Women's Weekly, 4 July 1942, p. 75.

The Beachhead News, Souvenier Edition, 15 October 1944.

The Billboard, Vol. 57, No. 37, 22 September 1945, p.36.

The Daily Courier, Connellsville, Texas, 18 July 1945.

The Delta Stage, Marseille, 3 October 1945.

The Guardian, D. Stafford, Nancy Wake Obituary, 8 August 2011.

The Guardian, Obituary of Francis Cammaerts, by M. R. D. Foot, 7 July 2006.

The Montana Standard, 'New York woman, heroine of French underground, helps Americans, Bute Montana', 12 September 1944.

The New York Times, 'Nancy Wake, Proud Spy and Nazi Foe, Dies at 98', 13 August 2011.

Vanity Fair, 'It happened at the Hôtel du Cap', by C. Beauchamp, 13 February 2009.

Var Matin, 'Le secret explosif de la poudrière de Saint-Pierre à Toulon', lundi 4 août 2014.

Var Matin, 'Raymond Aubrac, figure de la Résistance, a décoré
  Marcelle Zunino de la Légion d'honneur', 10 July 2010.
Var Matin, 'Un Varois retrace l'histoire d'un soldat américain: la
  dernière bataille du lieutenant Cornwell', 22 May 2017.
Von Rohr, M., book review, *Bandits in Uniform: The Dark Side of GIs
  in Liberated France,* in *Spiegel Online*, 29 May, 2013.
Warren Tribune, 'Warren paratrooper relates invasion leap over
  France', newspaper clipping, sn.
Yank, The Army Weekly, 'Down on the Riviera—GI's Relax in Nice,
  France', clipping, sn.
Yank, The Army Weekly, Vol. 2, No. 45, 'They want to go', p. 6, 27 April 1945.

Unpublished sources

Aimé Leocard's Story, speech given in Draguignan on 16 October
  1987, author's collection.
Aldani, B., unpublished testimony, Musée de la libération 15 août
  1944, Le Muy.
Ayral, X. J. R., *Heroisme: Jean Ayral,compagnon de la Liberation,
  histoire et carnets de guerre de Jean Ayral (18 juin 1940–22 aout
  1944),* private, 2013.
Boian, K. O. C., Major General Melvin Zais and Hamburger Hill, U.S.
  School of Advanced Military Studies, United States Army Command
  and General Staff College Fort Leavenworth, Kansas, 2012.
Bourhill, J. F., 'Red Tabs': Life and death in the 6th South African
  Armoured Division, 1943–1945, D. Phil. thesis, University of Pretoria.
Collection: Mémoire de la seconde guerre mondiale dans les Alpes-
  Maritimes, 11 juin 1944, les Fusillés de Saint-Julien-du-Verdon,
  Consiel General des Alpes-Maritimes.
Conseil général Député des Alpes de Haute-Provence, La répression
  allemande dans les Basses-Alpes de l'Occupation à la Libération,
  Septembre 1943-août 1944, author's collection.
Costello, H. G., Counterintelligence Corps, 36th Infantry Division,
  unpublished notes, Scottsdale, Arizona.
CSI Battle Book, Operation Anvil/ Dragoon, The Invasion of Southern
  France, 15 August to 1 September 1944, Combat Studies Institute,
  Leavenworth, Kansas.

SOURCES

Delta Base Section, unpublished history, Combined Arms Research Library, Digital Library, 2008.

Escape Statement, Chester A. Ray, Headquarters Fifteenth Air Force, 21 September 1944, author's collection.

Escape Statement, Robert M. Sanders, Headquarters Fifteenth Air Force, 15 August 1944, author's collection.

Gregory, F. E., History of 783rd Bomb Squadron (H) 465th Bombardment Group (H) (1943–1945) Pantanella, Italy, 1989, author's collection.

Guillon, J-M., Var 39-45, PhD thesis, University of Marseille, Aix en Provence, 1989.

Jones, B. F., Freeing France: The Allies, the Résistance, and the Jedburghs, doctoral thesis, University of Nebraska-Lincoln, 1999.

Libération d'Hyères 1ère partie, marche forcée le long du Gapeau, Les Bataillons de Marche et les Fusiliers Marins, publicity pamphlet for the 70th anniversary commemorations, author's collection.

Mehringer, P., Operation Union II: Marines land in France 60 years ago, The Official Web Site of the US Marines, 8 May 2007.

Operation Anvil/ Dragoon, The Invasion of Southern France 15 August–1 September 1944, Combat Studies Institute, Fort Leavenworth, KS, 1984.

Operational Groups Field Manual—Strategic Services (Provisional), Strategic Services Field Manual No. 6, April 1944, Section IV, Training.

Pocket Guide to France, US Government Printing Office, 1944, pp. 1-62.

Report on Airborne operations in Dragoon, After Action Report of the 1st Airborne Task Force, 25 October, 1944.

Rigg, S., Rural France, war, commemoration and memory, the relationship between the past and present a microhistory, research paper, University of Bristol, 2010.

Shaver, J. W., Office Of Strategic Services Operational Groups in France during World War II, July–October 1944, Master of Military Art and Science Thesis, Fort Leavenworth KS, 1993.

Smith, M., The Civilian Experience in German Occupied France, 1940–1944, History honors papers, Paper 6, Connecticut College, New London, 2010.

Zinsou, C., The Strategic and Operational Debate Over Operation Anvil: The Allied Invasion Of Southern France In August, 1944, MA thesis, University of North Texas, 2013.

Electronic sources

3rd Infantry Division Medal of Honor recipients, http://www.society3rdid.org

Anciens des Services Spéciaux de la Défense Nationale (France), www.aassdn.org

Août 1944: Une jeune fille raconte la Libération de Valence, https://unmondedepapiers.com

Association Pour un Maitron des Fusillés et Exécutés, http://maitron-fusilles-40-44.univ-paris.fr

Bailey, Frederick Arthur, IWM oral history, www.iwm.org.uk

Bernard Roger par Jean-Marie Guillon, http://maitron-en-ligne.univ-paris.fr

Brosset, Diégo, 1898–1944, www.cheminsdememoire.gouv.fr

Commando Order, Wikipedia, https://en.wikipedia.org

Diary of B. H. Seegmiller, http://57thbombwing.com

Jean-Pierre de Lassus Saint-Geniès (lieutenant colonel), http://museedelaresistanceenligne.org

L'Apocalyptique de la Libération de la Ville de Nice du 28 août 1944, http://politiquepaca.canalblog.com

Lacey, L. H., Peter Ortiz, The Man and the Legend, www.historynet.com

Le devoir de mémoire, Site official de la ville de Sainte-Maxime, www.ville-sainte-maxime.fr

Léon Dulcy, http://museedelaresistanceenligne.org

Les femmes dans la Résistance Azuréenne, resistance.azur.free.fr

Marcelle Zunino, unpublished memoir, www.resistance-var.org

Mémoire de Champsoar, http://champsaur.net/liberation-de-gap

Musée de la résistance en ligne, Massacre de Vassieux-en-Vercors en juillet 1944, http://museedelaresistanceenligne.org

Numero special dans les archives secretes de la Seconde Guerre mondial les, www.cheminsdememoire.gouv.fr

Operational Group Justine, Office of Strategic Services Operational Groups, http://oss-og.org

Operational Group Nancy, Office of Strategic Services Operational Groups, http://oss-og.org

Operational Group Ruth, Office of Strategic Services Operational Groups, http://oss-og.org

Operations May–June 1944, www.2ndbombgroup.org

SOURCES

Paratroopers' Odyssey, A History of the 517th Parachute Combat Team, http://517prct.org

Résistance, Devoir De Mémoire Pour Aujourd'hui Et Pour Demain, http://resistance.ftp.free.fr

Rostron, B., One Man's War, My Story 1939–1946, www.454-459squadrons.org.au

Tentative of History of In/Exfiltrations into/from France during WWII from 1940 to 1945: Parachutes, Plane & Sea Landings, www.plan-sussex-1944.net

Testimony of docteur Paul Raybaud à la ferme 'Boeuf', http://museedelaresistanceenligne.org.

Testimony of Monsieur Fortuné Ferrier, www.memoires-vives.mode83.net

The Death of Hélène Vagliano, Second World War Experience Centre, http://war-experience.org

War Diary of the 2nd Independent Parachute Brigade, National Archives Catalogue number WO 170/518, www.pegasusarchive.org

Yale Law School, the Avalon Project, Nuremberg Trial Proceedings Vol. 6, 31 January 1946, www.avalon.law.yale.edu

Zunino, M., Unpublished memoir, www.resistance-var.org

Notes

INTRODUCTION

1. J. Jackson, *France: The Dark Years, 1940–1944*, Oxford University Press, New York, 2003, pp. 7-8.
2. J-M. Guillon, 'Var 39–45', PhD Thesis, University of Aix-Marseille, 1989; H. R. Kedward, *In Search of the Maquis: Rural Résistance in Southern France 1942–1944*, Clarendon Press, Oxford, 1993.
3. R. Gilda, *Fighters in the Shadows, A New History of the French Resistance*, Faber & Faber, London 2015, pp. 12-19.
4. G. Sivirine, *Le Cahier rouge du Maquis, journal de résistance*, Editions Parole, Artignosc-Sur-Verdon, 2007.
5. Association Pour un Maitron des Fusillés et Exécutés, http:// maitron-fusilles-40-44.univ-paris1.fr

1. HUMILIATION

1. S. Sussna, *Defeat and Triumph: The Story of a Controversial Allied Invasion and French Rebirth*, Xlibris Corporation, 2008.
2. R. Gilda, *Fighters in the Shadows, A New History of the French Resistance*, pp. 12-19.
3. J. Jackson, *France: The Dark Years, 1940–1944*, Oxford University Press, New York, 2003, p. 328.
4. Ibid., p. 3.
5. J. Tickell, *Odette, The Story of a British Agent*, Chapman & Hall, London, 1949, pp. 144-5.
6. B. F. Jones, 'Freeing France: The Allies, the Résistance, and the Jedburghs', PhD Thesis, University of Nebraska-Lincoln, 1999, p. 96.
7. G. G. Kundahl, *Riviera at War: World War II on the Côte d'Azur*, I. B. Tauris, London, 2017, p. 91.
8. R. Forbes, *For Europe: The French Volunteers of the Waffen-SS*, Stackpole Books, Mechanicsburg, 2010, pp. 40-3.

9. J. Jackson, *France: The Dark Years, 1940–1944*, p. 534.

10. R. Forbes, *For Europe: The French Volunteers of the Waffen-SS*, pp. 41-2.

11. Archives départementales du Var – Draguignan, Cote/n° inventaire, 1 W 79, Tract de la Résistance rédigé par le mouvement 'Libération' contre le S.T.O (service travail obligatoire).

12. Conseil général Député des Alpes de Haute-Provence, La répression allemande dans les Basses-Alpes de l'Occupation à la Libération. Septembre 1943–août 1944, author's collection.

13. C. Pécout, *Les Chantiers de la Jeunesse (1940–1944): Une Expérience De Service Civil Obligatoire*, Presses de Sciences Po (P.F.N.S.P.), 2008/1 No. 47, pp. 24-33; A. Souyris-Rolland, *Les Chantiers de la Jeunesse dans la Résistance et les combats de la Libération, Mémoire des Chantiers*, CERPA, Paris, 2009.

14. C. Gritti, *Le temps de l'occupation au Coeur des Maures*, Claude Gritti, Le Lavandou, 2008, pp. 105-6.

15. *The Australian Women's Weekly*, 4 July 1942, p. 75.

16. J. Tickell, *Odette, The Story of a British Agent*, pp. 144-5.

17. M. Zunino, translated from unpublished memoir, www.resistance-var.org; *Var Matin*, Raymond Aubrac, figure de la Résistance, a décoré Marcelle Zunino de la Légion d'honneur, 10 July 2010.

18. *Pocket Guide to France*, U.S. Government Printing Office, 1944, pp. 10-11.

19. C. Gritti, *Le temps de l'occupation au Coeur des Maures*, pp. 85-90.

20. Testimony of Fortuné Ferrier, www.memoires-vives.mode83.net

21. C. Lloyd, *Collaboration and Resistance In Occupied France: Representing Treason and Sacrifice*, Palgrave Macmillan, New York, 2003, p.14.

2. HUMANITY

1. *Daily Telegraph*, Obituary of Elizabeth Furst, 15 October 2002.

2. *The Guardian*, D. Stafford, Nancy Wake obituary, 8 August 2011.

3. *The New York Times*, 'Nancy Wake, Proud Spy and Nazi Foe, Dies at 98', 13 August 2011; *The Telegraph*, Obituary of Nancy Wake, 8 August 2011.

4. Imperial War Museum, Boiteux-Burdett, Robert René, IWM Oral History, Catalogue number 9851.

5. R. Bailey, *Forgotten Voices of the Secret War: An Inside History of Special Operations during the Second World War*, Ebury Publishing, 2008.

6. M. R. D. Foot, *SOE in France: An Account of the Work of the British Special Operations Executive in France, 1940–1944,* London, Pimlico, 1999, pp. 224-5.
7. J. Grehan, & M. Mace, *Unearthing Churchill's Secret Army: The Official List of SOE Casualties and Their Stories*, Pen & Sword, Barnsley, 2012.
8. R. Gilda, *Fighters in the Shadows*, p. 329.
9. J. Goldsmith, *Accidental Agent: Behind Enemy Lines With the French Resistance,* Pen & Sword, Barnsley, 2016.
10. *Los Angeles Times*, Obituary of Marie-Madeleine Fourcade, French Resistance Leader, 22 July 1989.
11. Yale Law School, The Avalon Project, Nuremberg Trial Proceedings Vol. 6, www.avalon.law.yale.edu
12. *Paris Match*, 'Jacques et Lotka de Prévaux: Les amoureux de la Résistance', 28 August 2014; A. Yung-de Prevaux, *Love in the Tempest of History: A French Resistance Story*, Free Press, 2001.
13. C. Gritti, *Le temps de l'occupation au Coeur des Maures*, p. 195.
14. P. Churchill, *Duel of Wits*, Hodder & Stoughton, London, 1953, p. 155.
15. P. Churchill, *The Spirit in the Cage*, p. 26.
16. Ibid., p.15.
17. D. Martin, 'Vera Atkins, 92, Spymaster for British, Dies', in *The New York Times*, 27 June 2000.

3. MENACE

1. J-L. Gassend, *Operation Dragoon: Autopsy of a Battle: The Allied Liberation of the French Riviera, August–September 1944,* Schiffer Publishing Ltd., Pennsylvania, 2014, p. 24.
2. J. Robichon, *The Second D-Day*, Arthur Baker Ltd., London, 1969, pp.67-8.
3. *The Australian Women's Weekly*, 4 July 1942, p. 75.
4. Archives départementales du Var, Draguignan, 1 W 80, Correspondance du directeur de la police de Toulon au préfet du Var reproduisant le texte d'un tract, 2 May 1943.
5. E. Carles, *A Wild Herb Soup, the Life of a French Countrywoman,* Orion Books Ltd., London, 1996.
6. J. Goldsmith, *Accidental Agent*, p. 47.
7. A. de Tarle, 'In Occupied Provence: A Childhood Memory', Translated from the French by J. Weintraub, *Michigan Quarterly Review*, Volume XLIII, Issue 2, Spring 2004.

8. *Nice-Matin,* De l'occupation à la liberation, hors-série édité par le group *Nice-Matin,* Août 2010, pp. 8-9.
9. G. G. Kundahl, *Riviera at War*, p. 85.
10. *Nice-Matin*, De l'occupation à la liberation, p.15.
11. I. Levendel & B. Weisz, *Hunting Down the Jews: Vichy, the Nazis and Mafia Collaborators in Provence, 1942–1944,* Enigma Books, New York, 2011.
12. Ibid.
13. J. Jackson, *France: The Dark Years,* p. 378.
14. *Pocket Guide to France,* pp. 57-8.
15. A. de Tarle, 'In Occupied Provence: A Childhood Memory'.
16. J. J. Clark & R. R. Smith, *From the Riviera to the Rhine, United States Army in World War II, European Theater of Operations*, Centre of Military History, United States Army, Washington DC, 1993, p. 69.
17. J. Robichon, *The Second D-Day*, pp. 42-3.

4. DEFIANCE

1. *Daily Telegraph*, Obituary of Raymond Aubrac, 11 April 2012.
2. H. R. Kedward, *In Search of The Maquis: Rural Resistance in Southern France 1942–44*, (Oxford, 1993), p. 260; Cited in R. Harris Smith, *OSS: The Secret History of America's First Central Intelligence Agency*, University of California Press, Berkeley and Los Angeles, 1972, pp. 176-7.
3. B. de Gueyer, l'ora Dans Le Var, Memoire Vivre De La Résistance.
4. Marcelle Zunino, Unpublished memoir.
5. Les femmes dans la Résistance Azuréenne, www.resistance.azur.free.fr
6. Helene Deschamps-Adams, 'Behind Enemy Lines in France' in G. C. Chalou (Ed.), *The Secrets War: The Office of Strategic Services in World War II*, National Archives and Records Administration, Washington DC, 2002, pp. 140-64.
7. J. Goldsmith, *Accidental Agent:* p. 143.
8. Ibid., p. 7.
9. Cited in R. Harris Smith, *OSS: The Secret History of America's First Central Intelligence Agency*, pp. 176-7.
10. Ibid.
11. P. Churchill, *The Spirit in the Cage*, p.78.
12. G. Krivopissko, *La vie à en mourir: Lettres de fusillés, 1941–1944,* Points Seuil, Paris, 2006.

13. Ibid.

14. J-M. Guillon, 'Var 39-45', p. 486.

15. C. Gritti, *Le temps de l'occupation au Coeur des Maures*, pp. 22-3.

16. J-M. Guillon, 'Var 39-45', p. 504.

17. *Var-Matin*, Sainte-Maxime Les incroyables parcours de deux héros de la Libération, 16 août 2008.

18. J. Jackson, *France: The Dark Years*, p. 477.

19. C. Gritti, *Le temps de l'occupation au Coeur des Maures*, pp. 64-8.

20. J-M. Guillon, 'Var 39-45', p. 618.

21. Ibid., p. 512.

22. Conseil général Député des Alpes de Haute-Provence, La répression allemande dans les Basses-Alpes de l'Occupation à la Libération. Septembre 1943-août 1944, author's collection.

23. *Nice-Matin*, De l'occupation à la liberation, p. 44.

5. EVASION

1. Translated from G. Sivirine, *Le Cahier rouge du Maquis, journal de résistance*, Editions Parole, Artignosc-Sur-Verdon, 2007.

2. Ibid.

3. Ibid.

4. Ibid.

5. A. German, *Les chemins de la mémoire: 'Le Toubib Des Maquis Du Var', 65 ans au service social de la Résistance*, Bonnaud, 2007.

6. G. Sivirine, *Le cahier rouge du maquis, journal de résistance*.

7. Ibid.

8. Ibid.

9. Ibid.

10. J. Goldsmith, *Accidental Agent*, pp. 150-1.

11. G. Sivirine, *Le cahier rouge du maquis, journal de résistance*.

12. Cited in R. Harris Smith, *OSS: The Secret History of America's First Central Intelligence Agency*, The Lyons Press, Guildford Conneticut, 2005, p.175.

13. G. Sivirine, *Le cahier rouge du maquis, journal de résistance*.

14. Ibid.

15. J-M. Guillon, 'Var 39-45', pp. 622-3.

16. G. Sivirine, *Le cahier rouge du maquis, journal de résistance*.

NOTES

6. DUPLICITY

1. J-M. Guillon, 'Var 39-45'.
2. *La Gazette Locale*, Le 10 juin 1944 vu par le chef du Maquis Vasio, 11 June 2014.
3. E. le Chene, *Watch For Me by Moonlight, A British Agent With the French Resistance*, Eyre Methuen, London, 1974; Imperial War Museum, Boiteux-Burdett, Robert René, IWM Oral History, Catalogue number 9851.
4. R. Jenkins, *A Pacifist at War*, p. 145.
5. G. Sivirine, *Le cahier rouge du maquis, journal de résistance.*
6. Ibid.
7. J. Goldsmith, *Accidental Agent*, p. 162.
8. Collection: Mémoire de la seconde guerre mondiale dans les Alpes-Maritimes, 11 juin 1944, les Fusillés de Saint-Julien-du-Verdon, Consiel General des Alpes-Maritimes.
9. J-M. Guillon, 'Var 39-45', pp. 621-3.
10. G. Sivirine, *Le cahier rouge du maquis, journal de résistance.*
11. Monuments and memorials in Aups, http://museedelaresistanceenligne.org

7. DESPAIR

1. P. Churchill, *Duel of Wits*, p. 291.
2. R. Jenkins, *A Pacifist At War: The Silence of Francis Cammaerts*, Random House, London, 2009, pp. 4-5.
3. Imperial War Museum, Cammaerts, Francis Charles Albert, IWM Oral history, Catalogue number 33036.
4. *The Guardian,* Obituary of Francis Cammaerts, 7 July 2006.
5. R. Jenkins, *A Pacifist At War,* p. 172.
6. P. Jacobs, *Setting France Ablaze: The SOE in France During World War II*, Pen & Sword, Barnsley, 2015, pp. 200-1; B. F. Jones, *Eisenhower's Guerrillas: The Jedburghs, the Maquis, and the Liberation of France,* Oxford University Press, New York, 2016.
7. http://oss-og.org/france/justine.html; *After the Battle* No. 174, 'The Battle of the Vercors', Battle of Britain International Ltd., 2015, pp. 19-21.
8. R. Jenkins, *A Pacifist At War,* p. 171.

9. Ibid.

10. *After the Battle,* No. 174, pp. 30-2.

11. Ibid., pp. 26-7.

12. Ibid., pp. 34-5.

13. R. Harris Smith, *OSS: The Secret History of America's First Central Intelligence Agency*, pp. 171-2.

14. Musée de la résistance en ligne, Massacre de Vassieux-en-Vercors en juillet 1944; R. Jenkins, *A Pacifist At War*, p. 176.

15. P. Lieb, *Vercors 1944: Resistance in the French Alps*, Osprey Publishing, 2012, pp. 40-70.

16. R. Jenkins, *A Pacifist At War*, p. 183.

17. Ibid.

18. Ibid., p. 169.

19. A. W. Fielding, *Hide and Seek: The Story of a Wartime Agent*, Secker & Warburg, London, 1954, reprint by Paul Dry Books, 2013, pp. 150-1.

20. C. Mulley, *The Spy Who Loved: The Secrets and Lives of One Christine Granville, Britain's First Female Special Agent of the Second world War*, Macmillan, London 2012, pp. 237-9.

21. A. W. Fielding, *Hide and Seek*, pp. 172-4.

22. D. Martin, 'Vera Atkins, 92, Spymaster for British, Dies', *New York Times*, 27 June 2000.

23. L. W. Wylie, *Village in the Vaucluse*, Harvard University Press, Cambridge, 1977, p. 113.

24. J. Goldsmith, *Accidental Agent*, p. 75.

8. AUDACITY

1. R. Harris Smith, *OSS: The Secret History of America's First Central Intelligence Agency*, University of California Press, Berkeley and Los Angeles, 1972, pp. 166-8; M. R. D. Foot, *SOE in France*, p. xv.

2. E. Liptak, *Office of Strategic Services 1942–45: The World War II Origins of the CIA*, Osprey Publishing, London, pp. 6-7.

3. Commando order, Wikipedia, https://en.wikipedia.org

4. Operational Groups Field Manual – Strategic Services (Provisional), Strategic Services Field Manual No. 6, April 1944, Section IV, Training, pp. 10-13.

5. F. A. Bailey, IWM Oral History, www.iwm.org.uk, 1990.

6. J. E. St C. Smallwood, IWM Oral History, Catalogue number 17998, www.iwm.org.uk

7. Ibid.

8. A. L. Funk, *Hidden Ally: The French Resistance, Special Operations, and The Landings in Southern France, 1944*, Greenwood Press, Westport, 1992.

9. J. E. St C. Smallwood, IWM Oral History.

10. Office of Strategic Services Operational Groups, http://oss-og.org; A. L. Funk, *Hidden Ally*.

11. L. H. Lacey, 'Peter Ortiz, The Man and the Legend', www. historynet.com; P. Mehringer, 'Operation Union II: Marines land in France 60 years ago', The Official Web Site of the US Marines, 8 May 2007.

12. Ibid.

13. P. Lieb, *Vercors 1944: Resistance in the French Alps*, pp.40-70; www.militarymuseum.org/Ortiz.html

14. R. Gilda, *Fighters in the Shadows*, p. 330.

15. C. Mulley, *The Spy Who Loved*, p. 254.

16. Imperial War Museum, Boiteux-Burdett, Robert René, IWM Oral History, Catalogue number 9851.

17. J. W. Shaver, 'Office Of Strategic Services Operational Groups In France During World War II, July–October 1944', Master of Military Art and Science Thesis, Fort Leavenworth, Kansas, 1993.

18. G. G. Kundahl, *Riviera at War*, p. 220.

19. Ibid., pp. 394-5.

9. COURAGE

1. *Var Matin*, Un Varois retrace l'histoire d'un soldat américain: la dernière bataille du lieutenant Cornwell, 22 May 2017.

2. Missing Air Crew Report, Report on shot-down aircraft, Casualty Report for AGO, War Department Headquarters Army Air Forces Washington, 767th Bombardment Squadron (H) 461st Bombardment Group Apo 520 US Army, 28 September 1944, author's collection.

3. Ibid.

4. K. A. Mahoney, *Bombing Europe: The Illustrated Exploits of the Fifteenth Air Force*, Zenith Press, Minneapolis, 2015, p. 119; Operations May–June 1944, www.2ndbombgroup.org

5. Robert M. Sanders, Escape Statement, Headquarters Fifteenth Air Force, 15 August 1944, author's collection.

6. Ibid.

7. Chester A. Ray, Escape Statement, Headquarters Fifteenth Air Force, 21 September 1944, author's collection.

8. Ibid.

9. F. E. Gregory, *History of 783rd Bomb Squadron (H) 465th Bombardment Group (H) (1943–1945), Pantanella, Italy*, F. E. Gregory, 1989.

10. 'Tentative History of In/Exfiltrations into/from France during WWII from 1940 to 1945: Parachutes, Plane & Sea Landings', www.plan-sussex-1944.net

11. B. Rostron, 'One Man's War: My Story 1939–1946', www.454-459squadrons.org.au

12. Ibid.

13. Ibid.

14. Ibid.

15. J. Tagliabue, 'Clues to the Mystery of a Writer Pilot Who Disappeared', *The New York Times*, 11 April 2008.

16. Ibid.

17. www.telegraph.co.uk, 20 July 2004.

18. J. Robichon, *The Second D-Day*, p. 51.

19. C. Gritti, *Le temps de l'occupation au Coeur des Maures*, p. 211.

20. J. Robichon, *The Second D-Day*, pp. 45-8.

21. *Nice-Matin,* De l'occupation à la liberation, pp. 46-7.

22. J. Caver, J. A. Ennels, & D. I. Haulman, *The Tuskegee Airmen: An Illustrated History, 1939–1949*, NewSouth Books, Louisville, 2011.

23. A. Jefferson & L.H. Carlson, *Red Tail Captured, Red Tail Free: Memoirs of a Tuskegee Airman and POW*, revised edition, Fordham University Press, New York, 2017, pp. 106-7; J. T.Moye, *Freedom Flyers: The Tuskegee Airmen of World War II*, Oxford University Press, New York, 2012, p. 207.

24. J. Robichon, *The Second D-Day*, p. 207-9.

10. CRUELTY

1. P. Jacobs, *Setting France Ablaze*, pp.100-101.

2. Aimé Leocard's Story, Speech given in Draguignan on 16 October 1987, author's collecton.

3. Archives départementales des Alpes-de-Haute-Provence, Rapport du gendarme Boyer commandant provisoirement la brigade de gendarmerie d'Oraison, 17 juillet 1944 (42 W 105).

4. Léon Dulcy, http://museedelaresistanceenligne.org/media7953-LA

5. *Nice-Matin,* De l'occupation à la liberation, p. 26.

6. Conseil général Député des Alpes de Haute-Provence, La répression allemande dans les Basses-Alpes de l'Occupation à la Libération, Septembre 1943-août 1944, author's collection.

7. Testimony of docteur Paul Raybaud à la ferme 'Boeuf', http://museedelaresistanceenligne.org

8. Association Pour un Maitron des Fusillés et Exécutés, http://maitron-fusilles-40-44.univ-paris1.fr

9. Anciens des Services Spéciaux de la Défense Nationale (France), www.aassdn.org, 10 April 2017.

10. Ibid.

11. Archives nationales, 72 AJ 104, le Kommandeur de la *SIPO* et du *SD* de Marseille, Rapport final Affaire Catilina, Marseille, 6 juillet 1944, signé Dunker, *SS Scharführer*.

12. L'espion des nazis 'Erick' fait tomber le maquis de Ste Anne Les collaborateurs et criminels Nazis; Le rapport Flora, http://maquisdelaresistan.wixsite.com; Numero special dans les archives secretes de la Seconde Guerre Mondial, www.cheminsdememoire.gouv.fr

11. RECKONING

1. The exact number is not known because different sources state the total number of airborne troops to be more than 9,000 in total.

2. M. Zunino, Unpublished memoir.

3. G. Sivirine, *Le cahier rouge du maquis, journal de résistance.*

4. Ibid.

5. J. Robichon, *The Second D-Day*, pp.200-10.

6. J-L. Gassend, *Operation Dragoon: Autopsy of a Battle*, pp. 230-1.

7. The Death of Hélène Vagliano, Second World War Experience Centre, http://war-experience.org/lives/helene-vagliano-french-resistance/

8. G. G. Kundahl, *Riviera at War*, p. 266.

12. CONFUSION

1. B. Aldani, Unpublished testimony, Musée de la liberation, 15 août 1944, Le Muy.

2. Report on Airborne operations in Dragoon, After Action Report of the 1st Airborne Task Force, 25 October, 1944.

3. Interview with Oswald Baker, in J. Crwys-Williams, *Mood of a Nation: A Country at War 1939–1945*, Ashanti Publishing, Rivonia, 1992, pp. 378-81.

4. Ibid.

5. Ibid.

6. Ibid.

7. War Diary of the 2nd Independent Parachute Brigade, National Archives Catalogue number WO 170/518, www.pegasusarchive. org/dragoon/war_2bdehq.htm

8. J. T. Broumley, *The Boldest Plan Is The Best*, Rockey Marsh Publishing, 2011, p. 218.

9. J. Ludewig, *Ruckzüg: The German Retreat from France, 1944*, University Press of Kentucky, Lexington, 2012, pp. 67-9.

10. M. Georges, *C'etait hier au Muy,* Cultures Croisées, France, 2004.

11. W. J. Eldridge, *Finding My Father's War: A Baby Boomer and the Second Chemical Mortar Batallion in World War II*, Pagefree Publishing, Otsego, MI, 2004, p.176.

12. J-L. Gassend, *Operation Dragoon: Autopsy of a Battle*, pp. 104-7.

13. Ibid., p.108.

14. War Diary of the 2nd Independent Parachute Brigade.

15. J-L. Gassend, *Operation Dragoon: Autopsy of a Vattle*, p. 122.

16. Ibid., p. 123.

17. J. Robichon, *The Second D-Day*, pp.1139-40.

18. 517th Parachute Regimental Combat Team, Turner Publishing Company, Kentucky, 1998, p. 19.

19. J. Robichon, *The Second D-Day*, pp. 273-6.

20. The deputy commander of the 2nd Independent Parachute Brigade was Lieutenant-Colonel Thomas Pearson who was 30 years old in 1944 and at the time of writing is the oldest living full general, aged 104.

21. *Warren Tribune*, Warren paratrooper relates invasion leap over France, newspaper clipping, sn.

13. FORCE

1. R. D. Fisco, *Your Lives Will Be beautiful*, Arbor Books, New York, 2011, pp. 59-60.

2. J. T. Broumley, *The Boldest Plan Is The Best*, p. 216.

3. C. Gritti, *Le temps de l'occupation au Coeur des Maures*, pp. 249-53.

4. *Pocket Guide to France,* US Government Printing Office, 1944, pp. 1-62.
5. *The Daily Courier*, Connellsville, Texas, 18 July 1945.
6. Third Infantry Division Medal of Honor recipients, www.society3rdid.org/3rd-id-moh-recipients
7. J. Robichon, *The Second D-Day*, pp.188-90.
8. Le devoir de mémoire, Site official de la ville de Sainte-Maxime, www.ville-sainte maxime.fr/le_devoir_de_memoire.html
9. A. Kershaw, *The Liberator: One World War II Soldier's 500-Day Odyssey From The Beaches of Sicily to The Gates of Dachau*, Hutchinson, London, 2012, pp.138-46.
10. F. S. Fitzgerald, *The Complete Short Stories, Essays, and a Play*, Volume 1, Scribner, New York, 2004, p. 881-3.
11. Diary of B. H. Seegmiller, http://57thbombwing.com/321stHistory/321_BG_1944-08.pdf
12. J. Ludewig, *Ruckzüg: The German Retreat from France, 1944*, p. 70.
13. J. Robichon, *The Second D-day*, pp. 235-8.
14. P.A. Kennedy, *Battlefield Surgeon: Life and Death on the Front Lines of World War II*, University Press of Kentucky, Lexington, 2016, p. 140.
15. J-L. Gassend, *Operation Dragoon: Autopsy of a Battle.* p. 169.
16. R. Atkinson, *The Guns at Last Light: The War in Western Europe, 1944–1945*, Henry Holt & Co., New York, 2013.

14. FRATERNITY

1. R. Atkinson, *The Guns at Last Light*, pp. 200-5.
2. J. Robichon, *The Second D-Day*, pp. 262-3.
3. Diégo Brosset 1898–1944, www.cheminsdememoire.gouv.fr/en/diego-charles-brosset
4. Libération d'Hyères 1ère partie, marche forcée le long du Gapeau, Les Bataillons de Marche et les Fusiliers Marins, publicity pamphlet for the 70th anniversary commemorations, author's collection.
5. C. Gritti, *Le temps de l'occupation au coeur des Maures*, pp. 303-5.
6. S. J. Zaloga, *The Atlantic Wall (3) Sudwall*, Osprey Publishing, Oxford, 2015, p. 53.
7. Libération d'Hyères 1ère partie, marche forcée le long du Gapeau, publicity pamphlet for the 70th anniversary commemorations, author's collection.

8. C. Gritti, *Le temps de l'occupation au coeur des Maures*, pp. 308-9.
9. Libération d'Hyères 2ème partie – La prise du Golf-Hôte, publicity pamphlet for the 70th anniversary commemorations, author's collection.
10. Marcelle Zunino, unpublished memoir.
11. X. J. R. Ayral, *Heroisme: Jean Ayral,compagnon de la Liberation, histoire et carnets de guerre de Jean Ayral (18 juin 1940-22 aout 1944)*, Private, 2013.
12. *Var-Matin,* Le secret explosif de la poudrière de Saint-Pierre à Toulon, lundi 4 août 2014.
13. M. Stout & H. Yeide, *First to the Rhine, The 6th Army Group in World War II,* Zenith Press, St Paul, MN, 2007, pp. 114-15; Chars-francais.net, 5e Regiment de Chasseurs de Afrique; F. de Linares, Par les portes du Nord: la libération de Toulon et Marseille en 1944, Nouvelles Editions Latines, Paris, 2005, pp. 195-200.
14. F. de Linares, *Par les portes du nord: la libération de Toulon et Marseille en 1944*, Nouvelles Editions Latines, Paris, 2005, p. 266.
15. M. Stout & H.Yeide, *First to the Rhine*, pp. 125-35.
16. In the US Army C-ration, one particular can contained a combination of biscuits, sugar cubes, candies and a beverage – either coffee powder (Nescafé), cocoa or lemonade.
17. A. de Tarle, 'In Occupied Provence: A Childhood Memory', Michigan Quarterly Review vol. XLIII no. 2, Spring 2004.

15. PERSISTENCE

1. *Stars and Stripes,* Southern France, 21 August 1944.
2. Archives départementales du Var – Draguignan, Cote / n° inventaire, 132 PRS 1 23/8/1944, Journal clandestin, *La lutte patriotique*, Organe offociel de la section de Draguignan du Parti Communiste Français.
3. P. A. Kennedy, *Battlefield Surgeon*, p. 141.
4. G. G. Kundahl, *Riviera at War*, p. 199.
5. *Pocket Guide to France*, pp. 58-9.
6. Ibid., 24-5.
7. G. Orfalea, *Messengers of the Lost Battalion: The Heroic 551st and the Turning of the Tide at the Battle of the Bulge*, The Free Press, New York, 1997.

8. A. L. Maca, W. Folan & J. Reyman (Eds), *Prophet Pariah and Pioneer: Walter W. Taylor and Dissension in American Archaeology*, University of Colorado Press, 2010, pp.50-3.

9. Ibid., pp. 367-8.

10. Lieutenant Lawrence Swank should not be confused with Lieutenant Paul Swank of OG PEG who was killed in action on 17 August near Alet les Bains, south of Carcasonne in the Aude Department, and is buried in a rock-encased tomb on the side of the road. His wishes were to be buried on the site where he fell and although the US government had his body repatriated after the war, his family later returned him to his proper resting place.

11. Mémoire de Champsoar, http://champsaur.net/liberation-de-gap/

12. R. Jenkins, *A Pacifist at War: The Silence of Francis Cammaerts*, Random House, London, 2009, p. 169.

13. Ibid., pp. 177-88.

16. DESOLATION

1. C. Gritti, *Le temps de l'occupation au coeur des Maures*, pp. 269-70.

2. J. Goldsmith, *Accidental Agent*, p. 13.

3. Ibid., p. 10.

4. Ibid, pp. 9-13.

5. S. J. Weiss, *Second Chance: In Combat with the US 'Texas' Infantry, the OSS, and the French Resistance During the Liberation of France, 1943–1946*, Military History Publishing, 2011, p. 66.

6. G. G. Kundahl, *Riviera at War*, p. 240.

7. Jean-Pierre de Lassus Saint-Geniès (lieutenant-colonel), http://museedelaresistanceenligne.org.

8. *The Beachhead News*, Souvenier Edition, 15 October 1944.

9. S. J. Weiss, *Second Chance*, p. 82.

10. Ibid., pp.96-7.

11. Août 1944: Une jeune fille raconte la Libération de VALENCE (Drôme), https://unmondedepapiers.com

12. M. R. D. Foot, *SOE in France*, p. 413.

13. W. H. Maudlin, *Up Front*, Henry Holt & Co., New York, 1945, pp. 201-4.

17. MOMENTUM

1. J-L. Gassend, *Operation Dragoon: Autopsy of a Battle*, p. 147.
2. Ibid., p.148.
3. *The Montana Standard*, 'New York woman, heroine of French underground, helps Americans', Bute, Montana, p. 8, 12 September 1944.
4. *Nice-Matin* (Cannes), Les corps de deux héros de la Résistance cannoise finalement retrouvés 74 ans après la libération de la ville?, 23 août 2018.
5. J-L. Gassend, *Operation Dragoon: Autopsy of a Battle*, p. 270.
6. G. G. Kundahl, *Riviera at War*, 2017, p. 258.
7. J-L. Gassend, *Operation Dragoon: Autopsy of a Battle*, p. 298.
8. *Nice-Matin,* De l'occupation à la liberation, p. 68.

18. STAGNATION

1. J-L. Gassend, *Operation Dragoon: Autopsy of a Battle*, p. 435.
2. Le Maitron, Sospel (12 août 1944), http://maitron-fusilles-40-44.univ-paris1.fr
3. J-L. Gassend, *Operation Dragoon: Autopsy of a Battle*, pp. 460-61.
4. 'Paratroopers' Odyssey, A History of the 517th Parachute Combat Team', http://517prct.org
5. J-L. Gassend, *Operation Dragoon: Autopsy of a Battle*, p. 479.
6. Archives départementales du Var, 1 W 79, Tract de la Résistance rédigé par les Mouvements Unis de la Résistance (M.U.R) issu du fonds de la préfecture du Var, Draguignan.
7. A. de Tarle, 'In Occupied Provence: A Childhood Memory'.
8. L. W. Wylie, *Village in the Vaucluse*, p. 210.
9. G. G. Kundahl, *Riviera at War*, p. 333.
10. L'Apocalyptique de la Libération de la Ville de Nice du 28 août 1944, http://politiquepaca.canalblog.com/archives
11. J-L. Gassend, *Operation Dragoon: Autopsy of a Battle*, p. 441.
12. G. G. Kundahl, *Riviera at War*, p. 333.
13. *Nice-Matin*, Antibes Fusillés du Fort-Carré: 65 ans d'intérrogations, 20 septembre 2009.
14. J-L. Gassend, *Operation Dragoon: Autopsy of a Battle*, pp. 303-7.
15. G. G. Kundahl, *Riviera at War*, p. 85.

16. Archives départementales des Alpes-de-Haute-ProvenceLettre du milicien Maurice Giannardi à son épouse, Paris, 15 août 1944 (43 W 207).
17. R. Forbes, *For Europe: The French Volunteers of the Waffen-SS*, Stackpole Books, Mechanicsburg, 2010, pp. 41-3.
18. Ibid., pp. 176-80.

19. DELIVERANCE

1. G. G. Kundahl, *Riviera at War*, p. 281.
2. *Pocket guide to France,* US Government Printing Office, 1944, p. 20.
3. J-L. Gassend, *Operation Dragoon: Autopsy of a Battle*, pp. 486-7.
4. Ibid.
5. P. M. Coons, *Letters Home: From a World War II 'Black Panther' Artilleryman*, iUniverse Books, Bloomington, 2012, p. 304.
6. O. McCarthy, *Love and War: A Story of World War II in 268 Love Letters*, Travis Publishing, Canada, 2008, pp. 416-17.
7. 'History of Delta Base Section', Combined Arms Research Digital Library, 2008; D. Falgoux, J. Marnette, & A. Brusson, *L'Amérique en Provence, le camp de Calas 1944–1945*, Editions Persée, Aix-en-Provence, 2015, p. 58.
8. C. D. Bryant, *Khaki-collar Crime, Deviant Behaviour in the Military Context*, The Free Press, London, 1979, p. 178.
9. J. F. Bourhill, "Red Tabs': Life and Death in the 6th South African Armoured Division, 1943–1945', D.Phil thesis, University of Pretoria.
10. *Pocket Guide to France*, pp. 39-40.
11. J. Costello, *Love, Sex and War, Changing Values*, Collins, London, 1985, p. 89.
12. *Yank, The Army Weekly*, 'Down on the Riviera – GI's Relax in Nice, France', newspaper clipping, sn.
13. *The Billboard*, Vol. 57, No. 37, 22 September 1945, p. 36.
14. *Yank, The Army Weekly*, clipping.
15. J. Costello, *Love, Sex and War*, p. 360.
16. E. K. Pavalko & G. H. Elder, 'World War II and Divorce: A Life Course Perspective', *American Journal of Sociology* (95) 5, 1990, pp. 1213-34.

17. O. McCarthy, *Love and War*, pp. 416-17.
18. *Yank, The Army Weekly*, clipping.
19. J. F. Bourhill, *Come Back to Portofino: Through Italy With the 6th South African Armoured Division*, 30° South Publishers, Johannesburg, 2011, pp. 458-9.
20. W. R. Faith, *Bob Hope: A Life in Comedy*, Da Capo Press, 2003, p. 171.
21. *The Billboard*, p. 36.
22. D. M. Spragg, *Glen Miller Declassified*, Potomac Books, University of Nebraska, 2017, p. 306.
23. *Life* magazine, 'Life visits the GI Riviera', 9 July 1945, vol. 19, no. 2.

20. MONOTONY

1. G. Stuhlmann (ed.), *A Literate Passion: Letters of Anaïs Nin & Henry Miller, 1932–1953*, Harcourt Brace & Co., San Diego, 1987, pp. 170-1.
2. *The Delta Stage*, Marseille, 3 October 1945.
3. O. McCarthy, *Love and War*, p. 431.
4. D. Falgoux, J. Marnette, & A. Brusson, *L'Amérique en Provence, le camp de Calas 1944–1945*, Editions Persée, Aix-en-Provence, 2015, pp. 36-46.
5. *Stars and Stripes* (Marseille Edition), 4 December 1944, p. 3.
6. P. M. Coons, *Letters Home*, p. 299.
7. *Stars and Stripes*, 'Sweat-it-out-U, A unique GI school has sprouted up in old Biarritz', 16 September 1945, p. 7.
8. P. M. Coons, *Letters Home*, p. 305.
9. O. McCarthy, *Love and War*, p. 433.
10. J. Costello, *Love, Sex and War*, p. 118.
11. D. Falgoux, J. Marnette, & A. Brusson, *L'Amérique en Provence, le camp de Calas 1944–1945*, p. 101.
12. B. F. Jones, 'Freeing France: The Allies, the Résistance, and the Jedburghs', doctoral thesis, University of Nebraska-Lincoln, 1999, pp. 384-5.
13. R. Bailey, *Forgotten Voices of the Secret War*, p. 354.
14. J. Jackson, *France: The Dark Years, 1940–1944*, p.455.
15. J. Bourke, *An Intimate History of Killing*, Granta Books, London, 2000, p. 8.

Acknowledgements

Firstly, I must thank Pen & Sword and Claire Hopkins in particular, for bringing this work to fruition. As always, it was a pleasure to work with Chris Cocks, who was appointed as my copy-editor. As a former paratrooper, author and long-time publisher of military history, Chris brought the necessary skillset to this task. The maps were drawn by Loïc Jankowiak, an accomplished local historian, who also happens to be a qualified graphic designer. Jon Wilkinson must get the credit for integrating my muddled ideas into a compelling cover design. I am eternally indebted to my diligent proofreaders, Edward Bourhill and Loïc Laronche, for guarding against untold errors.

Cover Photography

The photograph on the front cover was taken in Saint-Tropez three days after the liberation. Standing on the left is Marc Rainaut, a leader of the Brigade des Maures. General Alexander Patch has just awarded him the Silver Star for his deeds on Dragoon D-Day. In the middle, with the pistol in her belt, is Nicole Célébonovitch, a courier for the Resistance, still unaware that her budding romance with a secret service agent has been snuffed out by the Gestapo. To the right is a member of the 509th PIB, Private Winifred D. Eason from Atlanta. The original caption says that Eason is thanking Marc Rainaut [Rainaut] for saving his life. A film clip exists of the trio puffing on cigarettes and reliving their D-Day experiences. Overshadowing this happy occasion was the loss of seventeen fit young paratroopers from Eason's company who jumped too soon and disappeared without a trace in waters of the gulf. (US Army Signal Corps Photograph Collection, Reference Number SC193052-S; US Army Heritage and Educational Centre)

Index